Head Masters

Head Masters

Phrenology, Secular Education, and Nineteenth-Century Social Thought

STEPHEN TOMLINSON

THE UNIVERSITY OF ALABAMA PRESS
Tuscaloosa

Copyright © 2005
The University of Alabama Press
Tuscaloosa, Alabama 35487-0380
All rights reserved
Manufactured in the United States of America

Typeface is AGaramond

∞

The paper on which this book is printed meets the minimum requirements of
American National Standard for Information Science–Permanence of Paper for
Printed Library Materials, ANSI Z39.48–1984.

Library of Congress Cataloging-in-Publication Data

Tomlinson, Stephen, 1954–
Head masters : phrenology, secular education, and nineteenth-century
social thought / Stephen Tomlinson.
p. cm.
Includes bibliographical references and index.
ISBN 0-8173-1439-3 (alk. paper)
1. Phrenology—History. [1. Education—History—19th century.] I. Title.
BF868.T66 2004
139′.09—dc22

2004010594

Contents

Photographs follow page 205

Acknowledgments

I want to recognize the reviewers and editors at The University of Alabama Press for their many helpful suggestions—this is a far better book thanks to their criticisms. I have also profited from the insights of colleagues and students at the University of Alabama, the Southeast Philosophy of Education Society, the American Educational Studies Association, and the Society for the Study of Curriculum History. But most of all, thanks go to my wife, Robin Behn. Without her constant moral support and editorial advice this project could not have been completed. It is to her, and to my son Simon, that this work is dedicated.

Frontal Matter

Do you understand Phrenology? The principles of Phrenology lie at the bottom of all sound mental philosophy, and of all the sciences depending upon the science of Mind; and of all sound theology, too. Combe's "Constitution of Man" is the greatest book that has been written for centuries. It shows us those conditions of our being without whose observance we cannot be wise, useful, or happy. It demonstrates from our very organization, and from our relation to the universe in which we are placed, that we cannot be prosperous (in any true sense of that word) unless we are intelligent, and cannot be happy unless we are good. It "vindicates the way of God to man" better than any polemical treatise I have ever read.

—Horace Mann, "Letter to a Young Lawyer,"
July 23, 1852. Published in *Dansville Herald*
and *American Phrenological Journal*

Horace Mann died in August 1859, just two months prior to the birth of John Dewey. This was also the same year, of course, in which Charles Darwin published *Origin of Species*. Therefore, not only did Mann and Dewey live during different times, their thoughts took shape in eras governed by radically different cosmologies. Both believed that the central problem of life was adaptation, but where Dewey, writing in the wake of the theory of evolution and the upheavals of modern urban-industrial life, rejected all moral and physical absolutes, Mann held an unquestioning faith in a divinely ordered and beneficent world. The Earth, Mann claimed, "is our automation." "Like Adam in a garden of Eden . . . man is born into a universe . . . redolent in treasures for the body, in grandeur for the mind, and in happiness for the heart."[1] "He finds . . . a vast and perfect apparatus of means adapted and designed to minister to his enjoyment and to aggrandize his power. The globe with all its dynamical energies, its mineral treasures, its vegetative powers, its fecundities of life, is only a grand and divinely wrought machine put into his hands; and on the condition of knowledge, he may wield it and use it as an artisan uses his tool."[2] Most importantly, Mann maintained, God had crafted the world according to the principle of virtue: actions that were good would be rewarded with pleasure; those that were bad would be punished with pain. The key to human happiness, therefore, was to understand and follow the moral imperatives woven into the laws of nature. Thus where Dewey pictured meaning and value as products of an open-ended transaction, Mann defended the "subjection or conformity of all our appetites, propensities and sentiments to the will of Heaven," God's providential economy of nature.[3]

In the months prior to his appointment as Secretary of Education to the State of Massachusetts, Mann found in George Combe's *Constitution of Man* a practical guide to life under this philosophical system.[4] Combe, the leading phrenologist of the day, demonstrated how the physiological laws of heredity and experience governing the structure and development of the brain could be employed to adapt human behavior to the moral laws of nature. From the choice of a spouse to the eradication of alcoholism, from the treatment of the insane to the reformation of the criminal, he brought every function of the modern world under the management of his mental science. Above all, with the aid of James Simpson, Combe worked tirelessly to establish a system of education grounded in the principles of phrenology—a cause that made him Britain's leading advocate of public secular schooling and a scientific curriculum based on Pestalozzian child-centered teaching methods.[5]

Sending a copy of the *Constitution* and a phrenological head to his sister, Mann confessed,

I know of no book written for hundreds of years which does so much to vindicate the ways of God to man. *Its philosophy is the only practical basis for education.* These doctrines will work the same change in metaphysical science that Lord Bacon wrought in natural.[6]

And, indeed, the *Constitution,* together with Simpson's *Philosophy of Education,* did become the basis for the reforms Mann championed in his common school crusade.[7] His arguments against the classics and corporal punishment, his advocacy of the object lesson and the teaching of physiology, his efforts to establish a nonsectarian school library and state Normal schools, and his insistence that moral education was the central task of public education were all prefigured in the writings of the British phrenologists.[8] When, in 1838, Combe traveled to the United States to promote his gospel of progress in the New World, the two men quickly established a close personal bond that matured into a lifelong friendship each would draw upon to further their respective reform efforts in Britain and America.[9] Mann even named his second son for "the philosopher."

According to Harold Silver, Combe and Simpson, "important figures in controversies and campaigns of the middle decades of the nineteenth century," have been repeatedly overlooked by British historians: a neglect, he claims, that has "resulted in profound distortions of the history of education, of social and cultural realities."[10] Similarly, although Lawrence Cremin has recognized that "the influence of phrenology on Mann's thought is universally apparent" neither he nor any other historian of American education has explained the meaning that this science had for reformers of the Early Republic.[11] Even Jonathan Messerli's magisterial biography, although acknowledging Mann's commitment to phrenology, fails to explain how he wielded physiological laws in his many reform efforts and is silent about the phrenologically based racism, sexism, and classism that permeated all of his writings. Michael Katz's *Irony of Early School Reform* (1968) only mentions phrenology in passing, whereas David Hogan confuses "affectionate authority" with moral treatment in a Lockian account of mind that Mann specifically rejects.[12] Indeed, the very idea that the founding father of the American common school was a committed phrenologist appears to be something of an embarrassment to historians who remember phrenology the way Mark Twain pictured it, as a pseudoscientific fad in which hucksters read character traits from the bumps on a person's skull. But this unfortunate and distorted perception is more a product of historiography than of historical fact. For although it is true that by the 1860s it had been largely relegated to fairgrounds and seaside piers, during the second quarter of the nineteenth century, phrenology was a widely accepted theory of human nature, embraced by prominent scientists and intellectuals—including leading members of the medical community who saw in its laws of heredity and exercise an explanation for insanity and the practice of moral treatment developed by Philippe Pinel and Samuel Tuke.[13] Having worked to establish America's first public asylum at Worcester, Mann was thoroughly conversant with the psychiatric theory of the 1820s. Indeed, as his second wife, Mary Peabody Mann, explains, "His interest and action in the cause of insane hospitals had deepened his insight into the primary causes and hindrances of human development: and the study of 'Combe's Constitution of Man,' which he met with in 1837, added new fuel to the fire of his enthusiasm."[14] By demonstrating how the principles of psychological management perfected on the insane could be extended to the entire community, the *Constitution* provided Mann with the pedagogic techniques necessary to engineer his vision of a virtuous republic supervened by God's laws. His many reform efforts can only be understood through the lens of this synthesis. As Combe himself boasted, phrenology's "influence in supplying him with guiding principles is conspicuous in every work that proceeds from his pen."[15]

PHRENOLOGICAL THEORY

George Henry Lewes observed in 1857 that although "phrenology is of German origin . . . it was in France that it acquired its European éclat," evolving from a physiological theory of brain functions into a middle-class social philosophy that—unable to flourish in the conservative atmosphere cast by the Restoration government—was quickly embraced by the more liberal thinkers of the new urban-industrial English-speaking world.[16] In many respects, phrenology was the heir of *Idéologie,* the medically based social science of the Revolution's bourgeois theorists. First formulated by Franz-Joseph Gall as a physiological theory of brain structure in which character and abilities could be determined from the size of mental organs (revealed by the contours of the cranium), it was effectively transformed into a progressive moral philosophy by Johan Gasper Spurzheim, who normalized the mind around middle-class values by defining human nature in terms of the balanced operation of faculties such as time, order, conscientiousness, adhesiveness, and love of approbation. Further elaborated and popularized by George Combe—in opposition to the environmental and socialist doctrines of Owenism—it flourished in Britain as a philosophy of practical Christianity and self-help that broadly endorsed a Whig program of political reforms aimed at improving the mind and habits of the working classes. It was Spurzheim's and Combe's powerful message of personal and racial improvement toward the religious ideal of physiological perfection that guided Horace Mann and Samuel Gridley Howe, his coworker in reform, in their remarkable efforts to institutionalize the early American Republic. The Normal school; the asylum; the prison; the reformatory; schools for the deaf, the blind, and the feebleminded; and the formation of the Freedmen's Bureau and the American welfare system were influenced by phrenology.

In recent years, phrenology has captured the interest of cultural historians who, following the insights of Foucault and other social theorists, have attempted to use this apparently implausible hypothesis as a lens by which to chart the epistemic contours of the nineteenth-century mind. This "external" history is certainly vital to an understanding of the role phrenology played as a focus of middle-class interests at a time of enormous social change. But there is also an important "internal" story to be told. How did phrenology unite physiological laws and moral imperatives? How was it tied to the natural theology of secularism? And how were its basic principles of human classification, inheritance, and development used to underwrite progressive pedagogic and disciplinary practices? This work attempts to answer these and similar questions by looking at phrenological theory from the inside—from the perspective of its leading advocates. Extending epistemological debates, it investigates the practical: what phrenology meant to Gall, Spurzheim, Combe, Mann, and Howe, and how these "Head Masters" wielded its doctrines in their many and various efforts to reform schooling and other institutional practices.

Anyone familiar with the history of British and American education will no doubt regard the claim that phrenology played such an important role in the development of schooling and other institutional practices with some skepticism. This book will challenge that orthodoxy. It will introduce new figures into the historical account, paint a different portrait of leading reformers, and attempt to make the implausible, phrenology, seem plausible. It will expose the way class, race, and gender stereotypes permeated nineteenth-century thought and show how views of nature, mind, and society supported a secular curriculum coupled with physiologically based disciplinary practices. It is hoped that this will lead to a new appreciation for the ideas and theories that motivated reformers such as Horace Mann and Samuel Gridley Howe and, equally important, a reassessment of George Combe, who, although hardly known by contemporary scholars, emerges as one of the most important and influential educators of the century.

Head Masters: Phrenology, Secular Education, and Nineteenth-Century Social Thought is a long book, with many meanders. It explores social and educational thought in three countries, sometimes attending to the big picture, sometimes focusing on details. Although there is an internal logic to this progression, the following claims may help keep the larger argument in mind.

- Any philosophy of education must incorporate some view of human nature and a conception of the social good. For Mann, Howe, and other followers of George Combe, the natural laws and moral imperatives of phrenology justified a secular scientific curriculum and a "softer" child-centered pedagogy as the means of correctly training a rational and virtuous citizenry.

- Phrenology came to prominence as the successor of Ideology, the positivistic social science developed by the liberal political theorists of the French Revolution. Drawing from the philosophical radicalism of Helvétius and the Lockian epistemology of Condillac, the *Idéologues* sought to restructure French society around principles derived from their physiologically based "science of man." Conceiving education as the process of perfecting human nature, they designed legislation, public festivals, and a hierarchical system of schooling to engineer a moral republic grounded in social and economic laws. Although these ideas were brought to Virginia by Thomas Jefferson, Ideology did not take root in America. It was only after the rise of practical phrenology in Britain, and its subsequent importation to the United States in the 1830s, that reformers embraced psychological management of the population.

- As in France, British phrenologists extended the economic and political agenda of middle-class theorists, the associationist psychology and utilitarian philosophy of James Mill and Jeremy Bentham—early advocates of monitorial education for the working poor. Inspired by the disciplinary practices devised by Robert Owen, George Combe and James Simpson rescripted Pestalozzian pedagogy around phrenological laws and, during the 1830s, spearheaded the Radical movement for a state system of secular schooling: the com-

petitive pedagogy and mechanical lessons of the Lancasterian system
were replaced by the intrinsic interest of the child, the appeal to
reason, and the religious imperative to follow God's will as manifested in scientific laws. A decade later Combe combined with Mill's
protégé William Ellis to establish model secular schools that would
demonstrate how the principles of political economy and physiology
could be taught to the working classes. Finally, it was Combe's popularization of Mann's work in Massachusetts that solved the religious
problem and provided the blueprint for the 1870 and 1872 Education
Acts of England and Scotland.

• Although nowhere recognized in histories of education, it was
Combe's practical physiology that Mann and Howe drew upon to
shape the institutions that shaped America. These principles funded
a classist, racist, and sexist political agenda. Convinced that the laws
of exercise and heredity could be used to eliminate the degenerate
and develop a more perfect Christian character, Howe and Mann
embraced the eugenic doctrines of phrenology in the search for a
superior New England bloodline. Phrenology provided the moral
technology necessary for the control—and ultimate elimination—of
the abnormal: the mad, the deaf, the blind, the mentally retarded,
the deviant, the criminal, and the mulatto.

This transatlantic story is told in three parts. Starting in France, the epistemological and pedagogic program of the *Idéologues* is explored through
the writings of Condillac, Cabanis, and Destutt de Tracy, and then traced to
America in the educational schemes of Thomas Jefferson. The second section explains how Spurzheim normalized Gall's neurological theory into a
middle-class moral philosophy. Promoted in Britain by Combe as an alternative to the radical environmentalism and utopian socialism of Robert
Owen, phrenology was then used to justify improving the mind and morals of the working classes through infant education and public schooling—
albeit, within a hierarchically ordered and scientifically managed middle-
class meritocracy. Finally, the third section of the book details Spurzheim
and Combe's visits to America and reveals the ways in which Howe and
Mann utilized phrenology to justify their sweeping social reforms.

Head Masters

I

"The Science of Man"

The memoirs published at the beginning of this century by Cabanis on the connection between the physical and moral nature, are the first great and direct effort to bring within the domain of positive philosophy this study previously abandoned entirely to the theological and metaphysical methods. The impulse imparted to the human mind by these memorable investigations has not fallen off. The labours of Dr. Gall and his school have singularly strengthened it, and, especially, have impressed on this new and final portion of physiology a high degree of precision by supplying a definite base of discussion and investigation.

Auguste Comte, *System of Positive Polity*, 1875

Postrevolutionary France, Frank Manuel claims, was the site of "one of the crucial developments in modern intellectual history . . . the reversal from the eighteenth century view of man as more or less equal . . . to the early nineteenth century emphasis upon human uniqueness, diversity, and dissimilarity" that culminated "in theories of inequality and organicism."[1] This transformation, from the egalitarian sensationalism and laissez-faire liberalism of the philosophes to the more interventionist social behaviorism of the positive sociologists Claude Henri Saint-Simon and August Comte, comprised at least three distinct assumptions: Metaphysical speculation had to be replaced by an anthropological "science of man" that explained the mind through the vital property of sensibility; the population was divisible into distinct physiological types according to factors such as sex, age, temperament, and inherited capacities; and medical and pedagogic practices could be devised to perfect more rational, moral, and industrious citizens. Like the differentiation and integration of parts with a living organism, this vision of human nature and the social good suggested that a well-ordered state had to utilize biological difference and coordinate a sense of solidarity. Equality and freedom were no longer seen as conditions for society, but as ideals toward which the individual and the social organization must progress. Although Manuel does not mention the work of Gall or Spurzheim, Comte's own phrenologically grounded writings clearly indicate the important role neurological accounts human diversity played in this intellectual evolution. By 1828, when the first phrenological society opened in Paris, Gall's new science had become a practical moral philosophy, offering a physiologically based system of classification and powerful disciplinary practices to normalize the population—the immature, the deviant, and the degenerate—in line with liberal bourgeois values.

The pivotal figure in the rise of physiology in French social thought was Pierre Cabanis, one of a loose and often contentious group of liberal intellectuals, popularly known as the *Idéologues,* who came to power as the Directory (1795-99) struggled to reestablish public institutions and secure stability in the years after the Terror.[2] From their seat in the Second Class on Moral and Political Sciences at the newly founded National Institute they sought to justify secular social policies that would help realize the rational and moral principles of the enlightenment. Civic laws, penal codes, welfare, health services, and especially education, they believed, had to be purged of the doctrinal dictates of the church and restructured in accordance with the natural laws governing the human mind.

A member of the Auteuil salon of Mme Helvétius, Cabanis was well acquainted with the materialist philosophers d'Holbach, Diderot, and La Mettrie, and had even met Condillac, the theorist from whom the *Idéologues* drew their central concepts of analysis and sensation. In a series of twelve reports, he fused Condillac's radical empiricism with advances in medical science to explain the relationship between the physical and the moral in human nature.[3] Men and women were situated within the animal kingdom, organic phenomena were reduced to the universal principle of sensitivity, and the transmutation of species were explained through environmentally induced inherited changes. Most importantly, Cabanis's materialism eschewed all metaphysical categories. The distinctively moral qualities, traditionally associated with the cogito or immortal soul, had to be understood as properties of a living organization. The production of thought by the brain, he famously argued, could even be compared to the secretion of bile by the liver. No longer the domain of the theologian and the metaphysician, the mind was now open to scientific study and medical control.

Following Helvétius, the *Idéologues* understood that the purpose of government was education: the Republic existed to improve the physical, moral, and intellectual character of the population. Although rejecting Helvétius's extreme environmentalism, Cabanis and his coworker in reform, Antoine Louis Claude Destutt de Tracy, were convinced that rationally and physiologically informed legislation could elevate the mind and the morals of all citizens. This demanded a scientifically educated cadre of civil servants who understood how to regulate thought and desire through education and other social institutions—much as a doctor might balance bodily health through diet, exercise, and climate. Tracy spearheaded this drive to create a *classe savante* through the scientific curriculum of the elite central schools established by the *Idéologues* in 1795. Pedagogy was also of paramount concern. Here Cabanis and his followers looked to the disciplinary techniques of Philippe Pinel, whose pioneering work with the insane demonstrated the power of therapeutic practices to restore alienated minds to reason—a psychological method, it was recognized, whose practices could easily be applied to the education of children. Roch-Ambroise Sicard, who drew upon Condillac's epistemology to construct a language of gestures for the deaf, also generalized his instructional strategies for future teachers at the *Ecole Normale*, which opened earlier the same year. Accordingly, when in 1800, Jean-Marc Itard attempted to apply these techniques to the education of Victor, the Savage of Aveyron, the *Idéologues* expected spectacular proof of their theory of mind and the power of moral treatment to transform society. As it turned out, Itard taught the world a great deal about pedagogy, but the mixed results he achieved with Victor only served to fuel growing skepticism about the plasticity of human abilities and the optimistic claims of social scientists.

Although supporters of the coup d'etat that established the Consulate, the *Idéologues* were quickly marginalized as Bonaparte consolidated power. Distancing himself from their efforts to analyze the mind, their strident anticlericalism, and their liberal policies, he embraced Catholic sympathies and in so doing helped to create the climate for a conservative reaction to the Revolution. The chaos of the Jacobin Terror was easily blamed upon sensationalism and its godless offspring Ideology. By reducing the mind to habits formed in response to pleasure and pain, faith in free will and the immortal soul had been undercut and the institutions that ensured social order displaced. Conservatives saw in Bonaparte the promise of stability; Bonaparte recognized in the church what his burgeoning bureaucratic state most needed: an instrument of public control. Alert to the threat that this pact posed to their liberal reforms, several leading *Idéologues* participated in fruitless efforts to overthrow the emperor's regime, the result of which was the suppression of the Institute's Second Class and the replacement of the central schools with lycées that restored traditional studies over the secular curriculum advocated by Tracy.

This reemergence of religiosity was not simply the result of political maneuvering. As the writings of Ideology's most prominent students demonstrate, the force of spiritual experience could not be denied. Pinel, for instance, sought to reconcile the "science of man" with the reality of the cogito. Joseph-Marie de Gérando—future statesman, social philanthropist, promoter of Lancasterian schooling, and early influence on the New England Transcendentalists—also rejected Condillac's vision of the faculties as transformed sensations. Turning to Kant, with Maine de Brian, and later Rolland-Collier and Victor Cousin, he helped justify the introspective analysis of thought central to the eclectic philosophy of the Late Empire and Restoration. Particularly influential was Pierre Laromiguière's assertion that attention was an active and independent power of the mind. This argument was embraced by Pinel's successor, Dominique Esquirol, and through his teachings, Edward Séguin, the so-called "apostle of the "idiots, who adapted Itard's methods to the training of the mentally retarded.

The phrenologists also attempted to preserve many of the scientific, social, and educational goals of Ideology, while offering a theory of mind compatible with religious sensibilities and—through their commitment to innate biological differences in intellect and character—the growing political acceptance of social hierarchies. Although framed in opposition to the basic tenets of Condillac's empiricism, Gall and Spurzheim's insistence that all mental functions have a somatic base in the structures of the brain appealed to medical theorists sympathetic to Cabanis's project. For spiritualists and emperor, however, this was old wine in new bottles. Phrenology was the child of sensationalism, yet another materialistic doctrine that undermined freedom, responsibility, and the religious foundation of community life.

SENSATIONALISM

Condillac composed his *Essay on the Origin of Human Knowledge* (1746) in order to render empiricism fully consistent with the scientific method.[4] Locke, he explained, had studied the understanding by observing how all ideas are derived from sense experience. But while correctly concluding men and women have no innate knowledge, Condillac found the assumption that the mind was prefigured with a faculty of reflection unsupportable and unnecessary. Had Locke been more systematic in his analysis, Condillac insisted, he would have discovered that the powers of comparison and combination central to intelligent thought were nothing but transformed sensations, habits of mind and action generated by the association of signs. Sensations, either pleasant or unpleasant, generated attention, and attention, in turn, made possible the association of ideas from which the faculties were constructed.

The central feature of consciousness was the ability to form perceptions independently of objects, as when, in imagination (the recollection of sense fragments from previous experiences) or memory (the recollection of signs or words associated with perceptions), a thought brings another idea before the mind. Both of these mental operations arose directly from bonds formed in experience. A need becomes associated with "something that will satisfy it; and this idea is connected with the place where the thing is found; to this place is connected the idea of persons that we have seen there; to the idea of these persons, the ideas of our past pleasures or pains," and so on.[5] In the end, "all knowledge forms a single chain whose smaller chains are united at certain links and separated at others."[6] Crucially, Condillac reversed the relationship that Locke had established between ideas and signs by arguing that language was not simply an instrument for communication, but rather the tool by which thoughts are assembled within the mind. In a state of nature, he argued, men and women had lived like animals—limited to imagination, they expressed their emotions through the "language of action" that accompanied sense experience. Gradually, however, they learned to use such cries and gestures as primitive metaphoric signs. As memory emerged, the capacity to control the imagination and communicate basic meanings developed. But it was not until the acquisition of arbitrary signs that the faculties really started to grow, as, freed from dependence on the real, the imagination and memory were able to work in concert, directing attention according to interests and desires. It was this power of reflection that enabled the mind to abstract, compare, compose, and decompose ideas—the basic powers that constitute the understanding. And reason? Following ordinary usage, this was simply "a knowledge of how to control the operations of the mind" and appreciate the limits and fallibility of human thought.[7]

Locke had cautioned that the greatest threat to human wisdom arose from the tendency to use words without meaning: Thought had to be built out of ideas derived only from the essential features of experience. To this end, Condillac introduced his concept of analysis, a process of decomposing complex ideas into clear and distinct perceptions. Any thought that could not be broken down into simple elements contained meaningless terms that had to be purged from language. Given these constraints, the assembly of ideas would preserve the intrinsic order of the perceived world. Not only a positivist program for the development of knowledge uncompromised by metaphysics, Condillac's principle was also a pedagogic strategy for the schooling of rational and moral citizens. Education had to lead in careful steps from the simple and concrete to the complex and abstract, in such a manner that students could understand and justify their own ideas by composing and decomposing thoughts without error.

To support this conjectural history of the mind, Condillac pointed to wild children and the deaf, who demonstrated that without language human beings would be trapped in an animal existence of purely imaginative thought. The story of a deaf mute who developed the ability to hear when aged twenty-three is illustrative. Until that time, Condillac reported, he lived almost without reflection, habitually following his sensations and imitating others with little or no idea of his own existence or the nature of the world into which he was born. The Abbé Epée's work with the deaf, which Condillac witnessed in the early 1770s, provided further proof of his thesis. Building upon the basic language of action, Epée systemized the spontaneous signs of his students and invented hundreds of other gestures to represent the words and grammatical structures of French. No longer limited to the immediate world of sensation, this artificial language of arbitrary signs allowed the deaf to form all the mind's faculties—there was not a thought or sentiment they could not entertain. Indeed, Condillac believed they had an advantage over the hearing, for Epée led his pupils "from perceptible ideas to abstract ideas by simple and systematic analyses" that avoided the haphazardness of normal learning.[8] Unlike spoken French, the signs of the deaf were firmly rooted in concrete experience.

Condillac elaborated his theory further in *Traité de Sensations* (1754), famously invoking the image of a human statue to explain how the mind gradually awakens to the world and itself as, one by one, the various senses are brought to life. Starting with smell, the weakest of the senses, he showed that the basis of all the faculties and passions could be derived from the simple pleasures and pains that attended the awareness of different odors. The other senses were then integrated into the developing mind, with touch playing the special role of helping the statue situate itself as a self-conscious and independent entity within a world of objects. Finally, though not as prominently as in the *Essay*, language was introduced to fashion the understanding. Although obviously hypothetical, Condillac's painstaking and careful construction presented a compelling justification of the sensationalist thesis: guided only by the desire to promote pleasure and avoid pain, the association of ideas could explain the formation of all the habits, talents, and passions that constitute human life.

Condillac's own attempt to bring the statue man to life in the education of the Prince of Parma flowed directly from these epistemological arguments. Working from the premise that all ideas come through the senses, he roundly rejected the rote memorization of texts and the teaching of principles and precepts. Much as Rousseau argued, Condillac believed that schooling had to start with the child. The "one true method," for the individual as well as for the species, "is to lead our pupil from the known to the unknown."⁹ Left to their own devices, of course, students would get no further than their primitive forebears. The key was to extend their first observations in an ordered and systematic way: a process, he believed, that would be greatly enhanced by teaching pupils the principles of sensationalist psychology. Alert to the nature of their own mind and the process of learning, they would then follow a kind of recapitulation theory, retracing an idealized history of civilization that led from simple agricultural and mechanical skills to a complex and abstract scientific knowledge of the world.

Other educators also sought inspiration in sensationalist epistemology, most notably the Abbé Sicard, Epée's successor and director of the National Institute for the Deaf. Following Condillac, Sicard taught that language was simply an artificial instrument for organizing thought. Forced to live outside of a linguistic community in which their faculties could develop, the deaf had became trapped in a preintellectual, animal-like state. Working closely with his star pupil, the celebrated Massieu, Sicard set about constructing a formalized language by transforming the crude and idiosyncratic gestures devised by Epée into brief, stylized, easily articulated signs that carried root meanings and syntax.

Sicard's fame soon rivaled Epée's. Touring Europe with Massieu and other students from the Institute, he put on a sensational show. Sicard would take questions from the audience and sign them to Massieu, who then responded by writing statements on a chalkboard. His answers were so spectacular that a book of his sayings was published. In one exchange, when asked to distinguish between desire and hope, Massieu replied "desire is a tree in leaf, hope a tree in bloom, enjoyment is a tree with fruit."[10] Sicard is even reported to have opened his theatrical show by announcing, "I have been waiting to introduce to you a new subject, almost an infant, a little savage, a block of unchiseled marble, or rather a statue, yet to be animated and endowed with intellect."[11] Summoning a deaf child from the audience, he would then reveal the basis of his system by teaching the meaning of a first elementary sign. Massieu stood to demonstrate the possible fruits of his educational scheme.

THE MORAL AND THE PHYSICAL

Cabanis attempted to provide a physiological foundation for sensationalism. Rejecting Condillac's philosophical dualism, he argued that all the faculties and emotions could be derived from the properties of organic matter and thus, as with the body, brought to their full realization and harmonious order through the laws of medical science. Schooled in the vitalist tradition of the Montpellier School, Cabanis was first and foremost committed to a vision of medicine based on an anthropological understanding of the human organism as a holistic system of discreetly operating parts, each subtly adapted to the physical environment. Adamantly opposed to the armchair speculations of textbook physicians and the quack cures of empirics, he insisted upon the careful systematic observation of disease suggested by Condillac's method of analysis. Illness was not to be treated by bleedings, tonics, and purges, but by the natural cures of diet, exercise, and climate that restored the natural equilibrium of animal life. Given the great diversity in physical organization and environmental conditions, this demanded doctors who had an intimate knowledge of their patients and a practical familiarity with the course and treatment of disease. These same Hippocratic principles could also be applied to the body politic to justify a liberal state guided by social scientists who understood how to help society function in accord with the natural laws of political economy.

What then could the physiologist say about the regulation of the mind? First and foremost, that thought is produced by the body: consciousness arises from feeling. Condillac had provided a philosophical proof that all ideas are derived from sensations, but the conceptual categories he and other metaphysicians had constructed—the faculties of attention, memory, and judgment—bore no resemblance to organic processes. Carried to the brain by nerves, the isolated and incoherent impressions received by the various sense organs were somehow transformed into the ideas "expressed in the language of physiognomy and gesture, or the signs of speech and writing."[12] It was as if "the brain in some way digests impressions" and "produces organically the secretion of thought."[13] Some day, Cabanis prophesized, the details of this process might be discovered, but the more pressing and practical concern was to see how the system functioned in relation to the subject's environment. Here he found a crucial mistake in Condillac's scheme. By considering only the role of sense data, he had ignored the impressions that originated from the brain, the stomach, the sexual organs, and other viscera. As the examples of intoxication, mental disorders, and puberty all indicated, both internal and external sensations combined in the composition of intellectual and emotional life. Throwing out Condillac's image of an undifferentiated statue, Cabanis rejected any metaphor—a slate or unchiseled marble—that failed to recognize how instincts and other physiological states mediated all interchanges with the world. This seemed particularly evident with animals. How could the complex species-specific behaviors displayed by many newborn creatures have been learned? Finding explanations involving narrow environmental conditions, tight social groupings, and experiences within the womb totally insufficient, he cast sensationalism on the evolutionary stage. Instincts, he asserted, were acquired habits learned within the population and passed on through the laws of heredity. As formalized by Cabanis's friend and colleague at the National Institute, Jean-Baptiste Lamarck, this process of "use inheritance" assumed that links in the animal's nervous organization strengthened by exercise would be transmitted to offspring. Under the pressure of environmental forces, such adaptive behaviors would then lead to organic changes that ultimately resulted in the creation of new species. Indeed, given the age and history of the Earth revealed by geologists, Lamarck and Cabanis were convinced that this gradual process could explain all organic forms, including the great variety of human types. (Unlike his friend Thomas Jefferson, he did not believe this process had progressed so far as to divide the different races into distinct species.) The inherent capacity of sensitive matter to adapt to a changing environment had enormous political implications. By following the correct medical practices, Cabanis claimed that "it was possible to alter the very habits of our constitution to an appreciable degree" and "to improve the particular nature of each individual."[14] He even lapsed into a eugenic fantasy. "If we are able usefully to modify each temperament, one at a time, then we can influence, extensively and profoundly, the character of the species, and can produce an effect, systematically and continuously, on succeeding generations."[15] It is time, he continued, to "practice upon ourselves what we have practiced with such success upon many of our fellow creatures," to get nearer "to a perfect type of human."[16]

Cabanis's materialistic behaviorism marrying the logic of utility and a commitment to natural rights perfectly complemented the laissez-faire policies of liberal revolutionary leaders—Condorcet, Seiyèrs, Garat, Danuou, and Voney—with whom he associated both at Auteuil and the Society of 1789. Indeed, it was thanks to these influential friends that Cabanis became a speechwriter for Mirabeau, authoring at least three papers on education, subsequently published under the orator's name after his untimely death in 1791. As Martin Staum explains, unlike the pivotal scheme of Condorcet, Cabanis did not call for a universal system of schooling, let alone the social leveling of the Jacobins. Civil rights did not imply political equality. He did propose scholarships for talented youth of the lower orders, much as Jefferson suggested in *Notes on Virginia*, but his main concern was to keep the state and the church out of the teachers' way. Relying solely upon fees, competition would improve instruction of its own accord. A more important task for government was the development of a national university that could train future leaders in the physical and moral sciences. In the following chapter we will see how many of these programmatic suggestions were implemented, albeit under the more direct control of the state, when the *Idéologues* came to power in the aftermath of Thermidor.

The same vision of expertise is evident in Cabanis's proposals to overhaul French medicine. In *Observation sur les Hôpitaux* (1790), he advocated the replacement of large and inefficient disease-ridden hospitals with more intimate home or hospice care where doctors could attend to patients in a healthier and more natural environment—and gain scientific knowledge of illnesses and their course of treatment. The following year, after the publication of his journal on the death of Mirabeau, Cabanis was appointed to a five-person committee charged to administer Paris's hospitals. Staum explains that without the resources to fund major reforms, the group concentrated on the most egregious abuses of the existing system. An immediate concern was the correct classification and treatment of patients, including the separation of insane from other dependents at the Bicêtré. Convinced that mental illness, like any other physiological condition, could be treated by a healthy regimen of diet, fresh air, and exercise, Cabanis helped secure the appointment of his friend and fellow *Idéologue* Philippe Pinel. It was at the Bicêtré, and later the Salpêtrière, that Pinel perfected the therapeutic technique of moral treatment that revolutionized the care of the insane and helped initiate the birth of the mental asylum.[17]

THE POWER OF PEDAGOGY

Sharing Cabanis's disdain for traditional medicine, Pinel sought to place the care of the mad on a scientific footing by establishing an anthropological understanding of mental illness grounded in Condillac's sensationalist epistemology. Sympathetic to Cabanis physiology, he nonetheless maintained a degree of independence between the moral and physical—a division that would split successors in the field. As Pinel explained in his *Treatise on Insanity* (1801), years of experience demonstrated that although many cases of alienation arose from organic causes (such as stomach disorders, brain lesions, and head injuries), the majority resulted from a functional imbalance of the mind.[18] These latter, nonmaterial causes were of two forms: either the individual was gripped by an inappropriate chain of ideas cemented by the imagination, or the individual's reason had been overpowered by the strength of their passions. Condillac, in fact, had defined insanity as "an imagination that, without our noticing it, associates ideas in a completely disordered way, and sometimes influences our judgments or behavior."[19] Not only did this suggest continuity between the normal and the alienated, it provided a key to the restoration of sanity in those cases where patients had became obsessed with certain thoughts—guilt over some deed or religious fanaticism, for example. Often Pinel would resort to theatre. By conducting a mock trial, an exorcism, or some staged event that resolved the patient's concern, he would attempt to shake their fixation and reestablish the rule of reason. In other cases moral treatment had to work directly on the passions. Certain emotions stemmed from basic physiological needs, but Pinel also pointed to other "artificial" desires—such as envy, pride, and the lust for property—that arose from social conditions. As many of his case studies demonstrated, there was a clear relationship between the excitement of the times and the rule of reason.

Condillac's analysis of sensations was of little help in understanding the dynamic relationship between thought and the emotions. Far better guides, Jan Goldstein explains, were Rousseau's *Discourse of Inequality,* with its penetrating analysis of the modern condition, and the pedagogic manual *Emile.*[20] "What an analogy there is between the art of directing lunatics and that of raising young people," Pinel declared.[21] "Both require great firmness, but not harsh and forbidding manners; rational and affectionate condescension, but not a soft complaisance that bends to all whims."[22] Indeed, it is remarkable to see how the asylum movement itself mirrors the structure of Rousseau's ideal education. Set in a natural and pristine environment free from the evils of the city, a paternal if not familial moral authority figure personifying order and stability carefully manages his patient's experiences to harmonize the passions and bring a true balance to faculties otherwise alienated by the unnatural pressures of urban life.

Despite their differences on the relationship between the moral and the physical, Pinel and Cabanis were united in the belief that abnormal states were simply an extension of normal functioning, and, as Tracy put it, "the art of curing madmen is the same as that of governing the passions of . . . ordinary men."[23] By catering to animal desires, society had become diseased, generating unnatural wants that perverted the mental and physical powers of the population. To ensure the health of the community, the doctor-politician had only to generalize the methods of moral treatment, creating, through schools and other institutions, disciplinary practices that would ensure that individuals developed the rational powers and moral qualities necessary for republican citizenship. As the next chapter explains, Tracy became the leading architect of this policy, pushing a differential system of public education that would train a scientifically informed intellectual elite and a psychologically compliant population.

PHILOSOPHERS AND WILD CHILDREN

In the hundred years from 1750 to 1850 popular attention was captivated by efforts to educate the deaf, the deaf-blind, the idiotic, and in the case of Victor, the wild boy of Aveyron, a feral child.[24] Certainly, these first experiments in the power of pedagogy were motivated by humanitarian desires, not least the religious imperative to redeem a soul lost to animality. But the education of the other, for so long an object of humor and distaste, was also motivated by the ambition to forward a political agenda. By providing empirical proof of a philosophical theory of mind and the effectiveness of physiologically informed methods, the successful training of a previously unmanageable subject presented an irresistible case for progressive social policies and institutional practices. Jean-Marc Itard's account of his efforts to educate Victor clearly reveals these underlying goals. A student of Pinel and an assistant to Sicard, he was convinced that the development of the mind resulted from initiation into language. After nine months following the pedagogic strategies of the sensationalist thesis, he confidently claimed that the boy's progress had answered "some of the most important inferences relative to the philosophical and natural history of man . . . truths, for the discovery of which Locke and Condillac were indebted merely to the force of their genius, and the depth of their reflections" and demonstrated that "the progress of teaching may, and ought to be aided by the lights of modern medicine, which of all the natural sciences can co-operate most effectively towards the amelioration of the human species."[25]

The details of Victor's discovery and subsequent life are well documented by Harlan Lane.[26] Captured by the villagers of Saint-Sernin in the province of Aveyron, the diminutive boy between twelve and fifteen years of age had come out of the woods to steal potatoes. Running naked, with matted hair and scars all over his body, apparently mute, possibly deaf, urinating and defecating indiscriminately, and with little concern for warmth, shelter, or human contact, he appeared more brute than human. This was clearly no ordinary case of abandonment. At a loss over what to do with the child, a local commissioner, Constans-Saint-Estéve, sent Victor to the orphanage in Saint-Affrique, near Rodez. A representative at the Republican Assembly in Paris some years earlier, he immediately recognized the scientific significance of the discovery and wondered whether the boy was a deaf-mute the celebrated Sicard could educate? Nor was the child's importance lost on the director of the orphanage who quickly composed a letter describing Victor for the *Journal des Débats*. Within two weeks Paris was buzzing with the news that someone had found Rousseau's noble savage wandering in the forests of Aveyron. And, as Constans-Saint-Estéve guessed, nobody was more excited than Sicard. Only two months earlier he and several other *Idéologues* had helped establish the Society of the Observers of Man, the world's first anthropological society dedicated to understanding the origin and differences of humankind. Victor's discovery could not have been more propitious.

Enlisting the support of Lucien Bonaparte, first the Society's secretary L.-F. Jaffret, then Sicard himself, wrote to the orphanage requesting custody of Victor and his immediate transfer to Paris. By this time however Victor had been placed under the care of the Abbé Pierre-Joseph Bonnaterre, a professor of natural history at the central school in Rodez. Apprehensive about the true status of the boy, the regional commissioner decided to put the ball back in Bonaparte's court. Explaining that Victor was probably not a savage after all and that his parents might still claim him, he suggested caution; in lieu of further instructions, Bonnaterre would continue to study the boy and report his findings. The authorities acquiesced, and Victor remained in Rodez for the next five months until Bonnaterre received a letter from Bonaparte demanding the boy be delivered to Sicard immediately. As he journeyed north to the capital, Bonnaterre prepared his report. Physically Victor differed little from children of his age. Although short and rather hairy, he was well proportioned with a pleasant face. He did not run around on all fours as rumors suggested, although he did have a strange gait and preferred to trot rather than walk. One oddity, common to other wild children, was Victor's long thumbs. More surprisingly, perhaps, the order of his senses appeared to be reversed. Relying mostly on smell, Victor seemed indifferent to cold, and, although not deaf, was unable to distinguish sounds normally. Oblivious to language, he would react to the noise of a nut cracked behind his back. Since entering society, he had started to make guttural cries, but he could not formulate words. Perhaps, as the scar across the boy's throat suggested, his vocal chords may have been damaged by an assailant, who then left him to die in the woods. Summing up, Bonnaterre reported that Victor showed few signs of intelligence; it was as if his mind and body were not connected. Devoid of purpose and with no powers of attention, he had the distinctive gaze of an imbecile, a human trapped in a purely animal existence. Whether or not Bonnaterre was truly optimistic about Victor's prospects or simply concerned to flatter his host, he ended his report with the rather absurd prediction that the "philosopher-teacher who has worked such miracles in this kind of education" offered "hope that the child who has just been confined to his care will become perhaps one day the rival of Massieu, Fontaine, and Mathieu."[27]

One can imagine Sicard's reaction when Victor finally arrived at the

Institute for the Deaf. More animal than human, the creature before him was totally unlike any child he had ever worked with. He quickly concluded his new charge was uneducable. But what could he and the Society do with the boy without tarnishing their reputations? A committee of five—comprising Pinel, Cuvier, Sicard, Jauffret, and De Gérando—was appointed to examine the reputed child of nature. Authored by Pinel, the report came straight to the point. After several months of observation it was clear that Victor was not a savage but an idiot who had probably been abandoned by his parents. Comparing him to the retarded children at the Bicêtré, Pinel argued that Victor showed no signs of perfectibility; beyond his desire for food, he paid no attention to his environment and seemed to live in a world constrained by the most primitive feelings. Bonnaterre's fantastic claims had to be forgotten; the boy, he concluded, was simply beyond help and should be institutionalized immediately.

Not everyone at the Society of the Observers of Man was convinced by Pinel's diagnosis. De Gérando argued that before concluding Victor's mental state resulted from some congenital abnormality a scientist should first determine whether long periods of isolation might not bring about a kind of *functional* idiocy. This possibility, after all, seemed to flow from Condillac's teachings. "Take away the use of all kinds of signs," the philosopher had argued, "so that [a child] cannot make even the least gesture correctly to express ordinary thoughts, and you will have an idiot."[28] Itard shared de Gérando's skepticism. Whatever similarities Victor might have with the children at the Bicêtré, he had survival skills no congenital idiot could ever acquire. He ran with astonishing swiftness, climbed trees, and, as his many bodily wounds demonstrated, he had the wit and physical power to defend himself in the wild. Evidently, a sufficient number of the Society's members were persuaded, and the group agreed to fund a trial that would determine the truth of Condillac's hypothesis.

What, Itard asked at the beginning of his first report on the wild child, "would be the degree of understanding, and the nature of the ideas of a youth, who, deprived, from his infancy, of all education, should have lived entirely separated from individuals of his species?"[29] Concluding that "the moral picture of this youth would be that of the Savage of Aveyron," he had approached Victor's condition as a case of functional insanity resulting from his social isolation. "Less like a simple youth than an infant of ten or twelve months . . . [limited by] anti-social habits, and obstinate inattention, organs scarcely flexible, and a very blunted sensibility," he adopted "that sublime art created by the Willis' and Crichton's of England, and lately introduced into France by the success and writings of Professor Pinel."[30] Following Condillac, he had awakened the boy's nervous sensibility, developed new interests, and commenced his socialization. By employing the power of speech to construct the faculties, Itard explained how Victor could acquire the mental operations necessary to understand the world. Instruction would then commence, and, who knows, the savage might even be turned into a savant.

When the experiment began, Victor's interests corresponded to his existence in a state of nature. He liked "to sleep, to eat, to do nothing, and to run in the fields."[31] He showed little concern for his new surroundings, but became extremely excited if the wind picked up or the sun appeared from behind clouds. When it snowed, he was overcome with joy and ran naked into the garden, apparently without regard to the weather. Physiologists, Itard noted, conjectured that a person's "sensibility is in exact proportion to their degree of civilization."[32] If this were true, the Savage of Aveyron was at the very lowest point of this scale. He ate food voraciously, however dirty, appeared indifferent to temperature, and, despite a keen interest in smelling almost every object he came upon, did not sneeze when a large amount of snuff was forced up his nose. Nor had anyone seen him cry. Most significantly, however, was the "complete insensibility" of Victor's ear, even to the sound of a pistol.

Because Itard's plan was "to develop the sensibility by every possible means, and to lead the mind to a habit of attention," with the help of his housekeeper, Madame Guérin, he set about exposing Victor's senses to "the most lively impressions."[33] This included several hours in a hot bath each day, until the boy showed an aversion to cold water. Within a year he could report that Victor was "sensible to the impression of all bodies, whether warm or cold, smooth or rough, soft or hard," his taste had been refined, and, much to the boy's consternation, he had even started to sneeze. Victor was not hard to please. He seemed to "delight, often almost to intoxication" playing with water and other "natural toys." Yet he showed absolutely no interest in the candies and playthings Itard hoped to use in order to multiply his wants and establish connections with the social world.[34] Itard remained in a quandary as to how he could advance the child toward civilization.[35] Following Condillac, something had to act as a reward or punishment. Returning to the basics, he hit upon a solution. He would take Victor to a restaurant and allow him to gorge himself on all his favorite foods. Combining these feasts with a ride in a carriage, he then established cues—wearing a hat, carrying a cane—that would trigger the boy's excitement. A similar strategy was used to regulate Victor's other great interest, taking walks in the countryside.

Having produced social desires in his pupil, Itard now turned to his main objective, teaching Victor the use of language. But the development of hearing presented a far greater challenge. There was no reason to think the ear itself was defective; after all Victor could discriminate those sounds he was interested in, even as he was indifferent to others. Related to his needs, Itard concluded, the organ must have "become an instrument of self-preservation, which informed him of the approach of a dangerous animal, or the fall of some wild fruit."[36] In sum, it had not been "apprenticed" to discriminate the subtitles of speech. In his new environment, Victor had become adept at expressing his needs through gestures, "the primitive language of the human species, originally employed in the infancy of society, before the labor of many ages had arranged and established the system of speech, and furnished to civilized man a fertile and sublime means of indefinite improvement."[37] As time passed, however, he started attending to human voices. It was thus with some enthusiasm that Itard caught his student responding to an "o" sound—the sound in the word "Victor" for which he was named. He also learnt the meaning of "no." But Victor could not form words, even though the scar on his neck indicated, contrary to Bonnaterre's hypothesis, that his larynx had not been damaged. Itard concluded that the organ had simply atrophied with disuse. This condition, he told his readers, presented a unique scientific opportunity: the chance to develop a method for teaching the mute to speak—Itard's great goal in his subsequent work with the deaf children at the National Institute of the Deaf. Trading on the "o" sound, he demanded the boy enunciate "eau" before receiving a drink of water. But however thirsty, Victor could do no more than grasp at the glass and produce an inarticulate hiss. Success seemed within Itard's reach when Victor was heard to utter "lait" after receiving a glass of milk. Yet try as he might, he could not get the boy to say the word first. This was a pivotal failure. "Instead of being the sign of a want," as the Condillac's theory demanded, "lait" "appeared, from the time in which it was articulated, to be merely an exclamation of joy."[38] Discouraged but not defeated, Itard elected to bide his time, hopeful that a more fortuitous opportunity would arise to establish a medium of communication with his pupil. His chance arrived as the trial neared completion. Believing

Victor's intellectual abilities had been stunted by the limited challenges of his physical existence, Itard invented a series of increasingly complex problems designed to strengthen Victor's attention and develop his memory and judgment. Following Sicard's pedagogical methods, he started by asking Victor to match common objects—scissors, a hammer, and keys—with chalk outlines drawn on a blackboard. Victor had no problem with this exercise, easily accommodating to changes in the position and orientation of the shapes, but completely lost the plot when Itard substituted words for the diagrams. Deaf students experienced no difficulty with this transition, but then, Itard conjectured, their perceptive faculties were more finely tuned than Victor's. Back to square one, he patiently taught Victor how to discriminate the various letters of the alphabet with cast metal characters, before demonstrating how L-A-I-T could be used to ask for a glass of milk. Victor grasped the idea almost immediately and readily arranged the letters whenever he wanted a drink. Itard was ecstatic. Contrary to Pinel's diagnosis, he had demonstrated Victor's capacity to learn. After only nine months, the boy was "endowed with the free exercise of all his senses . . . [gave] continual proofs of attention, reflection, and memory," and was "able to compare, discern, and judge, and apply in short all the faculties of his understanding to the objects which are connected with his instruction."[39] Having proven the truth of Locke's and Condillac's reflections and having demonstrated many facts useful to medical philosophy, Victor now stood ready to receive an education, the greatest experiment of all, and the supreme test of the new pedagogy.

Impressed by Victor's achievements, The Society of Observers of Man agreed to fund a five-year study to see what Itard could make of the boy. But by the time the experiment concluded, everything had changed. Under the influence of Napoleon, the Society had disbanded, and the Savage of Aveyron, no longer of interest to the curious, had become a forgotten being. Victor's education, moreover, although replete with minor achievements, was not the success Itard had dreamed of. "Less a story of the pupil's progress," he admitted in his second report (1806), "than an account of the teacher's failure," his student had reached a conceptual ceiling: Victor could not acquire the linguistic skills necessary for intellectual development.[40] This latter reveals both Itard's genius as a teacher and his single-minded commitment to oralism. Working in the school famous for the development of signing, he ignored the boy's spontaneous gestures and struggled year after year to teach him to hear and speak. One wonders, with Harlan Lane, what Victor's fortune might have been had he learned the language of the deaf? Especially because such instruction would not have compromised Condillac's thesis.

Itard commenced Victor's education in speech by training him to make increasingly finer discriminations between sounds. Starting with a drum and a triangle he gradually led his blindfolded student to distinguish vowel sounds, raising a different finger whenever he heard *a, e, i, o,* or *u.* This process came to a halt, when, much to Itard's annoyance, Victor started flashing his fingers randomly. Tapping his pupil's hand with a drumstick only brought greater merriment. In a moment of frustration Itard struck the boy—and the bond between them was lost. Fear replaced pleasure, and the course of instruction was totally undermined. Seeking to restore the boy's trust, Itard set about teaching him how to read. Victor had learned to use LAIT as an expression of pleasure rather than a sign. Determined to forge a stronger bond between word and object, Itard taught his pupil to fetch common objects from around the house that corresponded with printed labels. Eventually Victor was able to retrieve several items at once after being shown their names. But Itard had assumed too much, for, as he soon discovered, the boy interpreted each word as signifying a particular object, not a general term. Again he retreated and, through a series of ingenious exercises, gradually got Victor to appreciate that a name can refer to a class. Following Sicard's methods, he even taught the meaning of some adjectives and verbs and showed Victor how to arrange letters into simple words that could communicate his basic needs.

Given that Victor was unable to imitate sounds, Itard thought he might be able to teach the power of speech by sight. For "over a year," he confessed, "all my efforts and all our exercises aimed at this one end."[41] Sitting "face to face, grimacing as hard as possible . . . exercising the muscles of the eyes, forehead, mouth and jaw in every kind of movement . . . gradually concentrating on the muscles of the lips . . . and then the tongue," the pupil followed his teacher in what must have been a truly surreal ritual. But all to no avail; after twelve months the sounds Victor produced were no more distinct than on the day the experiment began. Finally reconciled to the futility of his quest, Itard admitted defeat and abandoned his "pupil to a life of incurable dumbness."[42]

Even more problematic for the teacher was the boy's increasingly violent behavior. Without any understanding of sexual roles, Victor struggled to ac-

commodate the torrent of emotions brought on by puberty. Habitually rest-
less, he would erupt into uncontrolled rages that never seemed to relieve his
tension. On several occasions Itard tried to calm Victor down by bleeding
him. He even considered "revealing the secret of his anxieties and the reason
for his desires," but demurred, recognizing that by identifying this need "our
Savage . . . would doubtless" seek to satisfy it "publicly as his other needs,"
thus leading "him into acts of great indecency."[43] Here was an obstacle no
amount of ingenuity could scale. Admitting defeat, he summed up the positive and negative results of his experiment. Victor had acquired the ability to
discriminate sensations and had greatly improved his intellectual faculties. He
had started to use symbols to communicate meaning. He had been socialized
and had developed affectionate relationships. Itard even claimed that he had
acquired a sense of justice—a knowledge of right and wrong that elevated
him to the "full stature of moral man."[44] But without speech or hearing
Victor's education was bound to be incomplete. Unlike normal children,
he had missed the critical period when learning is most natural. Consequently, every step demanded the most strenuous effort. Add to this Victor's
uncontrollable outbursts, and there seemed little hope that he could ever control his passions sufficiently to continue his education in a meaningful way.
All Itard could hope was that this unfortunate child of nature would receive
the support and protection of the government. On the bright side, whatever
the fate of Victor, Itard could at least boast he had discovered "a collection
of facts relevant to the illumination of the history of medical philosophy, the
study of uncivilized man and the organization of certain types of private
education."[45] A claim, it turns out, that Edward Séguin (and Samuel Gridley
Howe) proved true some twenty years later when he adapted Itard's pedagogy
to the education of idiots.

FROM IDEOLOGY TO ORGANOLOGY

In 1807, two years after Itard had terminated his experiment, Gall and Spurzheim visited Victor at the home of Mme. Guérin. The so-called savage of
Aveyron, they reported, was "weak-minded to a great degree."[46] "His forehead is very little enlarged laterally, and very much compressed from above
downward; his eyes are small and greatly sunken, his cerebellum little developed."[47] He had a tranquil disposition and behaved politely throughout, although "constantly balancing the upper part of his body and his head."[48]

They also noted his inattention to sounds. Despite all of Itard's training, he failed to respond when his name was spoken or a glass struck behind his head. As for his education, after years of patient and kind training, they noted that Victor was able to do little more than match a few words with objects and return some common household items to their proper place.

Condillac had pointed to cases of feral children to support his thesis that the faculties are constructed, through language, from the basic sensations of pleasure and pain. Outside of society, and without signs, he claimed, human beings would be consigned to the life of brutes. For Gall and Spurzheim, this was not the lesson of history and certainly not the conclusion to be drawn from Itard's experiment. Individuals of every species, they maintained, were uniquely adapted with behavioral traits necessary for participation in the social life of the group. Such instincts did not change with time or place. Throughout the past men and women had always lived in communities and always demonstrated exactly the same virtues and vices—the only progress was the objects to which these faculties were applied.

Far from supporting Condillac's argument, Victor's story revealed the truth of Pinel's diagnosis—that the boy was simply an idiot who had been left to die in the woods. Such children, Gall predicted, would always bear the same unmistakable physiological marks; their heads would be "either too large and affected with hydrocephalus, or too small, compressed and deformed; almost always with a scurflous constitution; eyes small, sunken, slightly opened upwards, closed horizontally; the mouth very large, the lips pendulant, the tongue thick, the neck swollen, the pace swaggering and insecure."[49] If a well-organized child had been left to wander in nature, he conjectured, their fate would be very different. They would certainly not have "adapted to the mode of living and the character of wild beasts" and, upon entering "society, [would] be seen to develop human dispositions, not only by a prompt imitation of social usage's, but by his capacity for instruction."[50] A fact, he took it, proven by the education of the deaf.

Turning sensationalism on its head, Gall and Spurzheim presented all desires and faculties as innate features of the brain. While opposed to the radical environmentalism of Condillac, this new physiologically based account of human nature nonetheless still resonated with the central mission of the *Idéologues*, explaining the moral in terms of the physical. Grounded in comparative neural anatomy, their study of the mind was also part of zoology. And, moreover, as medical men, they denounced metaphysics and strongly

supported the kind of scientifically informed social and educational practices
Cabanis and Tracy promoted. Of course, there were plenty of reasons for the
Idéologues to reject Gall and Spurzheim's work, not least of which was the
suspicion of fatalism, which might undermine aspects of Cabanis's progressive political agenda. There were also troubling questions about the scientific
validity of the Germans's research—a fear of charlatanry, captured in popular
accounts of cranial readings, that might further exacerbate Napoleon's skepticism about the value of the human sciences. Even so, for many physicians
seeking theoretical insight and professional standing, phrenology was a natural successor to the doctrines of Cabanis and Tracy. Certainly, spiritualist
thinkers were in no doubt that Gall's new science was an offspring of Ideology; yet another materialistic doctrine that suggested atheism and undermined the essential ethical principles holding society together. Both Gall and
Spurzheim strenuously rejected such charges, vigorously insisting that the
brain was simply an *instrument* by which the soul manifested itself within the
body. The intricate structure of the cerebral organs, Spurzheim would claim,
was proof that God had adapted men and women to the world and that the
natural laws governing moral behavior provided a *religious* justification for the
kind of progressive social policies and educational institutions envisioned by
the *Idéologues*. For the phrenologists, secularism, and the imperative to engineer human improvement through education, would become the gospel of
practical Christianity.

2
Ideology and Education in Virginia

Information in the last letter of M. de La Feyette that your eye sight has improved excites in me a hope that you might be able to finish your last work, and fill up the Ideological circle in which you made so great and happy a progress. I hope it for the benefit of a child of my old age, the University of Virginia. . . . It's [*sic*] misfortune will be that identity of language will confine the choice of it's [*sic*] professors to the countries speaking our own. But it will still be your science which shall get thro' that medium.

Thomas Jefferson to Destutt de Tracy, Nov. 5, 1823

In his 1957 introduction to *Living Thoughts of Thomas Jefferson*, John Dewey claimed that French political philosophy had little influence on Jefferson.[1] With the possible exception of laws governing the inheritance of property, Dewey maintained that "every one of Jefferson's characteristic political ideas . . . was definitely formulated by him before" he assumed the position of American Ambassador in Paris during the summer of 1784.[2] Jefferson's *Notes on Virginia*, composed in 1781 and 1782, seems to support Dewey's contention.[3] Responding to a number of queries from the French Legation in Philadelphia, he contributed to a statistical survey of America with a wide-ranging account of the geographical, economic, social, and political conditions of life in the state that clearly demonstrates the continuity of his early and later thoughts.

The scope of Jefferson's scientific learning, his classical erudition, and his articulate defense of liberal ideals—including the doctrine of natural rights and the separation of church and state—was immediately appreciated by the philosophes.[4] But while discussing history and government with Filippo Mazzei, the nature of species with Buffon, and race with Condorcet, Jefferson always kept an intellectual and social distance between himself and the French savants. Shocked by Parisian morals, and, it seems, his own errant passions, he could not emulate the flamboyant Franklin. Of all the societies he visited, he was perhaps most at home in the salon of Mme Helvétius. The meeting place of Condillac, Diderot, D'Alembert, and D'Holbach, during the 1780s, Auteuil became a retreat for materialist philosophers and liberal political theorists. It was here that the shy and retiring Virginian formed his closest bonds with Pierre Cabanis, Pierre de La Rosche (editor of Helvétius's collected works), and the economic theorist Pierre Samuel Du Pont de Nemours. Schooled in the writings of Locke, Shaftsbury, Bolingbroke, Hutchinson, and Kames, Jefferson was clearly sympathetic to the political and epistemological discourse of the salon. But he did not adopt a new master. Rejecting the radical implications of sensationalism, he returned home still firmly grounded in the Scottish moral sense philosophy and Whig political thought he had imbibed as a youth. It was only in the final two decades of his life, after his retirement from the presidency, that Jefferson became enamored with the work of Destutt de Tracy and an advocate for Ideology in America. Accordingly, Dewey and other commentators are somewhat wide of the mark in concluding that, if there were a stream of influence between the two nations, it was surely from America to France, for, as this chapter will show, Tracy's materialistic writings, especially his texts on economics, politics, religion, and public schooling provided a powerful philosophical justification for Jefferson's mature vision of a virtuous republic.[5] As he announced in 1820, after establishing a professorship in Ideology at the University of Virginia, he intended Tracy's works "to become the Statesman's Manual with us."[6]

THE IMPROVEMENT OF THE RACE

Jefferson's educational proposals are contained in Query 14 of the *Notes*, right after his discussion of race, an appropriate location given his views on the perfectibility of human nature and the fact that 40 percent of the states' population lived under the yoke of slavery. This authoritative account of the physical, moral, and intellectual capacities of the red, white, and black peoples of the New World shaped debates over the emancipation and schooling of African Americans for the next seventy-five years.[7] Indeed, it was the nest of legal and scientific arguments spawned by Jefferson's thoughts over the identity of the human species—the status of the mulatto, the relationship between climate and race, and the consequences of social integration—that Samuel Gridley Howe was forced to reconcile with Whig political ideology in the founding document of the American Freedmen's Bureau (see Chapter 16).

Jefferson opened his discussion of human improvement with an explanation of how the State of Virginia had revised colonial laws to fit the spirit of the new republic. Chief among these changes and contrary to Dewey's claim was an amendment to the rules of descent ensuring "that the lands of any person dying intestate shall be divisible equally among all his children" and legislation "to establish religious freedom on the broadest bottom."[8] Jefferson also explained that, although not yet brought before the government, a resolution had been drafted to emancipate the state's slaves, colonizing blacks to some distant land and recruiting white workers to take their place. "It will probably be asked," he continued, "why not retain and incorporate the blacks into the state, and thus save the expense of supplying, by importation of white settlers, the vacancies they will leave?"[9] He responded with two separate arguments: the deep-seated social prejudices of whites and the basic "distinctions which nature has made" between the races. After enumerating a number of physiological differences—skin color, hair, sweat glands, size of the lungs, and sleeping habits (all of which had important moral implications)—he turned to the intellectual capacities of blacks. Unlike Indians, who developed art and "astonish you with strokes of the most sublime oratory; such as prove their reason and sentiment strong, their imagination glowing and elevated," the African knew nothing of drawing and produced only the crudest music. Even the literary works of educated blacks were immature.[10] Their "imagination," he concluded, was "dull, tasteless, and anomalous."[11] If "in memory" they were "equal to the whites; in reason [they were] much inferior."[12] Could such differences be explained by the cruel and harsh terms of their confinement? Apparently not. Despite even harsher conditions, the classical world bore testimony to the achievements of white slaves. "Misery," Jefferson reflected, was "often the parent of the most affecting touches in poetry."[13] "Among the blacks is misery enough, God knows, but no poetry."[14] In any case, he insisted, the commonly recognized "improvement of the blacks in body and mind, in the first instance of their mixture with the whites, has been observed by every one, and proves that their inferiority is not the effect merely of their condition of life."[15] He conjectured therefore "as a suspicion only, that the blacks, whether originally a distinct race, or made distinct by time and circumstances, are inferior to the whites in the endowments both of body and mind." "Will not a lover of natural history," he asked, "one who views the gradations in all the races of animals with the eye of philosophy, excuse an effort to keep those in the department of man as distinct as nature has formed them?"[16] The purity of the white race was at stake. "Among the Romans," he noted, "emancipation required but one effort. The slave, when made free, might mix without staining the blood of his master. But with us a second is necessary, unknown to history. When freed, he is to be removed beyond the reach of mixture."[17] Torn between morality and practicality, he would spare no effort to prepare emancipated slaves for independent living—"sending them to a distant land with arms, implements of household and of the handicraft arts, feeds, pairs of useful animals etc."— but offered absolutely no hope of schooling for the blacks of Virginia.[18]

For white citizens, however, education was integral to Jefferson's political principles. He even claimed that his 1779 Bill for the More General Diffusion of Knowledge "was the most important bill in our whole code," completing, had it passed, the laws against entails and primogeniture and the separation of church and state.[19] As Montesquieu taught, he understood that corruption nestled in all societies and that a political mechanism had to be devised to prevent the degeneration of government. But rather than the widely vaulted checks and balances of the British system, Jefferson put his faith in representative government and the good sense of the common man to elect wise and virtuous leaders—or, more accurately, representatives who would elect wise and virtuous leaders. "Having put down the aristocracy of the 'clergy' and nurturing an equality of condition" among the population, he later told John Adams that "education would have raised the mass of the people to the high ground of moral respectability necessary to their own safety, and to orderly government; and would have completed the great object of qualifying them to select the veritable *aristori,* for the trusts of government."[20] Schooling in Jefferson's Virginia would thus have two components: the development of a literate population capable of making informed choices and the education of the moral and intellectual elite.

Where Adams saw the great aim of government as management of the passions, Jefferson put his faith in a basic moral sense common to all men and women. Conscience, he told his nephew Peter Carr, was as much a part of human nature "as the sense of hearing, seeing, feeling."[21] While given to individuals

in a stronger or weaker degree . . . [it] may be strengthened by exercise, as may any particular limb of the body. This sense is submitted, indeed, in some degree, to the guidance of reason; but it is a small stock which is required for this: even a less one than what we call common sense. State a moral case to a ploughman and a professor. The former will decide it as well, and often better than the latter, because he has not been led astray by artificial rules.[22]

Armed with this insight, and a basic knowledge of the natural and social worlds, the citizenry themselves could provide the moral foundation of a virtuous community. To this end, he proposed a system of free education for all (white) children. Situated within each ward (a five-square-mile miniature republic), schools would be erected and a teacher employed to provide three years of instruction in reading, writing, and arithmetic, together with lessons in the principles of civic virtue and Republican government. Study of the Bible—which was far too demanding for the immature mind—was to be replaced with "useful facts from Grecian, Roman, European and American history" that would teach the essential character of human nature and the basic hierarchical structure of a good society.[23] As reason strengthened, such knowledge would then enable each citizen "to work out their own greatest happiness, by shewing them that it does not depend on the condition of life in which chance has placed them, but is always the result of a good conscience, good health, occupation, and freedom in all just pursuits."[24] Jefferson's grand vision of a political community sustained through public schooling was thus quite different to the kind of embryonic democracy central to Dewey's educational philosophy: progress and stability would be achieved through deference to wise and noble leaders, not a faith in common intelligence and conjoint problem solving.

Jefferson's second concern was the selection and education of the elite. Conscious of the ethical problems of eugenic engineering, "for experience proves that moral and physical qualities of man, whether good or evil, are transmissible in a certain degree from father to son," he contented himself with the existence of an "accidental *aristori* produced by the fortuitous concourse of breeders."[25] This, he told Adams, was "the most precious gift of nature for the instruction, the trusts, and government of society."[26] He thus proposed a revolutionary scheme for the selection and training of his natural aristocracy. Each year the school's visitors would select the top boy and send him, at public expense, to one of twenty grammar schools established around the state. After one or two years of study in "Greek, Latin, geography, and the higher branches of numerical arithmetic," the most able would be selected for four more years of instruction. "By this means," Jefferson asserted, "twenty of the best geniusses [*sic*] will be raked from the rubbish annually."[27] Finally, at the end of their education, "one half are to be discontinued (from among whom the grammar schools will probably be supplied with future masters); and the other half, who are to be chosen for the superiority of their parts and disposition, are to be sent and continued three years in the study of such sciences as they shall chuse, at William and Mary college."[28]

The final part of this scheme demanded a radical revision to Jefferson's alma mater. As argued in Bill 80 for Amending the Constitution of the College of William and Mary, the original mission of preparing Anglican ministers had to give way to the civic needs of the people. This entailed replacing Latin, Greek, and Divinity with a more secular, scientific curriculum. Ancient languages, he complained in the *Notes*, "filled the college with children."[29] By restricting such preparatory skills to the previous educational level, professional schools in Law, Medicine, and Government could be established to transform traditional on-the-job training with knowledge of the principles governing human nature.

Although the legislature failed to approve Bill 80, Jefferson was able to institute elements of his plan in 1779, when, as governor, he became a trustee of the college. Under his guidance, the curriculum was reorganized around professorships in Law and Police; Anatomy and Medicine; Natural Philosophy and Mathematics; Moral Philosophy, the Law of Nature and Nations, and the Fine Arts; and Modern Languages. In the *Notes* he expressed hope that other professorships would soon be funded to offer specialized work in the sciences. But the college's charter, its lack of funds, and its increasing isolation from the political center of the state frustrated Jefferson's goals. By 1800 he had given up on transforming William and Mary. Virginia, he now understood, needed a new state university to educate its future leaders and offer the South an alternative to what he saw as the baleful influence of New England learning. Jefferson was also frustrated by the legislature's reluctance to fund public schools and religious opposition to his ward system, which was widely perceived as a threat to the basic parish structure. A much diluted form of Bill 79 did pass in 1796, but, Jefferson explained in his *Autobiography*, on realizing that the taxes levied for instruction "would throw on wealth the education of the poor . . . the more wealthy class were unwilling to incur that burden," and, as a result, schooling failed "to commence in a single county."[30]

As Jefferson's duties drew his attention to the national stage, he also considered a number of schemes to establish public education across the country. Most important was his plan for townships in the territories. Developed at the Continental Congress and passed into law in the land ordinances of 1785 and 1787, he divided each new community into thirty-six one-mile squares for sale at auction and dedicated the proceeds or rent of the sixteenth section to the construction of a common school. Congress later earmarked a further one hundred thousand acres of land for the establishment of a university.

While in France, Jefferson had explored the possibility of founding a national university with émigré faculty from the University of Geneva. Later, as president, he supported Joel Barlow's scheme for a national university and institute of learning based on the French model and commissioned Du Pont de Nemours to design a system of schooling for the entire country. Neither proposal was embraced by Congress; indeed, it seems that Jefferson had his own reservations about the federal control of knowledge. But he did establish the U.S. Military Academy at West Point—although, characteristically, he hoped this would serve to democratize the army and undermine federalism by teaching fidelity to his principles of Republicanism. However, it was after his return to Monticello, in the 1810s and 1820s, that Jefferson threw all his energy into the cause of educational reform, proposing once again the three-tiered system of public schooling outlined in Bills 79 and 80. Only now, influenced by the philosophy and social science of the *Idéologues,* his original plan was strengthened by the political philosophy of Tracy, who, in the years prior to Napoleon, had been instrumental in establishing a similar structure of schooling in France.

DESTUTT DE TRACY

When, in the aftermath of the Terror, Sieyès, Garat, Volney, and many of the other liberal reformers who met at the salon of Mme Helvétius gained power in the Directory (1795–99), they turned to the moral philosophy and disciplinary pedagogy sketched by Cabanis as the means to bring order and stability to the new republic. Public policy was to be informed by "the science of man," or what would later become known as "social science." This incipient movement acquired philosophical focus in 1796, when Cabanis's friend Destutt de Tracy was elected to the section on the analysis of sensations and ideas at the National Institute. It was Tracy who laid out the political agenda flowing from this physiologically based sensationalist epistemology and coined the ill-fated neologism *Idéologie.*

A youthful supporter of the American Republic and Turgot's liberal reforms, Tracy embraced revolutionary calls for greater representation of the Third Estate. As a delegate of the Bourbonnais nobility in the National Assembly (1789–91) he supported the Declaration of the Rights of Man, advocated the abolition of slavery in the French colonies, and strongly endorsed anticlerical legislation. Together with Cabanis, Du Pont de Nemours, Talleyrand, Garat, Sieyès, Condorcet, and the other intellectuals who met at the *Société* 1789, he envisioned a scientifically enlightened representative government that avoided the radical egalitarianism of the Democrats. Most troubling for Tracy was the spreading discontent in the army. A colonel under Lafayette (the future father-in-law of his daughter), he struggled to maintain discipline amid radical attacks on the privilege of rank. With the arrest of the king, and Lafayette's subsequent escape to Belgium, Tracy resigned his commission and retired to Auteuil, where, out of the public eye, he kept company with Condorcet and Cabanis. But Tracy's aristocratic background proved too much for the Jacobins. Imprisoned for eleven months, he was only saved from the guillotine by the fall of Robespierre. It was during this internment that he immersed himself in Condillac and the other philosophical works that would become the basis for *Idéologie*—literally, the science of ideas.

Like the epistemological and behavioral doctrines of the logical positivists, Tracy believed that a sound foundation for knowledge could be established by carefully assembling ideas out of the basic features of sense experience: thought had to proceed from simple to complex in steps immediately comprehensible to the attentive mind. In contrast to Condillac, however, Tracy did not view the faculties as an amalgamation of sensations, but rather, as Cabanis explained, basic responses of the human organization. Perception, memory, judgment, and desire were functions of the brain, the nervous system, and the bodily temperaments. Ultimately, Ideology was part of zoology. But it also suggested rational laws of mind and behavior. Fusing Condillac's analysis of signs with a moderate utilitarianism, he explained how social and moral codes could be constructed to foster happiness. The key to human well-being was the creation of a political order that properly regulated desires by rewarding virtue and punishing vice. For although direct instruction in moral principles might influence the behavior of more philosophic minds, the average person learned little from the classroom or the catechism: the legislator and the laws were the true teachers of mankind. Rejecting the concept of a moral intuition, Tracy was adamant that even the most basic notions of right and wrong were acquired through socialization in the family and other cultural institutions. It was thus incumbent upon political leaders to engineer public and private practices that would develop correct habits and teach the population the fundamental link between reason, virtue, and happiness. This included maintaining an economy that fostered small industry while eliminating debt, speculation, and the evils of extreme wealth; the abolition of primogeniture; and the removal of clerical influence over civil institutions.

Political economy was at the heart of Tracy's system. Grounded in his conception of human well-being, productive activity was to be measured by "goods" that promoted the full and harmonious development of the faculties. Following Jean Baptiste Say, he rejected the physiocrats' premise that wealth was measured by agricultural production. According to Du Pont de Nemours, for example, manufacturing and commerce contributed little to the creation of useful goods: the key to prosperity was simply to increase the efficiency of farming. Characterizing the efforts of the bourgeoisie as sterile, he promoted economic development through improved agricultural techniques and a centralized monarchy capable of coordinating the production and distribution of food. Say thought that this focus on agriculture was too narrow. The manufacturing and commercial classes were also involved in producing food and the many other goods that contributed to the country's wealth. Value, which reflected human needs, was best measured by the market. Tracy concurred. It was not the middle classes that were sterile, but the landowners who lived in luxury off the labors of the peasants. There were three actors in Tracy's economic system; the savant, educated to understand the scientific principles governing nature and society; the worker, who provided the physical power necessary for production; and the entrepreneur, who invested capital to make possible socially useful enterprises. While accepting the inequalities inherent in this organization of money, mind, and labor, he insisted that the interests of each class were best served by developing their talents in the position that fate had placed them—much as Jefferson had argued in the *Notes*. Under the guidance of the savant, modest industrialization could be encouraged without falling afoul of unrestrained capitalism and the gross inequalities that it produced. Tracy was hopeful that in an enlightened liberal state property owners would realize the value of well-paid and well-trained workers, while an educated populace, empowered with the kind of representative government established in America, would appreciate the importance of electing scientifically trained, virtuous leaders who would work for the common weal rather than for narrow class interests.

Indeed, Jefferson's Republicanism seems to have served as something of a blueprint for Tracy's political theory. In his *Critique of Montesquieu's Spirit of the Laws* (composed in 1805–6 as Napoleon consolidated power and disenfranchised the *Idéologues*), Tracy defended representative government as a modern solution to the problem of a just society.[31] Montesquieu identified three basic forms of government (republic, monarchy, and despotism) and explored the sentiments each created in order to retain authority over the population. In Tracy's mind this division failed to carve the political world at its joints. Governments, he believed, were more productively categorized according to whether they promoted the general will or special interests. In addition, rather than asking how each conserved power, it was far more important to examine how they promoted public or private good through the dissemination of knowledge. As Montesquieu noted, only "those governments which are founded on reason, can alone desire that education should be exempt from prejudice."[32] "In a hereditary monarchy," Tracy pointed out, a prince "ought to inculcate and propagate the maxims of passive obedience, and a profound veneration for the established forms."[33] There should be a "dislike for the spirit of innovation and enquiry, or the discussion of political principles."[34] And, "above all," Tracy continued, he should employ "religious ideas, which taking possession of the mind from the cradle, make durable and deep impressions, form habits, and fix opinions, long before the age of reflexion."[35] Conversely, in a republic, a government fearing "error and prejudice" would "constantly attend to the propagation of accurate and solid knowledge of all kinds" and

> prevent the poor class from becoming vicious, ignorant, or miserable; the opulent class from becoming insolent and fond of false knowledge; and should cause both to approach that middle point, at which the love of order, of industry, of justice, and reason, naturally establish themselves.[36]

Tracy gained a powerful weapon in his battle against the hegemony of the church with the publication of Charles Dupuis's twelve-volume *Origin of all Religious Worship* (1795).[37] As Tracy summarized Dupuis in his anonymous

Analysis, all the world's religions, including Christianity, could be reduced to myths of nature, allegorical tales, and metaphysical constructs that sought to explain the unknown forces governing events. Dupuis was particularly severe on the priesthood, which, he claimed, had constructed elaborate theological arguments to silence rational inquiry and defend the spiritualization of nature. Rather than elevating the population by teaching that happiness and virtue went hand in hand, it sought to maintain social privilege by spreading superstition and fear. In 1799, Tracy had an opportunity to correct this abuse and construct his own vision of a rational and moral society. Elected to the Council for Public Instruction, he poured his energies into fashioning elite schools for future leaders, convinced that a class of scientifically trained savants could craft the institutional practices, legal statues, and popular customs necessary to perfect the intellectual and moral powers of the masses.

THE GOVERNMENT OF MIND

One of the central pillars of the constitution drawn up by the National Assembly was a commitment to the education of all citizens.[38] Having eliminated the tithes and taxes that supported religious schools, nationalized church property, and suppressed traditional universities, the Assembly turned to the construction of a system of public education free from ecclesiastical control. This meant a radical revision of the religiously oriented Latin curriculum maintained by the church, in line with the theories of mind and secular ethics advanced by enlightenment thinkers. But while clear in their political aims and philosophy of education, the revolutionary planners struggled with the particulars. The philosophes had left no blueprints, and there was no other national system of schooling for them to draw upon. Should all children attend school beyond the elementary level? Should fees be assessed? Was education to be controlled by state or by local officials? Buildings, desks, books, and teachers—everything was open to debate. It is hardly surprising then that more than twenty proposals were submitted in the first two years of the Republic. Most influential were the schemes of Mirabeau (authored and published by Cabanis) and Talleyrand (1791), both of which proposed a four-tier system comprising elementary and secondary schools, technical colleges or lycées (to replace universities), and a National Institute.

To review these proposals the short-lived Legislative Assembly (1791–

92) appointed a Committee on Public Instruction under the leadership of Condorcet—who had roused popular opinion the previous year with a series of five memoirs on the necessity of education to the future of the Republic. Condorcet's report, *The General Organization of Public Instruction*, preserved this same basic structure while advancing a more egalitarian philosophy.[39] Not that he endorsed the leveling scheme of Robespierre, who, in 1793, advocated a nationwide system of boarding schools, Maisons d'Egalités, in which children from ages five to twelve could be raised without distinction. Condorcet's goal was simply to avoid the great disparities in education that underwrote the political oppression of the *Ancien Régime*. Similar in its details to Jefferson's proposal, but with two extra levels, he suggested primary schools to educate the masses free of charge; secondary education, with scholarships for the able poor; district grammar schools; and lycées. Finally, above and controlling all, would be a National Institute divided into classes for mathematics and physical science, the moral and political sciences, the applied sciences, and literature and the fine arts.

Condorcet's timing could not have been worse. Before any action could be taken, the Assembly turned to face the threat of the Austrian and Prussian alliance, and all enthusiasm for educational reform was lost in the tide of nationalistic spirit. It was not until the end of 1794, with the rise to power of the *Idéologues,* that the National Convention (1792–95) finally started to take action. Marked by the execution of Louis XVI (December 1792) and the Jacobin Terror (September 1792–June 1794), the intervening years had decimated cultural life. Schools, universities, and learned societies had been closed, and many prominent intellectual leaders and public figures, including Condorcet (who denied the guillotine by drinking a poison provided by Cabanis), had been put to death or ostracized. The need for order now superseded the need for equality. As the *Idéologues* saw it, schooling had to establish a secular morality necessary for a stable republican government and France's place as the leading center for science and the arts restored. Again, the Committee on Public Instruction was asked for its recommendations. This time, under the guidance of Garat, Joseph Lanakal authored a number of reports suggesting amendments to Condorcet's scheme in line with growing antidemocratic sympathies. Eventually passed into legislation, most importantly in Pierre Daunou's Law of the Third Brumaire (October 25, 1795), a comprehensive, if hierarchical, system of education was founded—and remained in place until Napoleon reorganized French schooling in 1802, and the National Institute in 1803.

The Daunou law required that one or more fee-paying primary schools be located in each canton and an *école centrale,* a center for learning and educational activities, established in every department. Unlike the secondary schools envisioned by Condorcet, these were not meant to be an extension of primary education, but rather separate elite academies for students beyond age twelve who wished to prepare for higher education or careers in the civil service. Indeed, in contrast to the more radical plans of the Assembly, primary schooling was not even compulsory, although, as in Jefferson's scheme, funds were provided for the advancement of the most exceptional students in the lower orders. This provision did little to satisfy democratic critics who bemoaned the loss of earlier, more egalitarian schemes. Thus, where the primary schools were charged to teach the fundamentals of reading, writing, arithmetic, natural history, and the basis of republican government to the working poor, the more academic curriculum of the central school—which comprised drawing, ancient languages, mathematics, physics, chemistry, general grammar, *belles-lettres,* history, and legislation—was designed for children of the middle classes. The next level of education also departed from Condorcet's plan. Instead of the lycées, ten higher specialized academies were to be founded. And, although a National Institute was established, it also differed in structure and mission to what Condorcet envisioned. Less a controlling body for the whole system than a center in which to celebrate French learning—a living encyclopedia of knowledge, as Daunou put it—the Institute, omitting the applied sciences, divided 144 of France's leading scholars into the remaining three of Condorcet's four classes.[40] Cabanis, Tracy, and several other prominent *Idéologues* were appointed to a section of the Second Class on Moral and Political Sciences devoted to the analysis of sensations and ideas.

At the height of the Jacobin dictatorship, plans had been drawn up to develop a corps of teachers armed with the knowledge and pedagogic skills necessary to educate a nation of republican citizens. Ten thousand men would attend a central seminary in Paris, and from there disseminate correct practices by opening Normal schools in their own departments. Supportive of this initiative to spread the art of teaching, Garat and Lanakal combined early in 1794 to advocate the establishment of what would become the *Ecole*

Normale. But with the change in political climate, their political interests gradually changed from preparing primary teachers to establishing a higher seat of learning to guide the education of an elite class. Accordingly, when the *Ecole Normale* opened in January 1795, a single auditorium in the Natural History Museum, the fourteen eminent professors engaged for the four-month semester did not have young children on their mind. Rather, their courses laid out the curriculum of the *écoles centrals,* established the following month by the Law of 3 Ventose. Among the many notable intellectuals, Lagrange and Laplace lectured on mathematics, Garat on "Analysis of the Understanding," and Sicard on general grammar. All of this must have appeared quite esoteric to the majority of students, who had been sent by local authorities in order to train as primary school teachers. By May, more than half had departed, leaving the faculty to justify their role as the guardians of higher education rather than masters of pedagogy.

As its first few years of existence soon revealed, the public school system created by Daunou's Law faced serious problems. Hindered by the lack of central authority, the *Idéologues'* plans were invariably subverted by local conditions. The chief concern was the existence of a large number of Catholic independent schools guaranteed by the right of conscience secured in Title X of the constitution. Often supported by charitable funds, this alternative system enrolled more than half of all pupils. Not only did this subvert Condorcet's goal of a unified system, but, for democratic critics within the Directory, it became a palpable threat to the Republic. Orthodox clergy, it was claimed in the debates of 1798, were using elementary schools in a counterhegemonic struggle against the political ideology of the Revolution. To combat this threat, laws were enacted to bring private education in line with public policy. Government officials had to enroll their children in public schools; local authorities were charged with monitoring private education to ensure that schools used approved textbooks; and, in order to exclude any priest not committed to civic codes, headmasters had to be married or widowers. As for the central schools, the confusing mission of educating both university and primary level students led to a hodgepodge of classes for all ages and abilities. Attendance was sporadic, lectures were disorganized, and teachers lacked training. With no bureaucratic mechanism to enforce its directives, most of the ministry's edicts fell on deaf ears.

Equally important to democratic critics was the divide between elementary and secondary schooling. The curriculum of the *écoles centrales* did not dovetail with the primary schools', and, by the Law 3 Brumaire, students were not permitted to enroll until age twelve, three years after their elementary education was completed. Fearful of creating a new aristocracy, Democrats called for sweeping changes. The *Idéologues* resisted. The staggering costs aside, they saw no purpose in expanding the education of the masses. What was the use of schooling millions of peasants in the higher branches of knowledge? Too much learning would only sour the worker for the life of toil to which they were destined. Primary education, Tracy explained, had to be short and sweet. It should ensure literacy and the most basic knowledge and values of the social elite. Unlike Jefferson, he did not even think it appropriate for the children of the *classe savante* to attend primary schools. Far better that the future leaders of society stay home and cultivate their tastes in a more refined environment until they had the maturity to pursue the more demanding curriculum outlined in his *Observations sur le Systême Actuel d'Instruction Publique,* an eight-year syllabus in language and literature, the physical sciences and mathematics, and the ideological, moral, and political sciences.[41]

But debate was mute. With foreign armies surrounding France, and the threat of a Jacobin revival, Liberals threw their support behind Bonaparte's coup d'état of November 1799. Led by Sieyies, the *Idéologues* helped engineer Napoleon's rise by designing the three-chamber scheme of the Legislative Body, the Tribunate, and the Conservative Senate—only to compromise their own authority in the final agreement by ceding executive power to the First Council. Napoleon did not have to answer to the Senate. Thus, on December 28, when Tracy, Cabanis, Garat, and a host of other *Idéologues* accepted the honored and highly paid role of senators, they lost a direct voice in the formation of government policy. From then on, as they ceased to be of value to the First Council, they gradually became Napoleon's scapegoats, idealistic metaphysicians, responsible for all the ills of the revolution. The faults of the school system would now be addressed by administrative fiat rather than parliamentary debate.

At first the *Idéologues* were confidant that Napoleon would help carry their scheme forward; a visitor at Auteuil and a member of the National Institute, Bonaparte had courted the approval of intellectuals and promised to maintain important political appointments. Crucial for their educational ambitions was the Council on Public Instruction, an advisory group formed in October 1798 to guide the Minister of the Interior. Originally comprising eight members of the National Institute, including four from the section on analysis of sensations and ideas, the ideological agenda of the group was strengthened the following February when Tracy joined their number.

In 1797 secondary teachers were instructed to submit their lesson plans and course notes, but few responded. Determined to see how Ideological principles were being enacted, Tracy issued a rather stern reminder together with a detailed questionnaire designed to assess the effectiveness of the nation's 100 central schools. He was not happy with the results, but mindful of the debates raging in the legislature, took care to press his principles without opening the central schools to political attack. Tracy was most concerned with the presentation of history, geography, legislation, and political economy, the social sciences necessary for the future savants of his secular state. In a number of circulars distributed just prior to Napoleon's coup, he reminded professors of the relationship between mind and language, and the system of laws, institutions, and social customs that arose from knowledge of human nature. As teachers of future legislators and administrators, it was their duty to prepare students with the ability to shape behavior in positive ways. Yet the materials they presented revealed either a total misunderstanding of Ideology or a stubborn commitment to Spiritualism. The fundamental problem, Tracy reported, was the failure to make the philosophy of language the basis for all learning. How could students understand the purpose of their studies if they did not appreciate the basic relationship between signs and thought? Recommending that they read Condillac, he outlined the Ideological project and explained how an ordered system of signs yielded knowledge free from conceptual confusion. Ideology itself had to become a subject of instruction if students were to be correctly prepared for classes in legislation, literature, and history.

Armed with an understanding of mind and character, pupils would explore civic codes, criminal law, and commercial regulations and critically evaluate their tendencies to promote freedom, prosperity, and happiness. They would then be poised to appreciate the development of societies through history. Like Condorcet, in his monumental *Sketch for a Historical Picture of the Progress of the Human Mind* (1795), Tracy viewed the past through the lens of ignorance and oppression. The traditional script of sacred tales, heroic stories, and political myths had to be replaced by a scientific study of peoples that revealed the causal structures underlying social progress.

Unfortunately for the *Idéologues*, secular social science was not popular with either students or faculty—grammar, legislation, and history were among the classes with the lowest enrollments. Many teachers reported that attention to writing skills left little time for philosophical study. Even those who did address the nature of mind tended to integrate Ideology and Spiritualism. Moreover, although teachers embraced the goal of political criticism, they stubbornly presented revealed religion or the dictates of the church as the basis of morality. As for history, Tracy noted a broad sympathy for studying the past as a ladder to civilization, but much to his chagrin, found almost no interest in Dupuis's masterwork.

Presenting the group's report to Lucien Bonaparte, Tracy maintained that the *écoles centrales* had proven themselves indispensable to the future of the Republic. Certainly, some changes were necessary. The minimum age of enrollment had to be lowered, prerequisites needed to be established, studies ought to be more carefully coordinated, and national examinations needed to be instituted—but the system was sound. By concentrating on the social sciences, the rigorous schooling of middle-class children between the ages of eight and sixteen would prepare elite students for careers in the civil service, or professional training in one of the special schools. It would even help develop a core of dedicated teachers capable of revolutionizing the primary education of the masses.

Tracy's report died on the minister's desk. Eight months passed without a word, then, in October 1800, Bonaparte dissolved the Council and took charge of its papers. Determined to preserve the existing system, Tracy joined the growing public debate on education by publishing the Council's findings and presenting his own textbook for the central schools, the first of his multivolume *Elements of Ideology*.[42] Dissatisfaction with the lack of organization and the confused mission of the central schools was growing. Determined to address this potentially volatile situation and meet Napoleon's political goals, officials from the Council of State crafted the bill eventually passed by the Legislative Body on May 1, 1802, as the Law of Eleven Floréal. It appears that Bonaparte was instrumental in shaping the most important provisions of the act. He did not share the secular goals of the *Idéologues* and certainly did not need an army of social scientists. Resurrecting elements of Condorcet's plan, the lycée was established to provide students between ages nine and sixteen with a general education prior to technical training in the special schools and *écoles secondaires* (while not a step toward the lycées) to foster social advancement for talented children of the lower orders. However, it was political patronage, not leveling, that underwrote the extensive system of scholarships that would make this new system possible. A lycée education was to be both a reward for the children of loyal government employees and a training ground for a future corps of dedicated and tough-minded public professionals. The same logic was then applied to the teaching body itself, when, in the laws of 1806 and 1808, Napoleon created the Imperial University, a hierarchically administered state-run bureaucracy that turned lycée and secondary school faculty into civil servants and standardized both public and private education.

By this time the *Idéologues* had lost almost all influence over government policy. Starting shortly after the coup of 18 Brumaire, the rift with Napoleon came to a head with their opposition to the Concordant of 1802. Fundamentally opposed to the reintroduction of the church into public life, they hoped to frustrate Napoleon's initiative in debate, but instead found themselves ostracized from power as Bonaparte pressured the Senate to purge the Tribunate and the Legislative Body of his opponents. Four months later the Senate was forced to name Bonaparte Consulate for life and accept a new constitution that effectively neutered its control of the executive. The final nail in the *Idéologues'* coffin came early the following year when Bonaparte reorganized the National Institute, dissolving the class on the analysis of sensations and ideas. Out of political favor, and with no voice in the shaping of educational policy, Cabanis, Tracy, and the other *Idéologues* gradually receded from public life. Ideology had become both passé and dangerous: there was simply no place for the "science of man" in a state that denied politics. Accordingly, although the school system of postrevolutionary France retained vestiges of the structural reforms suggested by the *Idéologues*—a two-track system that provided basic knowledge for the masses while preparing elite students for advanced training—it was shorn of the secular mission and social science curriculum fundamental to the positivist state envisioned by Tracy. The lycée, as Napoleon recognized, had become the great instrument for the maintenance of his bureaucratic empire.

THOMAS JEFFERSON, *IDÉOLOGUE*

It is not surprising that in struggling to consolidate authority within the Napoleonic regime the *Idéologues* would seek the endorsement of a powerful and sympathetic friend, the American president, and president of the American Philosophical Society (a group of scientifically minded men, including Benjamin Rush, Joseph Priestly, and David Rittenhouse, openly sympathetic to the physiological doctrines of sensationalism). In 1802 Jefferson was elected as an associate member of the class on Moral Science and started receiving texts from the movement's leading theorists. Say sent his two-volume *Treatise on Political Economy,* Cabanis his *Reports on the Physical and the Moral,* and Tracy the first two volumes of his *Elements of Ideology.* Encumbered by the demands of his office, Jefferson had little time to examine these works, especially, he later admitted to Adams, Tracy's rather dense and dry epistemological tract, but he did write back expressing his gratitude for the honor they had bestowed upon him and his interest in their future practical and theoretical labors. His retirement, he promised, would be sweetened by the careful perusal of his new library. In 1806, Jefferson received a second package from Tracy, the French manuscript of his *Commentary on Montesquieu.* Unable to publish under the eye of Napoleon, Tracy hoped the work would gain proper attention in America. Here was a topic much more to Jefferson's liking. As a student he had carefully dissected Montesquieu's masterpiece in his commonplace book. But while accepting the relationship between human nature, government, and institutions—even the physiological arguments about climate, temperament, and manners—he found the defense of monarchy totally unacceptable. Tracy corrected and updated Montesquieu's arguments: aligning the character of the state with the anthropological physiology of Cabanis, he presented a scientific justification of republican government. Apart from a small disagreement over the virtue of a single verses a plural executive, Jefferson was enthralled. Here was the principle political text of the generation. As Napoleon villainized the *Idéologues* for all the excesses of the Revolution, Jefferson had the work translated and published in America. He persuaded James Madison, rector of William and Mary, to make it required reading for all graduating students, and, in 1812, wrote to Thomas Cooper—the first professor appointed to the University of Virginia—expressing his hope that "the Review of Montesquieu . . . will become the elementary book of the youth at all our colleges."[43] He even suggested that students prepare for the text with "a mature study of the most profound of all human compositions, Cabanis's 'Rapports du Physique et du moral de l'homme.' "[44] In 1814 Jefferson received the fourth volume of Tracy's *Elements,* which, after much trouble with printers, he personally translated and published as *Treatise on Political Economy* (1817).[45] Convinced that Tracy had corrected and systemized economic thought from Quesnay to Smith and

Say, Jefferson wrote to Albert Gallatin, the Secretary of the Treasury, in 1818, offering the book as an antidote to the nation's profound ignorance of the science.[46] By "simplifying principles" it brought "the whole subject within a narrow compass."[47] Taken together, the *Commentary on Montesquieu* and *Political Economy* were to "become the Statesmen's Manual . . . elementary books of the political department" at the University of Virginia.[48]

In 1813, Adams wrote to Jefferson, excited by his recent acquisition of Dupuis's opus. Joseph Priestly had rejected the work and labeled its author an atheist. But Adams was more circumspect and challenged Jefferson to tackle the twelve volumes with him so that they could resolve for themselves the debate between materialism and spiritualism. Jefferson praised Adams's heroism, but reported that his appetite for Dupuis had been satisfied by Tracy's analytic review and sent on the "pithy morsel" for his friend's edification.[49] This debate, woven out of metaphysical and theological conceptions of nature, mind, and spirit, went to the core of Jefferson's thought. Following Priestly's deistic teachings, he formulated a vision of the universe that fused materialism and Christianity. Like Cabanis, Priestly believed that organic matter possessed sensitive properties capable of generating consciousness and free will. Jefferson found this conjecture far more plausible than the supposed existence of an immaterial self. Citing Locke's attack on spiritualists—that it was blasphemy to assert that God could not have endowed matter with the power of thought—he told to Adams that it was easier to swallow "one incomprehensibility rather than two . . . an existence called spirit, of which we have neither evidence nor idea" and which, lacking extension and solidity, "can put material organs into motion."[50] "To talk of immaterial existence," he later elaborated, "is to talk of *nothings*. To say that the human soul, angels, god, are immaterial, is to say they are *nothings*. . . . I cannot reason otherwise: but I believe I am supported in my creed of materialism by Locke, Tracy, and Stewart." (Stewart, whom Jefferson had befriended in Paris during the first year of the Revolution, supported a Baconian science of mind and society similar to Tracy's scheme, but tempered by a commitment to the doctrine of innate truths. Elie Halévy has written that Thomas Brown, Stewart's student and handpicked successor at the University of Edinburgh, "borrowed so much from Destutt de Tracy and Laromiguière that, he has been accused of plagiarism."[51] Both of these writers strongly influenced James Mill and other philosophic radicals, sponsoring liberal beliefs in the nature and structure of education remarkably similar to those of Tracy and Jefferson. Stewart, however, was no materialist.) "Why should the materialist be expected to explain the process by which matter exercises the faculty of thinking" when scientists are unable to account for the properties of gravity or magnetism? Only "on the basis of sensation," he told Adams, "erect all the certainties we can have or need. When this is quit all is in the wind."[52] Dupuis's *Origin* showed the truth of this dictum in the history of religion. A firm foundation for faith had to be established from the unquestionable design of the universe and the immutable principles of morality. Jesus, Jefferson insisted, was not a living divinity, but a profound teacher of moral truths. Eschewing Spiritualism, he confessed to being a Christian "in the only sense in which I believe Jesus wished anyone to be, sincerely attached to his doctrines in preference to all others; ascribing to himself every human excellence, and believing that he never claimed any other."[53] Later in life Jefferson even argued that the early Christians were themselves materialists and blamed St. Paul for infecting faith with mysticism and spirituality. Taken up by the church, these obscurities were then turned "by artificial constructions into a mere contrivance to turn filch wealth and power to themselves."[54] Charging rational men with infidelity, religions became "the greatest obstacles to the advancement of the real doctrines of Jesus, and do in fact, constitute the real anti-Christ."[55] Adams concurred. Praising Dupuis's history as the greatest fairy tale ever written, he too remained committed to the moral lessons of Christ. "The Ten Commandments and the Sermon on the Mount," he told the Virginian, "contained my religion."[56]

But who was this Tracy? "The ablest writer living on intellectual subjects, or the operations of the understanding," Jefferson replied.[57] Describing his three volumes on Ideology and his critique of Montesquieu, Jefferson explained that the *Idéologue* was now completing "the circle of metaphysical sciences" with a work on ethics. Tracy, he warned Adams, was a follower of Hobbes and adopted the principle "that justice is founded in contract solely, and does not result from the constitution of man."[58] He, like Adams, believed in an innate sense of right and wrong, but was nonetheless convinced that although they differed on foundations, "so correct a thinker as Tracy will give us a sound system of morals."[59] Although Adams found Tracy's *Analysis* "a feint [*sic*] Miniature of the Original," his interest was piqued.[60] What, he asked playfully in his next letter, was this Ideology?

When Bonaparte used it, I was delighted with it, upon the common principle of delight in everything we cannot understand. Does it mean idiotism? The science of *non compass mentuism*? The Science of Lunacy? The Theory of Delirium? Or does it mean the Science of Self-Love of *amour proper*? Or the elements of vanity?[61]

Most of all he wanted "to see his Ideology upon Montesquieu."[62] Jefferson promised to have a copy of the *Critique* delivered, explaining that by "Ideology," Tracy understood all the subjects that the French term *Morale*. Adams was delighted. The following year when he read the manuscript of *Political Economy* he found himself skipping from proposition to proposition, unable to leave the book unfinished. "It is a condensation into a little globule . . . of all the sound sense and solid knowledge of the grand master Quanay [*sic*] and all his redoubtable knights."[63] Delighted with this "high approbation of Tracy's book," Jefferson asked for permission to use his letter to help ensure the circulation of the work, and Adams happily consented.[64]

Tracy's moderate laissez-faire policies provided a theoretical justification for many of the issues that Jefferson had struggled with in his political career. His vehement opposition to government intrusion in economic affairs—to national banks, paper money, direct taxation, the setting of interest rates, and public debt—resonated perfectly with Jefferson's crusade against federalism. Most importantly, perhaps, Tracy helped temper the romantic image of pastoral life that Jefferson had presented in the *Notes*. True, he remained committed to the political importance of the land as the seedbed for the development of republican character, but events such as the embargo of 1807 taught the importance of small-scale manufacturing to America's economic independence. Fearing the excesses of the British industrial system, the debasement of labor, and the attendant evils of urban life, he defended Tracy's model of development through modest entrepreneurship: science and technology would be harnessed to improve the public infrastructure and the conditions of home and labor, but society was still to be agrocentric. One nagging inconsistency in this vision that cannot be overlooked was Jefferson's support of extending slavery to Missouri. Given his oft-repeated characterization of the institution as perverting the nature of both the master and the slave, its westward expansion—even if removing blacks from plantations to farms— hardly established the moral foundation on which to build an empire of reason. It did, however, promise to strengthen the political hegemony of the South through the application of the three-fifths rule.[65]

"A CHILD OF MY OLD AGE"

In addition to Tracy's political and economic writings, Jefferson was also extremely interested in his educational work. He even wrote to Tracy, in 1817, confessing that he had "availed [himself] of some of the leading ideas of . . . [his] luminous tract on public instruction" in the planning of Central College, at Albemarle. Like the *école centrale,* this was to be a secondary school—it was only later, when the site and buildings were developed into the University of Virginia, that Jefferson returned to his earlier three-tier system, albeit with much of Tracy's curricula still intact.[66] Jefferson's 1814 letter to Peter Carr, the college's future principal, reveals the extent of this debt. Every citizen, he explained, "should receive an education proportioned to the condition and pursuits of his life."[67] Dividing the population into "the laboring and the learned," he proposed elementary instruction in "Reading, Writing, Arithmetic, and Geography," and a secondary curriculum for his *aristo,* comprising the major divisions of language (languages and history, ancient and modern, grammar, *belles lettres,* and rhetoric); mathematics (pure and applied mathematics, physics, chemistry, natural history, botany, zoology, and anatomy); and philosophy (Ideology, ethics, the law of nature and nations, government, and political economy). With the exception of lessons in the theory of medicine, this was almost exactly the same grouping of subjects that Tracy had proposed in his *Observations* for the *école centrale.*[68] He even followed Tracy in advocating education for the deaf and the blind. Finally, as in France, he proposed professional schools to extend technical expertise in various theoretical, scientific, and practical fields.

Early in 1817 Charles Mercer's proposal for a system of public schools and a state board of education—which Jefferson opposed as federalist, fiscally unsound, and overly bureaucratic—was narrowly defeated in the state senate. Determined to push his own scheme, Jefferson wrote to his political ally Joseph Cabell with two proposals, designed to establish elementary schools and a state university in Virginia. Consolidated in *A Bill for Establishing a System of Public Education,* Jefferson's plan contained similar recommendations to his 1779 scheme, with the notable reduction in the number of natural aristocrats to be educated at public expense. But even with this concession, the Bill gained little support. Instead a subsequent proposal to use $45,000 of the literary fund to support the schooling of poor children was accepted. It was as a rider to this legislation that the construction of the University of Virginia was approved, thus setting off a four-year struggle for financing that pitted primary and higher education against one another. Moreover, Jefferson's project faced sectional rivalries within the state and bitter opposition from religious groups seeking to use the literary fund to support the construction of seminaries. In the end, he managed to win the day by rallying these disparate groups against the threat of northern federalists. Given the delicate political balance at the time of the Missouri Compromise, it seems that state's rights—and the power of slavery—were the most important issue on the minds of Virginians. Scholars have debated which end of the educational ladder Jefferson thought most important. Given his continuing petition for public schooling, even until his death, this seems an unfair question. But forced to choose, he told Cabell that it was better to pause primary schooling for three years and ensure that the university was properly established. As the epitaph he chose for his grave stone reveals ("Here was buried Thomas Jefferson Author of the Declaration of American Independence of the Statute of Virginia for Religious Freedom and Father of the University of Virginia"), he was convinced that this child of his old age would be one of the most significant projects of his life.[69]

By 1818, with the construction of Central College well under way, the legislature appointed Jefferson and twenty-three other commissioners to plan the location, structure, administration, and curriculum of the University of Virginia. Meeting at a tavern in Rockfish Gap, the group weighted two other sites before settling on the facility at Albemarle as the most convenient for the white population of the state. Written by Jefferson, the *Report* briefly outlined a plan for situating dormitories, classrooms, and faculty lodgings in a village-like academic campus that would facilitate the kind of mentoring relationships that had been so important in Jefferson's own youth. But this hardly captured the grandeur of Jefferson's architectural scheme. Convinced that beauty was a mark of eminence, he planned stately auditoriums around an impressive quadrangle. Virginia's grace would attract a faculty composed of the finest minds in Europe and stand as a citadel of learning for students across the South and West. The legislature worried about costs and balked at foreign-speaking teachers. But Jefferson was not to be denied. As America's most elegant campus started to take shape, a promising young lawyer, Francis Gilmer was dispatched to recruit faculty from Britain—the second generation of scholars would be homegrown. As for the curriculum, Jefferson laid out a table of subjects that would develop wise and virtuous leaders with knowledge of government, political economy, and the scientific skills necessary to engineer a happy and prosperous commonwealth. Structured around ten professorships, including a professor of Ideology, his curriculum remained essentially what he had advocated to Carr four years earlier. (In 1824, as funds became scarce, the scheme was consolidated to eight professorships, with Ideology, general grammar, and ethics included in moral philosophy, and government and political economy in the school of law.) Military training, gymnastics, manual arts, dance, and drawing were also mentioned, as was the need to preserve a secular foundation for studies. The ethics professor would offer proof of the existence of God, "the author of all the relations of morality, and of all the laws and obligations these infer," and from this common ground, each sect would be able to provide, in facilities surrounding the campus, "as they think fittest, the means of further instruction in their own peculiar tenets."[70] Not only did this respond to the severe criticism that Virginia lacked religious instruction to match the useful sciences "by bringing the sects together, and mixing them with the mass of other students," he told Cooper, now at the University of South Carolina, "we shall soften their asperities, liberalize and neutralize their prejudices, and make the general religion a religion of peace, reason, and morality."[71] To his dying day Jefferson was resolute in protecting the wall of separation between church and state— Virginia, the nation's first real university, would be a secular institution centered on the library, not the church. It would also, he told Tracy in 1820, "be based on the illimitable freedom of the human mind, to explore and to expose every subject susceptible of its contemplation."[72] Tenure, equality of rank, and the elective system would preserve the precious independence of thought. But as the selection of faculty continued, especially after Gilmer's untimely death, Jefferson's famed toleration hardened. Fearing the spread of federalism, preached in the northern colleges attended by so many of Virginia's youth, he sought to constrain teaching, especially in the all important subjects of law and government. Insisting that the legislature had the right to ensure future leaders were weaned on correct republican principles, he convinced the Board of Visitors to mandate a curriculum structured around the works of Locke, Sidney, the Federalist Papers, the Declaration of Independence, and Washington's Valedictory Address. He also insisted that the Board only hire a professor of law who would adopt the Whig *Coke on Littleton* rather than the Tory *Blackstone*. As for moral philosophy, he jumped on Madison's former student, George Tucker: a retiring senator from Lynchburg who had held the Jeffersonian line on Missouri. His lack of experience in metaphysics was not a problem, Jefferson explained, for "any person with a general education" could quickly master "Locke, Stewart, Brown, [and] Tracy."[73] In his first year, Tucker even taught economics from Cooper's text on Say until the professorship in law was finally filled by another member of Madison's coterie, John Lomax.

Without Jefferson's stewardship, Tracy's science of the mind gradually disappeared from the curriculum at Virginia—Tucker, for example, gravitated to the more standard college digest of Scottish Common Sense Realism. But a more enduring Ideology remained. For although it is true, as Pangle and Pangle suggest, that the renewed religiosity of the era favored the spread of denominational colleges rather than the secular and scientific studies pioneered by Jefferson, Virginia nonetheless proved a pivotal institution in the political culture of the antebellum South.[74] Party, rather than social science became "Old Sachem's" legacy. Four months before his death, Jefferson wrote to Madison determined to preserve his republicanism.

> It is in our seminary that that vestal flame is to be kept alive; it is then to spread anew over our own and sister States. If we are true and vigilant in our trust, within a dozen or twenty years a majority of our own Legislature will be from one school, and many disciples will have carried its doctrines home with them to their several States, and will have leavened thus the whole mass.[75]

If, as Jefferson claimed, the school of law, was the "nursery of our Congress," then Virginia had many influential sons.[76] For, as William P. Trent chronicles, in the first fifty years, Jefferson's institution trained hundreds of students who would take leading political and professional roles across the South, thus helping to legitimize the distinct sectional culture that would pervade the political contests of the next generation.

More troubling for Jefferson's legacy was the Old Dominion's failure to establish a system of public schooling until the 1870s, when the reforms pushed by Horace Mann in Massachusetts gradually spread across the country. Writing just a decade after Jefferson's death, Mann completely ignored the campaign for public schooling in Virginia. His view of human nature and the social good was sustained by a second transatlantic "science of man," Ideology's successor, phrenology. Here was a moral philosophy that America could not resist. In addition to political arguments for a wise and virtuous citizenry, phrenological principles provided a justification for every aspect of the educational system. From the physical design of the schoolhouse to the choice of textbooks and the training of teachers, Mann presented what Jefferson could only hint at, specific and compelling scientific explanations for the aims, methods, and content of schooling in the newly urban, rapidly industrializing world.

In an 1825 letter to Adams, Jefferson reports that he had "never been more gratified by the reading of a book than by that of Flourens."

> Cabanis has gone far toward proving from anatomical structure and action of the human machine that certain parts of it were probably the organs of thought and that consequently matter might exercize [*sic*] that faculty. Flourens proves that it does exercise it, and that deprived of the cerebrum particularly the animal looses all senses, all intellect, and memory, yet lives in health and for indefinite terms. It will be curious to see what immaterialists will oppose to this.[77]

A youthful disciple of Cabanis and Tracy, Flourens had praised Gall's efforts to identify and locate the brain's various mental organs. By 1822, his attitude had changed. Now under the orbit of Gall's nemesis, George Curvier, he presented a series of ablation and stimulation experiments that supported the Cartesian conception of mind. Dividing the brain into six distinct regions, he showed that each area performed a unique role in the overall mental economy: the cerebrum, for example, housed sense experience, memory, intelligence, and free will. But as he demonstrated so sensationally, even the removal of large sections of this material did not lead to the total breakdown of powers. Opposing Gall's localization thesis, Flourens was able to argue that thought was distributed throughout the entire region, thus proving the existence of an all controlling *a moi*. Ironically, what Jefferson read as an empirical demonstration of the physical causes of thought and feeling Flourens intended as a refutation of materialism and brain localization. It is to that theory, and the aims, methods, and content of education it sustained, that we now turn.

3

Gall, Naturalist of the Mind

Always, and every where, the human race has manifested the same propensities and the same talents; always and every where, there have resulted the
same virtues and the same vices, the same employments and the same institutions. . . . Sing your lines on the straw, or on the harp; dress your chiefs with
feathers or with purple; your women with flowers or with diamonds; inhabit
huts or palaces; it will still be the same faculties, which lead men to act within
the circle traced for him by his Creator.

Franz Joseph Gall, *On the Functions,* 1835

In *Physiology of the Nervous System* (1821), Etienne Georget, one of Gall's most
promising disciples, chided his master for not disclosing the intellectual an-
tecedents of his discoveries, "as if he alone has traveled the road of truth."[1]
With some justification, he complained that Gall had spared "of textual ci-
tations, where they might have lost him the character of originality."[2] Specifically, Georget drew attention to the writings of Charles Bonnet who, some
sixty years earlier, had prefigured Gall's thesis by maintaining that the brain
is a congeries of organs that determines the intellectual and emotional life of
animals and human beings. With the purity of his motives in question, Gall
responded that he and Spurzheim had quoted Bonnet extensively in their
response to the critical review of the 1808 *Memoire* they had submitted to the
French Academy of Sciences.[3] In his books and his lectures, Gall protested,
he meticulously demonstrated the similarity and differences between his
views and those of other leading theorists. Even so, he remained adamant
that he owed little to the Swiss naturalist or to any other thinker. "Indeed,"
he boasted,

it may be said, that to me only the physiology of the brain owes its
existence. That I have discovered it without the aid of anyone whatever,

the history of each of my discoveries sufficiently proves. It is with the physiology of the brain as with its structure. To unravel whatever might by chance have been found in the writings of authors, would have required infinitely more sagacity, than to divine, by means of observation, the mysteries of nature. I commenced, continued, and almost completed my discoveries without any previous instruction; and, if afterward I compiled quotations from others, it was rather to manifest my point of departure from them, than to strengthen my ideas.[4]

Like so many histories of phrenology written by phrenologists, Gall's scattered accounts of his life's work are presented as heroic personal struggles with the forces of ignorance and social prejudice.[5] He offers little in the way of a scholarly account of the intellectual context in which his thought matured and says next to nothing, for example, of what he learned as a student of comparative anatomy under Johann Hermann at the University of Strasburg, or from the positivist oriented physician Maximillian Stoll, when he completed his M.D. in Vienna. Yet, as Georget implied, Gall's work was deeply embedded in the biological arguments of his day and owes much, not only to the work of Hermann and Stoll, but most especially to the antimechanistic philosophy of Johann Gottfried von Herder, whose writings on nature, mind, and culture had a profound influence on German thought in the final decades of the eighteenth century.

According to Michel Foucault, biologists of the eighteenth century approached the problem of species through a taxonomic classification of external characteristics.[6] Every creature had to fit into a predetermined rational order, a great chain of being that revealed the design underlying the complex economy of organic adaptations established by God. In line with this Newtonian interpretation of the universe, Bonnet attacked the Aristotelian concept of a vital male force and argued that all organic structures developed from preformed homunculi embedded—like so many Russian dolls—within the female body. A close follower of Condillac, Bonnet also explored how individuality resulted from the assimilation of new material in the growth of the germ. In the case of humans, heredity determined species characteristics, but men and women developed unique thoughts and feelings as sense experiences shaped their nervous system. Drawing upon Condillac's model of an animate statue, he explained that objects acting upon the senses caused vibrations that created determinate configurations within the nervous fibers. With appropriate stimulation, these neural structures would then elicit memories of original events. Complex ideas arose from the connection of fibers and the faculties developed, as Condillac suggested, through the matrix of nerves coordinated by the use of signs. The brain, he summarized, is an "extremely compounded organ, or rather an assemblage of many different organs, formed themselves by the combination or interlacing of a prodigious number of fibres, nerves, vessels, etc."[7] This did not imply the reduction of the mind to physiological states. Like Condillac, Bonnet was convinced that men and women had a dual nature. Unable to say exactly how the spiritual and the corporeal interacted, he simply observed that the mind only influenced the body in response to alterations of the soul excited by the motions of the fibers.

Gall may have endorsed Bonnet's organology of the brain but he rejected his mechanistic ontology and sensationalist epistemology. "Precisely the inverse of the relation of . . . Bonnet . . . exists between the senses and the understanding. It is not the perfection of the senses which gives intelligence to the brain; but it is the perfection of the brain, which determines the employment of the senses."[8] He also rejected Bonnet's commitment to a *sensium commune*. Bonnet had argued "that we have ideas only by the aid of the senses;" that "ideas of every kind are chained to one another, and that this connexion belongs to the combination, which the fibres of the senses have together;" and that it "therefore follows, that the different senses with which we are endowed, have, somewhere in the brain, secret communications, by means of which they may act on one another."[9] This site, he continued, "must be regarded as the seat of the soul," the part at which the mind senses and acts upon the body.[10] Quite where this center was located remained a mystery. Frustrated by the complexity of the organ, Bonnet could only affirm its existence "from facts which cannot be called into question."[11] Gall demurred and pictured the soul operating through the brain's many discrete structures, a position totally unacceptable to the likes of George Cuvier and Pierre Flourens, who believed that the *moi* was both simple and indivisible.

In the second half of the eighteenth century, Bonnet's preformationism was challenged by discoveries in embryology and geology that suggested the transformation of forms over time. The fetus appeared to pass through lower stages of life in the process of maturation, and the fossil record pointed to the changes in species over time. For Herder and the German philosophers who followed Kant, nature was anything but mechanical. It was vital. The concepts of Newtonian science simply could not capture the teleological processes that permeated organic phenomena. When these thinkers looked at species, they did not see a mosaic of separate forms, but a single unifying pattern of modifications in which an underlying archetype gradually approached perfection. Most strikingly revealed in ontogeny, life ascended from an initial invertebrate state, through fish and reptile stages, to mammals, and then, human beings.

But if Herder spiritualized nature, he also naturalized spirit; *Kraft*, the force he believed immanent in matter, was more akin to Bergson's élan vital than the Hegelian *Giest*. Dismissing the *Naturphilosophie* of the German Idealists, he insisted that life and mind had to be studied through the empirical investigation of natural forms, not a metaphysical deduction of categories. Adopting a comparative approach to the question of species, he thus argued for a taxonomic classification grounded in physiology rather than morphology. "External form," Herder reasoned, "is fashioned by organic powers operating from within outwards."[12] His own anthropological study of mind, based on the writings of Diderot and Condillac, revealed how human powers emerged—mainly through culture and language, but also influenced by climate and diet—from the basic property of sensibility. Although Gall had no sympathy for sensationalist psychology, he completely embraced Herder's call for a naturalistic study of human nature. In particular, he was struck by his claim that function determined structure. According to Erna Lesky, Gall "felt summoned by Herder to pursue comparative anatomy, indeed to a very distinct comparative-anatomical method" aimed at explaining his own incipient beliefs about the diversity of human abilities "through the growth and differentiation of psychic functions by the progressive stages in the development of organs."[13] Most important were Herder's suggestions about the origin of the nervous system. As Charles Bell summarized, under the influence of Albrect von Haller, physiologists had concluded

that brain is a common sensorium; that the extremities of the nerves are organized, so that each is fitted to receive a peculiar impression. . . . It is imagined that impressions, thus differing in kind, are carried along the nerves to the sensorium, and presented to the mind; and that the mind, by the same nerves which receive sensation, sends out the mandate of the will to the moving parts of the body.[14]

Following Herder, Gall inverted this picture. The brain, he contended, must be understood from bottom up, not from the top down. If a single plan ran through nature connecting the simplest and the most complex organisms, the nervous system, like the developing structures of the embryo, must show a linear increase in complexity. The key to Gall's argument was the spinal cord. This was not simply a conduit between the brain and the body as Haller taught, but a confluence of independent nervous bundles that eventually grew into the cerebral mass. Thus the brain emerged treelike from the spine, a blossom of independent but communicating structures.

Tracing the genetic roots of this developing system in the first volume of their *Anatomie and Physiologie* (1810), Gall and Spurzheim explained how the vital organs of the simplest invertebrates generated a gelatinous gray substance containing white nervous fibers. In more complex animal forms, these knotty ganglionic areas fused into centers forming the spinal cords of vertebrates and, eventually, the brain itself. Here, according to Gall's principles of accumulation and reinforcement, the white nerves (he distinguished two kinds, converging and diverging), fostered by the nutritive gray substance, extended from the medulla oblongata into the cerebellum and the cerebral hemispheres, where the various mental organs were housed. It was by following this genetic track in their anatomical demonstrations that Gall and Spurzheim revolutionized brain anatomy, amazing even their opponents with their new methods of dissection.

Unlike Herder, whose writings combine an uneasy amalgam of scientific research and metaphysical speculation, Gall's works have a much more positivistic tenor. Certainly, he had important things to say about the soul, free will, and the existence of God, but his foremost concern was the scientific task of determining the various organs of the brain. Convinced that physiological functions were the key to anatomical structures, he presented himself as a naturalist of the mind, charting a taxonomy of intellectual, moral, and emotional powers. What distinguished Gall's theory was the assumption that these mental structures were largely determined by birth. Education and environment could certainly influence character, but unlike the sensationalists, he was adamant that the faculties were not determined by experience. This commitment, shared by many post-Kantians, dovetails with another popular theory of the day, physiognomy (the belief that a person's talents and abilities can be read from physiological features of the body, in particular the size and expression of the face), although, in contrast to Johann Caspar Lavater, Gall insisted that any explanation of behavior had to be grounded in a physiological account of the brain.

THE ROOTS OF ORGANOLOGY

As a boy, Franz Joseph Gall (1758–1828) spent much of his time collecting flowers and small animals in the countryside around his native Baden.[15] Indeed, gardening and the training of pets became lifelong hobbies. His house in Paris was full of dogs, cats, and birds; he even made use of a monkey in his lectures. The ethological understanding Gall acquired from these interests provided a wealth of behavioral knowledge that would support his claims about the structure of the brain. For, contrary to the metaphysicians of the day, he was insistent that men and women had to be understood as part of the animal kingdom, associated by virtue of their bodily and mental organization "with the boar, the bear, the horse, the ox—with the camel, the dolphin, elephant, and the stupid sloth."[16] Comparative physiology, not philosophy, was the key to understanding the human mind. Organic life, Gall argued in 1797, "from the zoophyte, to the simple polyps, up to the philosopher and the theosophist" was simply a composition and combination of basic forms.[17] Given the power of Jupiter, he could populate the Earth according to this master plan. Starting with "irritable vessels" then adding nerves, he would move on to higher beings that "look around upon the world by the organs of sense."[18] From "an arrangement of powers and instruments" divided "according to" his pleasure, he would "create insects, birds, mammilla . . . lap-dogs for your ladies, horses for your beaux; and for myself, men, that is to say fools and philosophers, poets, and historians, theologians and naturalists . . . [all] by putting into communication, in a strange manner, your body, and your muscles with your cerebral organs."[19]

By his own colorful account, the young Gall originated his naturalistic study of the mind by training his powers of observation upon his family and friends. Each, he quickly concluded, "had some peculiar talent, propensity, or faculty which distinguished him from the others."[20] It was easy to determine who "was virtuous or inclined to vice, modest or arrogant, frank or deceitful, a truth-teller or a liar, peaceable or quarrelsome, benevolent, good or bad."[21]

Some were distinguished for the beauty of their penmanship; some by their facility in calculation; others by their aptitude to acquire history, philosophy, or languages. One shone in composition by the elegance of his periods; another had always a dry harsh style; another reasoned closely, and expressed himself with force. . . . Some carved, and drew well; some devoted their leisure to painting, or to the cultivation of a small garden, while their comrades engaged in noisy sports; others enjoyed roaming the woods, hunting, seeking birds' nests, collecting flowers, insects, or shells. Thus each one distinguished himself by his proper characteristic; and I never knew an instance, when one had been a cheating and faithless companion one year, became a true and faithful friend the next.[22]

One trait held a particular fascination for Gall. Having been bettered at school by a number of "less able" students, he was struck by the fact that those adept in memorizing their recitations tended to have "ox-eyes," a feature, he later conjectured, that resulted from the power of a large language faculty in the frontal region of the brain. By 1777, when he enrolled at the University of Strasbourg, Gall was on the lookout for other students with prominent eyes and a facile memory—and, it seems, his suspicions were confirmed. Pondering this remarkable association of mind and body, he gradually formed the conviction that a whole range of moral and intellectual powers might be read from a person's head. Like the eyes, the brain was encased in a bony box that assumed slightly different configurations depending upon the organ within. Lumps, an asymmetrical cranium, and facial expressions were indicators of the brain's shape and size and thus, he concluded, different traits and talents. Carefully scrutinizing his peers, Gall soon added the abilities of painting, music, and mechanical arts to his cerebral taxonomy. And, because those in religious orders appeared to have larger than average crowns (as revealed by the practice of shaving), he placed the organ of veneration on top of the head. Other moral and intellectual faculties took their place, as Gall gradually completed his topological map of human nature on the surface of the skull.

But when Gall sought to reconcile his practical discoveries with theoretical knowledge of the mind, he found little support in the writings of either physiologists or philosophers. There was no agreement among medical theorists about the site of mental powers and propensities. Plato had located the affective and the cognitive faculties in the brain, but, following Aristotle, Descartes, and even Cabanis, many still believed that the emotions were a function of the whole bodily system and variously discussed the role played by the stomach, the heart, and the chest in the life of the passions. He also found that categories employed by epistemologists—perception, memory, judgment, and reason—were nothing like the practical powers he had delineated. Nor could he accept the overarching egalitarianism and environmentalism of the sensationalist theory of knowledge. His own experiences convinced him that human abilities were largely innate: no amount of training could make up for natural aptitude, and children brought up within the same household ranged widely in character. Casting tradition aside, he decided to retain his commonsense classification of behavior and resolved to pursue a naturalistic study of the inherent regularities of human character.

Gall was well placed to conduct such inquiries. Leaving Strasburg in 1781, he traveled to Vienna to complete his medical training and, upon graduation in 1785, set up a highly respected private practice. In 1794, he was even asked to become the emperor's private doctor, but declined, citing the time necessary to continue his scientific investigations. Vienna, with its many asylums, prisons, and schools, was a perfect place to explore the relationship between the form and function of the human mind. By 1796, with a wealth of empirical correlations to support his physiological hypotheses, Gall started giving public lectures. The following year, in a letter to Baron Retzer, he announced his intention to publish a treatise on the functions of the brain with implications for "medicine, morality, education, and legislation."[23]

As Gall's letter demonstrates, four years before he met Spurzheim, the basic concepts of his life's work were firmly in place. He would argue that the faculties are innate, that the brain is the organ of the mind, that each of the fundamental powers acts independently, that each is housed in a discrete neural region, that the size of an organ provides an index of its strength, and that different shaped brains (as revealed through human and animal skulls) correspond to unique moral and intellectual traits. He even promised to unravel the mystery of the female mind and account for national differences. Most provocatively, he would discuss free will and moral responsibility, explaining how right action resulted from the content of moral and rational faculties with the animal inclinations. By way of example, he noted that although Retzer had a "voluptuous disposition," with "good morals, conjugal affection, health, regard for society and for religion" as his "preservatives," he was able to resist his impulses.[24] "It was only this struggle against the propensities," Gall continued, "that gives rise to virtue, to vice, and moral responsibility."[25] But not everyone shared the Baron's preservative powers. Many were biologically prone to evil, and some, so absolutely incapable of controlling their desires, Gall was even willing to absolve of all responsibility for their acts. Such compulsives, he believed, belonged to the medical rather than the legal profession. It is not surprising, then, that by 1802, as popular and scientific interest grew, political leaders would seek to stem any radical movement that might flow from the study of brains and crania. No doubt fearing what had happened in France, the Austrian government labeled Gall a materialist and banned any discussion of his ideas as dangerous to religion and public morality.

It was during 1800 that Gall first came into contact with Johan Casper Spurzheim, an anatomy student at the University of Vienna. After attending Gall's lectures, Spurzheim was engaged to dissect brains at public and private demonstrations, a role he continued to 1804, when he became Gall's full-time assistant. Until then, he "was simply a hearer of Dr. Gall," but from that time forward became an equal partner, contributing, he reports, important discoveries in neurology.[26] Later, after their separation, in 1813, Spurzheim presented a philosophical reconstruction of Gall's research around a more liberal view of human nature. It was this progressive doctrine of individual and social perfectibility, adapted to institutional practices and middle-class mores, that was eventually popularized as phrenology.

Gall had come to realize that his physiological arguments had to be grounded in cerebral anatomy.[27] That is, he had to demonstrate how the various faculties that he hypothesized were physically embodied within the brain, and not, like the concepts of metaphysicians, simply linguistic constructs of his theory. But existing accounts of the brain, and the traditional method of dissection—slicing sections down the corpus callosum—revealed no evidence of the discrete structures he had conjectured. Not that cutting and probing such a complex organ would reveal its internal structure; Gall and Spurzheim always maintained that the secrets of the brain could only be discovered when anatomy was guided by physiology. Inquiry had to proceed from the association of behavioral traits and cranial features to the search for neural masses.

The autopsy of a fifty-four-year-old woman who had suffered all her life from hydrocephalus proved pivotal to the evolution of Gall's theory. According to leading anatomists, the cerebral matter of such patients was typically destroyed or dissolved by water—a condition that clearly undermined Gall's central thesis that the brain is the organ of the mind. After removing four pounds of fluid from the head, Gall and Spurzheim found that while much of the gray matter had indeed been lost, and the convolutions unfolded, the white fibrous structure remained intact. Nature had provided the key to unlocking its most complex treasure. In contrast to the smooth surface created by the "mechanical" slicing of the brain, they pointed to densely packed bundles of nerves encased in a gelatinous matrix. Given the expansion of these fibers, the convolutions were identified as the location "where the instincts, sentiments, penchants, talents and, in general, the moral and intellectual forces are exercised."[28] To demonstrate these structures, Gall and Spurzheim perfected the technique of unfolding the convolutions to reveal the path of the nerves from the surface down toward the brain stem. They also duplicated the natural maceration caused by hydrocephalus by boiling brains in oil and firing jets of water at the gray matter.[29] Finding no single point of convergence among the fibers, they rejected the existence of a *sensorium commune.* They also concluded that the number and compaction of convolutions was an index of each organ's power and, through the pressure exerted on the skull, the cause of the relationship between behavioral traits and head shape.

GALL AND HIS SKULLS

Having effectively coordinated naturalistic observations of animal and human behavior with anatomical structures, Gall and Spurzheim now had the confidence to actively promote their twin doctrines of "organology" (the mind is a congeries of independent faculties housed within the brain) and "cranioscopy" (neural features, hence character, can be read through the contours of the skull).[30] With their fame spreading—"Who has not heard of Gall and his skulls?" announced Charles Villers in a manuscript addressed to Georges Cuvier in 1802—the two elected to leave Vienna for Gall's home state and a highly publicized tour of universities, prisons, and asylums throughout Germany, Switzerland, Holland, and Denmark.[31] Two years later, in November 1807, they entered Paris as central figures in the raging debate between materialistic and spiritualistic philosophers.

In many ways this meandering tour proved to be an important phase in the intellectual and social development of Gall's doctrines. It introduced Gall and Spurzheim to new and extraordinary heads and, through debates with leading theorists, helped them hone their arguments into a consistent and empirically grounded theory. Gall won the admiration of Goethe and was honored in Berlin by the minting of a commemorative coin. But he also made some important enemies, most notably the eminent anatomists Walter in Berlin, Reil in Halle, and Ackermann in Heidleburg. Above all, the tour helped sensationalize the new science. News of the spectacular readings they gave in the Berlin and Spandau prisons, for instance, quickly spread across the Continent. For the *Edinburgh Medical and Surgical Journal,* the visit to the Berlin prison was the first official test of Gall's theories. In the presence of "the chief of the establishment, of the heads of the criminal department, and various counsellors [sic] selected by the Prussian government," Gall examined "two hundred prisoners, and described not only the nature of the crime, whether murder, theft, fraud, etc., for which each one was detained, but in many of them the special natural characteristics for which they were known to the authorities and their companions."[32] Walter was less impressed. After examining the head of one youth, he records that Gall advised locking the boy away for good, as he was predisposed to a life of crime. "What man of feeling for morality and religion," he asked, could read such reports "without amazement?"

A fanatic advises the perpetual internment of a child, which has stolen once and is supposed to have an imaginary organ of thieving. Mankind must revolt when it hears that a preacher of fatalistic theories promulgates teaching which would be abhorred even by the most savage people without morals and religion. . . . And we fill the pockets of such a man and engrave medals in his honor! It is lucky for Berlin that Dr. Gall held his Fatalism sermon in the presence of intelligent and just judges; in any other place it might have had dangerous consequences.[33]

With such notoriety, by the time they arrived in France with their crates of skulls and casts, Gall and Spurzheim were as much public celebrities as scientific figures. Enthusiastically received by the Paris literati, their public lectures sold out and, Richard Chenevix reports, their social calendar was booked for months in advance.[34]

All of this changed the following year when Gall and Spurzheim submitted a *Memoire* of their anatomical discoveries to the Académie des Sciences. Cuvier, who led the commission charged with responding to the work, had shown an early interest in phrenology. He attended Gall and Spurzheim's lectures and even invited them to dissect a brain in his rooms—his own inquiries, after all, had led him to study the brain and the shape of the skull. The two Germans were thus completely surprised when France's preeminent scientist publicly questioned the originality of their work and totally trivialized their findings. At the outset, Cuvier insisted that the commission would not consider those parts of Gall's theory associating brain structure with behavior, because such arguments "ultimately [depended] upon observations relative to the intellectual and moral disposition of individuals, which are certainly not within the sphere of any academy of sciences."[35] Although it was well established that the brain was the organ of the mind, he held that anatomists had absolutely no hope of discovering any link between its structure and function. How could they? Unlike the liver and the heart, the brain was subject to causes and effects that went beyond science, namely, "the supposed mutual, but always incomprehensible influence of the divisible matter and the indivisible mind (*moi*); a hiatus in the system of our ideas never to be supplanted, an eternal stumbling-block of all our philosophies."[36] The committee would thus confine its comments to anatomical claims. Here Cuvier applauded Gall and Spurzheim's surgical skill, but argued that their apparently novel method "was very long ago sketched by Varolius, and afterward more fully detailed by Vieussens."[37] As for their physiological claims, he noted that it was now a commonplace among physiologists that, far from being a "tree with a single trunk," the nerves form a network of relatively independent systems. What distinguished Gall and Spurzheim was their assertion that these structures had to be approached genetically, and that "the brain and cerebellum, far from being the origin and source of [the spinal] cord, are, on the contrary, an appendix or sort of deverticulum [*sic*]" to the system.[38] Without pretending to take sides on this issue, Cuvier identified ten distinct arguments cited in support of this thesis—including observations about the white and gray matter, the formation of the spinal cord, and the path of the fibers from the medulla oblongata to the convolutions. By and large what little Cuvier found to be true was already accepted by other anatomists. Moreover, the committee's own experiments failed to substantiate Gall and Spurzheim's claims about the spine. The conclusions they had drawn on the structure of the brain from hydrocephalous patients were erroneous, and the evidence they accumulated from embryology, comparative anatomy, and records of mental illnesses was inconclusive. Bringing the report to a close, Cuvier admitted that the Germans had distinguished two kinds of fibers in the hemispheres and demonstrated that the cerebral nerves ascend rather than descend from the brain, but cast against contemporary scholarship, they really had little new information to offer. Finally, as if to bury their scientific pretensions completely, he emphasized that the sensational claims for which Gall and Spurzheim were most commonly known simply could not be decided by anatomy.

Gall and Spurzheim replied that without a commitment to the underlying unity of nature and the rule of general laws, the commissioners would never appreciate the significance of their anatomical discoveries. Philosophy, not science, separated the two sides.[39] Privately, however, they blamed Napoleon for discrediting their work. The emperor, it seems, thought even less of Gall's theories than he did the doctrines of the *Idéologues*. "Nature does not reveal herself by external forms," he insisted, "she hides and does not express her secrets. To pretend to seize and penetrate human character by so slight an index is the part of a dupe or an imposter. . . . The only way of knowing our fellow creatures is to see them, to associate with them frequently, and to submit them to proof."[40] Originally "Gall's lectures [had been] attended by generals, senators, privy counsellors, and all the learned frequentors of the Court," but as soon as Napoleon's opinion was declared, Francois Broussais reported in 1836, those "who had received the doctrines of Gall with favor changed their tone, and either became his open enemies or sought excuses for their desertion of a cause which they had so recently espoused. But this was not all. Ridicule was employed, the journalists were let loose, and for several years Gall and his opinions were attacked in the most virulent and embittered manner."[41]

Persona non grata, Gall and Spurzheim retired from the public eye to work on their *Anatomie et Physiolologie du System Nerveux,* the first two volumes of which were published in 1810 and 1813. It was at this point that the two men went their separate ways, intellectually and socially. Having established a very comfortable medical practice, Gall remained in Paris, lecturing privately and completing the final volumes of "his large work." The lavish *Anatomie,* published in five folio volumes with an atlas containing more than 100 plates, went on sale in 1819 for the staggering price of one thousand francs.[42] *Sur le Fonctions,* a far cheaper, six-volume edition of his writings appeared in Paris between 1822 and 1826. As this "small work" reveals, Gall was far more interested in laying the foundation of a physiological psychology than the philosophical systemizing and moral reforms advocated by Spurzheim, who Gall complained "too frequently deviated from the pure path of observation and . . . [threw] himself into ideal-metaphysical and even theological reveries."[43] Gall, a lapsed Catholic who refused spiritual absolution on his deathbed, nonetheless retained an essentially conservative view that embraced original sin and denied the possibility of significant individual and social improvement. "Bad dispositions make part of the plan of Providence," he asserted.[44]

> Men always have been, and always will be, inclined to all sorts of perverse actions . . . besieged by temptations within and without . . . tormented by carnal desires, covetousness, ambition, pride . . . the world has never ceased and never will cease, to be the theatre of all vices; such as lying, calumny, jealousy, envy, avarice, usury, immodesty, vengeance, adultery, perjury, rape, incest, idolatry, drunkenness, discord, enmity, injustice, etc.[45]

By contrast, Spurzheim, a liberal Protestant, held a far more optimistic faith in social progress. Believing that Gall's research provided the physiological basis for his moral philosophy, he presented the brain as the normative instrument by which God had fashioned men and women for virtue and happiness. Evil was not an inherent characteristic of human nature, but the result of transgressing the moral laws of mind. To achieve this reconceptualization, Spurzheim introduced new organs and rearranged Gall's table of faculties into a hierarchical economy of powers that explained the positive function of each organ. The image of the ideal cerebral order thus stood as an ethical justification for progressive social policies. It was this fusion of natural law and moral values, not the details of brain anatomy, that would prove so attractive to aspiring middle-class professionals and upwardly mobile members of the working classes.

Among phrenologists, Gall would be revered as the founder of the new science, Spurzheim as its theorist and systemizer. Some, like Bernard Hollander, decried the vulgarization of Gall's scientific mission and painted Spurzheim as a schemer who, "unable to escape Gall's shadow in France," went to England determined to "reap a harvest for himself by an unprincipled misapplication of his master's researches and discoveries."[46] Others, most notably George Combe, believed that Spurzheim was the key figure in phrenology's development. But whatever their respective contribution, it is useful to separate physiological claims from moral imperatives and treat Gall's research (in the remainder of this chapter) and Spurzheim's moral philosophy (in the next chapter) as distinct phases in the evolution of the theory that would sweep Europe and North America.

THE FUNCTIONS OF THE BRAIN

"The greatest obstacle which has ever been opposed to the knowledge of man's nature," Gall asserted at the beginning of *On the Functions,* "is that of insulating him from other beings, and endeavoring to remove him from the domination of the laws, which govern his nature."[47] From birth to death, the soul is dependent upon the bodily organization for its expression. It is thus the physiologist, not the philosopher, who must investigate the mind. With this ringing rejection of metaphysics and the rational analysis of thought, Gall set out his own scientific study of human nature. Drawing on the positive knowledge that he had derived from a lifetime of anatomical, ethological, and anthropological research, he promised to uncover the basic determinates of all behavior and to offer principles that would revolutionize government, law, and education.

All organisms could be divided into two classes: the vegetative, whose existence is limited to automatic functions such as respiration and digestion, and the animal, which, in addition to these processes, also comprises the powers of sensation, consciousness, and volition. The actions of the first category could be explained through the irritation of muscles, and those of the second through sensibility, the fundamental property of the nervous system. Accordingly, insofar as animals shared similar nervous organizations to humans, Gall insisted that they must also share the same kinds of experiences. Who could deny that other creatures hear, smell, taste, suffer pain, experience pleasure, and form memories? Indeed, based upon the similarity of the anterior portion of the brain, he believed that some animals possessed up to nineteen of the twenty-seven mental organs in the human mind.[48] The primary difference lay with the upper anterior region not present in lower animals. It was here that Gall discovered the capacities for justice, sympathy, religious feeling, and reason that separated men and women from the beasts.

What were these mental powers, and how were they formed? Philosophers before him had analyzed the mind through a set of theoretical categories that bore little resemblance to the basic instincts and actions of any living creature. How could abstract faculties such as sensation, attention, memory, and reflection capture the impulses, talents, and dispositions, the capacities for art, poetry, music, mathematics, language, spatial orientation, physical dexterity, and the many other practical traits that constitute human nature? Could judgment account for the near universal desire of all animals to protect their offspring? Could reasoning explain the hibernation of animals, or memory explain the spider's web? Equally problematic was the philosopher's effort to explain the origin of these abilities through the sensationalist thesis. Take language, for example. Gall found the capacity for speech to be far beyond anything that could be acquired from experience. "However imperfect or perfect they may be," languages "are not the creation of the hearing, but of the cerebral organization."[49] In argument after argument, Gall sought to erode the theoretical bias of Condillac's epistemology. Focusing on the diversity of behavior, he asks how is it that animals (and idiots) who have keen senses do not develop (full) human powers; that creatures alter their behavior when the seasons change; that children raised together act so differently; and that some men and women seem destined to be geniuses or dolts despite their education? The profusion of universal species-specific traits in populations spread across the world presented an even greater challenge for the sensationalist. From insects to humans, environment seemed to have little fundamental effect on basic forms of behavior. This was not to say that climate, age, sex, diet, and temperament were insignificant. A doctor himself, Gall understood the value of medical therapeutics and even recognized the effect of such factors in generating national characters—he was especially attracted to the notion that altitude influenced pride. But such forces could not yield new faculties: they merely modified the existing organization. Lamarck's adaptation hypothesis, explaining how organs are gradually transformed through exercise and inheritance, was thus completely unacceptable to Gall. Quoting his assertion that "the mole preserves her little eyes, only because she exercises them but little," Gall asks "why does not the mole make use of its eyes . . . and adopt different habits of life?"[50] Clearly, he responded, because it is not in the creature's nature. It was "impossible not to believe that a supreme wisdom has not placed each animal in harmony with his external world."[51] Specialization was the law of nature. As Herder taught, each creature was uniquely adapted to the environment within a hierarchical progression of life. Without this preestablished harmony "animals would be found in a violent state of perpetual contradiction, or would have perished after a few moments of existence."[52] Species did not change—"as if man might descend to the rank of a monkey, or a monkey raise himself to the rank of a man"—because desires, needs, and interests all depended upon impulses "from within."[53] It was not survival that generated faculties, but faculties that assured survival.

The same argument also undermined Condillac's assertion that the faculties are nothing but transformed sensations, assembled in response to pleasurable and painful experiences in the world. Pointing out that the object for which "a man or an animal feels desire . . . is most in harmony with his propensities and talents," Gall insisted that it was the faculties themselves that generated pleasure and pain, not vice versa.[54] Laromiguière had argued that attention was necessary to the formation of reason and judgment. But again Gall objected: what we attend to depends on our propensities. "Children are interested in toys; females in fashion; and men follow horses, battles, and women. A fox will pay attention to chickens and a hawk to a field mouse, but try getting monkeys (or idiots) to learn etiquette or a sheep to appreciate the arts."[55] No less than pleasure and pain, interest depended on the determinate relations that exist between the inner organs of mind and the external world. An appropriate object could excite a given faculty, but if the organ did not exist, attention and desire could not be generated.

Gall's inquiries also pointed in the opposite direction of his French forebears on the relationship between human nature and society. Condillac believed that it was through initiation in language and other cultural symbols that the mind was formed, and he pointed, as we have seen, to cases of feral children to demonstrate that in a state of nature men and women would not display social impulses. But the behavior of many animals disproved this assertion. The remarkable cooperation evidenced in colonies of ants, flocks of geese, and packs of wolves clearly revealed that preordained drives fitted each individual for a definite role within the group. And so it was with humans. History demonstrated that "man has been destined to live in common," always and everywhere "united in families, tribes, and nations . . . his qualities must have been calculated for society"[56] Far from the mythic noble savage, wild children, such as Victor, were simply idiots, who, incapable of normal social intercourse, had been left to the mercies of nature.

As critics were quick to point out, Gall's thesis raised a number of challenging moral, religious, and political questions about human free will and the proper structure of social institutions. Indeed, given the "force of our propensities and talents . . . the primary motives of our actions," Gall confessed "that man, in many of the most important moments of his life, is subject to the power of destiny."[57] In fact, it was precisely in recognition of the power of such internal causes that civil law and religious codes were established. "In all ages and all countries men have robbed and murdered . . . [and] no education, no legislation, no religion, neither prison, nor hard labor nor the wheel, has yet been able to extirpate these crimes."[58]

Spurzheim, Combe, and later phrenologists would argue that character could be improved—in individuals and their descendents—through education and the ethic of self-help, but Gall remained convinced that "man cannot, in any manner, arrest the development of his organs, nor consequently, relax the energy of their functions and cause himself to be urged either more or less imperiously to do good or evil."[59] Was this fatalism? Prestaging Freud, Gall even speculated that the sense of freedom implicit in self-conscious thought might itself be an illusion generated by causal processes beyond or below our experience. There was an escape, however, if only for those blessed with superior brains. Drawing upon Bonnet, Gall defined moral liberty as "nothing but the faculty of being determined and determining oneself by motives."[60] Internal and external stimuli yielded sensations no man or woman could avoid—desires, impulses, and other emotions that entered even the most saintly heads. But unlike animals, human beings had "ennobled" faculties, magistrates of desire that traced the cause and effect of events, weighed responses, and chose actions, often against immediate impulses, for long-term goals more conducive to happiness. Before a man "throws himself into the arms of pleasure, the frightening image of his destroyed health and social conveniences, the shame of abusing confidences, the grievous consequences of his conduct for the beloved object . . . act on his mind and by their force or by their number finally get the upper hand."[61] Not everyone enjoyed this freedom of will to the same extent. "The man with great talents has more liberty than the ordinary man; and the more the faculties descend toward idiocy, the more also, moral liberty goes on decreasing."[62] Given this moral scale, Gall offered a social blueprint in which different biological classes would be assigned duties corresponding to their cerebral development. Assessing the relative size of mental organs, he concluded that "only a very small number would find, in themselves alone, the force, or sufficient motives, to make a law for themselves."[63] "The crowd of ordinary men," in whom "the organs common to the animal occupy the greatest part of the brain . . . remain limited to the sphere of animal qualities; their enjoyments are those of sense, and they never produce in any respect any thing remarkable."[64] "Plunged in profound ignorance, deprived of all that might have formed the qualities of his mind and soul," the worker "has but very inexact notions of morality and religion: even the obligations of society and the laws are unknown to him: solely occupied with earning his bread, gross and noisy amusements, gaming and drunkenness, make him a prey to base and violent passions."[65] It was thus incumbent upon the cerebral elite to use education and legislation to "develop and cultivate internal means, and multiply and fortify external motives."[66] Early schooling would bring "more energy to the superior propensities, feelings, and faculties, and render the idea of the fatal results of immoral actions, more lively and more habitual."[67] Gall was particularly interested in those criminals who, because of their unfavorable organization or wretched social condition, simply could not resist destructive urges. If an individual were impelled to vice by internal causes beyond their will, he argued, they should be treated according to their degree of culpability. Not that Gall dismissed the use of punishment—pain and suffering were powerful tools for teaching compliance to social and moral laws. Rather, he believed that retribution had to be balanced with the project of reforming character. Prisons had to be changed from schools of vice, where newcomers quickly learned the arts of villainy, to houses of correction in which, through hard work and moral guidance, offenders learned habits and vocational skills necessary to successfully reenter society. As for natural-born criminals—such as the boy examined at Berlin Prison—whose vicious tendencies were beyond control, Gall proposed permanent isolation.

FROM BRAIN TO BEHAVIOR

If Gall's organology derived anatomical structures from a knowledge of physiological functions, his cranioscopy took the opposite route of demonstrating that moral and intellectual traits could be read from physical features of the brain, as revealed by the shape of the head. Today it seems obvious that the brain is the organ of the mind, but at the turn of the nineteenth century many physicians were unsure about its purpose. Even Cabanis, who placed the intellectual capacities in the head, believed that the emotions were housed in the chest and abdomen. Others, most notably Pinel, although sympathetic to the science of man, did not embrace the union of the physical and the moral. Pinel recognized that some instances of insanity had bodily causes, but maintained that many cases were a product of erroneous mental associations. While deferential to Pinel's authority over the treatment of the mad, Gall was determined to assimilate his nosology to his own theory of cerebral functioning. Drawing passage after passage from Pinel's *Traite*, he illustrated how the many strange and aberrant behaviors Pinel had chronicled coincided with the effects of diseased neural organs and boldly asserted that there could be no mental illness without a physical cause in the brain. Pinel, a member of the committee that had rejected the *Memoire*, took strong exception to Gall's claim and dissected dozens of brains in search of negative evidence to prove him wrong. But Gall remained steadfast, insisting that Pinel's failure to find physical traces of the disease resulted from his lack of anatomical knowledge. Pinel may have understood madness, but he was no neurologist. Esquirol found a greater number of lesions, swellings, and discolorations, while his student, the "brilliant Georget," predicted "that in the course of a few years, the pathological anatomy of the brain will make great advances, and . . . few bodies of insane persons will be examined, without exhibiting appreciable traces of affection of this organ."[68] By the 1830s his prophecy was realized, and Gall's doctrine had become an integral part of the medical view of insanity.

Gall was not the first to argue that physical features of the brain were related to mental abilities; Boerhave, Haller, Soemmering, and even Cuvier had postulated relationships between the organ and human capacities. Size was an obvious approximation: the larger the cranial capacity, the greater the moral and intellectual powers, a correlation that seemed to justify the received Western account of the hierarchy of races. It did not, however, fit the diversity of brains and behavior in the animal kingdom. If size was all that was important, Gall asked, how was it that the monkey and the dog far outwitted the ox and the horse and that elephants and whales are not more intelligent than men and women? Other anatomists proposed measures based on the proportion of the brain's mass to that of the body, the face, the neck, the nervous system, and even the spinal marrow. Cuvier, closer to the mark, weighed the cerebellum against the cerebrum. Most famous of all, Peter Camper proposed a facial angle that charted the increasing slope of the forehead. Widely accepted at the time, indeed throughout the nineteenth century, this index was used to construct a scale of perfection from the lowest animal to the highest human.

Gall rejected all of these rules with numerous counterexamples. Against Camper, for instance, he argued that, although nearly three-fourths of all animals have similar facial angles, they display radically different behaviors. As for men and women, Camper's line started at the jaw (a part of the anatomy that had nothing to do with the brain) and completely ignored the majority of the cerebral mass. Nor did Gall buy into the progressive elevation of the races. People the world over had similar capacities. He claimed to know, for example, "many negroes, who, with very prominent jaws, are quite distinguished for their intellectual faculties."[69] Simply put, he "had no concern with the different forms of the head, except so far as they denote the form of the brain."[70] With this proviso, Gall was willing to make one claim about the size of the head, a hypothesis rejected by Pinel and his followers, which would become a crucial test for phrenology and an important point of contention among educators of the feebleminded. From his examination of microcephalic idiots at the insane asylum in Vienna, Gall was certain that unless the circumference of the skull exceeds fourteen inches in maturity, normal functioning is impossible. A fourteen-inch head, he reported, contains roughly half the mass of a typical brain. He had seen idiots with skulls measuring eleven to thirteen inches that "contained as much brain as the head of a new-born child, that is, a fourth, fifth, or sixth of the cerebral mass of an adult in the full enjoyment of his faculties."[71] In fact, with most adults having a circumference between twenty and twenty-two inches, Gall was even willing to assert that heads of "eighteen or eighteen and a half inches in circumference . . . although not incompatible with the regular exercise of the intellectual faculties" often indicate "a pitiful mediocrity, a slavish spirit of imitation, credulity, superstition, that species of sensibility, which, by a trifle, is raised to a height of joy, or plunged into an abyss of tears, a judgment rather fallible, an extreme difficulty in discerning the relation of cause and effect, a want of self-control, and frequently, what is a happy circumstance, few desires."[72] Gall did not make the converse claim: large brains did not mean great intellectual power. There were many "remarkable for nothing but love of conquest, desire of ruling, love of destruction, inordinate vanity, a rage for combats, cruelty, an irresistible desire for beastly pleasures etc., [who] have the superior-anterior part of their heads but slightly developed," the other parts being "remarkable prominent."[73] It followed that moral character and genius was not determined by mass alone, but by the development of the various cerebral parts that perform so many discrete and diverse functions. A single index of the brain might explain idiocy, but the normal or superior mind could only be measured by charting all of the faculties.

Believing that "the art of interpreting forms of the head supposes . . . a knowledge of the functions, both of the brain and its several parts," Gall developed his taxonomy of the mind's organs by correlating distinctive behaviors with cranial protuberances.[74] Today the very idea that a person's character can be read from the form of the skull seems ludicrous, an obvious mark of quackery that could only fool the most gullible. Yet, in its time, this sensational procedure did have an element of plausibility. It was based upon sound arguments about the plasticity of the cranium and a persuasive account of the brain structure. And, as so many skeptics found, the readings provided by skilled phrenologists were remarkably insightful. Spurzheim, in particular, often staggered his audience with analyses of previously unviewed brains and skulls—many reported that he knew their secret nature. Quite how this was achieved is impossible to say. But it was not—at least in the case of Gall, Spurzheim, and Combe—a confidence trick. These men were seeking scientific respectability; any taint of commercialism or charlatanism would have been anathema to them.

What, then, was the evidence in favor of cranioscopy? First, the shape of the brain itself, which Gall and Spurzheim convincingly demonstrated was uneven, with bumps and depressions generated by the thickness and density of the convolutions. Because their surgical technique revealed that the fibers emanating from these surface features lead to the central nervous system, they were also able to argue that the brain is divided into sectors (each corresponding to an organ), the size of which, in line with basic physiological principles, provides an indication of its power. Second, the cranium. Composed of eight distinct bones, the skull is extremely thin and plastic at birth and does not become rigid until after puberty, when, Gall reported, it is often still only half a line thick. Given its constant contact with the brain, was it unreasonable to conclude that the pressure exerted by the convolutions could form a surface configuration that matched the organ below? Certainly the shape of the head changed radically as the brain altered form in the passage from infancy to maturity. No doubt cranioscopy would become more difficult as a person got older—the physiological influences of sex, temperament, and environment would also have to be factored in—but these observations did suggest that a trained physician could determine something of an individual's cerebral endowment from the contours of their head.

In any case, it worked for Gall. He collected casts from the living and skulls from the dead, examined paintings, and studied sculptures to identify the cranial landscape. Each bump had to be associated with a distinct behavioral characteristic. Unfortunately, Gall admitted, the majority of his collection came from hospitals and asylums without any of the biographical details necessary for his research. It was thus the heads of animals that yielded the majority of his insights. The habits of cats, birds, dogs, and numerous other creatures provided a natural laboratory from which to chart the primitive powers underlying the multifarious forms of life. The account of the discovery of the love of offspring is typical of Gall's reasoning. Having noticed that "in most of the heads of females, the superior part of the occipital bone recedes more than the heads or crania of men," he started to ponder the nature of the faculty beneath, gaining a flash of insight (in the middle of a lecture) from similar shapes in the skulls of monkeys.[75] Reflecting on the common characteristics of women and apes, he was struck "with the extreme love that these animals have for their offspring."[76]

> Impatient of comparing instantaneously the crania of male and female animals, in my collection, with all those of females, I requested my class to leave me, and I found, in truth, that the same difference exists between the male and female of all animals, as existed between man and woman. This new idea appeared to me as much more plausible, as the organ of this instinct is found placed very near that of the instinct of propagation. What could be more in conformity with the order of nature?[77]

Clearly, not every common sense term corresponded to a primitive power: cowardice and bravery, for example, resulted from the underdevelopment and overdevelopment of the instinct of self-defense. Accordingly, to complete the phrenological map of the head, Gall set out to discover an underlying set of motives and talents capable of yielding all behavioral traits. Each fundamental organ had to grow and act independently of the others. Drawing upon comparative physiology and anatomy, embryology, cases of brain damage and mental disorders, sex-based differences, and the peculiar abilities of idiot savants and geniuses, he used the abnormal and the pathological as keys to unlock the structure of the human mind—ensuring, in every instance, that the faculties he identified corresponded with a distinct localized cerebral mass. Occupying nearly a thousand pages, Gall's empirical findings contain hundreds of fascinating and bizarre stories. Among this potpourri: the public official who could not stop stealing kitchen utensils, a diminutive friend who loved to start bar fights, cases of female erotic mania, a beggar too proud to eat, the numerical abilities of animals, a cat that could not find its way home, the cunning of ducks, and the courage of a deer in a staged fight against a bear. The result, a list of twenty-seven fundamental faculties, which, although not exhaustive of all abilities, provided a key to the basic grammar of human action:

Gall's Twenty-Seven Organs
  1. Instinct of Propagation
  2. Love of Offspring
  3. Attachment
  4. Instinct of Self-defense
  5. Murder, the Carnivorous instinct
  6. Sense of Cunning
  7. Theft, the Love of Property
  8. Pride
  9. Ambition
  10. Cautiousness
  11. Memory of Things (or Education)
  12. Sense of Locality
  13. Recollection of People
  14. Verbal Memory
  15. Spoken Language
  16. Faculty of Color
  17. Faculty of Music
  18. Faculty of Number
  19. Mechanical Ability
  20. Comparative Sagacity
  21. Metaphysical Thought
  22. Causality, Inductive Inference.
  23. Talent for Poetry

24. Moral Sense
25. Faculty of Imitation
26. God and Religion
27. Firmness
Adapted from *On the Functions.*

Gall admitted that his list might not be complete, that other organs could be added to the mosaic he had charted, but was confident that the majority of primitive powers had been identified. Like the almost infinite assembly of letters into words, the different combination of these twenty-seven faculties could easily explain the myriad forms of human culture and the almost limitless diversity among individuals. Finally Gall was beginning to see the logic of God's handiwork. Those faculties that men and women have in common with animals were all collected at the rear of the brain, whereas the distinctively human powers were placed in the forehead: organs that cooperated—such as the instinct of propagation and the love of offspring, color, tune, and number—were also found to be adjacent. This was no haphazard arrangement. From the most basic instincts to the most refined and delicate capacities, the building blocks of the mental world were unfolding in a mathematical pattern across the surface of the skull. Under Spurzheim's systemizing influence, the busts produced to illustrate the phrenological organs would become increasingly idealized. Smooth and well proportioned, they indicated not an actual head, but the harmonious physiological order that God had implanted in the brain—perhaps even the head of Christ.

The configuration of the skull was not the only sign of the brain's organs. Gall also believed that a person's thoughts and feelings could be read from the natural language that accompanied all mental activity. Not that he approved of physiognomy, which, based upon the idea that the soul expressed itself through human features, totally ignored the laws of physiology. What, he asked, do the nose, the ear, and the mouth have to do with the brain, the organ of the mind and source of all actions? In its place he suggested pathognomy, the science of gesture. "Pantomime," he asserted, "is the universal language of all nations and all animals: there is no beast, there is no man, who does not learn it; it accompanies language and strengthens its expressions; it supplies the defects of articulate language; words may be ambiguous, but pantomime is never so."[78] What made Gall's treatment of this important insight so bizarre was his belief that the entire range of bodily movements could be explained by twelve geometrical rules of motion stemming from the location of active faculties within the brain. The organ of cunning, for instance, situated in the lower part of the temples, directs

the head and the body forward and downward. When the double organs act alternatively, the head and the body are gently turned from right to left, and from left to right. While turning thus, the cunning man looks aside, and accompanies the movement of his head and body by an analogous movement of his forefinger, which he holds extended. Hence the expression, *a low, vile flatterer, a cringing man.*"[79]

Similar movements could be seen when a cat stalked its prey, or when dogs in play try to surprise one another. Actors, artists, and, of course, the deaf, all understood that the language of gesture was a powerful instrument for communicating ideas and emotions—oftentimes more vividly and subtly than the spoken word. "The intimate and immediate connexion . . . between the language of action and the operations of the organs of the brain" being "the source of that sympathy, which . . . gives rise in us to the same sentiments and the same thoughts, with which pantomime is itself animated."[80]

It was not until 1835 that Gall's works were translated into English. By this time Spurzheim had successfully marketed his own version of their anatomical studies. The differences were profound. Eliminating one and adding eight new organs to the original table of faculties, he completely reorganized Gall's empirical findings around the principles of his progressive faith in human nature. Most importantly, in line with Cabanis's project, Spurzheim promoted the idea that knowledge of the mental organs and their development could be used to shape the character of men and women for the greater good of society. Like Gall he believed that moral evil infected the world, but this, he insisted, resulted from the corrupting influences of society, not the work of the Creator. Education—by which he meant the improvement of the human organization—was the key to progress. "If an agriculturalist wishes to cultivate plants, trees, and fruits . . . does he not train his trees and place them in certain situations favorable for his purpose?"[81] So it was with children. Like any other creature, the full and harmonious development of an individual's powers could only occur in an environment structured around the natural laws of mind and body. Even more importantly, given that the living organization is determined by the act of procreation, the perfection of the race demanded a careful attention to the principles of propagation. Phrenology, as the following chapter explains, thus developed in the English-speaking work not as the physiological science envisioned by Gall, but as the broad eugenic social philosophy formulated by Spurzheim.

4

The Birth of the Normal

Now it is true that the whole constitution is propagated from parents to children. . . . This is the most important thing a man can attend to; and if the
time should come when the laws of propagation shall be attended to, more
good will be done to perfect man than hitherto has been done by all the institutions, and all the teachers, of present or past ages, not only with respect to
individuals, but families and nations.

Spurzheim, *Lectures on Phrenology*, 1837

By 1813, as the fifty-five-year-old Gall settled into his comfortable medical
practice, ministering to the health of counts, princes, and ambassadors, the
thirty-six-year-old Spurzheim decided to go his own way. Determined to escape Gall's shadow, Spurzheim completed his M.D., studied English for six
months, and crossed the channel convinced that his reformulated theory,
soon to be christened phrenology, would flourish among the more progressive
minds of Britain. Gall, who believed that Spurzheim had perverted his life's
project, bending science to philosophical ends, is reported "to have spoken
violently against him, calling him a plagiarist and a quack."[1] The break was
complete. Even though Spurzheim returned to Paris for several years, the two
did not associate with one another. In 1828, hearing news of Gall's imminent
death, Spurzheim rushed from Scotland in search of a reconciliation, only to
find Gall too weak for visitors. He did not even get the skull.

Arriving in London during March 1814, Spurzheim faced an extremely
skeptical audience. The leading journals had kept readers abreast of Gall's
theory but had uniformly ridiculed cranioscopy and been highly suspicious
of its materialistic implications. Spurzheim labored to reverse this popular
opinion. He dissected a brain at the offices of the *Medico-Churiological* journal and presented a series of lectures to small audiences in Dr. John Abernathy's auditorium. As Abernathy recalled, "he met but with very few who
would give the subject he proposed to them that patient attention and con-

sideration which are necessary for its clear comprehension."[2] Spurzheim's writings, however, did create something of a stir. Published early the following year, his *Physiognomical System of Drs. Gall and Spurzheim* drew the attention of several critics, most notably, the Edinburgh surgeon John Gordon, whose scathing assessment appeared anonymously in the June issue of the *Edinburgh Review*.[3] Certainly, in the years following the Napoleonic Wars, radical ideas from the continent were not warmly received. But as Spurzheim read the *Review* he must have bristled at his and Gall's labors being characterized as "trash," "despicable trumpery," "a piece of thorough quackery from beginning to end," and "a mixture of gross errors, extravagant absurdities, downright misstatements," which "can leave no doubt . . . in the minds of honest and intelligent men, as to the real ignorance, the real hypocrisy, and the real empiricism of the authors."[4] A gentleman and a scholar, Spurzheim resolved to confront his accuser with the truth of his discoveries. As fate would have it, this encounter, at the seat of Scottish medical science and academic philosophy, initiated an interest in phrenology that would blossom into the leading organ of the movement, the Edinburgh Phrenological Society. Most importantly, in George Combe, Spurzheim would find an ardent and sincere disciple with a gift for clear thought and crisp prose. It was only when this "most able and eloquent advocate came forward," Abernathy reports, that "general attention" to phrenology was awakened.[5]

As he made his way north, lecturing in Bath, Bristol, Cork, Dublin, Liverpool, Manchester, Glasgow, and a number of other towns, Spurzheim planned his confrontation of mind and morals carefully. A letter to the Irish physician Andrew Carmichael, an early and ardent disciple, explained his strategy. Notes of introduction in hand, Spurzheim had visited the most eminent men in Edinburgh—including Gordon, who feigned no knowledge of his guest— ingratiating himself in their company and studying their character. "*I shall never know the reviewer;* but keep everywhere the same free and open language, and provoke him to appear if he like truth."[6] The melodrama came to a climax the following week when Spurzheim showed up at his adversary's afternoon lecture and was granted an hour to demonstrate his method of dissection before "his own class at his lecture table in presence of himself, Drs. Thompson, Barkley, Duncan, jun., Irwin, Emery, and many others."[7] With a brain in one hand and the *Edinburgh Review* in the other, Spurzheim then refuted all of Gordon's substantive criticisms, point by point, without ever mentioning the author's name.

I only stated: *This is denied,* and then made the preparation. We are accused of such a thing, or blamed for showing such and such a structure. And then I presented the structure in nature. At the same time I have our plates in hand, and asked the audience, whether, they represented the preparations as I have made them. The answer was always affirmative.[8]

Upstaged in front of his colleagues and students, Gordon furiously defended his review by "denying what others had admitted" and "disputing words and definitions."[9] But now Spurzheim had the stronger position and calmly demonstrated that Gordon's remarks were either contrary to nature or based upon a shallow reading of his work. He may not have converted his audience to phrenology, but the moderate and disinterested manner in which he presented his findings impressed many that Spurzheim was indeed a man of science and that his arguments were worthy of objective investigation. "Our doctrine is no more quackery or trash," he told Carmichael. "On the contrary there is more anxiety here to become acquainted with it, than in any other city of the united kingdoms. Since I left Germany, I have not observed a greater enthusiasm."[10] Moving to capitalize on this interest, he quickly scheduled lectures on the physiological and philosophical components of his doctrine and reported that, even though advertised privately, by the sixth class "Dr. Barkley's lecture-room was scarcely large enough. They stood even to the staircase."[11]

For George Combe, a young lawyer from the lower echelons of the middle ranks who had studied the philosophy of Reid and Stewart and taken several courses in anatomy and physiology, Spurzheim's professionalism and positivism were a potent combination. Socially disadvantaged in a community governed by strict religious, class, and family ties, Combe was naturally receptive to a philosophy that questioned irrational and authoritarian structures without undermining the rule of faith, reason, and morality. By legitimizing observation over introspection, Spurzheim helped Combe problematize the traditional categories of ruling elites and carefully nurtured his own dispassionate evaluation of the new science. It took a meticulous study of casts and skulls to complete the conversion, but within a year, Combe was lecturing friends and writing articles. By 1819 he had released his first book, *Essays on Phrenology,* later expanded and published as *A System of Phrenology* (1825) and the following year, together with his brother Andrew, James Simpson, and a number of like-minded men, opened the Edinburgh Phrenological Society.

After seven months in Edinburgh, Spurzheim returned to London, leaving a small but growing band of enthusiastic followers. If he expected a similar response to his doctrines in the capital, he must have been disappointed, for although gaining a few converts and being admitted to the Royal College of Surgeons, he continued to face a largely skeptical press that lampooned his work at every opportunity. In addition to lecturing, he then spent much of 1817 extending the later sections of his *Physiognomical System* into what would become his most influential book, *Observations on Insanity*. By the fall, despairing that his cause would not after all take root in Anglo-Saxon soil and buoyed by the liberal opposition to the Restoration government, he gave in to the wishes of his future wife, Madame Perier, and returned to Paris, where he opened a private medical practice and started lecturing at the Athénée.[12]

Unlike Combe, who directed his teachings to political leaders and popular audiences, Spurzheim struggled to make converts in the medical community. In time this strategy did bear fruit, as, on both sides of the channel, a new generation of physicians and alienists sought the scientific knowledge necessary to establish their professional standing. *Observations on Insanity*—with its celebration of medical expertise, its comprehensive and authoritative account of the diagnosis, prognosis, and treatment of mental illness—proved a timely and perfectly positioned text in this social confluence. Thomas Forester, the man who invented the term "phrenology," was correct when he told Spurzheim, "Although you have left Great Britain without establishing so fully in the minds of British Anatomists the truth of the doctrines regarding the Organs of the Brain, as the clearness of the proofs seem to warrant . . . yet the valuable Observations on Insanity and its periodical aberrations, which you have given the World in your late Work, will give rise to a better knowledge and treatment of that disease."[13]

In *Console and Classify* (1987), Jan Goldstein explores the genesis of the psychiatric profession in the politically and religiously contested landscape of postrevolutionary France. Her study reveals just how potent phrenology's fusion of physiological laws and a meritocratic social order was for young physicians with radical sympathies. Alienists had to make "the philosophical choice" between a state-sanctioned spiritualist psychology and the antimetaphysical doctrines associated with the followers of Cabanis. Both positions endorsed moral treatment, but the latter, which became increasingly tied to phrenology, extended the domain of medical expertise to cover mental illnesses, a shift in the ownership of the mind that clearly challenged the authority of the church. A social order grounded in a religious conception of free will and responsibility simply could not accommodate medical theorists who wanted to transform sin into disease. It was in an effort to undermine these "atheistic" forces that the conservative government purged the Paris medical faculty during 1822–23 and restricted all unauthorized lectures within the city. But this move only elevated phrenology into a political cause.[14] By the time of the July Monarchy, the new science had evolved into a powerful social credo endorsed by leading physicians, men such as Jean Baptiste Boulillard, J. V. C. Broussais, Félix Voisan, and Joseph Vimont. The Société Phrénologique was formed in 1831, and over the next ten years it became a prominent organ for liberal-minded reformers seeking to extend bourgeois policies over welfare, criminal justice, health, and education. Moreover, as with its British counterparts, the Société also served as an important theoretical conduit for biological notions of race, class, and gender differences, influencing, through the work of Adolphe Quételet, Paul Broca, and others, the future development of eugenic philosophies among the social theorists of Europe's colonial powers. It was only as the Orleanist Regime took an increasingly conservative turn in the years leading up to the 1848 revolution that the charge of materialism, spearheaded by Flourens's attack on Gall, would gradually discredit phrenology as a public philosophy.

As phrenology grew in popularity among French physicians, so, in a like manner, it matured in the British medical community. Largely through the efforts of George and Andrew Combe; the anatomist John Elliotson; and the sympathetic editors of *The Lancet, The British and Foreign Medical Review,* and *The Medico-Chirurgical Review,* by the mid-1820s, phrenology had become a powerful and practical theory for doctors seeking to establish themselves in a society still fettered with the vestiges of patronage. Paralleling Goldstein's analysis, Roger Cooter details the important role that phrenology played in the development of British psychiatry. The country's leading authority on the care of the mad, William Ellis; his successor at the Hanwell Asylum, John Conolly; W. A. F. Browne; and a host of lesser known superintendents all followed Spurzheim's teachings in their diagnosis and treatment of insanity. Their remarkable successes with these techniques ensured, as in France, that the insane became the responsibility of medical professionals, not layman or the church. "As lecturers on phrenology and writers of both popular and specialist medical works," these men had a "considerable impact on the rest of the profession."[15] Indeed, Cooter continues, "the phrenological endeavors of Spurzheim, Combe, Ellis, and Browne, in particular, greatly contributed to the education of students and practitioners alike and their influence on leading American alienists like Brigham, Samuel Woodward, and Pliny Earle soon resulted in a reciprocal transatlantic influence on British psychiatrists."[16] Influences, moreover, that were quickly exported to the allied fields of penal reform, education, and social policy.

In March 1825, a year after the French government's crackdown on public lectures, Spurzheim returned to Britain and a very different reception. Now in favor among medical writers, his publications and lectures received sympathetic reviews. Over the next three years, as he shuttled between capitals, he once again took his message to the nation, lecturing in London, Bath, Bristol, Hull, Dublin, and numerous other cities to increasingly large and enthusiastic audiences. He was even embraced by the faculty at Cambridge. By January 1828, when he arrived triumphantly in Edinburgh to help Combe in his debate with Sir William Hamilton, Spurzheim could at last celebrate the success of his theory. A decade after his confrontation with Gordon, he was toasted in a lavish banquet arranged by the Edinburgh Phrenological Society as "an individual whose name would rival . . . Galileo, Harvey, or Newton . . . in brilliancy and duration."[17]

THE DOCTRINE OF MIND

After reviewing Spurzheim's *Physiognomical System,* later edited and published as *Phrenology, or the Doctrine of Mind,* it is hard not to be sympathetic with Gall's charge of plagiarism. Page after page reads like a vast summary of *On the Functions,* in which Gall's meandering thoughts are replaced with pithy explanations and well-chosen examples. The tone is altogether more authoritative. Far from a chronicle of struggles to found a new science, *Phrenology* is a philosophical treatise that assembles knowledge in a cohesive and coordinated structure.

Repeating Gall's reflections on the history of anatomy, Spurzheim argued that it was not the complexity of the brain that retarded the advancement of knowledge, but the negative influence of metaphysicians. Like Galileo, the physician had to overcome the ignorance of spiritualists and theologians.

Human beings had to be situated in the animal kingdom and the mind explored through the canons of Baconian science, not the introspective psychology of the armchair philosopher. This did not imply endorsing materialism; neither he nor Gall searched for final causes. As "the eyes are the organs of sight, but . . . not the faculty of seeing," so the brain was the instrument by means of which the soul was manifested.[18] Like physical events, all mental acts had a causal structure—without such necessity in the world, how could we predict events or judge a person's actions? But except for the insane, he did not think this implied a lack of free will. As Gall argued, men and women had the reflective powers to weigh their various motives, assess consequences, and chose actions that were in their long-term interests.

Dividing organic functions, he distinguished irritability from sensibility, showing, as Gall had, that experience depends on the genetic development of the nervous system. Phrenologists, he pointed out, were concerned with all organic laws, including the effects of temperature, air, nutrition, and various other environmental factors. But, following Cabanis, special attention had to be given to how the internal organization influenced the intellectual and emotional life of a person. Assembling evidence from comparative anatomy, child development, and cases of insane and brain-damaged patients, he ridiculed suggestions that the stomach or the chest could be the site of the intellectual and affective powers. The brain was clearly the organ of the mind. Objections based upon ossified or dissolved brains were quickly dismissed, as was the evidence of Pinel's autopsies. Mental derangement, he assured his readers, always had a physical cause that would be found in the cerebral mass—one only had to know how and where to look.

Having established the seat of the soul, Spurzheim then turned to the problem of its measurement: did any physical features indicate a person's intellectual and emotional powers? Like Gall he quickly swept through gross comparisons based upon brain size and relative weight to other parts of the body or nervous system. Camper's angle was rejected as "perfectly useless," again because it incorporated the nonrelevant factor of facial area. To understand human talents and character, all of the mind's powers had to be considered. This meant identifying the various organs of the brain, their direct influences, and their interactive effects. Against those who rejected the plurality of the mind, Spurzheim offered a variety of philosophical and physiological arguments to prove that specific functions have distinct organic sites. As the history of anatomy demonstrated, it was not easy to untangle the complexities of the brain. The mutilation experiments of Flourens and Magendie were a case in point. How could normal physiological functions be observed in an animal that had undergone such a massive trauma? Gall's comparative physiology, he concluded, was the only valid approach. His painstaking observations had demonstrated the plausibility of cranioscopy and the direct relationship between the size of an organ and its power.

Circumstances had favored Gall's inquiries. His visits to the asylum provided a remarkable range of heads, and of course, Vienna itself had no shortage of criminals, artists, musicians, and other exceptional types whose skulls could be explored. With the addition of casts and crania from their European tour, an unassailable body of proof now existed that the brain was indeed a congeries of discrete organs whose strength could be read through the shape of the head. But an important caveat had to be observed. In his efforts to chart the mind's organs, Gall had focused on the protuberances he found around the surface of the skull and, in many cases, Spurzheim asserted, confused bumps with the size of the organs below. The overall shape of the brain had to be taken into consideration. This was an important distinction. Was it not possible that the neighboring organs were equally well developed, thus masking the size of the faculties beneath? Before feeling the skull, Spurzheim cautioned, the phrenologist should first ascertain the basic proportion of the cerebral parts. This was achieved by dividing the head along two lines that indicated the separate regions in which different classes of organs were housed. A trained eye could then determine the overall nature of a person's character—whether, for example, they were driven by their passions, morality, or reason—before examining specific faculties.

After praising Gall's pioneering labors, Spurzheim came to the fundamental fault at the heart of his master's system. By focusing only on the most talented, the most wicked, in short, the most extreme behaviors he could find, Gall had identified the primary powers with extraordinary states of activity. For Gall, "individuals are, from birth stubborn, proud, courageous, or thievishly, murderously, religiously inclined" because their behavior was determined by "organs of pride, firmness, courage, theft, murder, religion."[19] But "no organ," Spurzheim maintained, "should be named after any action, and certainly not after an abuse of its function."[20] Gluttony, drunkenness, and adultery all resulted from organic causes, but this did not mean that there were special organs for these disorders. It was true that "individuals who steal from infancy, notwithstanding the most careful education and the severest punishment, have one portion of the brain particularly developed, but all persons in which the same part is large, are not thieves in the common acceptation of the word," for other organs within the cerebral economy could combine to control such vicious tendencies.[21] Actions, therefore, had to be understood through an underlying grammar of motives. Faculties combined, interacted, and drew upon one another in set ways. Most importantly, Spurzheim insisted, God had crafted each organ to perform a positive function in human life. Smuggling liberal norms into his physiological account, he found virtue, not vice, to be the natural state of the mind. But after generations of abusing the principles governing this organization, men and women had inherited imbalanced, deranged, and diseased brains, the physical embodiment of human sin. The moral order implicit in the architecture of the faculties thus became the ideal toward which human beings had to be normalized, both individually and generationally, through adherence to natural laws.

Given that the faculties could not be read directly from the head, Spurzheim had to draw upon theory to reveal the brain's fundamental powers. Gall, he believed, was correct to reject the abstract categories of the metaphysicians, but wrong to think general abilities inhered within each organ. With a keener appreciation for philosophy, Spurzheim set about dividing the cerebral parts into distinct classes according to their "special and characteristic functions," separating "that which belonged to each power itself from what depends upon its combinations with other faculties."[22] Parsing the mind into affective and intellectual functions, he further subdivided these orders into distinct genera, classifying each organ as a species of the propensities, sentiments, and perceptive or reflective faculties. Each kind played a different role. The propensities were blind instincts; the sentiments more circumspect impulses that incorporated moral feelings; the perceptive faculties gave form to the information provided by the senses; and the reflective organs, operating upon this knowledge, yielded general truths about the world. A new nomenclature was demanded to illustrate the positive role each faculty played within this systematic economy. This meant introducing new names into the English language, an arrogant move for a foreigner! But, as Locke had asserted, words were tools, and Spurzheim claimed the right to construct terms that best captured his ideas. The ending -*iveness* would designate the abstract and productive qualities of the propensities, and -*ousness* would characterize the operation of the sentiments. Thus, impulse to propagation became amativeness; love of offspring, philoprogenitiveness; murder, destructiveness; theft, acquisitiveness; and goodness (the moral sense), conscientiousness. These may have been awkward expressions, but they did make the point that the mind's powers were fundamentally good and that only the abuse of destructiveness, secretiveness, or acquisitiveness would lead to murder, lying, and theft. Finally, Spurzheim introduced seven new organs to the list of primary powers. For example, embarrassed by Gall's peculiar fascination with altitude and morality—which, much to the amusement of his critics, led him to talk of the elevated character of mountain goats and eagles—Spurzheim decided to take a closer look at the skull. Discovering that the cranium was raised or lowered at the top or bottom of the region that Gall had identified, he concluded that there were two organs, not one. Saving the system from ridicule, he thus replaced pride with the new faculties of self-esteem and inhabitiveness. Similar reasoning led him to divide music into tone and tune, and poetry into ideality and marvelousness. Gall found Spurzheim's phrenology monstrous, a departure from the implicit order of nature. The "system of M. Spurzheim," he claimed, "shines in sub-divisions, sub-sub-divisions, etc.; and this is what he calls infusing more philosophy into physiology of the brain than I had the ambition of introducing."[23] But for Spurzheim, taxonomic classification went hand in hand with moral order and the purposive design that he saw in the works of God.

Having established the basic function of the faculties, it was easy for Spurzheim to explain human behavior and assess its merit. Diversity flowed from the almost infinite combination of the variously sized organs, norms of conduct from the Aristotelian mean of behavior. The harmonious balance of the faculties thus became the standard of a well-adjusted mind. As illness was an abnormal condition of the body, so wickedness resulted from disequilibria of the brain. Cowardliness, stupidity, jealousy, pride, and all other vices were simply departures from the ideal or normal state brought about by the over-development or underdevelopment of one or more organs.

Although the relative strength of the different organs was largely determined at birth, Spurzheim believed that developmentally appropriate experiences were necessary to ensure the balanced growth of the cerebral order. Like the rest of the body, the brain was subject to physical laws governing nourishment, exercise, and pleasure. Because every organ was stimulated and strengthened by its natural object (destructiveness by scenes of violence, philoprogenitiveness by the sight of children, and so on), the maturing mind had to be nurtured within an environment that trained the higher but weaker moral and intellectual faculties to control the impulsive lower propensities. Not only would this inner government of desire promote social order, it would also help individuals find happiness that flowed from reaping the greater pleasures produced by the proper functioning of the higher powers. With these basic principles of difference and development in place, Spurzheim could then turn to his applied tracts on insanity and education, and to the social project of normalizing the population according to the laws of exercise and inheritance.

INSANITY

Like all diseases, insanity was caused by the aberration of an organ from its healthy state. Given the wide variety of human behaviors, Spurzheim wondered if the whole world might not be considered a madhouse. It was important, therefore, both for medical and legal reasons, to establish a criterion of deviation that would mark the point at which a person loses their will. Two conditions presented themselves: "*the incapacity of distinguishing the diseased functions of the mind*" from normal states (as when a patient truly thought he was the emperor of France) and "*the irresistibility of our actions*" to the morbid activity of some feeling (as when a person cannot stop stealing).[24] Such dysfunctions could be total or partial and did not imply the total breakdown of reason: there were many examples of otherwise cogent individuals who seemed fixated by a single idea or passion. Moreover, there was hope that, with the aid of phrenology, the various manifestations of the disease could be understood and, in many cases, cured.

The almost infinite range of abnormal behaviors complicated diagnosis. The same cause, Spurzheim explained, could affect several faculties, and every faculty could be deranged by numerous causes. In addition, as with other illnesses, factors such as temperament, sex, and climate meant that the same disease would take a different course in each patient. Sometimes the afflicted would be extremely agitated and exhibit enormous strength; on other occasions they might display weakness, moroseness, and an almost complete lack of feeling. There were those that hallucinated or became obsessed with some compulsive desire, whereas others were lucid, even creative, apart from some peculiar set of beliefs. What is more, such states were often observed as phases in the behavior of a single patient passing from frenzy to despondency. The traditional division of insanity into mania and melancholia simply did not capture this plurality of forms.

Rejecting moral causes, Spurzheim insisted that a true nosology had to be grounded in the organic conditions of the illness, and this demanded an intimate knowledge of the healthy and diseased brain. A far more useful division was that of inactivity, underactivity, and overactivity. In idiotism, for example, the brain's organs are so damaged that they cannot function. Partial or full, this condition was beyond treatment—patients would have to be committed to hospitals specially designed for incurables. However, insanity, especially in its early stages, could be treated. Resulting from inappropriate stimulation, the key was to employ a pharmaceutical and therapeutic regimen that lowered or heightened the activity of affected organs and reestablished the natural economy of the mind. Although heredity seemed to predispose individuals to mental illness, head trauma, climate, pregnancy, and other environmental factors could also upset the delicate cerebral balance. Spurzheim was particularly concerned about the demands of modern life, especially in the politically and economically free atmosphere of early industrial Britain. Madness, the "English malady," was reaching epidemic proportions. Amariah Brigham, fearful of the overexcitement of the young mind and the terrible stress exacted by religious fanaticism, introduced *Insanity* to American readers with the cautionary note that "had he lived to have traveled through the United States and made inquiries respecting insanity," Spurzheim would no doubt "have found it to prevail to a still greater degree here, than even in England."[25] Never was there a more urgent need for medically trained alienists.

To harmonize the mind and restore the correct functioning of the faculties, patients had to be placed within a highly structured environment. The traditional treatment of the mad only exacerbated their condition by further inflaming the very feelings that caused insanity. An institution designed according to the principles of phrenology would have the opposite effect. Inmates would be separated according to their illness and housed in sanitary, clean, warm, and well-ventilated cells. Some would spend time isolated in darkness to avoid stimulation; others would listen to music that stirred the emotions. There would be access to fields and gardens, and inmates would be gradually drawn into a variety of practical occupations. With signs of progress, they would be organized within family units and encouraged to make friendships. Daily contact with the superintendent was essential. Playing the role of a wise and benevolent father, the physician had to exert his moral character on the entire life of the asylum. On occasion, coercion would be needed to protect an individual from hurting himself or herself, but, by and large, kindness was always the guiding policy, and patients would earn personal liberty commensurate with their improving condition and safety.

To coordinate these therapeutic experiences, the physician had to understand the rule of motives. There was nothing more fruitless than trying to reason or shock the mad back to sanity: "One insane will behave well by veneration; another, by fear; a third will be guided by the love of approbation, often by attention paid to his self-esteem; many by gentle manners and Kindness; melancholic, anxious and fearful patients, by the greatest mildness," and so on.[26] As a rule, everything that might "excite the deranged feelings must be removed."[27] "How injudicious to give books to persons insane from religion, or to let them hear sermons, which nourish their disorders; or to keep with melancholics a conversation on the objects of their despondency!"[28]

The impact of Spurzheim's *Insanity* did not flow from the book's many practical recommendations, for there was little in his account of treatment that was not common knowledge among doctors of the mad. It was rather his *theory* of madness that proved popular among physicians. Reducing derangement to general principles of pathology, he explained how the brain, like any other organ, was subject to organic laws. Not only did this provide doctors with a disciplinary and systematic approach to the diagnosis and treatment of mental illness, it also justified their professional standing. With the remarkable success of the asylum movement, this same authority over the mind became a powerful force in penal reform and the movement to establish a progressive system of common schooling, fields of social engineering also influenced by Spurzheim's teachings on the nature of mind.

EDUCATION

Because Spurzheim understood education as "embracing every means which can be made to act upon the vegetive, affective, and intellectual constitution of man," he opened his work on *Education* with an examination of the extent to which human nature can be perfected.[29] On the whole he was optimistic. There had been great improvements in the arts and sciences since ancient times and, he believed, clear advances in religion and morals. The Christian ethic of love and charity was far superior to the Old Testament code of fear and retribution. Even so, he could not endorse the radical environmentalism of Locke's French followers, Helvétius in particular, who thought that all children could be molded into rational and moral agents. Such exaggerated claims, he observed, were simply not borne out in practice. Siblings grew up with very different traits and, as all teachers knew, there were limits to what some students could learn. The mind and body were fashioned with a determinate organization. Education could weaken or invigorate these innate powers, but it could not shape human nature at will. This commitment to the primacy of heredity presented an important challenge when Spurzheim faced up to the problems created by the rise of urban-industrial society. A new degenerate class was starting to appear in the midst of the city that promised to frustrate social progress unless sweeping educational policies were enacted. The laws of propagation and exercise that governed the human organization had to be applied to the moral management of the masses.

It was obvious, Spurzheim asserted, that in addition to "gout, sofula, dropsy, hydrocephalus, consumption, deafness, epilepsy, apoplexy, idiotism, insanity, &c." there were "many examples on record, of certain feelings, or intellectual powers, being inherited in whole families."[30] Given the danger of such disorders, he placed the greatest premium on the careful choice of a partner. Inbreeding had to be avoided at all costs, moral and intellectual traits had to be compatible, and children were not to be born before parents reached an appropriate age—and certainly not conceived while they were intoxicated. More progressive than Gall, he accepted Lamarck's principle of use inheritance but cautioned that "it is infinitely more easy . . . to keep up natural changes, and even deformities, than to produce them by art."[31] Given that at least "three successive generations appear to be necessary to produce an effectual change be it for health or disease," he restated the importance of observing the principles of inheritance not only to "the condition of single families, but of whole nations . . . who by attending to them . . . might be improved beyond imagination, in figure, stature, complexion, health, talents, and moral feelings."[32] "He who can convince the world of the laws of hereditary descent, and induce all mankind to conduct themselves accordingly," Spurzheim prophesied, "will do more good to them, and contribute more to their improvement, than all institutions and all systems of education."[33]

Knowledge of physiology was also essential after the child had been born. The healthy development of the mind and body demanded fresh air, cleanliness, nutritious food, warmth, and appropriate exercise. Ignoring these vital conditions, as so often happened in the home and the workplace, greatly depleted the vital energies of the population. Of first importance was the mother's health during pregnancy and breastfeeding. Parents had to understand the effects of certain foods, alcohol, and temperature on the baby's delicate organization. The age, bodily condition, and morals of the wet nurse were also important, though Spurzheim dismissed the possibility of transmitting character traits through the milk. He also presented some interesting observations about teething and a long discussion on the dangers of overtaxing the young child's brain with excessive verbal instruction—an argument developed and popularized by Brigham.

To ensure the healthy development of the faculties, it was essential that parents and teachers understand how to exercise the mind's organs in due proportion. "Exercise strengthens powers" was a general principle throughout nature; it explained the blacksmith's arm, the improved hearing of the blind, and the superior reason of the philosopher. But training had to be coordinated with the natural unfolding of the brain and the innate talents and dispositions of the child.[34] "Too little or too much does great harm, but applied in proper degree, it makes the organs increase in size, modifies their internal constitution, and produces greater activity and facility."[35] These principles demanded a complete overhaul of the traditional Latin-based curriculum, which did little more than strengthen the organ of language. Some defended the classics for the mental discipline they imposed, but Spurzheim was adamant that causality and comparison could be trained in science, history, and even phrenology—branches of knowledge that had far more practical value in the modern world. More generally, he objected to the neglect of moral education. Virtue was not learned by reciting precepts; it had to be cultivated by constructing situations that would bring the moral sentiments into action. To develop benevolence, for example, a child "should not . . . learn by heart descriptions of charity; he must experience for himself and contemplate the painful situations of others."[36]

Each faculty, then, had to be excited by its own natural object, not some verbal or written sign representing it. Starting in the home and on the playground, children ought to learn about the world into which they are born. As she made the family supper, a mother could tell her children about potatoes, how they were cultivated, and the various ways in which they could be cooked; while exploring nature, boys and girls could be taught "physical properties such as form, dimensions, weight, color, distances, phenomena of hydraulics, mechanics and chemistry."[37] Schooling would then continue these first object lessons with a more systematic examination of "the most common objects and events, Forms, Measures, Weights, Colors, Coins used in the country, the general division of beings into minerals, vegetables, animals, the great and common phenomena of nature."[38] Words and ideas, as Locke argued, would be associated through concrete experiences. So it was with the affections. "Hunger and Thirst, Warmth, Cold, Anger, and Fear, and all other emotions had to be felt before their signs could be fully understood."[39] Here the importance of the teacher's natural language could not be overestimated; voice, gait, and posture had a powerful impact on the child.

With the caveat that "it may still be improved and more adapted to the nature of man," Spurzheim identified Robert Owen's infant school at New Lanark as "the practical application of these principles. Uniting physical and intellectual education . . . no one can observe the happiness and intelligence which reigns among the children there, without wishing this mode of instruction generally adopted."[40] Owen's environmentalism was unacceptable, but his pedagogy, suitably adapted to the plurality of the brain's organs and their order of unfolding, dovetailed perfectly with the moral dictates of phrenology. Spurzheim envisioned

> schools for infants, children, and youth, where positive notions of things, their usefulness and means of improvement, are communicated by way of mutual instruction; where at the same time morality is shown in action and imposed as a duty; where refined manners are inculcated; and where physical education is particularly taken care of. I hope the time will come when everyone will learn to read, write and cipher . . . when all knowledge, extended according to age and particular classes of society, will be practical . . . when the religious feelings will be cultivated in everyone, not by words but in deeds, not by superstitious formalities, but in harmony with reason and with the intention to improve the fate of mankind; when even animal feelings will not be neglected, but only employed as powerful means to assist the faculties proper to man, which alone are the aim of our existence; finally when all the powers of the physical, intellectual, and moral nature will be cultivated in harmony.[41]

At the elementary level, Spurzheim favored the monitorial method, introduced by Joseph Lancaster, where a single master instructed a large number of students with the aid of older children. Owen found this technique narrow and mechanical, but Spurzheim was impressed by its economy and the method of mutual instruction at the heart of Lancaster's scheme. It would, he believed, permit children of all classes to be educated under one master. Moreover, rather than repeating their lessons or waiting in boredom as other pupils struggled to keep pace, brighter students could develop their intellectual and social faculties by teaching their peers. He even advocated incorporating the method into the university, contemplating a level of instruction between professor and students comparable to the classes currently taught by graduate assistants. Teachers would need careful training, especially in the use of rewards central to the system. He recognized, for example, that "if two boys possess the same natural endowment of the faculty of language, but the one double the love of approbation of the other, he, by the influence of the latter faculty, may be rendered the more excellent scholar of the two."[42] Yet schools were not to be breeding grounds for vanity, pride, and greed. Because self-esteem and love of approbation were the most powerful of all human motives, responsible for the majority of social ills, he cautioned that praise should only be given for clear demonstrations of talent and virtue. Moral regulation was far more important than intellectual instruction.

Developing this insight, Spurzheim explained that a truly virtuous society would only be formed when each individual was trained for a life suited to their phrenological development. That is, the population had to be divided into distinct biological classes according to the ascendancy of their intellectual and moral faculties. There were those "who, from the felicity of their natural constitution, desire only what is good, who act from love, and show pure morality in all their actions."[43] The rest of mankind, however, were forced by nature to constantly battle their inferior feelings. Three groups could be identified. Those with strong superior and inferior faculties who were prone to vacillate between vice and virtue; those with more active lower organs who were in perpetual danger of criminality; and, by far the largest proportion of men and women, those with medium-sized organs who acted good or ill as a result of the education they received. "The great mass of mankind," he continued, could not be left to their own guidance; common people, when tempted, easily yield. "Education, therefore, in all its details, legislation, and all public institutions, ought to contribute to accustom them to regularity and order."[44] Quite how this normalization process was to be achieved, he did not explain, other than to assert, rather chillingly, that he supported "the use of all possible inducements to produce virtuous conduct."[45]

> We may reason with those who understand the laws of the Creator, and feel their importance, whilst others, who cannot comprehend these laws or perceive their utility, should be restrained by inferior and selfish interests even by disagreeable impressions or their senses, or by feeling the pains of hunger, or solitary confinement.[46]

What was true of moral education also followed for the development of the intellect. All children had to learn how to make wise and informed decisions appropriate to their future station in life. Divided into intellectual classes corresponding to their natural proclivities, Spurzheim proposed a general curriculum comprising "physical . . . chemical . . . [and] vital phenomena . . . history, geography, geology, and cosmography . . . anthropology, the mother tongue, printed and written signs, calculation, and finally, moral and religious principles."[47] The classics were out, positive knowledge was in. Although the vast majority of children could only hope to attain a rudimentary conception of these ideas, at least their limited understanding would dovetail with the wisdom of their intellectual superiors who would continue these same studies at university.

In discussing schooling and the natural organization of the community, Spurzheim also paused to consider the arguments of Mary Wollstonecraft and others who demanded the equal education of girls on the grounds that the differences between men and women were a product of enculturation—a suggestion he found socially dangerous and contrary to the basic facts of physiology. He too celebrated women's contribution to "morals and manners," but found them "weak and delicate creatures" in no way the equal of men in mind or body.[48] God had made "the two sexes different but concordant, so as to produce together a delicious harmony . . . prepared for their future destinations by a particular modification of feelings and intellectual faculties."[49] Of course, there were exceptions. In Mary Wollstonecraft, for example, he found "a manner of feeling and thinking, which resembled that of a man."[50] And herein lay the fault of her argument: she was simply "wrong to take herself as the standard of her sex."[51] As a child *she* may not have wanted to play with dolls, but clearly other girls did. With larger love of offspring than males, young women everywhere "delight to dress and undress a baby" while boys were more inclined "to noisy amusements" and "seldom thought of such a pastime."[52] Consider also the distinctive failings of women. A strong sense of attachment led them to covet exclusive ownership, whereas their love of approbation fueled a need for attention that knew no bounds. "Some would suffer pain in order to be pitied, rather than remain unnoticed."[53] With intellectual faculties widely different in power to men's, he found "the conduct of females in general is unstable" and "moved by momentary impressions."[54] "Whenever great combinations, deep reflection, discrimination, and general abstraction are required, when principles and laws are to be established, females in general remain behind. A shawl or a ribbon will soon absorb their minds, and make them easily neglect any philosophical discussion."[55] Not that Spurzheim regarded women as toys for or slaves of men. Their physical, moral, and intellectual nature was also to be cultivated. They should receive gymnastic training, but not to make them the physical equal of men; their sentiments should be nurtured, but not in preparation for the social and political duties of men; and they should develop their understanding with useful knowledge, but again, not to mimic the rational powers of men. In short, females should be schooled for their future station as wives and mothers, the role they were appointed to by God and nature.[56]

Finally, turning from the education of individuals to the education of nations, Spurzheim returned to consider how the welfare of a community could be promoted by implementing social policies grounded in physiological laws. The *Idéologues* understood that customs, institutions, and legislation could shape populations with distinctive behavioral traits. But rules controlling propagation would have an even more powerful impact on national character. No government had the moral right to impose such legislation on the general public, but they did have a duty, he believed, to at least "inculcate the natural laws of hereditary decent, and find various ways to favor its practice."[57] He was particularly disturbed by military conscription, which sacrificed "all the better heads" while "the inferior [were] allowed to propagate."[58] "If only those with inferior moral and intellectual organizations are employed as soldiers, and prohibited from marrying," he predicted, "the military line may be very useful to society."[59]

Without wars to cull the worst minds from society, Spurzheim turned to the positive practical measures by which governments could promote health, morality, and intelligence. Three central causes of degeneracy cried out for attention: illness, idleness, and ignorance. Hoarded into the cramped, noxious, and squalid confines of the urban slum, the masses were growing old and feeble before their time. Drained of vital energies, it was only the infusion of fresh blood from the country that kept many of Europe's major cities going. Ignored for too long, here was a vast field of legislation by which politicians could contribute to the physical well-being of society. "The salubrity of habituations, the purity of air in the streets and houses, food, cleanliness, bodily exercise"—and, of course, temperance—had to be addressed with all possible means.[60] He even advocated provision of "gymnastic amusements for all ages and classes of society."[61] On the issue of public welfare, Spurzheim agreed with Herbert Spencer, who, in his early phrenological writings, saw the Tory Poor Laws as instruments for promoting social degeneracy. The undeserving poor, he observed, "are undoubtedly a burden to themselves and to the community at large."[62] Arguing that alms houses should be transformed into institutions of correction, he demanded disciplinary practices that would teach the lazy and worthless how to support themselves in the world. Here, at least, he concluded, "those who cannot provide for a family should be prevented from propagation."[63]

5
George Combe and the Rise of Phrenology in Britain

The world was a chaos. From the pulpit and catechism I learned that human nature was altogether prone to evil, and the knowledge of the world I gained by induction from this kind of observation and experience confirmed me in this faith. . . . There was neither within nor around me any atmosphere of consistency, goodness, and truth . . . the vivid recollection of the unhappiness in which I passed many days and hours of my early life, gave intensity to my subsequent desires to assist in the introduction of a better order of things.

George Combe, *Life of George Combe,* 1878

The remarkable flowering of phrenology in 1820s Edinburgh has been the subject of much scholarly attention.[1] Commencing in 1803 with Thomas Brown's scathing rejection of Gall; followed in 1815 by Gordon's attack on Spurzheim; P. M. Roget's "Cranioscopy" in the supplement to the 1819 edition of the *Encyclopedia Britannica;* Francis Jeffrey's commentary on Combe's *System* in the *Edinburgh Review;* and, in 1825, Sir William Hamilton's lectures before the Royal Society, Edinburgh's leading academics issued a series of searching criticisms designed to stop phrenology in its tracks. Along with the standard accusations of atheism, materialism, and determinism, and questions about the nature and number of the faculties, the chief objections raised concerned the anatomical foundations of organology and cranioscopy—most challenging among which were assertions that the brain did not parallel the cranium, that the apparent fibrous structure of the gray matter was actually produced by Spurzheim's method of dissection, and that the frontal sinuses altered the shape of the skull and thus made character delineations impossible. Hamilton, a self-confessed interloper in physiology, even experimented with live animals, piercing their heads with needles in an effort to show that localized damage to the brain would not produce the kind of aberrant behaviors predicted by phrenology. It is a testament to Combe's ingenuity that he could respond effectively to these criticisms and, in the eyes of many, undermine the authority of prominent intellectuals in one of Europe's greatest centers of learning.

Writing to his brother Andrew in 1819, Combe laid out the two principles with which he would "defend the system. . . . *First,* Dissection never reveals functions. . . . *Second,* Reflection on our own consciousness never reveals organs."[2] Most importantly, the court of appeal had to be shifted from the judgment of elites to the opinion of the ordinary (informed) person; when observation of facts and issues of usefulness ruled debates, he declared, the truth and value of phrenology would be unassailable. These were formidable arguments, given the public interest in the contest, and Combe wielded them with subtlety. Even the *Edinburgh Review* was forced to admit "it is impossible not to admire the dexterity with which he has evaded the weak, and improved the plausible part of his argument, and the skill and perseverance he has employed in working up his scanty materials into a semblance of strength and consistency."[3] In Combe's final debate with Hamilton it was suggested that the conflict could be resolved by submitting arguments to a panel of experts. Combe insisted on a public audience and the verdict of common sense; Hamilton, who saw no value in the opinion of a layperson, demanded university-trained physiologists. Here was an impasse that served both sides. After Combe published the *Constitution of Man* (1828), the contest changed. Moving ground from physiology to moral reform, phrenologists invoked Galileo's struggles with the church to characterize these debates as a rite of passage necessary to justify reason and observation over an entrenched authority blinded by metaphysics. Conversely, the antiphrenologists, fearing the erosion of cultural and political norms, painted their opponents as dangerous quacks, bent on undermining the religious basis of society. Originally viewed with some sympathy, by 1830, Combe had been transformed into an infidel.

According to G. N. Cantor, it was only when phrenologists realized they could not win these debates outright that they changed their strategy, turning from their assault on the metaphysical foundations of the mind to political agitation and the field of moral reform. Stephen Shapin disagrees. Rejecting Cantor's "intellectualist" account, he explains the technical differences over brain structure and skull formation as a more deep-seated struggle between the city's ruling literati (insiders) and its class of aspiring professionals (outsiders). Pointing to the incommensurability of each side's ontological and methodological assumptions, Shapin maintains that these increasingly esoteric and acrimonious disputes are not to be understood as disagreements over rationally decidable facts, but rather as hegemonic clashes in which socially opposing groups vied for control in politically fluid times. In a sense, the brain was incidental. "They did anatomy, and developed the anatomy of their canon," he maintains, solely "in an attempt to secure social credibility and to conceal the role of their social interests."[4]

Social credibility was certainly very important to Combe—he always courted political and religious leaders, even royalty. But it was not an end in itself. Above money and status, Combe was driven by a genuine religious commitment to improve the physiological condition of humankind. As he explained his secular faith in the *Constitution,* only by understanding and following the laws by which God constructed the world could men and women enjoy happy, healthy, and productive lives. The key to this practical Christianity was education, in Spurzheim's broad eugenic sense of the word. Everything flowed from the *Constitution,* Combe's bible of secularism. From birth to death, moral principles were deduced from the physiological laws of mind to govern every practical decision—whom to marry, when to have children, the length of the working day, and even the choice of servants. Meeting objections to the anatomical principles of phrenology became increasingly irrelevant, a nuisance to be silenced or passed over rather than debated. Much more important to Combe's developing agenda was gaining the political ground from which to push reform. As it became increasingly apparent that this could not be achieved within the existing status quo, Combe sought an alternative site of authority among the rising professional classes with Whig political sympathies. He even took his message of rational enlightenment and happiness to the working classes themselves.

The single most important reform issue generated by Combe's philosophical synthesis was the necessity of establishing a system of public schooling that would train the developing faculties and provide the population of industrial Britain with a knowledge of the scientific principles that governed their physical and social existence. As the following chapters reveal, Combe and his lifelong coworker James Simpson pursued this goal on many levels. Building upon the doctrines of the *Constitution,* they formulated a sophisticated justification for child-centered teaching methods geared to the needs of the maturing mind, they opened and ran model infant and elementary schools in Edinburgh, they played a leading role in the radical movement to establish a national system of secular education, and they participated in the development of adult education programs for the working classes. Through their writings, lectures, and correspondence they exerted a profound impact on the debates of the day, influencing leading social theorists, educators, and politicians on both sides of the Atlantic. Yet, as Harold Silver acknowledges, "George Combe and James Simpson, important figures in the controversies and campaigns of the middle decades of the Nineteenth Century, have vanished with their phrenology or their secularism."[5]

Silver's own *Popular Education in Britain* demonstrates the pivotal role that Robert Owen played in the development of progressive pedagogy and infant schooling. But this and other works fail to explore Owen's influence on Combe. After several visits to New Lanark and Orbiston (the Owenite community established by his brother Abram) Combe was convinced of the power of education to shape character. Already a disciple of Spurzheim, he could not accept Owen's utopian socialism or his views on the extreme plasticity of human nature, but he did embrace his disciplinary pedagogy. Suitably modified by phrenological theory and his secular theology, Combe was convinced that Owen's rational system of schooling could greatly improve the physical, moral, and intellectual health of the country.

Although Combe's involvement in the theory and practice of social reform did not come of age until after the publication of the *Constitution*, his lifelong commitment to human improvement was born out of the religious and educational experiences of his youth—his terror of Calvinism and the brutal and irrational discipline of traditional schooling. It was only with his conversion, first to phrenology and then to liberal Christianity, that these psychological wounds healed. Awakening to a real sense of mission, he realized that education could break the chains of fear and force and lead individuals into a rational and loving relationship with God. Men and women of all stations would enjoy happier, more purposeful lives, if only they had the knowledge and habits to conduct themselves in accord with the laws of nature. Spreading this gospel was far more important than defeating academics, once the plausibility of phrenology had been established in the public mind.

COMBE'S EDUCATION

There was nothing exceptional in Combe's early life; it contained all the miseries and privations others of his day were forced to suffer. What singles out Combe's chronicle of violence, hunger, sickness, toil, despair, and death is his effort to demonstrate how the horrid conditions into which he was born wounded the organs of his growing mind. At times, this theorization of his own cerebral development is obviously contrived (as when he jumps straight into a description of his mother's brain); on other occasions it is hopelessly romanticized (he was always a good boy in a cruel world). In his seventieth and last year, it was impossible for Combe to look back on his childhood dispassionately; the events of his youth, he believed, had left him emotionally and physically wounded for life.

One of seventeen children, of whom eleven survived, Combe grew up in the family's modest five-room house located at the foot of Edinburgh Castle.[6] The crowded and suffocating internal conditions he describes— Combe shared his bedroom with five brothers—were matched by the dark, dank, and filthy surroundings outside. Nestled between his father's brewery, a tanning factory, and a magnesia works, Combe's home was adjacent to a public ditch filled with their byproducts; an open sewer ran past the front of the house and a swamp full of dunghills sat at the rear. A market gardener and the fields beyond made up the circumference of the young Combe's world. Here, at least, was a hint of the natural order and beauty of the world God had created. His social environment was equally depressing. Structured by the gloomy doctrines of Calvinism, Combe was taught the inherent evil of human nature and the necessary misery of life. His parents, although good and dutiful people, were emotionally distant; sparing affection, they raised their children not to "complain, but to accept suffering as the will of God."[7] "Both highly moral . . . they had an abhorrence of debt, never shrank from their duties, and were kind to the destitute people around them, and to their poor relations."[8] But while setting "excellent practical examples" for their children, Combe lamented, they never gave us "any instruction . . . they only ordered us to do or not to do certain things, and scolded us heartily if we failed."[9] This did not include beating. George senior had resolved never to inflict upon his children the injuries of his own youth. As a result, "calculating on impunity," his boys continued to defy his orders in the face of threats, until Abram would whisper, "He is near the striking pitch we had better go."[10]

> Dear, good, old father . . . we went; but I went sullenly, the love of self indulgence pulling one way, conscience another, and fear only supporting conscience . . . yet I was not vicious; and my moral and intellectual

faculties were naturally so strong; and my Love of Approbation and Adhesiveness so vigorous, that one word of moral council accompanied by kindness, approval, or commendation, would have subdued my selfishness and made me docile as a lamb: but it never came. With a nature highly affectionate I never received a caress; with an ardent desire to be approved of, and to be distinguished for being good and clever, I never received an encomium, or knew what it was to be praised for any action, exertion, or sacrifice, however great.[11]

Nor was Combe to find any loving guidance from the church. Strict Calvinists, his parents devoted the day of rest to religious observances. Starting at 11 A.M. with an hour for lunch and dinner, the family attended two services before settling down for an evening reciting the Catechism and memorizing psalms. Communal reading of the New Testament rounded out the night. Composed from "the terrors of the Gospel," Combe "trembled" before the sermons of the Rev. Paul.[12] "The whole world appeared . . . to reflect the Fall and the sinfulness of man," and although some might feel the ecstasy of being among the elect, he numbered himself one of the damned, doomed to a future of eternal suffering.[13] "The religion . . . he learned from the pulpit and Catechism appeared a matter for Sunday only . . . never . . . as a practical rule of conduct."[14] "On the contrary," he recalled, "I was systematically taught that that my religion and my world were at open war; and truly all observed facts and personal experience confirmed the truth of this assurance."[15] "While Abram threw . . . the dogmas of Calvinism . . . to the winds, and framed many a witty sarcasm and joke out of the materials which they afforded him," George, being more serious, continued to suffer under the yoke of predestination until manhood.[16]

Nowhere was the irrationality of his childhood more fearful than in the daily tyranny of his schooling. It is impossible to read Combe's autobiography without sensing the terror he felt recalling his experiences in Mr. Fraser's classroom. Forced to sit still for long hours in stuffy, cramped, and uncomfortable conditions, he endured lessons that consisted solely of memorizing and translating Latin texts. There was no outlet for the natural energies of childhood and no stimulation for an active mind, just the constant tedium of verbal exercises enforced by the ever-present threat of savage punishment. "The Rod of Correction," as Fraser called it, was a riding whip with a knotted cord that would lash around his victim's limbs producing vicious welts and frequently drawing blood.

> In the morning Mr. Fraser began with the *dux,* he then translated the first sentence, the next boy the second, and so on. If any fault was committed, the first boy below who could give the correct words came up above the defaulter. Among these boys the lessons went on pretty smoothly; but when the incapable were reached, then beating took the place of teaching. Mr Fraser exhausted his muscular strength, which was great, in inflicting blows, and saved his brain all the effort of thinking. The torture and screams, and reckless injustice of this rule made us High School boys, when we met many years later in society, ask each other "under whom did you suffer?"[17]

Combe's strategy for survival was to occupy the middle rows and learn his lessons by repeating the words of the boys above him. Although this helped him avoid punishment, it did not promote understanding. When, after four years, he advanced to the senior class and the more benevolent care of Dr. Adam, he was ill prepared for real instruction. With an "intellect . . . trained to repeat words without thinking of their meaning," he read passages "without interest or comprehension."[18] Only at the end of schooling were the beauties of the classics opened up to him. Had he been taught rationally throughout, Combe was sure he "had both the inclination and capacity to learn."[19] Instead he had wasted his own time and his father's money. He had often asked, "What is the use of this education? but never received a satisfactory answer."[20]

Combe's parents seem to have seen things differently, for education was prized at Livingston's Yards. As Scotland struggled through the famine of 1800, and the brewery teetered on failure, the family continued to support George's schooling, employing a private tutor to help with Latin and enrolling him in evening classes in order that he could learn sufficient mathematics and geography to enter Edinburgh University. In return, George served as teacher to his younger brothers and sisters, imposing, he later regretted, the same regimen of verbal learning and physical discipline Fraser had modeled for him: "I ordered my pupils to learn, and scolded and beat them when they would not say their lessons."[21] Once at University, Combe experienced a very different method of teaching. Those who sought knowledge moved to the front with the professor, while he and others of the same mind "voluntarily took seats on the back benches . . . sat quietly, listened and learned what [they] could."[22] He made little progress in language, but derived "considerable pleasure from hearing the classics read and explained . . . Cicero, Horace, and Virgil" being his "great favorites."[23] Ever justifying his own inner nature, Combe explained that his sympathies always turned to the victims. Whereas other students reveled in the exploits of the hero, he asked what right had the Romans to invade England. His moral sentiments, he concluded, must have been rebelling against the evil and brutality of the classics, scripts of "conquest and domination" that served to "sow the seeds of Toryism in the yet undeveloped average mind."[24]

Apart from these "accusations of conscience," this was a period of rest and recuperation for Combe's brain. As his reflective organs matured free from the pressures of the schoolroom, a new set of feelings started to occupy his mind, "the desire to obtain distinction by doing good."[25] No doubt excited by the pressing need to find a calling, he was gripped by the fear that his life would amount to nothing. He had no distinguishing talents and had learned little from his years of schooling. His prospects were bleak. Even the tailor with whom George senior had arranged an apprenticeship turned him away. It was while en route to a second interview that fate stepped in, as, by chance, they ran into one of their in-laws, a city bailiff. Convincing Combe's father that, having spent so much on his son's education, he should aim for a more respectable profession, the relative promised to line up a position in the law offices of John Higgins. Upon successful completion of college, Combe would train as writer to the Signet. His years of anonymity paid off. With a standard note from his Latin teacher that his studies had been prosecuted "with diligence and success," Combe entered the legal world in May 1804. This proved to be a most fortuitous arrangement, for in contrast to a life in commerce, his new duties encompassed activities that helped develop the latent powers of his mind. Abram had "made a shipwreck of his life and fortunes," becoming a tanner when "nature had given him an active brain and the organs of an engineer."[26] "Had I been placed in a smallware shop," Combe reflected, "it is probable that my history might have been written in similar terms."[27] With the warm support of Higgins and his new colleagues, Combe soon mastered the basics of his office duties, including shorthand and a working knowledge of French. He also attended elocution lessons, smoothing his native Scotch brogue into the more refined tones of Standard English essential to his new profession and, as he reports, readily embraced the manners and morals of middle-class life. A serious and studious bachelor, it seems that after a long day at the office, he preferred evening classes in philosophy and literature, the *Edinburgh Review*, and *Cobbitt's Register* to the company of friends. By the time his apprenticeship was complete, Combe could look forward to a life of "comfortable mediocrity." A new post as a bookkeeper permitted a good deal of lucrative private work and, by 1812, he had established his own home and respectable income of £130.

And yet he sought fame. Cautious about what others might think of him, he was possessed by the belief that he "had powers of mind to write some useful book on human nature, and especially on the education and intellectual state of the middle ranks of society."[28] Summarizing the early 1810s, Charles Gibbon writes that Combe

> found pleasure in his profession, in his social surroundings, and in his studies. He was busy reading history; and attending lectures on geography as applied to history. He devoted some time to chemistry and became a member of Dr. Murray's class. He also became a student of anatomy and physiology under Dr. Barclay, then the most esteemed teacher of these sciences in Edinburgh.[29]

Combe, it seems, was particularly interested in the physiological conditions of mental health. His diary contains quotes from Cabanis and reveals how he experimented with vegetarianism in order to improve his intellectual powers and control his emotions. In philosophy he had read "Locke, Francis Hutchinson, Adam Smith, David Hume, Dr. Reid, and Dugald Stewart."[30] Most likely Ferguson, Robertson, and Kames could also be added to this list, for one of the distinguishing features of Combe's writings, first included in his *System of Phrenology*, is a description of the development of nations, in which the accounts of explorers and travel writers are woven into a hierarchical ranking of the world's peoples according to their mental and moral progress—a phrenological version of the conjectural history of civilization developed by the philosophers of the Scottish Enlightenment. Accordingly, in 1815, when Combe encountered Spurzheim, he was both intellectually and socially primed for the doctrines of phrenology. Sympathetic to the existence of a relationship between the moral and the physical; critical of the irrationalism and injustices of the Scotch social order; and, above all, troubled by the grim realities of the Calvinist worldview, he was naturally receptive to the scientific moral philosophy, reformist political agenda, and progressive liberal Christianity that Spurzheim presented. Phrenology not only explained the travails of his own life, it promised the rational society and benevolent loving God that he craved.

THE BIRTH OF A PHRENOLOGIST

Although Combe did not attend Gordon's lecture, he saw Spurzheim repeat the same presentation at a friend's house. With a handful of others in attendance, "the brain and the Edinburgh Review were laid upon the table," and everyone was encouraged to contrast the reviewer's assertions with the evidence of their senses. Persuaded by the testimony of his own eyes, Combe then attended Spurzheim's six lectures to hear the author's account of the system.[31] Here, Combe later recalled, "I attained the conviction that the faculties of the mind he had expounded bare [sic] a much greater resemblance to those which I had seen operating in active life, than did those which I had read about in the works of metaphysicians, but I was not convinced that these faculties manifested themselves by particular parts of the brain."[32] It took a meticulous study of casts and skulls to complete the conversion, but within a year, carefully nurtured by Spurzheim, Combe was lecturing friends and writing articles in defense of the theory. As he tells the story, it was while studying the casts he had ordered from London—gradually becoming convinced that there was indeed something to cranioscopy—that he noticed every article on the subject was full of ridicule for Spurzheim and his discoveries. When the Statistical Magazine called for an open discussion of the topic, he waited anxiously for a public debate, but nobody responded. Finally he offered the editor his own paper "the careless production of a leisure hour."[33] After publication, another article was requested, then a third and a fourth. Combe's career as a writer was launched.

Throughout this time Combe was in close contact with Spurzheim. They met regularly during Spurzheim's seven-month stay in Edinburgh and corresponded when he returned, first to London, and then to Paris. Combe also spent a month with Spurzheim, in 1817, during the French stage of his first European tour. As much interested in the cranial landscape of the continent as its countryside, Combe divided the French into a number of distinct races, just as Spurzheim had partitioned the Scots. He was particularly impressed by the high foreheads of French women, but was informed by his mentor that this was only an illusion caused by the comparatively lower heads of the country's men.

By 1819, with the publication of *Essays on Phrenology,* Combe had gained national recognition as one of the movement's leading authorities. Careful not to parade the political and theological implications of Spurzheim's thesis, his early writings focused on the scientific foundation of phrenology—social reform would come later. The first of the three long chapters in his *Essays,* for example, attacked the speculative techniques of metaphysicians and anatomists, recommended the observational methods championed by Gall and Spurzheim, and attempted to demonstrate that the premises of the new theory did not imply materialism, atheism, or the loss of free will. The second chapter enumerated the various faculties and their functions. It was only in the final essay that Combe turned to phrenology as "a system of the philosophy of man." But while announcing its power to revolutionize criminal legislation, the treatment of the insane, and a various other social practices, he restricted his remarks to proving the hereditary nature of genius and the importance of restructuring education around the developing needs of the child's faculties.

His central concern was to describe how teachers and parents might "modify the innate powers, and regulate their manifestations . . . restrain such of them as may be too energetic, or to call forth into greater activity those which may be naturally languid."[34] This demanded knowledge of the human organization, the developmental unfolding of the organs, and the means by which the various faculties might be excited (and strengthened) or constrained (and weakened). One of the chief lessons he drew from phrenology was the independence of the feelings and the intellect. Because the reasoning powers matured later than the affective organs, teaching through precepts would never ensure virtue; the passions themselves had to be trained. This had to be approached with care, for the physical and emotional trauma brought on by punishment or emulation might destroy the cerebral balance that educators aimed for. Mental management was a delicate affair that demanded treatments appropriate for each personality. A child with "powerful faculties of conscientiousness, cautiousness, and love of approbation," Combe explained, "will naturally be prone to timidity and bashfulness. The treatment proper for such an individual is not to scold and ridicule him for being timid; for this only produces pain and increases the evil; but to inspire him with confidence, by kindness and affability."[35] Educators had to be guided by the "general rule, [that] whatever you wish your child to be or do, be that or do that to him."[36] "It was not sufficient merely to excite the sympathetic activity" of the faculties by example."[37] To ensure "the full measure of cultivation," the faculties had "to manifest themselves externally in actions as frequently as possible."[38] To develop benevolence, for example,

> we must make our children the actual administrators of benevolence themselves. We must allow them to do acts of charity, and not merely to give alms, but to court acquaintance with poverty, misery and distress in its bodily form, and to feel the sympathetic glow which can be experienced in its full fervor, only when we see the objects of our charity in all their misery, but at the same time "in possession of all the feelings which unite them to us by ties of a common nature."[39]

The grand object was to "repress the energy of the faculties common to man and animals, so as to place them under the guidance of the faculties proper to man."[40] This goal was within reach of the majority, but certain individuals were born with an innate organization that would never permit the ascendancy of reason and morality. "Such persons," he believed, "ought to be looked upon rather as patients than as objects of wrath."[41] Their behavior would have to be controlled externally by teachers adept at manipulating emotions—the fear generated by Cautiousness, for instance—to check unruly impulses. In addition to elevating character, education also had to develop the knowing and reflecting powers. As Combe knew well from his own school days, the traditional classroom focused mainly upon Language, ignoring the essential role other organs played in the acquisition of knowledge about the world. The intellect had to work with ideas that corresponded as directly as possible to facts. Following Spurzheim's law of exercise, this implied that children must think for themselves. Starting with the tactile exploration of objects in the early years, the maturing higher powers would be trained to yield a reasoned understanding of the causal laws governing all events.

Some critics objected that educating the working poor would only breed discontent, giving those who labored aspirations beyond their station. Such fears, Combe insisted, rested on a misunderstanding of human nature. "The effects of education," he declared,

> are always bounded by the natural capacity of the mind to be educated; and nature has taken care to provide a sufficient supply of men and women for every rank of life, by making a large majority of the race so moderate in degree, that they will never be enabled by the efforts of others, to aspire to anything much above the level of moderation.[42]

The cost of not educating the poor was unimaginable. Slaves to their passions, the vast majority of Britain's underclass were in the same miserable state as primitive savages. Such suffering could not be ignored. Not only would training the faculties render the masses happier, it would also reduce crime and teach them to appreciate their station and duties in life. Turning to the middle class, he focused on the education of women and the parallel charge that too much learning would make them unfit for their role in life. This, too, was simply absurd. Women needed both intelligence and high moral feelings to discharge their domestic obligations. Elevating the female mind and character, he concluded, would not undermine the social fabric, but render women more useful and a greater delight to their family and friends.

THE EDINBURGH PHRENOLOGICAL SOCIETY

These early thoughts on education reveal Combe's growing interest in the application of phrenology to issues of social reform. But although his political sympathies were firmly established, he remained uncertain about the basic principles of organology and cranioscopy. Determined to ensure the scientific basis of phrenology, he sent his younger brother Andrew to study medicine in Paris. In letter after letter, he implored him to learn everything he could from Spurzheim about the anatomy of the brain so that they could be certain that the laws of physiology would provide a secure platform for expounding their moral philosophy. (After the death of their father in 1815, George acted as guardian to Andrew, his great favorite, supporting him financially through years of study and illness.) It worked. Like his brother, "the doctor" converted to phrenology. A lecture by Spurzheim proved pivotal. A member of the audience produced a brain and challenged Spurzheim to explain the dispositions of the deceased. Spurzheim "took the brain without any hesitation" and

> proceeded to point out peculiarities of development which it presented, and desired his auditors to remark the unusual size of the cerebellum, or organ of Amativeness, and the great development of the posterior, and part of the middle lobes of the brain, corresponding to the organs of the propensities, the convolutions of which were large and rounded, forming a contrast with the deficient size of the anterior lobes, which are dedicated to the intellectual faculties. The convolutions situated under the vertex, and toward the top of the head, belonging to the organs of Self-esteem and Firmness were also very large, while those of Veneration and Benevolence were small. These peculiarities were so well marked that Dr. Spurzheim felt no difficulty in inferring that the individual would be very prone to sensual indulgences; that "his natural tendencies would not be toward virtue"; . . . that "*he would be one to whom the law would be necessary as a guide.*"[43]

When Combe found out that the brain belonged to a patient he had known at the hospital where he studied, he reported that the exact coincidence

> between the facts with which I was familiar, and the remarks of Dr. Spurzheim, who had never seen the skull, and judged from the brain alone, as it lay misshapen on a flat dish made a deep impression on my mind, as it went far to prove, not only that organic size had a powerful influence on power of function, but that there actually were differences in brains, appropriate to the senses, and indicative of diversity of function.[44]

Dedicating his life to phrenology, by the time of his death, at age fifty, Andrew Combe was almost as famous as his brother. An internationally respected physician and acclaimed author, his *Observations on Mental Derangement* stood alongside Spurzhiem's *Insanity*, while his *Principles of Physiology* and practical guides to health and child care sold in the tens of thousands.[45]

With the positive reception of the *Essays* and Andrew's return to Edinburgh later the same year, Combe developed the confidence to start promoting phrenology. Together with James Simpson and a number of other interested men, the two brothers established the Edinburgh Phrenological Society (1820), commenced public lectures, and engaged critics in debates about the nature of mind and morals. The society and the science thrived. By 1825 more than eighty of the city's professional and literary elite had submitted to the phrenological tests for membership, Combe's house had become a museum of casts and skulls for the curious, his public lectures (now opened to women) were drawing large audiences, and the *Phrenological Journal* (established in 1824) had a healthy circulation. Calls came for lecture tours of London and the provinces, and a growing stream of fashionable and famous visitors presented themselves for examination—all of which made Combe an increasing object of attack within the orthodox press. His works were even banned from the University of Glasgow library.[46]

As articles in the *Phrenological Journal* and his *System* illustrate, one of Combe's earliest interests was to account for the formation of racial traits. Extending Spurzheim's speculations about national character, he crafted a systematic account of mental cultivation that integrated the primitive, the barbaric, and the exotic into a physiological account of brain development, greatly contributing, through the measurement and comparison of skulls, to the birth of race science in Britain and America. His starting point was the rejection of Dugald Stewart's environmentalism, the claim that "the capacities of the human mind have been, in all ages, the same; and that the diversity of phenomena exhibited by our species is the result merely of the different circumstances in which men are placed."[47] The casts of the Edinburgh Phrenological Society, he believed, told a very different story. Sketching outlines of aboriginal skulls on a rectangular grid, Combe traced the relative proportions of the various faculties, revealing how the ascendancy of the animal appetites over diminutive moral and intellectual organs led to the base and corrupt practices of savages reported by Captain Cook and other travelers. The people of Asia had sat stagnant for centuries, Africa was "an unbroken scene of moral and intellectual desolation," and the "aspect of native Americans [was] even more deplorable."[48] "Surrounded for centuries by European knowledge, enterprise, and energy, and incited to improvement by the example of European institutions," they remained "the same miserable, wandering, houseless, and lawless savages as their ancestors were, when Columbus first set foot upon their soil."[49] Lowest on the scale of humanity was the Charib, with large areas if combativeness and destructiveness and almost no reflecting organs, they lived a life of unbridled violence based upon immediate gratification. "Blind to every consequence," they were "incapable of tracing the shortest links in the chain of causation."[50] Above them came the New Hollander, the New Zealander, the North American Indian and the Negro. Here Combe disagreed with Thomas Jefferson. The savages of the New World had rejected Christianity and fled civilization like "bears and wolves," but Africans, with a higher forehead and stronger moral organs were capable of improvement.[51] Blessed with large areas of philoprogenerativeness, concentrativeness, veneration, and hope, they showed the capacity to settle and assume sedentary employment—although deficiencies in "Conscientiousness, Cautiousness, Ideality, and reflection" meant that this would have to be under the guidance of Europeans.[52]

While the *System* and the *Phrenological Journal* established Combe as Britain's leading exponent of phrenology, his writings in the early 1820s gave little indication of the moral philosophy for which he was to become famous. This sea change in his work came about as Combe finally shed the Calvinistic worldview of his youth for the rational theology promoted by his Owenite brother Abram. Spurzheim's manuscript on the *Natural Laws of Man* provided the inspiration. Building upon the scientific rationalism of enlightenment thinkers, Spurzheim suggested that the social world, no less than the physical, was governed by an underlying grammar of natural laws. Here was the solution to the chaos Combe had experienced in his youth: God had adapted men and women to virtue. Actions that were good ennobled the faculties and led to happiness; actions that were bad distorted the ideal cerebral balance and resulted in misery. By masking this moral ordinance, Calvinism and its bleak discipline distorted the practical imperatives of life, stunted mental growth, and frustrated the possibility of enjoyment written into the human organization. In the end, he reasoned, Calvinism produced a kind of madness in the population.

Unifying science and liberal theology, Combe developed a practical Christianity in which human actions were dictated by knowledge of God's will as revealed in the laws of nature. The *Constitution,* then, was to be "an introduction to an Essay on Education," a justification of the need to correctly train the faculties and disseminate positive knowledge about the world and the self necessary for individuals to make intelligent choices about the conduct of their lives.[53] It would also justify social and institutional reforms in those cases—such as treatment of criminals and the provision of welfare—where the ethic of self-improvement could not reach. Above all, the *Consti-*

tution would justify a new loving relationship with God and vouch, through the bounty of science, that the world was indeed a comforting home, a site of health, happiness, and prosperity for all. If the realities of urban-industrial life contradicted this blissful promise, Combe pointed to the future. Men and women had a long way to go before they would be perfected as Christian beings, but they could at least take solace in the knowledge that each step forward brought them closer to true happiness.

As Roger Cooter observes, this synthesis may have helped Combe reorganize his social world into a more personally and emotionally satisfying order, but it did not replace key elements of the value system that he had imbibed as a youth. Turning orthodox theology on its head, Combe effectively secularized the key Calvinist concepts of original sin, the elect, and the damned in a temporal account of physiological states: those born with good brains experienced the joys of living salvation; those with deranged brains, the torment of a living hell. Most important, Cooter notes, was the revolutionary change of authority implicit in Combe's new scheme. Rejecting the metaphysical speculation of privileged elites for common sense and the open and transparent testimony of the senses, he utilized the potent power of nature to scientize middle-class values and gain ideological command of the working poor. Projecting the division of labor encoded in the phrenological head onto society, he defended a hierarchical political order in which classes were defined according to the innate structures of the brain. The working poor would have to accept the laws of political economy, but this did not mean that the dismal predictions Malthus or the evils of capitalism were part of God's plan. With the development of science he was sure that the world had the physical recourses to secure the moral and material elevation of all. Combe could not promise working men and women equality, but he did offer self-respect and the hope of a brighter future. In return, by accepting secular theology and middle-class values, the masses would have to learn to regulate their own behavior in line with the morals of their new masters.

Immediately recognized as a threat to orthodox theology and the aristocratic social order, Edinburgh's ruling elites did everything in their power to discredit Combe and suppress his "infidel book." With few friends in the city, by the mid-1830s, Combe had turned from debating the truth of phrenology to lecturing working-class audiences on his moral philosophy. Helped by the publication of an inexpensive edition, sales of the *Constitution* soared. As Harriet Martineau observed, with more than a quarter of a million copies sold by 1860, it joined *The Bible, Pilgrims Progress,* and *Robinson Crusoe* as one of the most widely read books of the day.[54] It was a reflection of the times. More than any other text, the *Constitution* became the principle source of practical wisdom for the working classes, providing them for the first time, as Martineau put it, a true vision of "man's proper place in the universe."[55] In concert with this effort to raise the minds and morals of the masses through the doctrines of self-help, Combe and Simpson also rose to prominence as the leading proponents of public schooling. Extending the utilitarian program of radical theorists, they presented secularism as a solution to the religious impasse frustrating the expansion of education. Combining a progressive pedagogy keyed to the child's developing faculties with a scientific curriculum designed to impart knowledge of the natural and social worlds as examples of God's will, they promised a disciplined, intelligent, and morally compliant populace. Cooter simply states, "Combe's views on education . . . were reiterations through phrenology of contemporary ideas that were gaining currency."[56] But this generalization masks a complex and fascinating story that should be explored by anyone seeking to understand mid-nineteenth century debates on public schooling. Born out of the disciplinary practices developed by Owen and nurtured on the principles of phrenology, Combe's philosophy of education matured in the 1830s, a powerful justification for the Whig agenda of public school reform in both Britain and America.

6

Schooling for a New Moral World

Any character, from the best to the worst, from the most ignorant to the most enlightened, may be given to any community, even to the world at large, by applying certain means; which are to a great extent at the command and under the control, or easily made so, of those who possess the government of nations.

Robert Owen, *A New View of Society,* 1816

Socialism, as Robert Owen conceived it, was an experiment in human engineering. Following the philosophical teachings of the French philosophes and their English followers, he was convinced that poverty, brutality, and widespread debasement of men, women, and children were the products of social institutions that perpetuated ignorance and selfishness. Individuals, he came to believe, would only live happy and fulfilling lives within scientifically ordered communities that fostered mutual cooperation and a concern for the well-being of all. The key to this transformation was education. Starting with infant schools for children as young as eighteen months, he devised teaching methods to fashion the moral, rational, and productive citizens of a new moral world. A self-made industrialist who had become rich through the application of disciplinary strategies to factory production, by 1820 he was poised to demonstrate the power of education not only to improve the worker but to remake the entire social order. Although this utopian scheme inevitably fell foul of human nature, the power of Owen's pedagogy was not lost on George Combe. Harnessing Owen's rational methods to a Whig political philosophy, he defended the instruction of the working classes in the laws of economics and physiology and the training of their minds to virtue. Perhaps the most potent weapon in this disciplinary armory was the "eye of the community." Like the silent monitor Owen devised to ensure the efficiency of factory operatives, the "eye" utilized the moral force of approbation and disgrace flowing from the public scrutiny of behavior to ensure psychological control of the child. Combined with a secular scientific curriculum, this technology of management—foreshadowed in the Lancasterian system of monitorial instruction—became a central pillar of the phrenological philosophy of education that drove the radical petition for a state system of schooling during the 1830s.

THE ONE IDEA

Given Owen's insistence that character is a product of circumstance, it is important to know something about the origin of his own thought. Born in May 1771, the son of a saddler in Newton, Montgomeryshire, Owen was a strong-willed and precocious child with a love of reading—he especially enjoyed tales of explorers, histories, and intellectual biographies. At the age of ten, he claims to have realized that "there must be something fundamentally wrong in all religions, as they had been taught up to that period"; three years later, after studying the foundations of the world's faiths, he was an avowed atheist.[1] All religions emanated from the same dubious source, the human imagination. Ignorant of nature, ancient peoples had projected their fears and vanities into a Supreme Being, and these myths had been perpetuated through the ages by language and culture. Duly naturalized, Owen's youthful religious feelings were then "immediately replaced" by "a spirit of universal charity . . . for the human race, and with a real and ardent desire to do them good."[2] It should be noted that Owen's *Autobiography*, written at age 86, presents a rather romanticized account of his life and work.[3]

Owen's lifelong skepticism was cemented during his apprenticeship in the Lincolnshire drapery shop of James McGuffog, whose "well-selected" library and liberal attitudes afforded him "upon the average about five hours a day in which to read."[4] McGuffog and his wife also set an important practical example. Along with Owen, they cheerfully attended one another's church every Sunday. After listening to competing and antagonistic sermons for three years, Owen realized that small differences in doctrine were undermining great commonalties in religious sentiment and that, as the harmonious lives of his guardians demonstrated, sectarian dogma need not create the divisions he witnessed in society. Owen also proved to be an alert and industrious worker—McGuffog even tried to retain the ambitious sixteen-year-old with the promise of half-profits in his highly successful business. But having learned the basics of shop management and a good deal about the cloth trade, Owen set his sights on a wider field of achievement. Moving first to London, then to Manchester, by the age of twenty-one he had enough experience and self-confidence to be hired as a manager in one of Peter Drinkwater's cotton mills. Here, despite his youth, Owen was able to establish an effective relationship with the operatives, introducing systematic and standardized controls over the manufacturing process. He rewarded efficiency and, imposing conditions of conduct, helped further the aptly named Drinkwater's crusade to improve the moral habits of his workforce. Over the next ten years, through a series of partnerships, Owen extended and applied these techniques of "kindness and cooperation" in his own mills, becoming one of the most successful owners in the spinning business and one of the leading men in the city.

Owen reflected in his *Autobiography* that it was during this period that he first perceived the "constant influence of circumstance over my own proceedings and those of others."[5] "Man," he realized, "could not make his own organization, or any of its qualities."[6] His character, as he later expressed his one idea, was "formed for him, not by him."[7] A new spirit of understanding was demanded. The great error of the existing order, perpetuated by religious tales of eternal rewards and punishments for freely chosen acts, was to see alcoholism, crime, pauperism, and all other vices as the responsibility of individuals rather than the world into which they were cast. Only when the traditional conception of moral responsibility was replaced with an appreciation of how the social environment shapes human nature, could men and women be molded into rational citizens. Education was the key to this new moral order. It could no longer be asserted, he maintained,

> that evil or injurious actions cannot be prevented, or that the most rational habits in the rising generation cannot be universally formed. In those characters which now exhibit crime, the fault is obviously not in the individual, but the defects produced from the system in which the individual was trained. Withdraw those circumstances which tend to create crime in the human character, and crime will not be created. Replace them with such as are calculated to form habits or order, regularity, temperance, industry; and these qualities will be formed. Adopt measures of fair equality and justice, and you will rapidly acquire the full and complete confidence of the lower orders.[8]

While mysteriously silent about the intellectual sources of these psychological and political views—claiming only that he had discovered the laws of human nature in the course of his efforts to reform the habits of a "large population of the working classes under my direction in Manchester from 1791 to 1799, and a still larger number at New Lanark from that period"—it is evident that Owen was influenced by the ideas he encountered at the Manchester Literary and Philosophical Society. A center for provincial nonconformists, the Society was led by John Dalton, Thomas Percival, and a number of other scientifically minded men openly sympathetic to the works of radical writers such as Erasmus Darwin, Joseph Priestly, and William Godwin. Like the philosophes, from whom they drew inspiration, this group of associationist and utilitarian thinkers were all committed to education as an instrument of social change and promoted a scientific pedagogy—grounded in observation, experiment, and questioning—as the means of developing a practical knowledge of the world and the intellectual powers necessary for independent thought and conduct. Later, in Scotland, his friendship with professors at the Universities of Glasgow and Edinburgh and his membership in the Glasgow Literary and Commercial Society reinforced these environmental arguments. Dugald Stewart's analysis of mind and society, in particular, recognized the importance of education to the moral and economic future of the nation—a message crystallized in the work of his students Henry Brougham, James Mill, and Lord John Russell, the leading promoters of public schooling in Britain over the following decades.

Godwin, in particular, seems to have exerted a great deal of influence on Owen.[9] In common with Priestly, through combining an even more strident critique of government, he merged the environmentalism of Helvétius with the tradition of English dissent to explain how mind and character would gradually be perfected by the inevitable forces of truth and reason. The chief impediments to progress, he believed, were institutions such as the church and aristocracy that created a dependent childlike population. But education was more powerful than government, and Godwin was convinced that, freed from state control, schooling could shape all children into independent citizens able to act on the central maxim of his social philosophy, that personal well-being coincides with the happiness of all. Perhaps the greatest of ancient errors was the belief that people inherited different abilities according to their station in life. Godwin was adamant "that the actions and dispositions of mankind are the offspring of circumstances and events, and not of any original determination that they bring into the world."[10] Reason, character, and virtue all flowed from the association of sensible impressions. There was "no essential difference between the child of the lord and of the porter," and if switched at birth, each would naturally learn to "fulfill their appointed roles in life."[11]

Priestly had interpreted the American and French revolutions as instruments of Providence, historical events that, by instituting radical principles, would bring about a time of peace and Christian piety. Godwin took this argument a step further. Extending the nonconformist commitment to free thought and independent action, he rejected all forms of political organization that placed private interests before public virtue—love of country, friends, even family were not to interfere with moral duty. He envisioned a society free of specialization and hierarchical divisions. Unencumbered by excessive wealth or poverty, people would live off the land in small face-to-face pastoral communities that promoted intellectual independence, and, through intimate social arrangements, moral dependence. Society was to behold the behavior of all in its gaze. "There is no terror" he asserted, "that comes home to the heart of vice, like the terror of being exhibited to the public eye . . . [and] no reward worthy to be bestowed upon eminent virtue but this one, the plain, unvarnished proclamation of its excellence in the face of the world."[12] Sociability, not coercion, had to be the engine of social reform.

It was not until the severe social distress of the late 1810s that Owen started to advocate the kind of economic and political arrangements proposed by Godwin. As the quote at the head of this chapter indicates, his first major work, *A New View of Society* (1813), was addressed to governments and suggested reforms that would improve the character of workers in order to promote the well-being of nations. At this stage in his life, Owen walked in high circles. Respected as a successful industrialist with a proven record of ameliorating the condition of the worker without challenging the class structure of society, he won the ear of the prime minister, Lord Liverpool, and members of his cabinet. Indeed, convinced of the merits of Owen's disciplinary practices, Lord Sidmouth even sent copies of Owen's book to leading members of the church and several European governments. But Owen's credibility among political elites began to evaporate the moment his thought took a millennial turn. Painted as an atheist and a subversive by industrialists and property owners opposed to his factory reforms, Owen's plan to construct alternative, small-scale agricultural communities to combat the widespread unemployment and famine resulting from the failure of capitalism in the years after the Napoleonic Wars was widely received with a mixture of incredulity, ridicule, and fear. Such responses were not surprising, for in addition to replacing money and the ethic of self-interest with labor notes and cooperation, Owen also proposed a radical revision of even the most basic social institution, the family. Openly opposed to the traditional marriage contract, which, he argued, reflected unions based on financial gain rather than bonds of affection, he painted the home as a breeding ground of vice and self-interest. It was here that children

> *acquired all the most mean and ignorant selfish feelings that can be generated in the human character.* The children within these dens of selfishness and hypocrisy are taught to consider their own individual family their own world, and that it is the duty of all within this little orb to do whatever they can to promote the advantage of all legitimate members of it. With these persons, it is *my* house, *my* wife, *my* estate, *my* children, or *my* husband . . . thus is every family made a little exclusive world seeking its own advantage, regardless, and to a great extent in opposition to all other families.[13]

To secure genuine communal spirit, the whole of society had to become the child's family. Accordingly, in addition to a system of education designed to cultivate rational powers, Owen advocated separating children from their parents at an early age so that they could be raised as wards of the commune. Perhaps such radical ideas seemed feasible to social philosophers writing during the breakdown of the old order, but, as the Owenite community that Abram Combe established at Orbiston demonstrates, when translated from paper to practice, they inevitably clashed with basic human impulses.

THE FORMATION OF CHARACTER

As the eighteenth century drew to a close, Owen's commitment to radical principles led him to expand his interest in factory discipline to the broader field of social engineering. During a 1799 visit to David Dale's mills at New Lanark, he met and later married Dale's daughter, Caroline. Although this was not a happy union, Owen did fall in love with the idyllic setting on the banks of the Clyde, a perfect site on which to build a model community and demonstrate the effectiveness of his disciplinary techniques to the world. With the aid of several partners from Manchester, he purchased the whole enterprise from Dale, and on the first day of the new century established himself as manager of the New Lanark Twist Company.

The mills at New Lanark had already gained a national reputation for the progressive child-labor practices initiated by Dale. Indeed, Owen had first learned of Dale in 1796 when, as a member of the Manchester Board of Health, he participated in an inquiry to determine the causes behind the spread of fever among factory children. Pointing to the cramped, unventilated, and unsanitary working conditions of most textile mills, the group wrote to Dale to discover details about his facilities and the working hours, diet, exercise, cleanliness, and education of the children in his care.[14] It was as a result of this investigation that the first Robert Peel, himself a successful cotton manufacturer, carried the issue of child labor to Parliament and secured the legislation of 1802 commonly known as the First Factory Act.

Now Owen was set to push his father-in-law's humanitarian efforts even further. Dale had built up his business by employing orphans from the workhouses of Glasgow and Edinburgh. Although the picture of six- to ten-year-olds toiling eleven hours a day, six days a week, may seem barbaric to the modern reader, their lot was nonetheless superior to that of other destitute children who struggled to survive in the streets and squalid slums of the city. Dale provided warm, comfortable clothing, nutritious meals, clean dormitories, and, at the end of the workday, two hours of instruction. He even constructed schools for the village children who were too young to work—as W. A. C. Stewart and Philip McCann point out, possibly the first nursery and infant schools in Britain.[15] Even so, in Owen's mind, Dale's was still "a very partial experiment." Rather than importing so many children from the city, Owen focused on transforming the community around the mill, where, as he soon discovered, "the population lived in idleness and poverty, in almost every kind of crime; consequently in debt, out of health, and in misery."[16] These conditions demanded a total reform of the workplace and the home. Reorganizing the factory, Owen instituted systemwide controls on labor and processing; materials were closely supervised and the output of operatives recorded. Central to this scheme was the silent monitor, a four-colored block of wood suspended above the machinery to publicly display each worker's level of productivity. "Gradually the blacks were changed for blue, the blues for yellow, and the yellows for white."[17] Soldiering and theft were greatly reduced; productivity and profits soared. "Never perhaps in the history of the human race," Owen boasted, "has so simple a device created in such a short period so much order, virtue, goodness, and happiness, out of so much ignorance error and misery."[18] He even claimed that a distinctive "expression of countenance" corresponded to the color shown, as under the public eye workers gradually learned to comply with the moral order.[19] A similar moral gaze soon governed the village. Under the watchful eye of inspectors, waste and ashes were collected, the streets cleaned, and houses whitewashed. A curfew of 10:30 P.M. was imposed and the village patrolled for drunks—first-time offenders were fined, and repeated intoxication led to expulsion. Owen even imposed financial penalties on men responsible for illegitimate births. An extremely popular measure was the opening of a factory store, the first co-op, where goods were sold at prices well below those of local retailers. If the villagers resented Owen's intrusions in their private affairs, they nonetheless grew to accept his paternalism in exchange for the real advantages of life at New Lanark.

Having established a moral and rational code, in 1809 Owen turned his attention to schooling and the construction of his Institution for the Formation of Character—which would include his soon-to-be-famous infant school. Why he waited so long before reforming the education of the village is puzzling. He had, he claims, earnestly tried to persuade the master appointed by Dale to adopt his views, but this "good obstinate 'dominie' of the old school" was under the influence of the local parish and resisted "what he deemed to be such a fanciful new-fangled mode of teaching."[20] When at last he retired, Owen looked around for someone with a love of children and an unprejudiced attitude. And so it was that he came upon James Buchanan, "a simple-minded kind-hearted man" who "had been previously trained by his wife to perfect submission to her will."[21] Although "scarcely able to read, write, or spell," Owen reports preparing Buchanan and his somewhat sharper assistant, Molly Young, into the instruments of his theory. "Without an idea of the office in which they were placed, or the objects intended to be attained," the two "produced results, unconsciously to themselves, which attracted the attention of the advanced minds of the civilised world."[22] Later, in 1820, when Buchanan was employed as master of the first infant school in London, Owen was confident that this "willing servant" would be able to repeat all that he had learned at New Lanark, but soon found "he had not the mind nor the energy to act for himself."[23] Owen's description of Buchanan is hardly credible. Why would he hire such a person to conduct his most important social experiment? Why recommend him to his prominent associates in London? And how, despite his quirks and working-class background, was Buchanan able to retain his position of responsibility and the trust of his new employers? As Philip McCann and Francis Young demonstrate, the evidence suggests that Buchanan was indeed a competent teacher who successfully introduced a number of original ideas into the schooling of infants.[24] It seems more likely that Owen's criticisms of Buchanan flowed from his "lack of system," his occasional use of corporal punishment, and his strong commitment to Swedenborgianism.[25] Likewise, David Hamilton argues that Owen's initial interest in schooling was as much a product of economics as philanthropy: a measured response to Scottish labor problems that included replacing orphans with more cost-effective female operatives.[26]

With the foundation of Owen's impressive Institution laid, several of his Manchester partners started to balk at the spiraling costs of his grandiose plans. Other manufacturers were not educating their child labor. Was the purpose of the mills at New Lanark to produce textiles or conduct a social experiment? Recognizing their differences, Owen agreed to purchase the business from his colleagues by establishing a new company with a number of local investors—men, he believed, who had greater sympathy with his social goals. From the outset, however, this arrangement proved an absolute disaster. The new partners objected to Owen's investments and blocked every move he made to further his educational experiment. By 1812 the group had reached an impasse, and the mill was put up for auction, the majority thereby expecting to acquire the company and force Owen out. It was at this point that Owen turned for support to the leaders of the Lancasterian movement— a religiously disparate and often contentious group that included Francis Place, James Mill, Jeremy Bentham, William Allen, Joseph Fox, and Henry Brougham. His radical friends would provide the financial backing necessary for him to retain control of New Lanark, and Owen would prove the value of early education. Even so, as events unfolded, Owen still found it impossible to enact all of his educational ideas; Allen, whom he later called "a bigoted persecutor of my opinions during our partnership," saw to that.[27]

THE RADICAL MOVEMENT FOR EDUCATION

Owen's ideas about schooling have to be read against the background of debates between the church and radical reformers over the most appropriate method for educating the nation's poor. At the core of this oftentimes fiery contest was the question of human nature and the social good. Both sides embraced an essentially conservative desire to ensure a hierarchical social order, but where one focused on instilling piety, humbleness, and domestic virtue, the other stressed utility and the need for a disciplined workforce with the moral habits and practical wisdom to contribute to a productive economy. Although an early supporter of the radical cause, Owen soon rejected the mechanical practices and competitive social values inherent in the system of education they promoted. Increasingly critical of capitalism, he demanded a "rational" pedagogy that promoted understanding and taught the ethic of cooperation.

In 1798 Joseph Lancaster set out to improve the condition of poor children by opening a makeshift school in his father's South London house. Promoting his successes, Lancaster soon secured sufficient funds from his fellow reform-minded Quakers to establish larger accommodations on Borough Road. Here, faced with several hundred students, Lancaster hit upon the idea of monitorial instruction as a cheap and effective way for a single master to teach the basics of reading, writing, and arithmetic and, most importantly, to discipline children in the appropriate conduct for industrial life. Assiduously nondenominational, he taught the scriptures and read the Bible without comment. What was truly revolutionary, as David Hogan illustrates, were precise militaristic rote and drill procedures that he devised to regulate every aspect of the system.[28] Replacing individual recitation with group instruction, pupils, classed by age and ability, were constantly tested to determine their progress. Performance was meticulously recorded and rewards—often visible tokens of esteem—presented to the most productive students. Like Owen's silent monitor, pride and shame helped to instill the knowledge and dispositions essential to the new moral order.

By 1805, with royal support, Lancaster was traveling the country publicizing his scheme as a national plan. But unable to match the economy of the classroom, his personal extravagances almost shipwrecked the project. Rescued by a group of wealthy businessmen led by Joseph Fox and William Allen, the Royal Lancasterian Society (RLS) was formed. Lancaster was then paid to open schools, train teachers, and lecture on his system. Fearing the threat of dissent, the church responded in 1811 with its own National School Society (NSS), employing similar methods, developed in India by Dr. Bell, to educate the poor in the principles of the Anglican creed. The rivalry between the two groups quickly proved destructive. Rather than expanding education in the most needy areas, schools were built to compete for enrollment and promote denominational interests. Frustrated by this sectarian contest and what they regarded as an egregious waste of funds, in 1812, Mill, Place, and Brougham sought to reignite the movement by establishing the West London Lancasterian Association (WLLA). As explained in Mill's programmatic *Schools for All*, after a careful survey, a network of monitorial schools based upon nondenominational teaching would be built to serve the capital's children.[29] The following year, as Place collected statistics, Lancaster's continuing financial mismanagement came to a head. He was finally pensioned off, and the RLS was renamed the British and Foreign School Society (BFSS). Now more directly under the control of Allen and Fox, a more rigorous religious regimen was instituted: the Bible was the only book permitted in the Society's schools, and children who did not attend church on Sundays were to be expelled. This brought the goals of the WLLA into conflict with the parent body: subscribers withdrew, and Mill's ambitious project, itself proving overly expensive, was terminated.

Mill and Place quickly turned to another Lancasterian scheme: promoting Bentham's plan for a "Chrestomathic" school in Leicester Square. Based upon the design of the Panopticon, the school would present useful scientific knowledge to 600 high school students of the middling classes. (The monitorial method was also adopted at the Edinburgh High School by James Pillans, who found it a far more effective method for teaching Latin than the traditional system of taking places described by Combe.) Although funding and Bentham's eccentricities eventually foiled the plan, the radical's drive to disseminate practical wisdom eventually flowered in the 1820s as Mill, Place, and Brougham worked to establish the London Mechanics Institute, the Society for the Diffusion of Useful Knowledge, and, in 1828, London University. This movement was then continued in the 1840s by Mill's protégé, William Ellis, who, along with Combe, established model secular schools around the nation to teach the working classes the principles of political economy. Only now, supported by the principles of phrenology, the competitive and rote tasks of the monitorial system were replaced by the appeal to reason and the imperative to observe God's will, as manifested in the laws of nature. Finally, the radicals were also strong supporters of early moral instruction. Brougham, in particular, was convinced that the infant-school practices developed by Owen, suitably modified to include religious instruction, could be a panacea for ills of the crime-ridden city.

In all these endeavors, James Mill provided the theoretical basis and political rationale for the radical view of schooling—and, by editing *New View of Society,* helped clarify the metaphysical and practical implications of Owen's environmentalism. He began thinking earnestly about education in 1808, when he commenced the private schooling of his son, John Stuart Mill, and his views matured during the 1810s as he turned his mind to psychology and the developing science of economics. As his 1815 article *Education* reveals, Mill embraced sensationalism and the moral philosophy of Helvétius. Combining the insights of Cabanis with the writings of Hartley and Darwin, he defined the task of education as forming character by establishing sequences or trains of ideas in the mind of the child. Paramount was the development of intelligence and virtue, the ability to govern the appetites for the greater happiness of oneself and the community. Following Helvétius, he insisted "that all the difference which exists, or can ever be made to exist, between one *class* of men, and another, is wholly owing to education."[30] The laws of economics, however, demanded different kinds of workers. A disciple of J-B Say, he thought it "absolutely necessary for the existence of the human race" that "a large proportion of mankind" must labor to produce food.[31] For these men and women, the acquisition of knowledge would be limited by their duties. "The intelligence, industry and wealth of the state" depended on the middle classes. Here was "the heads that invent, and the hands that execute; the enterprise that projects, and the capital by which these projects are carried into operation." "The people of the class below are the instruments with which they work," whereas "those of the class above" were parasites on their achievements.[32] Much as Tracy had argued, Mill believed that the happiness of all demanded a population compliant with social leaders trained to understand the natural laws of nature and society. What were the educational instruments for shaping the future worker? Dividing the physical and the moral, he considered how internal and external factors influenced the bodily organization (e.g., temperament, climate, food, and exercise) and how thought and behavior could be controlled by organizing experience. It is a fact, he asserted, "that the early sequences to which we are accustomed form the primary habits; and that the primary habits are the fundamental character of the man."[33] He also spoke of technical education for the various demands of working life and social and political education for effective participation in the community.

RATIONAL PEDAGOGY

In 1812, when Owen first met Mill, he had enthusiastically supported the founding of monitorial schools for the poor of Glasgow. At a banquet held in Lancaster's honor, he demanded that every child of this class "must learn the habits of obedience, order, regularity, industry and constant attention which are to them more important than merely learning to read, write, and account."[34] He donated £1000 to the BFSS and £500 to the NSS (promising a further £500 if they opened their doors to children of all sects)—not a small sum, even for the prince of spinners. But Owen's attitude quickly changed. By the time *New Views* was published, with the ownership of the mills at New Lanark secure, he was openly critical of the monitorial education. Personal experience had revealed the practical reality of a pedagogy based upon mindless drills and rote learning. Students, he observed, "are taught to read, write, account and sew, yet they acquire the worst habits and have their minds rendered irrational for life."[35] He was particularly severe on the church. "Enter any school denominated National," he challenged, and "request the master to show the acquirements of the children; these are called out and he asks them theological questions to which men of the most profound erudition cannot make a rational reply: the children, however, readily answer as they had been previously instructed, for memory in this mockery of learning is all that is required."[36] Owen shared Mill's views on the value of education, but by 1815 he openly opposed the monitorial system as an effective method for developing reason and virtue.

The opening ceremony of the Institution for the Formation of Character on New Year's Day 1816 provided Owen a timely opportunity to explain his educational philosophy to those assembled villagers willing to brave the elements and the aftermath of Hogmanay celebrations. Starting with the measures he had introduced over the past fifteen years, Owen outlined his mission at New Lanark. All peoples, he insisted, were a product of their time and place. "Has the infant any means of deciding who, or of what description, shall be its parents, its playmates, or those from whom it shall derive its habits and its sentiments?"[37] "Has it the power to determine for itself whether it shall see the light within the circle of Christendom; or whether it shall be so placed as invariably to become a disciple of Moses, of Confucius, of Mohammed; a worshiper of the great idol Juggernaut, or a savage and a cannibal?"[38] Every society that ever existed has assumed that the individual is responsible for his or her own character, that crime, poverty, and suffering are the result of personal failings. But the principles upon which the new moral world would be founded made it evident that

> when men are in poverty,—when they commit crimes or actions injurious to themselves and others,—and when they are in a state of wretchedness,—there must be substantial causes for these lamentable effects; and that, instead of punishing or being angry with their fellowmen because they have been subjected to such a miserable existence, we ought to pity and commiserate them, and patiently trace the causes whence the evils proceed, and endeavor to discover whether they may not be removed.[39]

This had been Owen's policy since he took charge of the mills. He had not punished workers for their sloth, immorality, and intemperance. Rather, he informed the villagers, having "dispassionately investigated the source of the evils with which I saw you afflicted" and found it to lie in a social system perpetuated by ignorance, he was now trying to ameliorate their condition by introducing more rational and moral practices.[40] But the complete transformation of human character demanded even more radical measures.

Experience showed that infancy was the crucial period in which every individual's language, value system, and character were formed. "Much of the temper or disposition is correctly or incorrectly formed before [a child] attains his second year; and many durable impressions are made at the termination of the first twelve or even six months of his existence."[41] Indeed, it was this powerful law of nature that prevented people from recognizing the truth of Owen's theory. But thanks to this new Institution, the children of the next generation would understand the blindness of their predecessors and free themselves from error and the torment of angry passions. They would learn to view the world with reason and charity. It was sad that such a happy and virtuous state could not be created overnight, for children would still acquire many of the old habits and values of their parents. But a start had to be made; the world had to be convinced that the great errors of history could be avoided. By governing the passions and removing the animosity generated by class, cast, and other artificial divisions, "the period of the supposed Millennium [would] commence, and universal love prevail."[42]

Because Owen spent far more time castigating the evils of traditional schooling than he did explaining his own positive practices, the methods of instruction developed at the Institution have to be pieced together from a variety of sources, foremost among which is the account of his son Robert Dale Owen, who became a manager at the mill on his return from Fellenberg's school in 1822.[43]

The building itself, which would bring about the "improvement in the *internal* as well as the *external* character of the whole village," had two stories with enough space to accommodate 300 children.[44] The top floor was divided into a large chamber (90 feet by 40 feet) "fitted up with desks and forms, on the Lancasterian plan" (as Allen insisted) and a second hall, half the length, with space for an orchestra at one end and seats at the other.[45] The downstairs comprised three equally sized rooms, the middle of which opened up to a paved playground. No expense was spared to furnish the school. A London teacher, Catherine Vale Whitwell, decorated the walls of the smaller chamber with "representations of the most striking zoological and mineralogical specimens," and Owen had "a very large representation of the two hemispheres" constructed, "each separate country, as well as the various seas, islands, etc.," his son tells us, "being differently coloured, but without any names attached to them."[46] The only constraint on the experiment was space. With just three classrooms on the lower level for reading, natural history, and geography, and the use of the second floor chamber for dancing and singing, the older children, split by gender, were forced to share the remaining large room—a far from perfect arrangement, he acknowledged.

Children were to be admitted "as soon almost as they could walk"; not to receive lessons, but to amuse themselves in play.[47] Under Buchanan this comprised games, music, rhymes, and storytelling to engage interest in nature and introduce the rudiments of language and number. Dunn, the teacher who followed, was more organized. Establishing a set curriculum, formal activities were designed to teach the alphabet and introduce spelling to the youngest students. Between ages four and six, pupils were taken to the lower wing rooms for regular instruction "in the rudiments of common learning," and from six to ten, when they were permitted to work in the mill, lessons in "reading, writing, arithmetic, sewing, and knitting" were conducted on the upper floor.[48] Throughout, they learned interesting facts about history and geography, and studied nature by exploring objects. A firm believer in physical exercise, Owen also included dancing and military style marches in the curriculum. Children with a good voice were given singing lessons, and those "among the boys who have a taste for music . . . taught to play some instrument."[49] Education was not confined within the walls of the Institution. "Whenever possible pupils would derive knowledge from a personal examination of the works of nature and art."[50] In the evenings the building would be turned over to adolescents and those adults seeking to extend their knowledge and pursue useful hobbies. There were also occasional lectures, weekly musical events, and religious services.

Pedagogy had to follow the dictates of nature. Lessons were kept short, keyed to children's interests, and alternated with sessions of physical activity. Learning focused on understanding the world, not the memorization of words. Moreover, because no knowledge was to be accepted on authority, students were encouraged to question their teachers—who, if unable to answer, were instructed to admit their ignorance before leading a student into error. Owen agreed with Rousseau that books ought to be reserved for the age of reason, but in deference to the wishes of parents and his agreement with Allen, the Bible was used to teach reading. Fridays, it is reported, were devoted to the Catechism and Sundays to the Scriptures, prayer, and hymns.[51] As for discipline, punishment and emulation were replaced by intrinsic motivation and appeals to the child's natural curiosity. Above all, children would learn to live "without party." Free of class distinctions, they would appreciate that their personal well-being coincided with the good of the community. Much of this regulation would occur in the playground, where, as Combe eagerly noted, the free play of the child's passions could be monitored and corrected by an observant teacher.

As Robert Dale Owen takes care to explain, the form and content of schooling at the Institution flowed directly from utilitarian and sensationalist principles. "If happiness be our being's end and aim," he writes, "then a simple and intelligible definition of right and wrong . . . is this: *whatever in its ultimate consequences, increases the happiness of the community, is right; whatever, on the other hand, tends to diminish that happiness, is wrong.*"[52] Unaware of this principle, men and women sought to satisfy their needs by gaining social distinction and wealth, only to suffer the consequences of "pride, vanity, ambition, and their concomitant irrational and injurious feelings and passions."[53] Social progress demanded that children be taught "by *natural* rewards and punishments . . . the *necessary consequences,* immediate and remote, which result from any action."[54] Such a program would soon lead every individual to understand that personal happiness coincides with the good of the community and that "the pleasures resulting from the exercise of sincerity and of kindness, of an obliging, generous disposition, of modesty and of charity" far outweigh the "consequences of hypocrisy and ill-nature, of a disobliging, selfish temper, and of a proud, intemperant, [*sic*] intolerant spirit."[55] Those brought up amid the irrational structures of the old world were thus suffering a kind of insanity that absolved them of moral responsibility for any evil act. Instead of blaming a wrongdoer, Robert Dale would pity, then educate him "to recognize the intimate, irreparable, and immediate connection of his own happiness, with that of those around him," a principle he confidently asserted, "which to an unbiased mind, requires only a fair statement to make it evident; and the practical observance of which, confers too much pleasure to be abandoned for a less generous or more selfish course."[56]

In 1824 this experiment in rational education was terminated. Owen's London partners, originally content to support his efforts from afar, were gradually drawn into a long running dispute with the Lanarkshire clergy over the school's irreligious and immoral influence on the villagers. Allen was deeply troubled by Owen's skepticism and, indeed, only agreed to the partnership in the first place on the condition that teaching followed the BFSS system, that religious instruction be given to all workers, and that "nothing shall be introduced tending to disparage the Christian religion or underwrite the authority of the Holy Scriptures."[57] Owen's scathing attack on monitorial education in *New View of Society* and subsequent pronouncements about the negative influence of religion were a cause of great consternation for Allen. He was mortified by the thought that his money was being used to spread atheism. So when, in 1818, Allen and fellow partner Joseph Foster traveled north to investigate these charges for themselves, they may well have been expecting the worst. What they saw certainly did not harmonize with the ascetic principles of Quakerism. Owen gently mocks the two men enjoying the natural delight of children as they danced, marched, and sang. But although won over by the possibilities of early education—he opened an infant school of his own four years later—Allen was deeply disturbed by the military tone of the exercises, the pervasively secular curriculum, and the sight of boys wearing tunics cut like kilts. Despite Owen's protests that children did study the

Bible, learn the Catechism, and attend church on Sundays, Allen was insistent that the school be infused with more religious instruction. He even assembled the villagers to deliver an address on the necessity of following faith rather than reason. Recommendations were made and warnings delivered, but Owen paid little attention. Finally, after a second visit in 1822, Allen could no longer tolerate Owen's prevarication and, with the help of several other partners, drew up his own plans to restructure the school. Catherine Vale Whitwell was dismissed to make way for a Lancasterian master; secular songs, marching, and dancing were banned; religious education was stressed; and boys were forced to wear pants. Eight years after opening his Institution with such promise, Owen was forced to resign and watch the mills pass into new hands. Increasingly occupied with the project of constructing a socialist utopia and persuaded that rational schooling could never succeed in such an irrational society, he turned his energies to the most ambitious and flawed project of his life, establishing the New Harmony Society in Indiana.

THE SPREAD OF INFANT SCHOOLING

People from around the world flocked to see Owen's model society and the revolutionary infant school at New Lanark; according to his son, the village had some twenty thousand visitors in ten years.[58] Although much has been made of British reformers traveling to Switzerland in order to learn the techniques of Pestalozzi and Fellenberg, until recently, insufficient attention has been paid to the impact of Owen's experiment. As Harold Silver explains, Pestalozzian pedagogy did not sweep the Anglo-Saxon world until the mid-1820s, and then in the context of an already blossoming infant school movement that grew out of the practices that Owen had devised at New Lanark. True, in the years after the Napoleonic Wars, Bell, Brougham, Allen, and James Kay-Shuttleworth, among others, all visited the Swiss pedagogs, but their observations did little to influence the methods of schooling in Britain. It was only in the following decade, through the writings of James Pierrepoint Greaves (who published Pestalozzi's *Letters on Early Education*), Charles Mayo (who opened a Pestalozzian school in Cheam), and Edmond Biber (editor of the *Christian Monitor* and the popular book *Henry Pestalozzi*) that a distinctive Pestalozzian pedagogy started to take shape. Mayo, and his sister Elizabeth, were particularly influential. Founding the Home and Colonial Infant School Society, they trained teachers and popularized Pestalozzi's object lesson in a series of textbooks that became an integral part of the elementary school curriculum for more than fifty years—and a central feature of the phrenological view of schooling. Owen himself visited Pestalozzi in 1818 and, according to his son, incorporated his method of teaching arithmetic into the curriculum at the Institution. But by this time the basic practices of infant schooling were firmly established.

Troubled by Thomas Malthus's dismal predictions of uncontrolled population growth, Brougham, Mill, and their fellow radicals saw the infant school as a prophylactic for the soaring rates of inner-city crime. Convinced that the young mind could be turned to virtue, they presented an apocalyptic choice: build infant schools now or construct prisons for a future army of criminals. After further discussions with Owen, Mill and Brougham established a committee of political leaders and wealthy businessmen to raise funds for an experimental infant school in Brewer Street, Westminster. Opened in 1819, James Buchanan was secured as the school's first teacher. Yet from the outset, it was clear that squalid conditions of urban London presented a very different set of challenges to the bucolic environment of Lanarkshire. At the Institution Buchanan had relied on his natural charm to engage pupils in imaginative and amusing games. Now, with his wife and several monitors, he struggled to control large numbers of inner-city children and turn their interest to reading, writing, and arithmetic. Naturally, he adopted more regimented activities. The result, according to Owen, was a mechanical copy of New Lanark, "governed in the spirit and manner of the old irrational schools."[59] "Founded on falsehood and supported solely by deception," children were pressed into "believers and slaves of the system."[60] The new school's owners—keen to distance themselves from Owen's religious and social views—were less concerned. Far more problematic for them was Buchanan's lack of fiscal sense and his public commitment to Swedenborgianism. And yet it was from the ranks of the New Church that the altogether more promising Samuel Wilderspin was recruited to carry the movement forward. A textile worker by trade, the thirty-year-old Wilderspin had taught Sunday school since the age of sixteen and, in line with Swedenborg's teachings, was deeply interested in ways to develop the rational and moral capacities of the young.[61] Drawn to his fellow church members' school, it was on one of his frequent visits to Brewer's Green, during the summer of 1820, that he met the wealthy silk manufacturer Joseph Wilson, who, on Buchanan's advice, offered Wilderspin the position of master at his newly opened infant school in Spitalfields.

Visiting Wilderspin later that year, Owen found him "much more teach-able than my first master."[62] "Very desirous and willing to learn," he eagerly accepted "general and minute instruction" on the aims and methods of infant education perfected at New Lanark.[63] And, according to Owen, in the years that followed, Wilderspin implemented these recommendations faithfully, even though he seemed unable to grasp the rational system of mind and society behind them. Indeed, the next year, when Wilderspin wrote up his experiences as a practical handbook for teachers, *Infant Education* (1823) con-tained a warm tribute to Owen. It also demonstrated his own significant adaptations to the needs of his school and the interests of his employer, in-cluding innovations that increased the number of mechanical exercises. Later writers criticized this regimentation of Owen's rational pedagogy, but, forced to discipline large numbers of children from one of the poorest and most troubled districts of London, Wilderspin had few options. Walking the streets of Spitalfields incognito, he claimed to have seen sights of depravity beyond the comprehension of the normal mind. Yet, with few resources, Wilderspin worked miracles. As his remarkable public demonstrations show, in just a few short weeks he could transform 100 or so boys and girls from the most dire slums into tidy, efficient, and polite pupils. Audiences were amazed. Beaming with health and joy, his charges sang, danced, and recited the rudiments of learning and Christian ethics.

In 1822, Wilderspin helped Allen open London's third infant school in Stoke Newington. Within a year similar requests for assistance were arriving from every part of the country. In an effort to channel this growing interest in early education into a national movement, Brougham and Mill helped form the Infant School Society (ISS). A model school was proposed, with Wilderspin as its future master, and James Pierrepoint Greaves was appointed as the group's secretary and chief publicist. It was under Greaves's influence that the movement gradually restructured around Pestalozzian theory. Wait-ing for his future school to materialize, Wilderspin criss-crossed the country opening dozens of infant schools in every corner of the nation.

For many of the movement's backers, turning Wilderspin into a peripatetic was a far more effective use of funds than establishing a costly model school. Yet ironically, McCann and Young argue, it was this lack of an institutional base that proved to be one of the two main reasons for the demise of infant schooling in Britain. Wilderspin could enter a community, give speeches and demonstrations and get the public committed to his project; he could identify an appropriate site, oversee the construction of the school building, and order its furnishing; he could even help select a promising master. But the training of new teachers proved problematic. Without a center in which they could learn methods thoroughly, future instructors were generally sent to observe other schools and left to follow the principles laid out in Wilderspin's book. But then, once Wilderspin had gone, many reverted to traditional methods of rote learning and physical discipline. The second major problem was a growing awakening to the religious dimension of early education. Owen, a socialist, Buchanan and Wilderspin, Swedenborgians, and Greaves, following Pestalozzi, a transcendentalist, were easily associated with irreligion, and the infant school tarred as a first step toward atheism. These fears soon spread concern, and by 1827, Wilson, Allen, and other leaders were calling for the replacement of Buchanan and Greaves—Wilderspin, more discrete in his views, was too useful to dismiss. The housekeeping that followed split and ultimately destroyed the ISS. The following year, "deserted by the Society," Wilderspin relocated to Cheltenham, where he opened a store for school supplies and established himself as a private educational consultant. It was in this capacity, later in 1828, that he first met George Combe and began a decade-long association with James Simpson.

The phrenologists were among Wilderspin's most ardent supporters. Believing that the mind was most pliant during the first years of life, they embraced the child-centered teaching methods and disciplinary practices that had evolved from Owen's experiment—especially the use of the playground as a moral theater in which to observe and train the developing passions. But to be of practical and political value, infant schooling had to be grounded in a moderate view of human nature—there could be no taint of environmentalism, socialism, or atheism. Combe's solution was a gradual meliorism. Echoing Brougham's concerns, he warned against the destructive force of a criminal population. Ignorance and wickedness could not be eradicated in a single generation, but with the correct phrenological management, the masses could make the first steps toward moral improvement—and ultimately, through the laws of heredity, the biological advancement of the race. So much was evident from Spurzheim's teachings. But Combe added a powerful religious justification for the importance of public schooling, the natural theology of secularism. First expressed in the *Constitution of Man*, he insisted that human happiness required submission to God's will as revealed by the laws of nature. This element of Combe's thought was clearly influenced by the teachings of his brother Abram, whose ill-fated community at Orbiston was guided by the conviction that Owenism was the rational gospel of Christ. As the following chapter shows, this failed experiment in practical Christianity helped Combe justify his vision of human nature and provided compelling proof of the power of education to refashion the social order.

7
The Eye of the Community

There is no vice or crime from that of mere personal or domestic filthiness, to the foulest robbery or murder, to which [the Laws of Nature] do not attach an adequate and corresponding punishment. And [Nature] does this by merely leaving the individual to the feelings which naturally arise within him when the action is made known. . . . The Eye of the Community, and the inward feeling produced, will soon either create a change of conduct, or make the individual retire from the Society.

Abram Combe, *The Register for the First Society of Adherents to Divine Revelation, at Orbiston,* 1826

As Robert Owen brought his educational innovations before the villagers of New Lanark, he was also drawn into a national campaign to revise child-labor laws in the textile industry. During 1815, he and a number of other Scottish manufacturers had petitioned the government to reduce taxation on imported cotton. Owen also wanted to add resolutions calling for the improvement of working conditions, but found absolutely no sympathy among his peers. Determined to pursue the issue, he drummed up support among Parliamentary friends for legislation that would ensure, among other provisions, a minimum working age of ten and two hours of schooling during the first four years of employment. Peel's act of 1802 had only served to regulate the work of apprentices in cotton mills, a system that had all but died out by this time. As a result, all manner of horrific abuses had arisen. Many years later, Robert Dale Owen still recoiled at the scenes he and his father witnessed during their fact-finding tour of British industry. Children as young as six were forced to work up to fifteen hours a day in hot, dangerous, and poorly ventilated rooms for little more than a pittance. "In some large factories, from one-forth to one-fifth of the children were either cripples or otherwise deformed, or permanently injured by excessive toil, sometimes by brutal abuse. The younger children seldom held out more than three or four years without serious illness, often ending in death."[1] Believing the government would support his reforms, Owen called on Peel to bring his bill before the Commons. But rather than acting directly, Peel began a process of negotiation and compromise with manufacturers that, over a two-year period, gradually stripped Owen's proposal of all its major demands. When it finally became law, in 1819, the measure, now restricted to the cotton industry, instituted a minimum age of nine and a twelve-hour working day—but without any official method of inspection, even these modest provisions were unenforceable.

By this time Owen had washed his hands of the whole project. Disgusted by the suffering he witnessed and alarmed by the government's inability to stem the unemployment and poverty sweeping the nation, he developed a powerful critique of the capitalist system and the social order that supported it. Human well-being had to be placed before the demands of profit. Building upon his work at New Lanark, he proposed an imaginative solution: the construction of small, self-sustaining agricultural communities. By 1820, as the economic and political situation worsened, Owen became increasingly and more openly critical of the government and the church. No longer content simply to advocate for a new form of poor relief, he now presented a plan for "villages of cooperation" and a new kind of communal life based upon reason and mutual interest.

OWEN'S PLAN

The late 1810s were a time of extreme hardship for Britain's laboring classes. The end of the Napoleonic Wars brought a glut in the market that resulted in price-cutting, wage reductions, and extensive layoffs. Strained by large numbers of dependent ex-soldiers, the meager relief of the Poor Law was the only protection many had from starvation. At a loss over how to deal with the economic forces generating this dire situation, the government cast about for solutions. "Owen's Plan" was one such proposal. First elaborated before a committee convened by the Duke of York and the Archbishop of Canterbury, Owen proposed a kind of Copernican revolution in economics. The demands of wartime, he explained, had brought two fundamental changes in British society: a largely agricultural population had been turned into factory operatives, and scientific advances in chemistry and mechanics had vastly increased the power of production. With just 2,500 workers, a single factory could now match the manufacturing power of Scotland only fifty years earlier. When peace was declared, the artificial bubble sustaining these developments burst. Supply outstripped demand, and with industry tied to the power of machines, the worker suddenly became superfluous. Thousands were laid off or forced to labor for subsistence wages. Moreover, Owen pointed out, with less money circulating in the population, the demand for goods was diminishing, causing prices to be lowered and costs reduced. Cycling out of control, capitalism thus presented an impossible choice: either discard the machine or allow millions to starve. Owen's solution to this impasse was the creation of a new economic system in which technology was made subservient to human interests. Proclaiming advances in agricultural science as great as those that had transformed the cotton industry, he explained how William Falla's method of deep-spade cultivation could easily support 1,200 people on less than 1,800 acres of land. Engineering social harmony through geometric order, he designed homes and communal facilities in rectangles around public spaces. There would be a large dining room, a common school, a nursery, public lecture theaters, meeting places, and churches, and, pressing his views on the formation of character, dormitories for children over the age of three. With a modest investment to get the project under way, Owen was sure that such a community could be fully independent within a couple of years and able to pay back the initial loan within a lifetime.

Unsure what to do with such a radical suggestion, the committee referred Owen's report to a parliamentary committee recently established to examine changes to the Poor Laws—possibly on the recommendation of his friend Brougham, who was a member of both groups. But after two days of heated deliberation, this body voted not to hear Owen's evidence. Snubbed by official channels, he took his plan to the public. In a series of pamphlets and lectures he attacked the government's Malthusian policies for focusing on the containment of popular unrest rather than the amelioration of economic ills. His rhetoric grew increasingly more strident. How could he persuade the current generation, whose "minds and habits" had been fashioned "by the powers of this world—rightly declared to be the 'powers of darkness?'"[2] Resolving to take "the bull by the horns," he faced up to the uncomfortable task of explaining that "the populations of all nations had been, and even now are, governed by a thick mental darkness."[3] One biographer, C. D. H. Cole, argued, "Owen went a little mad in 1817 . . . and gradually lost . . . that firm grasp on the world of facts that made him the greatest practical social innovator of his day."[4] Never again could he "argue a cause—he could only see visions and dream dreams."[5] While this made him "appear as a visionary in the eyes of ordinary men," to the "political and religious figures he had so assiduously courted, he gradually became a fanatic."[6] The pivotal moment came at a public meeting that Owen had called at the City of London Tavern. Before an audience studded with political and religious leaders, he revealed the full depth of his social critique. Why, in the long course of history, had this plan never been tried? Because of religious bigotry! "Hitherto," he declared, humankind "have been prevented from knowing what happiness really is, solely in consequence of the errors—the gross errors—that have been combined with the fundamental notions of every religion . . . and, in consequence, [have] made man the most inconsistent, the most miserable being in existence . . . a weak, imbecile animal; a furious bigot and fanatic; or a miserable hypocrite."[7] Such prejudices, he promised, would not be allowed into his villages of cooperation, which he now advocated as a mode of life for all poor workers, not just the unemployed. The fallout was fierce. Owen lost all favor with the church and, from that time forward, was publicly branded an infidel by his opponents and pilloried as a danger to the morals of the nation. A number of sympathetic aristocrats and a few leading Whigs stood by him, but Owen's public standing was irrevocably compromised.

Owen's attack on the evils of religion did not diminish the flow of influential visitors to New Lanark. Ambassadors, counts, barons, dukes, grand dukes, and numerous other dignitaries all traveled north to see for themselves the advantages of his moral discipline. One visitor, Professor Pictet of Geneva, a renowned scholar and former Commissioner of Education for France, became so enamored with Owen's pedagogical innovations, that he persuaded him to promote the system on the Continent. Joining Pictet and his close friend Cuvier, Owen sailed from London to Paris and, in the space of six weeks, was introduced to the prime minister, Louis Phillipe (the future king), and many leading scientists and intellectuals. Owen and Pictet then proceeded to Switzerland, where they toured the schools of Oberlin, Pestalozzi, and Fellenburg. Owen found Oberlin and Pestalozzi good and benevolent men, laboring under great difficulties to realize advanced ideas, though without the guidance of a sophisticated theory of human nature. He was far more pleased with Fellenburg, who, he reports, soon became a disciple of the "new views." Only able to speak English, in these and other meetings, it appears that Owen did far more talking than listening. After short stays in Germany and Italy, Owen then returned to France, where he presented *Two Memorials on Behalf of the Working Classes* to the postwar Council of Sovereigns at Aix-la-Chapelle.[8] He was heard with interest, his theories were discussed, but, as might be expected, no action was taken.

Events in Britain had not stood still. The Factory Bill had stalled, and, outraged by Owen's antireligious tirade, William Allen was pressing for changes at New Lanark. After rushing home to placate Allen, Owen spent much of the following year agitating for the reform of labor laws and campaigning for a trial of his planned community. In *Address to the Working Classes,* for example, he attempted to soothe the fears of social disorder by instructing the poor that their future wealth would not come at the expense of the middle and upper ranks. He even tried standing for parliament. But the worsening economic crisis and events such as the Peterloo Massacre pushed Owen's thoughts in an even more radical direction. Certain of the imminent collapse of capitalism, he transformed his scheme for poor relief into a blueprint for an alternative social order. No longer seen as a mechanism for protecting the worker within a corrupt system, his new social philosophy caught the imagination of radical reformers, spawning Owenism and the movement to found a new moral world through the construction of socialist communes.

Consulted by local authorities on the growing problem of unemployment in his home region, Owen articulated his mature views in *Report to the County of Lanark* (1821).[9] Attributing the increasing economic woes of the day to the arbitrary valuation of commodities, he described how villages of cooperation could solve the problem of poverty by abolishing all artificial measures and establishing a system of payment based on the natural standard of human labor. Rather like the concept of horsepower, each job would be assessed by the amount of energy it required and rewarded with labor notes. Fixing value in this way would prevent speculation and so avoid the excessive wealth and poverty generated by capitalism. It would even prevent the formation of a class society and its concomitant evils. Current conditions were not caused by an increase in population or a lack of productive power but by the inherent flaws of a market that prevented the equitable distribution of wealth. By harnessing advances in agriculture, home, and industrial technology, Owen saw no reason why a large number of people could not live off small tracts of land. Indeed, he predicted, surplus goods could be traded with other groups, securing, contrary to the bleak predictions of Malthus, a future of material wealth for all. The time had passed for small-scale enterprises such as New Lanark. Poverty demanded action. If only one such community could be founded, Owen was sure it would set an example that would be followed around the world, spreading peace and prosperity within a generation.

Quite overwhelmed by the scope and scale of Owen's scheme, the county council appointed a committee to consider its feasibility. Delivered six months later, their report praised Owen's successes at New Lanark but asked for further proof of his agricultural claims. In the meantime, a second proposal was presented to the council by A. J. Hamilton, the son of a local landowner willing to rent some 600 hundred acres of his property for the construction of an Owenite community. Apparently, the county was planning to build a prison near the family estate, and Hamilton reasoned that Owen's scheme would make this unnecessary; rather than incarcerating the down-and-out, a model community could transform them into moral citizens.

Hamilton was no ordinary squire. A former lieutenant in the Scotch Greys, he had returned from Waterloo deeply disturbed by the carnage of war and resentful of the corruption and cronyism that infected the British military. Claiming to have been cheated out of half his pension, he grew increasingly frustrated with the callous authoritarianism of the Tory government and was appalled by its harsh indifference to the widespread suffering of 1819 and 1820. Searching for some way to alleviate the condition of local villagers, he had provided fieldwork for a group of unemployed weavers and experimented with methods of intensive agriculture—heavy manuring and deep-spade cultivation, which he had witnessed on the continent. Although the rigorous labor and inclement conditions proved too much for the weavers (who were not accustomed to outdoor work), he remained adamant that landowners and capitalists had to do something to address the suffering of the poor. Living just ten miles west of New Lanark, Hamilton was no doubt familiar with Owen's achievements and industrial philosophy. Indeed, the two had met at a dinner party in 1816, debated the causes of poverty and vice, and agreed on the importance of educating the masses. After reading Owen's *Report,* he found the solution to his dilemma. Converting to Owenism, all his resentment for the evils of the old world were quickly refocused into a zeal for the new, as he threw himself into the task of raising the funds necessary to build a village of cooperation.

When it became evident that the council could not raise the £40,000 necessary for Hamilton's proposal, and Parliament refused to help, the two men sought private backers for their plan. A company was proposed to oversee operations, and two thousand shares paying 5 percent interest were offered at £25 apiece. When all debts had been paid off, it was promised, members would be granted total ownership of the community. Failing to attract a sufficient number of investors, Owen and Hamilton established the British and Foreign Philanthropic Association. In its one and only meeting, on June 1, 1822, pledges totaling £55,000 were secured, a sizable sum, but short of the £100,000 Owen now thought necessary to complete the project. Quite why Owen and Hamilton did not pursue other sources of funding is unclear. Despite their friendship and commitment to the socialist enterprise, they did have their differences. Most importantly, Hamilton rejected Owen's demand for absolute equality. The equal division of property and funds, he believed, had to be a goal rather than a precondition of membership. This disagreement seems to have arisen after 1821 when Hamilton, then a student at the University of Edinburgh, came under the orbit of George and Abram Combe. Converting to the younger brother's phrenology appears to have tempered his commitment to strong environmentalism, if not to community building. Like so many other followers of Owen, he seems to have believed the two systems were compatible; after all, both promoted the perfectibility of human nature and a society governed by natural law. Hamilton was also captivated by the older brother's argument that "a society might commence upon the old system and gradually get into the new, as soon as it was found that the minds of the members became adapted to the change."[10]

With William Allen continuing to exert pressure over the running of New Lanark, Owen's interests started to wander, first to Ireland and then America, for sites where a settlement could be constructed unencumbered by the orthodox structures of the old world. Hamilton and Combe recognized that they would have to go it alone. Without Owen or his financial support, the two set about establishing the first socialist community in Britain. Situated on the banks of the river Calder, close to its union with the Clyde, some nine miles east of Glasgow, Orbiston drew 300 men, women, and children to live and work under Owen's theories—and Abram Combe's rational theology.

ABRAM COMBE AND THE DOCTRINE
OF DIVINE REVELATION

Less serious than his younger brother, Abram Combe was known by family and friends for his rebelliousness, humorous pranks, and sarcasm. He was, George reminisced, "very cleaver at all boyish games, tricks, and small mischiefs."[11] Later in life, Abram also proved himself a man of principle, building a reputation as a fair but tough manager in the tanning trade. It was during the fall of 1820 that the thirty-five-year-old Abram accompanied his younger brother George on his first visit to New Lanark. Greatly impressed by the order and efficiency of the village, he experienced something of a moral epiphany. After studying Owen's writings, he quickly dedicated himself to realizing the principles of the new system.

Joining with Hamilton, he first ventured into community building during the fall of 1821, opening a cooperative shop in Edinburgh styled after the company store at New Lanark. As the subscription card indicated, "by our works shall we be judged," this was a practical society in which members pledged abstinence from alcohol, tobacco, and profanity. George Combe reported that within the first year more than five hundred families were enrolled, "a school on the plan of those at New Lanark, was established for the children," and adults met in "the evenings for mutual instruction and social enjoyment; conversation, music, and dancing constituted their amusements."[12] "At first," he continued, "the society prospered amazingly. The members, full of moral enthusiasm, experienced delightful emotions and anticipated vast advantages; some conceived that Earth was immediately to be changed into heaven and that sin and sorrow were about to be banished from the land."[13] Abram is even said to have bet a friend that Edinburgh's Royal Circus would be converted into Owenite communities within five years. He lost his wager. In less than twelve months the practical society was dissolved. According to his brother, the severe economic conditions undermined the project. Hamilton pointed to a storekeeper who embezzled funds. But whatever the final cause of the failure, Combe lost none of his enthusiasm for social reform. Putting this first setback behind him, he then established a small commune in his tanning factory. Workers lived together, sharing directly in the profits of their labor. Yet again personality seems to have undermined principle, and after a series of acrimonious disputes, this scheme also had to be abandoned. "It was evident," he later reported, that while professing their commitment to mutual cooperation, the workers "were not really *inclined* for 'equal distribution.'" Their "feelings and inclinations . . . [could] not be forced prematurely into such a state."[14] At Orbiston, he would ensure that each member was prepared for the new system as, through education and character formation, they were gradually adapted to virtue.

Over the next two years, as plans for the Orbiston community developed,

Combe published numerous pamphlets promoting Owenism and explaining his religious principles. But because commentators have been more interested in the events at the community than Combe's writings, little attention has been paid to these works. Alexander Cullen, for example, dismisses them as "so involved and wordy as to be scarcely readable."[15] It is true that Combe's major work, *Metaphorical Sketches*, presents his fusion of Owenism and practical Christianity through a long and rather abstruse historical tale in which Owen, the servant of Common Sense, helps Nature, Truth, Experience, and other personified characters defeat the likes of Ignorance, Error, and Force by educating the infant mind to understand the dictates of reason. But his practical creed, provocatively called "The Doctrine of Divine Revelation," was clearly spelled out in many letters and lectures that he prepared for the community. Identifying the laws of nature as the instruments of God's will, Combe named Christ the first and greatest teacher of the secular gospel. As Jesus was Owenized, so Owen was Christianized: already the messiah-like individual in *Metaphorical Sketches*, he became the prophet of the one and only true religion, that which was *unobjectionable to all sects*. To distill truth from error, Combe proposed eliminating all doctrines, ceremonies, and practices that contained *unnatural* or *irrational* beliefs. The mind had two sources of knowledge, the outer experiences of the physical world perceived by the senses and the inner moral voice of reason. Nature revealed the unerring regularity of God's works, whereas in the private realm of thought, he found the imperatives of reason—fundamental moral principles such as "that whatever augments human happiness is right, and that whatever diminishes this happiness is wrong," and "we ought to do unto others on all occasions as we would that they should do unto us."[16] Whatever was contradicted by experience or could not be understood by reason had to be the product of the human imagination, a power most evident in religious myths and social traditions that distorted reality to match human desires. No doubt such stories contained a germ of truth, but as he playfully demonstrated, they also included much fantasy and error. Review the world's sacred tales, he suggests in his *Seven Lessons*.[17] "Have similar facts ever come under the cognizance of your senses. . . . [D]o you understand the way in which they were accomplished?"[18] If men and women could not see this in their own beliefs, he suggested that they first look at the customs and tales of others. After exposing the absurdities of the Muslim and the Hindu, they might then be in a position to critically examine their own beliefs. Large tracts of the Bible clearly deviated from this principle; Jonah could no more have entered the belly of a whale than God could have commanded Abraham to kill Isaac. Such manifestly erroneous stories were perpetuated by the indoctrination of the infant mind and religious prohibitions that made it a sin to question doctrine. This did not mean the practical Christian should despise other sects. The correct attitude, derived from an understanding of human nature, was one of forbearance and sympathy. The irrational and unnatural products of the imagination could not oppose experience forever. In time, he predicted, the ministers of all faiths would shed their superstitions and embrace "the one true and undisputable Religion," the will of God as revealed through the regularities nature and the force of reason.

Orbiston then, would not only solve the problem of poverty by a more judicious economy of land, labor, and capital, it would also demonstrate to the world "the utility and inestimable value of the practical precepts of Christianity."[19] It would, Combe insisted,

> demonstrate that UNION is better for all, than division and opposition is for any . . . that all children may be trained to prefer Temperance and Industry to Dissipation and Idleness, and Charity and Good-Will to anger and Animosity . . . that at least nine tenths of the misery that has so long afflicted humanity, is not a necessary consequence of the work of our Creator in our nature; formation; but that it proceeds from the removable Ignorances of Man, on account of which he has been induced to listen to the evidences of his own imagination, in preference to the knowledge which God has revealed to his sense and to his understanding.[20]

The fundamental goal of the Orbiston experiment was thus the formation of character; the transformation of men, women, and children from the self-centered and sensual creatures of the old world to the rational, moral, and Christian beings intended by God.

THE FIRST SOCIETY OF ADHERENTS TO DIVINE REVELATION

Drawing together the agricultural, architectural, economic, and educational principles laid out in Owen's writings, Combe presented his scheme to investors in *The Sphere for Joint Stock Companies; or the Way to increase the Value of Land, Capital, and Labour* (1825). Convinced that the plan would be both profitable and worthy, he led the way, borrowing £20,000 to purchase 291 acres of land from Hamilton's father. In addition to this mortgage the project required a capital investment of £50,000, which he sought to raise by selling 200 shares at £250 each—£100 of which would help pay for the building, £50 help establish the workers, and the remainder, paid in quarterly installments of £10, help meet the developing needs of the society. At the first meeting of the proprietors, in October 1826, it was announced that sixteen people had purchased a total of 125 shares. By May the following year, Hamilton had put up £13,000, Combe £1,500, and several other investors—including Captain Robert O'Brien, William Falla, William Combe, and a Mrs. Rathbone of Liverpool—somewhat smaller amounts.[21] The beauty of the community was that it overthrew nothing. "It proposes to enrich all," Combe promised, "not by dispossessing the present wealth class of their riches, and distributing them amongst the poor . . . but by placing all in a condition to create new wealth for themselves, and society at large."[22] The entrepreneur was not to blame for the ills of the market, he assured investors, but the distributor, whose disproportionate profit taking, unjust dealings, and chancy speculations robbed owners of their rewards and kept operatives in a state of artificial poverty.[23] By putting money directly into a working community geared to self-sufficiency and moral education, lenders would be sure to enjoy handsome dividends and the reward of improving the degraded state of the lower orders. What was there to lose? Workers were bound to be more productive without a middle man, and if the experiment did fail, the property could always be sold and debts repaid. The members had even more to gain. Allowing for certain adjustments, Combe would match whatever they were paid in the old world. Although this meant considerable differences in income, equality would be preserved by limiting all members to the same weekly allowance at the Society's store: the residue accumulating as stock in the community, with a 5 percent annual interest payment in cash. Lastly, any profits earned by the Society would be divided equally and added to the shares of everyone over the age of eighteen. No one could draw their investment from the company, but stock could be sold to another individual.

Comprising seven departments of industry and public works, the community would employ the latest technology, scientific practices, and rational methods to ensure productivity and social order. Deep-spade cultivation and other modern farming techniques would help produce food more efficiently; a clothing section would manufacture cheap tunics; and a common kitchen, dining room, laundry, and central heating system would avoid unnecessary duplication of domestic recourses. The nonprofit general store would sell products for labor notes, and a sense of solidarity would be fostered through open management, communal meeting halls, and integrated living spaces. As at New Lanark, the nucleus of the system was the formation of character. Adults would gradually be adapted to the superior habits required for full membership within the community, whereas children would be educated from infancy according to the principles pioneered by Owen. "The right education of the rising generation . . . under DIVINE PROVIDENCE . . . [was] the base upon which the future prosperity and happiness of the community must be founded."[24]

To enter Orbiston, applicants had to accept eleven articles of agreement.[25] The first indicated that no distinctions would be recognized "except those of Nature and which arise from superior habits and attainments."[26] Men and women, it stated, were to be regarded as having equal rights in all respects. In practice, however, Orbiston was very much a male-dominated society. There were separate meetings and facilities for the two sexes, and Combe stipulated that women would only be allowed half the credit men received at the store. Old society, he asserted, had corrupted female nature, training women "to live entirely secluded from their fellow creatures, in a state of sloth and negligence, and in the daily practice of many pernicious habits" and "irrational notions."[27] Other articles explained that members had the freedom to work as and when they pleased; that everyone would value their own labor; that the education of the children would be paid for by the community; and that Orbiston would be run by an elected general manager, seemingly styled on Owen, who, although not subject to the majority's wishes, could be removed if he or she lost the confidence of the group. Finally, article XI required that all applicants had "to give, to the Spirit of Religion, of Loyalty, and of Ambition, which exists in the Human Mind, the direction which Experience proves to be most conducive to the general welfare and happiness of Mankind."[28] Here was Combe's license to engineer character in accord with the principles of the new system. The members of the Orbiston community would become adherents to divine revelation as they slowly but surely learned to follow the dictates of reason and experience.

Like other Owenites, Combe proposed to improve character through the use of a psychological eye. C. T. Craig, for example, adapted the silent monitor, producing an abacus-like board of colored cubes that displayed every student's behavior at the front of the classroom. These readings were then entered into his register, the "Classometer." Together, he reported, these devices "powerfully stimulated the pupil to moral and intellectual exertion and rectitude of conduct, by appealing to those faculties of the mind which are the best instruments in the hands of a judicious teacher for the rational development of the superior faculties."[29] Similarly, George Mudie, editor of the *Economist* (1821–22) and a founder of the London Cooperative and Economical Society, explained how members earnest on moral improvement would team up to regulate one another and admonish any faults that might endanger the "general harmony and mutual esteem and goodwill."[30] Owen had proven Godwin correct; there was no more powerful stimulus than public approbation. "All that is requisite" in regulating human desire, Combe confidently asserted, was to let "individuals know the nature of the impressions which their conduct makes upon the community," or rather, as he later qualified his argument, "the rational portion of Society."[31] "The Eye of the Community, and the inward feeling produced, will soon either create a change of conduct, or make the individual retire from the Society."[32]

His own analysis of motives infused Owen's teachings with phrenological insights. "The Phrenological mode of arranging the faculties," he argued, promised to revolutionize education, teaching children "in a few hours, to have a more correct idea of the powers of the human mind, than those 'philosophers' have been able to obtain, by their own system, devoted to this one object."[33] Yet Combe's classification of instincts remained somewhat heterodox and obviously colored by his overriding commitment to the plasticity of human nature. The key to happiness was to tie these natural impulses to the concrete realities of life, as revealed by experience, rather than the artificial desires manufactured by the imagination. To manage this process, each member's character was to be quantified on a scale of goodness. If positive and negative habits on a given trait balanced, a score of 4 would be awarded, yielding a composite of 28 for all seven instincts. This number would then be recorded and each individual ranked in the Society. As a person's behavior improved, a committee of peers would then vote to elevate his or her standing. The same practice would also be adopted with children, rendering, Combe believed "all other rewards and punishments unnecessary."[34] At first a natural aristocracy would rule the community. But as character improved, and individuals rose in rank, a society of equals would emerge. Whether or not these exact procedures were followed at Orbiston is unclear, but there is ample evidence in the pages of the Society's biweekly newspaper, the *Register,* to show how public praise and disgrace were used to shape behavior.

Combe knew that the long-term future of the community rested with the education of the children. Aware that

youth, like the softened wax, *with ease* will take
Those images which *first impressions* make

he had embedded the Owenite principle that infants should be separated from their parents into the very structure of the Orbiston estate.[35] On either side of the main building dormitories were to be constructed with accompanying rooms to house "the infant children of both sexes, and the females under 18 years" at one end, "the children above six years of age, and males under 18 years, at the other."[36] Breaking down the family was both a pivotal and a controversial axiom of the community. In addition to promoting a sound constitution, "good tempers and habits," the school's curriculum would ensure facility "in reading, writing, and accounts . . . the elements of most useful sciences; including Geography and Natural History" and a practical knowledge of agriculture and domestic economy, plus "a trade useful for employment and the improvement of mental and physical powers."[37] Children would be eased into the work of the community, an hour a week at age eight, two at nine, and so on until they reached full-time labor at fourteen. He did not think anyone should toil more than six hours a day. Finally, the child was to "acquire a knowledge of himself and human nature" so as to "form him into a rational being, and render him charitable, kind, and benevolent to all his fellow creatures."[38] As for pedagogy, Combe embraced the methods employed at New Lanark and promised to establish a Normal school so that the science of character formation could be refined and developed for other communities.

Secure in the revealed truth of God's moral government, Combe was in no mood to wait for investors. On March 18, 1825, with the sale of stock just beginning, 100 men were hired to construct the main building using stone mined from a quarry just 500 yards away. The dining room, kitchen, bake house, and the majority of one wing were completed in only six months. Next came the erection of the workshop, a five-floor complex situated close by on the banks of the river containing space for blacksmiths, weavers, carpenters, wheelwrights, printers, painters, shoemakers, and tailors. As the work progressed, Combe commenced publication of the *Register* to teach his doctrines to new members and provide the world an accurate account of his momentous experiment. The first issue, on November 10, explained the meaning of the term "divine revelation" (distinguishing the truths of reason and sense from the contents of the Bible) and laid out the principles the community would follow. There was an account of the building's progress addressed to the London Cooperative Society and some discussion of drinking among the workers. The second number contained a lighthearted dig at Hamilton's organ of wit for his reaction to hearing that Orbiston had been nicknamed "Babylon" by the locals, an exposition of how each individual could wield the principle of divine revelation as the "line and plummet" of truth, a justification for the Society's name, and some discussion of the character of the people applying for residence. This was to become an important issue for Combe in the following weeks, as he struggled to reconcile his principles with the obvious dangers of admitting applicants of low character and ability. Unwilling to blame an individual for the effects of the old system, he refused to turn away anyone who professed a sincere desire for membership. Those that faked interest, he consoled himself, would soon leave when they found the eye of the community upon them. More positively, he distilled his views on knowledge and character formation into a series of seven lessons so that adherents would understand where their interests lay and how they might bring their physical and mental desires under rational control. He also published a catechism of his rational creed, to which all who entered Orbiston had to assent. There was provision for applicants to explain in writing why they could not accept any of Combe's doctrines, but given the background of those who enrolled, it is doubtful that many took this step seriously. In the third number, published as the roofers were busy laying slates and the carpenters modeling the interior, Combe tackled the thorny issue of justifying the ambitious educational plans laid out in the *Joint Stock* proposal to those who entered Orbiston without children. His solution was to advance each child a loan, repayable with interest, through future labor within the Society. A sound investment for friends of the society, he was sure this small debt, equivalent to six months of labor, would be gladly repaid by the future citizens of the community.

By April, as the first stage of the project neared completion, Combe dismissed the workers and opened Orbiston to anyone willing to help finish the construction and start life under the new system. This proved to be something of a mistake, for as the *Register* indicates, without proper training, residents were still struggling to complete the building a year later. Originally the plan had been to advertise for members, but as word of the site spread, people flooded to Orbiston of their own accord, and to Hamilton's disgust, none were turned away. Combe himself recognized that most "had come to avoid the evils of the old system, rather than obtain the advantages of the new"[39] Some were physically incapable of labor, others had no trade or useful skill, and many had absolutely no clue what life in an Owenite community entailed. At the end of the first week, for instance, several residents approached Combe demanding a cash payment for the days they had spent preparing their apartments. Calling a general meeting, he explained the principles of Owenism and organized members into departments according to their talents and interests. Each would be paid in labor notes for the value of the work they chose to perform. But a month on this system proved a disaster. After an initial burst of enthusiasm, listlessness and discontent quickly pervaded the community. Essential tasks went undone, and, fueled by factional divisions, members started avoiding the communal spaces. Trouble seems to have erupted in the dining room where, according to one resident, the grander of the room's two tables was occupied by a self-elected elite who railed against the manners of "Brawny armed labourers."[40] The laborers, for their part, objected to what they regarded as second-class service and the unequal distribution of food. At first Combe thought it best to wait until individuals came face-to-face with the consequence of their actions; after all, that was natural logic by which God governed the world. But after discussions with more orthodox Owenites within the society, he hit upon the idea of restructuring Orbiston along military lines. The community, he reasoned, was rather like a group of raw recruits who needed to be drilled in squads and organized into companies before it could operate harmoniously. This new scheme had hardly gotten off the ground when Combe overexerted himself digging in the fields. Physically and emotionally spent, he was forced to return to Edinburgh and the care of his brother Andrew. Two weeks later, as reports of the chaotic situation reached his bedside, Combe faced up to the task before him. The population was coarse, boisterous, and plagued with revolting habits. Drinking and the use of tobacco were on the rise, and, even though the proprietors had employed a local man to empty pots, dunghills were appearing below windows. Calling the population "a herd of animals," the resident and proprietor Captain Robert O'Brien wrote to Combe cautioning that "*complete failure* was now inevitable, unless we dismissed a great proportion of the present inhabitants, and supplied their places with a selection of superior workmen."[41] Given the tenor of these remarks, it is understandable why O'Brien was so annoyed when Combe broke confidence and published his letter in the *Register*. Combe felt obliged to air all viewpoints openly, but the resulting fallout only served to fuel growing class tensions. To make matters worse, property values had dropped in the slump of 1826, and the land was mortgaged way beyond its value. Such conditions presented a severe test, Combe admitted in a letter to the community. But he would not waver in his commitment. Orbiston would meet all challenges. It would reform the character of the most wretched and promote the interests of the capitalist, even in an economic recession.

Combe desperately sought ways to stimulate members to work. His chance came when a number of tenets asked permission to establish an iron foundry. Valuing union and cooperation over the principle of equal distribution, he agreed that it would be inappropriate for them to sink their labor and capital into such a project without any opportunity of reward. Suspending the community's rules and breaking a fundamental axiom of Owen's scheme, he turned the group into an independent company that paid workers double the stock from the profits of their labor. Not everyone was happy with the introduction of individual enterprise, but given the pressures on the community, Combe carried the day. The change was instantaneous. In a few weeks the industry and intelligence of the group surpassed his fondest expectations. Similar plans were devised for other departments, and in short order the gardeners, shoemakers, printers, weavers, and masons all had their own companies. By late August Combe was nearly ecstatic about the possibility of commercial success—the community would soon be able to afford holiday homes in Edinburgh and the Highlands, and workers might even retire at age thirty-five! Recognizing that success still rested with the development of character, Combe redoubled his efforts to mold new citizens. He implored sobriety and pleaded with parents to curb the loud and boisterous behavior of their children. But his greatest hope for moral reform came with the addition of Catherine Whitwell, the teacher whom William Allen had dismissed from the school at New Lanark. A committed Owenite with strong religious sentiments and a resolute nature, she brought energy and experience to the task of schooling the community's younger children. She also lectured on the Christian duty of parents, revealing to the Society that the entire history of vice and virtue could be accounted for by the kind of character training individuals received in their first seven years. This was an important lesson. With one-half of the building yet to be constructed, and parts of the existing wing still unfinished, many of Orbiston's eighty-six children were still forced to sleep in their parents' quarters. Those who were housed in the dormitories lacked adequate supervision: washing facilities were inadequate, and, according to later accounts, many were dressed in dirty or torn clothing. Add to this the problem of loud and rowdy games in the corridors and hallways and truancy and rebelliousness in the schools, and it becomes obvious why education became such a pressing problem. Most important was the behavior of a few older boys whose unruly actions had been observed and reported by a correspondent from the *Glasgow Free Press*. These lads, Henry Kirkpatrick (the new editor the *Register*) explained, were in the most unfortunate position of "having been born a little too soon."[42] Because of its disorganized state, the community had done nothing to address all the bad habits they had acquired from their infancy and childhood in the old world. But now, as reason was developing, positive efforts were under way. Miss Whitwell had undertaken evening instruction in good habits and morals, "writing and arithmetic, geometry, drawing, music and dancing, geography, general history, etc.," and Alexander Campbell—a Glasgow carpenter who later joined the Ham Common Socialists—was superintending them during the day.

In a letter to the *Register*, Campbell explained that, after outlining the essentials of order to twenty of the boys, all agreed to record cases of misconduct in a book and elected superintendents to report on their behavior at each general meeting.[43] Their conduct, he later reported, continued to improve. They met every Sunday to discuss the events of the previous week, and the majority was soon gainfully employed learning useful trades. "So ardent were they in their proceedings," he cheerfully concluded, "that I am completely convinced that these boys, under proper management, will, in the course of a few years, be the most useful members of the community."[44] Life was improving at Orbiston. Every day, Kirkpatrick added, brought new and exciting evidence that their great experiment in human nature was a resounding success. The "power of public opinion, so concentrated as it necessarily is under our present arrangements," was improving both young and old. Drunkenness, swearing, and smoking were declining; industriousness and virtue were on the rise. He was "very much inclined to think, that *no character whatever* could long resist the improving effects of *this* manner of living together."[45]

Restricted to his bed in Edinburgh, after a second collapse, Abram Combe also had reason to be hopeful. His belief that, as members of the community became increasingly enlightened, they would choose the new system for themselves seemed to be coming true, although rather sooner than he expected. In his absence several of the more orthodox Owenites had crashed a meeting called to consider whether the carpenters should form a company patterned after that of the foundry men. Determined to stem the spread of capitalism, they challenged the ethicalness of policies that undermined the original principles on which Orbiston was founded. Defenders of individualism argued that the minds of some members were not yet prepared to go the full length of the system and that without the stimulus of profit it would be impossible to maintain productivity. The Owenites responded that "the generous motive would always far surpass the selfish" and that, if anyone were found remiss in his duty, the eyes of the whole community would be upon them."[46] In the end, collectivism won the day, with the compromise that all members "according to the time occupied by each" would share any surplus. Despite the opposition of the foundry workers, gardeners, and other company men, this principle was then embraced by a majority of the community. Fired with enthusiasm, the Owenites predicted a rosy future. Individuals could be fairly remunerated for their efforts while working for the common good and, by instituting more careful controls, expenditures could be trimmed, providing funds with which to purchase the community from the proprietors. Although Combe thought this all rather precipitous, he wrote supporting the move to equal distribution, but cautioned the group not to force its will on the approximately one-third of the Society that opposed the new system. They had to learn the value of this principle for themselves. Even so, he agreed that greater order must be brought to the enterprise and, extending his earlier notion of squads, directed the community to institute a system of supervision that broke down all work into divisions and branches. Invoking Owen-like industrial controls, he mandated weekly meetings in which directors and superintendents would report productivity, expenditure, and the performance of all the workers.

The proprietors cautiously embraced the tenants' declaration, but demanded proof of a firm commitment to the new arrangements. All members, they insisted, had to assent to Owen's doctrine that "character is formed for and not by the individual" and meet the test of reelection in a secret ballot. Although none were ostracized, this bloodless revolution was not without its wounds. Anger with the new regime and the course of the community's affairs soon boiled to the surface when the outspoken O'Brien submitted a fiery letter to the *Register*. Published in the first issue of the new year, he declared himself and his friends fundamentally opposed to equal distribution (a scheme, he charged, that had been instituted to profit the elite who directed the community), the selection of tenants, and the care and education of children. He also resented being "impressed, into a Society under the nickname of Adherents to Divine Revelation, where nothing was meant, than natural religion, to the exclusion of revelation, as received amongst mankind."[47] Evidently considering himself a cut above the "brawny labourers" whose idle ways, course language, and rude manners had subverted the entire experiment, he feared for the mind and morals of his children. Education was dear to O'Brien's heart. Without casting any aspersions on Catherine Whitwell, "whose zeal, disinterestedness, good feeling, perseverance, and talents" were beyond question, he deplored the lack of organization and investment in what was after all the community's most important division.[48] O'Brien had a bold solution: he proposed establishing a boarding school, "a manufacture of mind," for between 100 and 200 fee-paying students. The money generated would then fund all the expenses of rearing Orbiston's children, including a "school of labour."[49] He had no "objection to the amalgamation of the two classes of children, as soon as their habits of cleanliness and acquirements justified such mixture."[50] In fact, the same teachers could run both schools—he had in mind a fully qualified assistant for Miss Whitwell and two gentlemen from Switzerland who had studied with Pestalozzi for nine and twelve years respectively. The sticking point, he explained, was that to accommodate the new inmates, the Society's children would have to vacate their dormitory and sleep in the attic until the new wing of the building was completed.

Combe, who admitted neglecting children while he struggled to ensure the economic security of the Society, responded that he "felt a considerable aversion to hire teachers at a high salary, both because our funds required to be managed with economy, and because I thought that men who required to be tempted with money to engage in such an undertaking, were by this very circumstance disqualified for this office."[51] As for O'Brien's views on the admission of tenants, Combe responded that it was *he* who was unacceptable! Orbiston had been established "to Banish Poverty and Vice, and to ascertain to what height the *lowest* of the working classes could be raised by their own industry, under a system of Justice and Equity."[52] How could this object be achieved if he was forced to "look upon a poor or even vicious individual as unworthy of admission?"[53] "I am still compelled to think I acted judiciously in *rejecting none* of the applicants," he concluded.[54]

Such public battles did not help heal the divisions within the community, which, as time passed, appear to have solidified into three distinct camps: the Owenites who ruled the management committee and through the press controlled the official voice of the society; the defenders of individualism, who grew increasingly unhappy with the financial arrangements, the strict supervision, and the austerity measures; and the laborers, who, less concerned with ideological struggles, remained in the community only to meet their immediate needs. Orbiston limped along. Generally, reports were optimistic. The *Register* pointed to the Society's increasing refinement, its theatre, choral music society, and public lectures. With more than a thousand pear and apple trees planted, and a dairy and piggary established, it boasted that the agricultural department could easily support 100 families on 300 acres of land. The press even apologized for its failure to publish the *Register* due to a backlog of printing orders. When Abram Combe finally succumbed to illness on August 11, 1827, he died believing that Orbiston "was established beyond the point of failure."[55] "If *any* epitaph is written on me," he pleaded, "may it simply be . . . THAT HIS CONDUCT IN LIFE MET THE APPROBATION OF HIS OWN MIND AT THE HOUR OF HIS DEATH."[56] Owen, back in Britain from New Harmony, arrived at Combe's deathbed just six hours later. His greatest disciple had passed away and, as he soon discovered at Orbiston, the nation's first experiment in socialism was facing a similar fate.

With William Combe now in charge of finances, it became evident that the hefty interest payments left little profit with which to pay off the community's £40,000 debt. The foundry, for example, reported only a small surplus of £232. Fueled by O'Brien's warnings that the community was on the verge of breaking up, several proprietors refused to meet their financial obligations. In March, William Combe wrote to Hamilton complaining of the Society's lack of funds. Without an immediate infusion of cash, he warned, "the consequences may be very serious."[57] Money was advanced to carry the group until harvest time but was evidently either insufficient or poorly managed. As gloom spread, Orbiston's problems were exacerbated by the rise of soldiering, the reporting of false hours, and the pilfering of food from the Society's storehouse—presumably given or sold to family and friends in the locality. Preaching more self-denial and generous conduct, the *Register* asked how, under such burdens, the Society could ever hope to create wealth? Workers started to lose confidence in the enterprise, and the value of the stock plummeted. Robert Hicks, for example, left the community selling his shares at 50 percent of their original value. As austerity measures were increased, life under the eye proved too much for many residents. Positive until the end, the final issue of the *Register* followed George Combe's "Memoir of Mr. Abram Combe" with a bucolic picture of residents eagerly and cheerfully reaping the corn. As if to salvage what it could from the experiment, it reported none "of that brutal swearing and obscene jesting which are most commonly so disgusting in the harvest field," but a polite and intelligent discourse "on interesting topics related to the community."[58] The whole tenor of the place had changed. Men, women, and children showed striking improvements in character. Where once residents spent their Sundays idling in their rooms, they were now found on the benches clean and well dressed, quietly "reading books or contemplating the beauties of the scenery, being evidently pleased and satisfied with the circumstances in which they are placed."[59]

The whole affair finally came to a head when the Society defaulted upon its mortgage payments, and the Scottish Union Insurance Company decided to call in its loan. This meant the immediate liquidation of the company and all its assets. Just three months after Abram's death, an eviction note was served upon the residents. Taking charge of the auction, George Combe sold the community's produce and machinery without reserve and placed the property up for sale. Of little use to other manufacturers, Orbiston remained on the market for more than two years. Finally, a neighboring landowner purchased it for £15,000. A longtime opponent of the community, she immediately had the building razed. Not a stone remains to mark the site. Several members of the foundry company wound up in debtor's prison, and William Combe fled to America, where, as his brother George later put it, "he displays the same want of energy on the other side of the Atlantic that formed so striking a feature of his character on this."[60]

In 1841, Owen presented *A Development of the Principles and Plans on*

Which to Establish Self-Sustaining Home Colonies.[61] As his subtitle indicated, the father of socialism was still convinced that "Ignorance, Poverty, and Crime" could be permanently removed and the material benefit of all classes assured "by giving a Right Application to the now Greatly Misdirected Powers of the Human Faculties." To support his argument, Owen included in his appendix a chapter from George Combe's *Moral Philosophy.* Owen clearly approved of Combe's analysis of the old world, his critique of capitalism, and the social institutions that brutified the minds of the population. Turning men and women into "labouring animals" was hardly God's plan for humankind. Throughout history, Combe observed, certain individuals have glimpsed a more natural state in which justice and benevolence could reign. Plato's *Republic* was perhaps the first example of such a utopia; leaders of religious sects, such as George Rapp of the Harmonites in Indiana, had envisioned others. More recently, Combe continued, Owen had drawn on the social sciences in his efforts to engineer the same end. Blessed with favorable conditions and a strong leadership that ensured complete solidarity to religious principles, the Harmonites had enjoyed great prosperity and the delights of life governed by the moral and rational faculties. Owen's scheme at New Harmony proved less successful. By opening his doors to all who professed his principles, he admitted men and women who were constitutionally incapable of acting "in accordance with the dictates of the moral sentiments and intellect."[62] The same was true of Abram's experiment. Without "efficient direction or superintendence . . . and no habitual supremacy of the moral and intellectual powers . . . to animate [operatives] with a love of the public good . . . the result was melancholy and speedy."[63] Combe reiterated the same conclusion in his private correspondence. "The great error in Orbiston" he told William, "has been the putting the cart before the horse."[64] "To produce union and cooperation there must be harmony of principle," and this demanded "highly *enlightened* and *moralized*" individuals.[65] A person of "great and commanding mind, who is thoroughly persuaded of its truth himself" could hold individuals together by strong religious enthusiasm.[66] But this was not Abram's nature. There was a great difference

> between *feeling* in favor of union and co-operation, and *intellectually understanding* the principles of human nature and *percieving* [sic] *how* to suit external circumstances to its wants. I have considered our late lamented brother Abram, and the founder of Orbiston more in the first

condition than the last. In short, as reason and benovelence [*sic*] were to form the bonds of union, the establishment should have been delayed until, by education or by books, a sufficient number of individuals had been prepared—by the ascendancy [*sic*] of these principles in their minds—for carrying their principles into practical effect.[67]

"A higher, purer, and happier state of society" was possible if, as "the success of Mr. Rapp" demonstrated, "the animal propensities [could] be controlled by the strength of moral and religious principle."[68] Owen agreed, pointing to the success of fifteen other communities in North America that had banished private property. But Combe was more circumspect. Before submitting to "poetical fancies" on the basis of "this almost solitary example," he suggested a careful examination of human nature to determine "whether such capacities were "laying dormant within us."[69] His conclusion, as the next chapter illustrates, was less optimistic. Men and women would advance to this superior state, but it would take generations following the laws of inheritance and exercise.

8

The Philosophy of Christianity

I see an immense field of practical application of the principles before me, and feel convinced that my philosophic labors, if life and health remain, are only beginning; and now all fear and doubt and hesitation are removed. I have got hold of the principle of divine administration, and most holy, perfect and admirable it appears. Now I can say for the first time in my life that I love God with all my heart and soul and mind; because now I see Him as an object altogether gratifying to Benevolence, Veneration, Hope, Ideality, Conscientiousness, Comparison, and Causality.

George Combe, *Life of Combe*, 1878

George Combe, who claimed to have "perused with attention Mr. Owen's printed works . . . heard that gentleman publicly expound his system, and . . . frequently conversed with him in private," first visited New Lanark in September 1820. He was "exceedingly delighted," especially by the educational arrangements Owen had made for the village's 400 children. Recalling the noise of the students "romping and playing in great spirits," he assured his brother Andrew that this was "a chorus of mirth and kindness, and not the early growl of selfish passions."[1] At ten o'clock the children were assembled for marching, followed by music and dance. An hour later they settled down to lessons on the "Lancasterian plan," before finishing the day as it had begun. "Mr. Owen," Combe noted approvingly, was "well aware of the difference betwixt words and things" and had "ordered £500 worth of transparent pictures representing objects interesting to the youthful mind" so that students would "form ideas at the same time they learn words."[2] Everything was directed by the great lesson "that life may be enjoyed, and that each may make his own happiness consistent with that of all the others."[3] If Owen's pedagogy captivated Combe's imagination, Combe's science of mind was equally interesting to Owen. "Astonished at the facility and correctness" with which he determined the student's characters, "Mr. Owen ordered two books and two casts to be sent out by the first coach" and invited Combe to return another time to register the children's heads in a book so that he could "see how they turn out."[4] Owen's own head, however, was something of a disappointment. The height and length were fair, but the breadth was narrow: "Dominated by the sentiments, he had the brain of a moral enthusiast rather than an intellect."[5]

The theory and practice of education was an important concern for Combe in the early 1820s. In the *Essays* he had explained the importance of training the faculties and disseminating useful knowledge, but, although endorsing the education of the lower orders, he had nothing substantive to say about curricula or pedagogy. It was after editing Spurzheim's *Education* that his thoughts turned to the broader issue of moral reform and the social significance of schooling. Two further visits to New Lanark, in 1822 and 1823, provided the opportunity to assimilate Owen's methods to Spurzheim's science of mind. Glimpsing a widening field of practical activity, he wrote to his friend, the theologian and phrenologist David Welsh, sharing his ambition to open a school based on a reformulated version of Owen's educational scheme. The key was to separate Owen's pedagogy from his socialism, environmentalism, millennialism, and atheism and structure teaching around the gradualist view of human nature and the social good implicit in phrenology.

This assessment, which Combe presents rather bluntly in his 1824 article "Phrenological Analysis of Mr. Owen's New Views," clearly upset Owen, who, having shown sympathy to phrenology, was probably not expecting such a thoroughgoing critique from the brother of his most ardent disciple.[6] He may also have been disturbed to read that the morally correct elements of his new system flowed directly from his large organs of benevolence and love of approbation, while the lack of scientific proof and logical order in his writings resulted from his "decidedly deficient Causality."[7] "Owen," Combe revealed, "views the mind through the Knowing faculties, and sees it as a 'passive compound,' while a person endowed with Causality in adequate degree intuitively perceives it to consist of a combination of *active energies* which may be regulated, but not extirpated or fashioned according to our will."[8] Contrary to Owen's assertions, men and women were not born equal, nor was their character uniformly plastic. As Spurzheim suggested, so Combe believed that "human beings may be divided into three great classes."[9] "The first, in which the animal propensities pre-dominate so much over the moral sentiments and intellect, that naturally they are extremely prone to vicious indulgences hurtful to themselves and society"; the second, in which "the animal propensities are nearly equally balanced by the moral sentiments and intellect, and the *habitual* preponderance of either depends upon the influence of external causes"; and third, the smaller, rarer "elect," in which "the propensities are so powerful as to serve their necessary purposes in life, and in whom the moral sentiments and intellect so greatly predominate, that a perpetual serenity of temper and benignity of disposition reign within, and who seem already to have realized in themselves the *beau ideal* of a perfect human being."[10] According to Combe, Owen was simply wrong to think that the first group could be schooled into rational and moral citizens. A threat to any society, their lower organs had to be constrained by a mixture of external government and moral training. The second set was more susceptible to improvement, under appropriate moral leadership. But such training could not follow Owen's simplistic calculus in which all human motives are reduced to the promotion of pleasure over pain. Phrenology demonstrated that men and women are compound creatures driven by a variety of intractable impulses. Ignoring basic drives such as acquisitiveness, love of approbation, self-esteem, secretiveness, and veneration only frustrated human needs, leading, Combe announced prophetically, to an explosion of emotions that would destroy society. Take, for example, love of offspring. According to Owen's plan, the community must assume responsibility for all aspects of education, and parents must delight equally in the advancement and happiness of all the society's children. Although such feelings might be possible for one, such as Owen, "in whom benevolence is stronger than philoprogenetiveness," it was obvious to Combe that "nature has constituted man with a sentiment of self-love, and combined it with a love of offspring" such that, "impelled by these instinctive impulses," he would "cherish his own offspring as part of himself."[11] Any "system which should attempt to limit or control such feelings, will be regarded as an intolerable restraint upon the best of our natural affections."[12] In a footnote, Abram protested that Owen's system would diminish "those instances in which children are *troublesome* to their parents" and promote "the pleasure of all without destroying the natural affection of either side."[13] But as events at Orbiston demonstrated, Combe had the stronger argument.

As for Owen's pedagogical innovations, great improvements could be made by grounding the methods of infant and elementary education in phrenological laws. In his letter to Welsh, written after his third visit to New

Lanark in 1823, Combe explained how he would teach children the laws of nature outlined in Spurzheim's book on education. "Let them see from infancy the real situation in which they stand as created beings; and point out to what extent they are arbiters of their own fate, or at least how conduct and happiness are joined."[14] "In addition to the natural sciences, to which Owen's Symbolic Instruction is confined," he also advocated teaching students "the principles of hygiene or dietetics, of political economy, and of the law of the country in which they live. I see a great suffering produced from a want of a slight knowledge of this last kind," which, he added, "might be given in a few pages and quite intelligible to youths below seventeen."[15] Owen, Combe reported, taught morality "independently of the Bible and Catechism" by relating actions to natural circumstances. But the accounts he gave of good or evil behavior did not prepare students for the future. Phrenology would provide a far better guide to individual conduct, and, by revealing the rules governing the cerebral organs, would better inform students of the dangers to society posed by the inherently wicked. Finally, unlike Owen, Combe would structure education around religion.

> Having explained nature's laws, I would lead them up to God; in obeying His laws you obey Him. If children have not 30 (Comparison) and 31 (Causality) sufficiently strong to see the advantages of obedience, perhaps they have enough of 14 (Veneration) and 15 (Hope) to venerate the laws and to yield obedience on account of the lawgiver, and to expect in the spirit of faith that reward which they cannot realise by positive perception. This would not exclude the duties of repentance, prayer and praise; nor ought the view of good and evil to be limited to this life. At present half the benefits of 14 are lost to practical results.[16]

THE CONSTITUTION OF MAN

By 1826, as Abram struggled to realize his own Christianized version of Owen's social philosophy, George Combe had even given up on "repentance, prayer and praise" for a thoroughgoing natural theology, secularism. Even if the soul were not immortal, he had told David Welsh in the summer of 1825, "I would regard the works of the Supreme Being, and religion both in practice and in spirit, as rational and delightful."[17] Indeed, he continued, the belief in immortality, combined with the notion that this world is all ajar, has a bad effect on ignorant minds. They attribute evils which result from their own gross errors in conduct to the system of things, and fly to dreams of future happiness as compensation for their miseries instead of proceeding to obey the dictates of nature and remove them.[18]

Chief among the abuses of religion was "trusting to the efficacy of prayer instead of . . . obedience to the laws of the moral and physical world."[19] What difference would it make to the justification of the Christian life, he challenged Welsh, if there were no hereafter? Nature and divine revelation had to be in complete harmony.

The previous year, Spurzheim had given Combe a manuscript, later published as *Philosophical Catechism of the Natural Laws of Man,* in which carefully chosen passages from Scripture were used to justify that men's and women's duty to God was to obey the laws of creation.[20] Building upon these arguments, Combe composed "On Human Responsibility as Affected by Phrenology," a radical attack on the Calvinist view of the human condition that deeply disturbed orthodox members of the Phrenological Society.[21] But if Welsh and other evangelicals were shocked, their bewilderment turned to horror and indignation when, in the final months of 1826, Combe developed his argument into the series of essays that would become the *Constitution of Man.* Pressed on one side to publish, on the other to withdraw, Combe agreed to hold his manuscript for six months in order that someone might offer a cogent refutations of his thesis. William Scott, editor of the *Journal,* distributed a lengthy critique of Combe's principles. Combe responded, Scott fired off a rejoinder—and the infidel book, as it became known, hit the presses.

When the dust settled, the Society had split down religious lines. "Fundamentally erroneous, and contrary both to sound natural reason and to sound Scriptural doctrine," Scott claimed Combe doctrines were no different to the materialism and atheism of the *Idéologues.*[22] It is worth pausing to consider why. Combe had set out to reconcile the causal necessity of the physical world with the moral necessity of human responsibility. Phrenology taught that all actions were produced by the excitement of the organs. The sight of money, for example, might engage acquisitiveness, producing a desire to steal. But this did not lead directly to theft, as the resultant feeling also aroused the disgust of the moral sentiments. It was at this stage that the intellect weighed in, siding with the stronger motives to yield the person's will, a force accompanied by a vivid sense of freedom that masked the underlying causal sequence of mental events. As anyone familiar with phrenological laws understood, a given person in a given situation would always be compelled to act in a given way. So what then of responsibility? Combe dropped a bombshell. Responsibility had nothing to do with free will! It followed solely from the relations of cause and effect established by the Creator. Two kinds of responsibility could be distinguished: internal and external. The former referred to the way in which individuals suffered the torment of their own conscience; the latter, the consequences that followed from the effects of an individual's behavior on others. Here Combe took aim at the criminal code. In nature, he observed, animal interactions were totally governed by the propensities. So it was with the law, which, ignoring the cause of events, visited violence with violence. A scientific understanding of the mind suggested replacing such punishments with moral treatment. By subduing the passions and stimulating the sentiments, he was certain that many criminals could be trained to manage their own animal nature. For a Calvinist, equating responsibility with internal and external consequences totally distorted the meaning of the term, which, Scott pointed out, "implied answering to someone, as a child answers to parents, a servant answers to a master, and all men and women answer to God."[23] Moreover, he maintained, knowledge of God's will could not be derived through science, only through the reading of the Scriptures. Combe assumed that God had crafted the world in such a way that the pleasure and pain of experiences served as a guide to human happiness. This was absurd. No doubt knowledge of natural laws could be used to improve the human estate, but this did not imply *every* event was designed to promote our well-being. In what way did the agony of a child writhing in pain after mistakenly swallowing arsenic reveal God's benevolent design? As for Combe's ideas on punishment, Scott bitterly objected to the apparent equation of criminal behavior with misfortune, as if guilt were something that happened to a person. And, far from being animalistic, Scott insisted, the law was a wise institution, carefully designed to protect decent individuals.

But Combe's break with Calvinism was complete: phrenology had become the philosophy of Christianity. Freed from a system of thought that excited only the base emotions—promising eternal torment or everlasting bliss—he found salvation in his new loving relationship with God. "True religion," he wrote in his journal, "had to recognize that God created man that he might be happy," and this implied discovering and obeying "the divine laws, from conviction that they alone are suited to gratify all our faculties."[24] Sin was not a wicked act to be forgiven through prayer, but a physical evil to be eradicated from the body. This meant amending brains and adapting external circumstances so that the desire for virtue and intelligence could blossom within each individual. The final nail in the coffin, as far as the evangelicals were concerned, came when Combe pushed these insights into a thoroughgoing attack on Calvinism in his 1831 essay "On Human Capability of Improvement."[25] Rejecting the concept of original depravity, he blamed traditional institutions for relegating the mind to perpetual savagery. Only a phrenologically informed practical religion could elevate men and women to their full potential as Christian beings. The orthodox simply could not tolerate such radical doctrines; Welsh resigned as president and many others deserted the Society. Under the guidance of the orthodox, Combe complained, the *Journal* had stopped all efforts to "render [phrenology] more than a subject of mere scientific or literary curiosity."[26] It was now time to reveal his "stupendous discovery in relation to the moral world."[27] If the evangelicals could not be convinced to join him, he could at least take his secular philosophy to those in the population who would like to see a little more of the kingdom of heaven here on Earth.

Combe opened the *Constitution* with the assertion that the world had been adapted to virtue. Every object, including the body and the brain, was crafted with a precise set of powers that caused events to follow independent, universal, unbending, and invariant laws. Obedience to these laws was "attended with its own reward, disobedience with its own punishment."[28] As Bishop Butler argued, so Combe reasoned that human beings were thus "under God's government, in the same sense as we are under the government of civil magistrates."[29] After considering the human organization as revealed by phrenology, he thus presented the fundamental axiom of his moral philosophy: those who obey God's ordinance "enjoy the intense internal delights that spring from the active moral faculties . . . while those that disobey that law are tormented with insatiable desires, which, from the nature of things cannot be gratified."[30] The details of this naturalistic commandment had to be deciphered and disseminated if people were to realize their place in God's grand design. This implied educating the population about physical, organic, intellectual, and moral laws that supervened from their nature. For instance, to maintain health and cultivate the mind, several hours each day had to be devoted to physical exercise and mental activity. Moral and religious exercises were equally important. The problem was that society constantly disregarded this providential order; the upper classes, adopting a sedentary life, had become indolent, slaves to the love of approbation, whereas the masses, forced to labor "in habitual infringement of the important laws of their nature" had become "organized machines" rather than "moral, religious, and intellectual beings."[31]

Given the inherent goodness of the world, Combe had to demonstrate that all miseries and misfortunes resulted from the infringement of natural laws. Ignorance was no defense. God had provided animals with superior frames and an instinctive understanding of natural dangers, but human beings had to learn from their mistakes. At first glance, this might seem a cruel arrangement—how, as Scott protested, could the accidental death of an innocent child be reconciled with the concept of a beneficent universe? But, after much reflection, Combe found wisdom in God's plan. The regularity, blindness, and unbending consequences of nature provided a stern lesson that would help prevent further suffering. Abram's death provided another painful illustration of the same principle. Had he rested after his collapse, the haemoptysis in his lungs might have healed. Instead, despite the continued effusion of blood, he continued to exert himself directing the Orbiston community from his bedside. Only later, when the laws of the organ were explained to him, could he recognize his own ignorance and lament "how greatly he would have benefited if one month of the five years he had been forced to spend in a vain attempt at acquiring a mastery over the Latin tongue, had been dedicated to conveying to him information concerning the structure of his body, and the causes which preserve and impair its functions."[32]

Perhaps the most important of all natural laws were those related to the original organization and subsequent development of the human organism. To fulfill God's design, the germ from which men and women spring had to be "complete in all its parts, and sound in its whole constitution."[33] Thereafter, "as long as it continues to live it shall be supplied with food, light, air, and every physical aliment necessary for its support, including due exercise of its functions."[34] "If the corn that is sown is weak, wasted, and damaged, the plants that spring from it will be feeble, and liable to speedy decay."[35] So it was with human beings. "The feeble, the sickly, the exhausted with age, and the incompletely developed, through extreme youth, marry, and, without the least compunction regarding the organization which they shall transmit to their offspring, send into the world the miserable beings, the very rudiments of whose existence are tainted with disease."[36] The sins of the parents would be written into the very being of their children, a misery to themselves and a burden to society. What could be done? First, the laws of heredity had to be understood. Here Combe departed somewhat from Spurzheim, stressing the role of a progressive mechanism of inheritance. Recognizing that "mutations" and "other additions to, or abstractions from, natural lineaments of the body" are not transmitted to offspring, Combe drew on the observations of animal breeders and numerous personal anecdotes to support the Lamarckian formula that "the qualities of the children are determined jointly by the constitution of the stock, and the faculties which predominate in power and activity in the parents, at the particular time when the organic existence of each child commences."[37] How else could the differences between children of the same parents be explained? And, as Esquirol had observed, did not the children conceived at the height of the Terror turn out "weak, nervous and irritable in mind, extremely susceptible to impressions, and liable by the least extraordinary excitement, to be thrown into absolute insanity?"[38] Imagine then Combe's fears as he considered how many children were conceived while parents were intoxicated. Men and women alert to their Christian duty would recognize the importance of "preserving the habitual supremacy of the moral sentiments and intellect" once they realized that, by so doing, "improved moral and intellectual capacities may be conferred upon the offspring."[39] It was also common knowledge that the first offspring of a young marriage "inherits a less favorable development of the moral and intellectual organs, than those produced in a more mature age."[40] This was a particular concern, given that in Scotland women were allowed to marry at twelve and men at fourteen. Phrenology, Combe noted soberly, taught that the higher powers did not evolve for another ten years! Children born with a hereditary disease or a handicap might not regard God's system of rewards and punishments as just, but at least, Combe consoled himself, they would learn to "bow with submission to an institution" with such "blessings to the race" and form a "reverential acquiescence . . . so delightful, that it would diminish, in great degree, the severity of the evil."[41] Death was another of God's mercies. "I have departed from the natural institutions and suffer the punishment," Abram declared, "but in death, I only see the Creator's benevolent hand, stretching out to terminate my agonies, when they cease to serve any beneficial end."[42] The feeble and sickly child who passed away in infancy was no exception. Here too God's love and wisdom was apparent, preventing needless suffering and "protecting the race" by "cutting short . . . the transmission of its imperfections to posterity."[43]

Having identified many of the conditions that promote well-formed progeny, Combe turned his attention to nurture and the steps parents and society should take to ensure the full and healthy development of each individual. What most interested him were the social laws by which nations regulated the behavior of citizens. Working from the assumption that "the world is arranged on the principle of the supremacy of the moral sentiments and intellect," he set out numerous examples to show how observance of this natural directive is "attended with external advantages, and infringements of it with positively evil consequences."[44] Chief among the latter was the mental and physical condition of the population brought on by industrialization. God had not intended the mass of humankind to be turned into instruments for gratifying the selfish propensities of property owners. They too were rational and moral creatures deserving the same opportunity to realize their nature as Christian beings. But after "exhausting their muscular and nervous energy . . . for ten, twelve, and some even fourteen hours a day," there was "no time or energy for moral and intellectual pursuits."[45] Further compounded by the craving for alcohol that this state excites, the lower orders sunk deeper and deeper into an animal nature. As the economy continued to fluctuate between cycles of poverty and growth, the country reaped the grim predictions of Malthus and ever-increasing levels of crime and social degeneracy. The capitalist system was equally severe on the middle ranks, producing an insatiable lust for wealth and petty amusements that left them void of morality and intelligence. As for the higher classes, lacking any active pursuit to exercise their faculties, they were subject to "the evils of ennui, morbid irritability, and the excessive relaxation of the functions of the mind and body, which carry in their train more suffering than is entailed even on the operatives by excessive labour."[46]

Combe even phrenologized nations. Had countries followed the principle that the world was arranged in harmony with the moral sentiments and intellect, each would live together in peace, cooperatively exploiting their natural resources and promoting the advancement of its citizens. But instead they have followed their propensities. England led the way:

[She] invented restrictions on trade, and carried them to the greatest height; she conquered colonies, and ruled them in full spirit of selfishness; she encouraged lotteries and fostered the slave trade, carried paper money and the most avaricious spirit of manufacturing and speculating in commerce to their highest pitch; and defended corruption in Parliament, distributed churches and seats on the bench of Justice, on principles purely selfish.[47]

Even more egregious were the consequences of war. Fueled by acquisitiveness, self-esteem, and destructiveness, Britain had invested its great wealth in combat, incurring massive debts that trapped the nation in a well of economic blight. Consider if just one "twentieth part of the sums" expended in the wars with America and France had been spent on "instituting seminaries of education, penitentiaries, making roads, canals, [and] public granaries . . . how different would be the present condition of the country?"[48]

The advancement of the physical sciences contributed greatly to the possibility of improving material conditions, but this was nothing compared to the advantages that would flow from a science of morals. Politics, legislation, and especially education could all be revolutionized once the phrenological view of mind was accepted. Sectarian disputes would dissipate when it was understood that each individual's faith was determined by the distinctive organization of his or her mental faculties; the different classes would learn to work in a social and economic system that promoted the well-being of all; and nations, so long at one another's throats, would learn the advantages of justice and cooperation.

As the failure of Owenism demonstrated, such transformations would take generations. There was "no practical error," Combe warned, "greater than that of establishing institutions greatly in advance of the mental condition of the people."[49] Human improvement demanded the formation of a new character, and this, as Owen had understood, must begin by teaching the young the natural laws of God's universe.

Their minds, not being pre-occupied with prejudices, will recognize them as being congenial to their constitution; the first generation that has embraced them from infancy will proceed to modify the institutions of society into accordance with their dictates; and in the course of ages they may at length be acknowledged as practically useful . . . a perception [which] . . . will lead to their observance, and this will be attended with an improved development of the brain, thereby increasing the desire and capacity for obedience.[50]

"Education" was thus "valuable in the exact degree in which it communicates such information, and trains the faculties to act upon it."[51] "Reading, writing, and accounts," the subjects that made "up the instruction enjoyed by the lower orders," together with "Greek, Latin, and mathematics which are added in the education of the middle classes," were "merely *means of acquiring knowledge,*" and so almost useless to the intelligent conduct of life.[52] Schooling, at all levels, had to be organized around the scientific study of the physical and moral world. This did not mean omitting the Bible; knowledge of the revealed will of God was also essential to a Christian life. But surely, Combe reasoned, these two sources of wisdom could be reconciled. If not, he warned prophetically in the final sentence of the *Constitution,* "the religious instructors of mankind" would "retard, by a century, the practical adoption of natural laws, as guides of human conduct."[53]

THE EDINBURGH INFANT SCHOOL

Expressing such views in a city dominated by the Scottish Kirk must have taken some courage. But Combe's position was made even more difficult when he joined with Wilderspin to establish an infant school in the city, a move clearly and correctly seen by the establishment as an attempt to put his secularist credo into practice. Combe explains the whole affair in an 1829 letter to Spurzheim. Returning from Liverpool the previous September, he had met Wilderspin on his way to open an infant school in Glasgow.[54] Persuading him to continue his mission in Edinburgh, Combe "provided the Clyde Street Hall free to lecture in, introduced him to Richie and MacLaren of the *Scotsman* . . . and got the public mind roused to the resolution of forming an infant school."[55] According to the *Scotsman,* which had carried several articles describing Wilderspin's work, his first lecture on November 27, although short on "philosophical principles," presented "a clear and practical illustration of a method of dealing with the infant mind."[56] And this, if not completely satisfying to phrenologists, was sufficient to encourage those present four days later at Wilderspin's second lecture to organize a committee to promote the establishment of a school in the Scottish capital.

Religious tensions quickly surfaced. At the committee's first meeting in early January, several evangelicals objected to the "name and interference" of the author of the *Constitution*. Combe offered to withdraw so as not to "shipwreck the measure," but Simpson and other friends, bristling at this infringement of religious liberty, pushed the issue to a vote and successfully demanded that the committee should have a broad representation from all denominations. A public meeting was planned, and leading citizens of all parties assembled to publicize the project. The *Scotsman* even carried a review of *Infant Education* on its front page. A steering committee was formed after several speeches outlined the positive effect of schooling on public morals. Once again there was opposition to Combe on religious grounds, but he was eventually named a director, and Simpson, already on the board of the Edinburgh Monitorial School, the group's chair. Yet despite the inclusion of church members, aristocracy, and even Francis Jeffrey of the *Edinburgh Review,* Combe could still report to Spurzheim, "Through all the town the cry is raised that the infant school is an infidel and phrenological job," adding "nevertheless the scheme goes on, and my book is selling all the better for the discussion."[57]

The project soon ran into problems, however, as a dispute over building rights, coupled with attacks in the Tory press, started to erode support for the school. With subscriptions falling behind costs, Wilderspin was called back to answer his critics and supervise the construction. This time his presentation was nothing less than sensational. Parading twelve pupils from the Glasgow infant school, he demonstrated how in only a few weeks children of the lowest orders could master the rudiments of arithmetic, reading, and spelling. Choreographed with marching and singing exercises, his demonstration delivered an irresistible message of order, efficiency, obedience, and cheerfulness. After this "astonishing exhibition of intellectual progress," as the *Edinburgh Courant* put it, money poured in, and the school was completed within a year.[58] Opened in April 1830, fully equipped with the latest teaching apparatus, it was, Wilderspin claimed, the best of its kind, and in Simpson's estimation, "a model to the whole country."[59] At a final cost of more than a thousand pounds, it must also have been the most expensive in the nation and, as Simpson soon found, without the continued assistance of philanthropists, totally incapable of meeting its own operating expenses.

Authored by Simpson, the *First Report* reveals just how extensively phreno-logical principles underwrote practice at the school. Without mentioning the science by name, the six assumptions enumerated on the opening page explained the central task of infant education as the training of dispositions through "PRACTICAL EXERCISE IN MORAL HABITS" at the time when human character is most pliable.[60] This was to be achieved by forming the infants into a society of equals—"unrestrained, but well observed"—so that their selfish feelings could be managed and essential traits such as "cleanliness, delicacy, refinement, good temper, gentleness, kindness, honesty, justice, and truth" instilled.[61] The innate dispositions were thus "prepared as a soil for the precepts and spirit of Christianity . . . so that in after life, they would not be listened to merely as abstract ideas on Sundays . . . but will be felt as practical laws, regulating every part of everyday conduct."[62] Simpson even advocated a phrenological version of the silent monitor, a daily character report designed to record the action of the various mental organs.

Although considered less important than physical and moral development, intellectual education was not neglected. Rather than tasking them with letters and words, students studied objects and their properties. William Wright, the school's teacher, had "collected a little museum of articles, calculated to impress, in a systematic manner, a great number of natural qualities and effects," and Simpson called upon his readers to make donations of any miscellaneous items calculated to "surprise, amuse or instruct children from two to six years."[63] "Model ships, manufactured products, raw materials, zoological and mineralogical specimens, and artifacts from other cultures, especially from rude tribes" were particularly welcome.[64] After just one year Simpson was proud to announce that "the whole economy and system of the playground has fully answered the most sanguine expectations entertained of it. . . . Dirtiness, indelicacy, and filthiness are unknown; and habitual kindness, civility, justice, and scrupulous honesty rule the intercourse of the little community."[65] Typical among the many anecdotes of moral training was the story of J. H., a boy who, having spied another child's lost penny under the stove, returned two hours later to claim his prize. When his crime came to light, J. H. was put on trial before the school. Humiliated before his peers, the power of shame and disgrace proved more effective than the "few pats on the hand" to which he was sentenced. Asked some time later what he had learned from his experience, the boy replied that he had never stolen since. Why? Because "I listened to the *thing in my breast,* and that told me it was a crime."[66] One parent wrote that "before my children attended the Infant School, they were slow, dull, and unmanageable; they are now active, lively and obedient."[67] Another explained that his son's morals were very much improved, "For he [now] has a true sense between right and wrong, and the greatness and goodness of God."[68]

If phrenology had to be read between the lines of the *Infant School Report,* it was explicit and center stage in the anonymous articles that Simpson published in the *Phrenological Journal.* In his review of the work of Dr. Charles Mayo, "Lessons on Objects as Given in a Pestalozzian School at Cheam, Surrey," and in his "Phrenological Analysis of Infant Education on Mr. Wilderspin's System," he carefully assimilated modern pedagogy to the laws governing the developing mind. Wilderspin, who was "utterly unembarrassed by theory," had presented "practical views of human nature" that were in the "minutest point, coincident with that analysis of man's animal, moral, and intellectual nature, which it was reserved for Phrenology to *demonstrate.*"[69] Indeed, after hearing Spurzheim lecture at Glasgow, Simpson claimed that Wilderspin was now a believer, publicly confessing, that, "had he known it years ago, [Phrenology] would have incalculably abridged his labours, and shortened his road to his present position."[70] Wilderspin's system, Simpson continued, conformed to "ALL the faculties yet known to belong to man."[71] The architecture of the infant school and its furnishings were fully in accord with the organic laws, while frequent exercise in an open playground provided an outlet for the child's natural energies. The senses were trained, the knowing faculties strengthened, and the reflecting organs stimulated. The museum, in particular, offered a "feast . . . for all the faculties which take cognizance of . . . the material world," its many natural and artificial exhibits presenting "forms, sizes, weights, colours, [and] sounds" to delight the young mind.[72] But the greatest and most novel aspect of the plan was its "harmony with the MORAL LAWS of Nature."[73] Moral education had to start as soon as possible. "In many cases," Simpson declared, character training was "next to impossible, at least with the lower classes, after six years of age."[74] Infants were creatures of impulse. Driven by acquisitiveness, self-esteem, combativeness, and destructiveness, they seized and destroyed possessions, fought one another, and hurt animals. Such spontaneous acts had to be regulated by a watchful teacher who understood how the higher feelings of benevolence, love of approbation, and justice were brought into play. The playground was thus a "world in miniature" where the "barbarian" could be tempered into a moral being. "No instance, however trifling, [was] too in-significant for inquiry."[75] Every "unkind, coarse, insolent, cruel, and unjust" act had to be addressed.[76] Mostly, this would flow from the loving words and gestures of the teacher, but on occasion Wilderspin assembled a jury of peers to assess the rights and wrongs of a dispute. Rarely failing "to take the just view of the occurrence," the judgment of fellow children "had a much more powerful practical effect than the master's."[77] The higher feelings invariably dominated, and offender and jury alike profited from the rule of justice and the humanitarian emotions that invariably followed. There was no physical punishment (other than a symbolic slap on the hand) and no prizes or place taking to overexcite the dangerous organs of acquisitiveness and self-esteem. Finally, Simpson observed the religious foundation of infant schooling. No opportunity was lost to direct the faculties of wonder and veneration to the author of nature and prepare the young mind through secular knowledge and moral lessons for the truths of revelation professed by the various denomina-tions. True, Wilderspin taught the Scriptures, but this was done in exactly the same way as profane history, by presenting principles without creed.

Even though Simpson could not claim Charles Mayo as a disciple of phre-nology, he found the doctor's development of the object lesson equally sound. By carefully investigating the material qualities and social uses of leather, glass, cork, India rubber, sponge, wool, various foods, and numerous other everyday objects, children would train their senses, gain valuable information about the world, and exercise their "Individuality, Form, Colour, Resistance, Order, Language, and Comparison."[78] Locality, number, tune, and causality "were not left unsurmounted, and it was easy to see how Eventuality and Time could be added to Mayo's plan."[79] Indeed, as the phrenological theory of schooling matured, Mayo's lessons became central to the whole enterprise of leading children from basic sense experiences to an understanding of natu-ral laws and the moral order of nature spelled out in the *Constitution*. As Combe summarized,

Children should be taught to examine every object minutely, and to mark its hardness or softness, its solidity, its form, size, weight, colour, the number of its parts, its place of growth or production, its liability to suffer change from the influence of other objects, and its powers of producing changes in them. They should be taught to try experiments and note the consequences, and be trained to perceive and comprehend

that life is a series of processes, each of which has an inevitable consequence of good or evil attached to it, which they cannot alter or evade,
but to which they may, within certain limits, accommodate their own
conduct and position.[80]

Simpson even envisioned extending this process by introducing pupils as
young as "ten . . . to the constituent parts of their own minds."[81]

RAISING THE POPULAR MIND

Here, then, were all the pieces—physical, moral, and intellectual—from
which to construct the kind of scientifically based secular education demanded by the doctrines of the *Constitution*. For Combe and Simpson there
was no more pressing problem: the nation had to awaken to the practical and
ethical necessity of popular schooling built around the laws of human nature.
Vast sums had been poured into foreign wars and millions spent on jails,
hospitals, and poor relief. Was not a similar investment warranted for the
improvement of the population? An investment, they reasoned, that would
surely be repaid many times over through the conduct and industriousness of
a virtuous citizenry.

Both men were thus greatly dismayed when, in 1833, J. A. Roebuck was
forced to withdraw his bill committing the government to consider a comprehensive system of public schooling similar to that established in Prussia.
Yet they took heart from a speech delivered by Brougham just two months
later. As Combe explained in "On National Education," in Brougham's estimation, Parliament could not pass such sweeping legislation until "the people
themselves take the matter in hand with energy and spirit."[82] But how could
the masses be awakened from their ignorance? Rather optimistically, Combe
suggested that the clergy might devote a portion of their Sunday service to
promotion of secular knowledge. An altogether more promising avenue was
the public lecture. Combe had been deeply impressed the previous year when,
after attending his phrenology series, a group of mechanics and tradesmen
had banded together to form what became the Edinburgh Philosophical Association (EPA), a society dedicated to "the promotion of instruction in useful and entertaining science." These men were not interested in the erudite
and showy presentations delivered in most scientific institutes and literary
societies; they had a thirst for positive knowledge. This experience convinced

him of the need for a new breed of instructors to disseminate practical wisdom in a form the working classes could understand and utilize.

The kind of practical ethics that Combe had in mind for the masses can be seen in his weekly addresses to the EPA between November 1835 and April 1836, later published as *Lectures on Moral Philosophy*. Here he explained to audiences of more than 500 the principles of health and happiness, guidelines on how to choose a spouse and care for children, the causes of pauperism and crime, the duties of citizenship, and the reformation of the criminal. Every decision in life was deduced from the laws of organization, exercise, and heredity laid out in the *Constitution*. He even boasted that his own (happy) marriage two years earlier to Cecila Siddons (daughter of the famous actress Sarah Siddons and cousin of Fanny Kemble) had been planned and executed on these principles. Combe also presented two courses on education during 1833, which, at the EPA's request, were complied into *Lectures on Popular Education*—a work that gained national attention when serialized in *Chamber's Edinburgh Journal*.[83] Neatly and elegantly weaving progressive thought on education with phrenological theory, the *Lectures* explained the advantages of schooling to the individual and to society. Saying little about the specifics of schooling or the practical measures that the government ought to take to improve the education of the nation, Combe focused on the value of self-help and the possibility of improving the population and reforming the malefactor.

Combe opened his discourse by pointing out that every approach to schooling presupposes some conception of mind. Even those who had not thought philosophically about human nature held tacit assumptions that influenced their practices and colored their judgments in morals, politics, and religion. The key to social progress, therefore, was to ensure that these naive and unreflective views were replaced by a scientific understanding of the human organization and the advantages of life under God's moral government. Schooling, he continued, should have two central aims: preparing future citizens with the positive knowledge necessary for rational self-government and ensuring the harmonious growth of each child's physical, moral, and intellectual capacities. Ideally, these ends would be achieved by fusing instruction and training in a single process that simultaneously leads students to a

> knowledge of our creator, of ourselves, of external nature, and the formation of those habits of religious, moral, and intellectual enterprize

[sic] and activity, which are indispensable to the evolution of our faculties, and the performance of our parts with intelligence and success.[84]

Traditional schemes of education fell short of both these goals. Whereas Latin and Greek may have been essential for scholars during the Middle Ages, modern English works contained more useful knowledge than the wisdom of the ancients. For the average child in industrial Britain, the enormous amount of time necessary to acquire such *instrumental* skills was simply wasted. Focusing on dead languages only left the pupil "ignorant of things, ignorant of men, and ignorant of the constitution of the social system in which he is destined to move."[85] Nor was there any truth to the "mental gymnastics" argument presented by those who saw the classics as the best medium for training intellectual faculties. By setting out the various organs of the brain, the phrenological map demonstrated the diversity of activities needed to exercise the mind. At most, verbal learning would excite language. But because this organ was typically small in the average child, not maturing until adolescence, Combe believed that the teaching of foreign tongues, ancient or modern, should be reserved for gifted students and interested adults. Phrenology also demonstrated that teaching which drew upon the spontaneous interests of the child would make learning as pleasurable to the mind as food was to the body. The maturing brain simply could not assimilate the verbal culture of traditional schooling. Expecting children to memorize meaningless words was like forcing them to eat on a full stomach. Moreover, the threat of punishment and the promise of reward only compounded the problem by promoting the unhealthy growth of the propensities. More important than intellectual education was moral training. With the exception of amativeness and veneration, both of which matured during adolescence, the sentiments and propensities had to be correctly cultured from infancy. Adults had to be models of honesty, duty, and kindness, but because teaching by example and by precept, like verbal learning, only stimulated the organs indirectly, Combe strongly endorsed the kind of moral exercises developed by Wilderspin.

In his third and final lecture, Combe turned to the education of women. "The great secular business of female life" was "the nurture and rearing of children; the due management of domestic affairs; and the cultivation of those graces, virtues, and affections, which shed beams of happiness on all members of the family circle," occupations, he asserted, that were as important to women as the professions were to men.[86] These were no mean tasks.

Women needed extensive knowledge to fulfill the duties of life. They had to know the laws of health in order to promote the family's physical well-being, and, in the case of children, they needed to understand the principles governing the proper development of the intellectual and moral faculties. The vast majority of children, "nineteen out of every twenty," he explained, "are not gifted with originating powers of mind" and "reflect slavishly, when they grow up, the impressions and ideas which their mothers, nurses, companions, teachers, and books, have infused in them."[87] Depending on their own attainments, therefore, women would either sow seeds "of superstition, prejudice, and error" or those of "piety, universal charity, sound sense, philosophical perception, and true knowledge."[88] The future of the nation was in the balance; the evils of ignorance must not be inflicted upon the next generation. First and foremost, women should study physiology—to those who thought it unseemly for ladies to learn about the body and its functions, Combe responded that there could be nothing coarse in the exploration of God's creations. Next, they should gain knowledge of "the elements of Chemistry, natural History, natural Philosophy . . . [and] the social institutions of our country, and the civil history of nations."[89] Only when fully armed with this practical wisdom ought mothers to turn their attention to the domestic circle and the cultivation of those arts of elegance and refinement—music, drawing, and manners—that graced the female character and added charm to the home.

Combe's involvement in the cause of education during the 1830s has to be read in concert with his broader effort to promote the practical implications of his moral philosophy. Certainly, in his writings and lectures, he was a strong advocate of popular schooling, and, as his correspondence with the likes of Thomas Wyse, Thomas Whatley, and Richard Cobden demonstrates, he worked behind the scenes promoting educational reform. But despite their overtures, Combe resisted the opportunity to play a more prominent role within the secular education movement. When Wyse wrote in 1835 asking that he testify before his Select Committee on Education, Combe declined and instead proposed Simpson. Given the incident with the Edinburgh Infant School and the continuing attacks on the *Constitution,* perhaps he thought it wiser not to tie the cause of education to the fortunes of phrenology in a field so rife with religious tensions. In any case, a natural division of labor emerged: Simpson, who had mastered the art of presenting phrenological arguments without drawing attention to the theory, would push the issue of schooling, whereas Combe made the wider case for improving the population and disseminated his moral philosophy to the masses.

In the wake of Spurzheim's death, Combe's national and international reputation started to rise. By 1836 there were ninety-tow phrenological societies in Britain. Applied moral philosophy was proving far more interesting than scientific discourses on the structure of the brain. Sales of Combe's books also started to skyrocket. Combining a 45 percent cut in royalties with funds from a £5,000 bequest, he joined with Robert and William Chambers to publish a people's edition of the *Constitution* for one shilling and six pence, a quarter of its previous price. Where only 1,500 copies had sold by the end of 1834, with nine new editions over the next four years, sales reached 60,000. Together with increasing requests for his other works, lecture fees, and the interest from his and his wife's investments, by November 1836 Combe was able to retire from the law and devote his energies full-time to phrenology. But what finally seems to have convinced Combe to take on Spurzheim's mantle was the intense animosity he faced in the wake of his unsuccessful bid to obtain the vacant Chair of Logic at Edinburgh University. Respected and admired abroad, by the end of 1836, he was an object of odium in his own city.

Quite why Combe put himself forward for the Chair of Logic, a position he had almost no chance of winning, is unclear. After all, this seat was at the very center of the established community he had struggled against for the past twenty years. Gibbon suggests that he saw the contest as an opportunity to promote phrenology. But the portfolio he published—containing more than 100 testimonials from leading national and international figures—reveals a more radical agenda: the desire to force recognition of his own achievements and set up phrenology as an alternate site of social authority. The time had passed for persuasion. Combe was now preaching to a new audience that prized very different configurations of knowledge and society. As Thomas Gieryn explains in his cartographical analysis of this political space, Combe set the learned wisdom of the academic against the common-sense understanding of the layperson, metaphysics against positive knowledge, mental philosophy against physiology, and divine revelation against natural theology—lines of demarcation, Gieryn points out, that were clearly visible as a potent threat to the social map of the city. By contrast, the eventual winner, David Hamilton, defended the *status quo;* his testimonials "in effect reproduced brick-and-mortar Edinburgh, preserving in cultural form geographic distances between the institutions of church and politics . . . the space between different scientific disciplines at the university . . . [and] . . . the separation of the Royal Society from the Canongate slums."[90] The rhetoric quickly escalated. In the press and from the pulpit, Combe was painted a godless infidel and ostracized by polite society. "With the exception of Maclaren and Robert Chambers," he told a correspondent, "there is no man pertaining to literary attainments here that does not shun my society."[91]

Persona non-grata in Edinburgh, Combe's star was rising in the rest of Britain and abroad. His chief interest lay with Germany and America. Should he introduce phrenology to the land of Gall or continue Spurzheim's mission to the New World? Language was obviously a key issue. After taking German lessons, the Combes successfully navigated their way through the elite society and institutions of Hamburg, Berlin, Dresden, and Leipzig during the summer of 1837 (much the same route he would plan for Horace Mann some six years later). But while falling in love with Germany and its big-headed people, he was far from comfortable with the prospect of delivering public lectures in a country that had yet to awaken to the new science. If, by contrast, America seemed wild and dangerous, its free institutions and incipient interest in phrenology were more welcoming. With renewed assurances of the widespread public interest in his teachings from William Ellery Channing, Charles Caldwell, and his Boston publisher, Nahum Capen, Combe weighed desire and duty. Finally, settling on the United States, he pledged to improve his language skills and continue his mission in Germany on his return from America.

In August 1838, on the eve of his voyage from Bristol to New York, the fifty-year-old phrenologist mused in his diary that perhaps the science that could not take root in a society fettered by the Scottish Kirk could bloom in the more hospitable ground of Republican America. "The seed I carry," he reflected optimistically, "is of noble stock; the soil, I am assured will prove fertile; and it is God who gives increase. If we act in conformity with His laws His blessing is never withheld. May I be enabled to walk in His ways and teach His truths to men."[92] As fortune would have it, Combe's labors did bare fruit, not so much through the direct influence of his lecturing, but through the agency of men like Samuel Gridley Howe and Horace Mann, disciples who nurtured the theoretical germ of his moral philosophy into practical policies that shaped the institutions of the Early Republic.

9
James Simpson and the Necessity of Popular Education

[The Constitution of Man is] a book which, professing a regard for the Bible, treats all the fundamental doctrines of the Bible as absurd dogmas; speaks of the fall of man as "an hypothesis in an age when there was no sound philosophy;" talks of the doctrine of the corruption and disorder of human nature as a "theological dogma;" speaks of death not as the punishment of sin, but as the dissolution of nature; tells us that disease and misery are the consequences of sin, but may be easily removed from the earth; destroys all notion of human responsibility, referring man's character to the formation of his organs; treats the idea of prayer as preposterous, and the influence of the Holy Spirit as absurd; and in fine, eviscerating the Bible, leaves it as a useless skeleton, the object of professed respect, but of real contempt.

James Colquhoun, quoted in James Simpson, *Anti-National Education, or, the Spirit of Sectarianism Morally Tested by Means of Certain Speeches and Letters from the Member for Kilmarnock,* 1837

Building upon the educational schemes of the utilitarians, during the mid-1830s, Thomas Wyse and James Simpson led a national campaign for a state-run system of public secular schooling. Despite five years of writing, lecturing, and lobbying, their efforts failed to secure the widespread support necessary for a sympathetic Whig government to enact meaningful changes. The dissenting factions could not embrace education without scriptural teaching, the working classes were distrustful of middle-class radicals ("Broughamite" was rapidly becoming a term of derision), and the church vehemently opposed any erosion of its traditional role as guardian of the religious and moral well-being of the nation. In the fall of 1838, the home secretary, Lord John Russell, sought to capitalize on the momentum for change. After all, each group spoke of the need to promote common schools, improve teaching, and make lessons more relevant to industrial life. Attempting to head off the church's own far-reaching plan for a national system of Anglican schools, he prepared legislation calling for a Board of Education and inspectors to monitor the distribution of government grants. Tasting the strength of the Tory opposition, he withdrew the bill and secured his goals by administrative fiat, creating a Committee of the Privy Council on Education (four ministers and a secretary). Conservatives were outraged. Believing that a radical-liberal alliance had undermined the historical mission of the church, they battled its every move—including its first motion to establish a national teacher training college and model school. Over the next few years, by refusing to cooperate with the government, the church managed to engineer special privileges over inspection and schooling. Alienated by these arrangements, many dissenters came to reject any state involvement in education. Fired by laissez-faire social policies and the ethos of self-help, voluntaryists argued that schools had to be supported through the efforts of individuals. By 1843, Britain stood alone among the advanced nations of Europe with no public system of education—only a council of ministers to distribute meager funds between religious parties so resentful of government incursion that they were not always prepared to accept them.

What role did the phrenologists play in this contest? According to James Murphy, the arguments of Simpson and Wyse provided the foundation for Russell's scheme.[1] J. L. Alexander paints Russell as an apostle of the BFSS, determined to impose its religious standards on the country: secularism then became a scapegoat, an Aunt Sally, used by the church to castigate the government's plot.[2] In either case, Simpson and Wyse set the agenda. They popularized the idea of a Board of Education; the importance of inspection and public returns; the establishment of local taxation; the need for a scientific curriculum, stressing health, hygiene, and political economy; and the founding of Normal schools to improve the quality of instruction. If their secularism did not provide a suitable solution for the religious anxieties of the day, this expansive scheme did provide a blueprint for Horace Mann in Massachusetts and a later generation of radicals who took up the challenge of public education in the years after the repeal of the Corn Laws.

SCHOOLING THE MASSES

A Whig politically aligned with Brougham, James Simpson was convinced that the root cause of Britain's social problems lay with the ignorance of the masses. Physically plagued by feeble constitutions and perpetual sickness, intellectually "creature[s] of impressions and impulses" and morally unable "to restrain their . . . propensities, or to call forth, cultivate, and exercise their moral sentiments," he found the lower classes "not greatly more under the guidance of reason than . . . inferior animals."[3] A condition, moreover, that was being compounded every generation by the laws of heredity. In only "a few generations," he cautioned in his highly influential *Philosophy of Education,* "the stock, the very source of such a population" would be "extinguished."[4] Yet he was optimistic that with appropriate training and instruction, the children of the working classes could develop their innate powers and acquire the knowledge necessary to lead a healthy, intelligent, and virtuous life. Scotland, of course, already had parochial schools for the poor, but when Simpson examined their curriculum he found the entire focus to be on language and the instruments of learning. Was this education "of a kind," he asked rhetorically,

> to impart useful practical knowledge for resource in life; does it communicate to the pupil any light upon the important subject of his own nature and place in creation; on the conditions of his physical welfare, and his intellectual and moral happiness; does it, above all, make an attempt to regulate his passions, and train and exercise his moral feelings to prevent his prejudices, suspicions, envyings, self-conceit, vanity, impracticability, destructiveness, cruelty, and sensuality? Alas! No. It teaches him to READ, WRITE, and CIPHER, and leaves him to pick up all the rest as he may![5]

An education tailored to human powers had to start in the home and continue in the infant school, the period between ages two and six, when the "feelings are incomparably more easily bent and moulded to good . . . than in after years . . . [when] their effectual culture is, in many cases, nearly hopeless."[6] Heeding Amariah Brigham's warnings about overtaxing the delicate structures of the growing brain, Simpson was careful to assure his readers that in the Edinburgh Model Infant School, children's "studies varied with healthful exercise and constant amusement, story, song and fun; nothing like a task annoys them, and they obtain, without an exertion, much fundamental knowledge to serve them for life."[7] As the work of this institution demonstrated, the correct management of the faculties had to be grounded in a knowledge of physiology. Parents and teachers had to understand that the LAW OF EXERCISE IS OF UNIVERSAL APPLICATION. It is a fundamental law of all nature, that ALL the capacities of man are enlarged and strengthened by being used. From the energy of a muscle, up to the highest faculty intellectual and moral, repeated exercise of the function increases its intensity. The efficiency of the blacksmith's right arm and of the philosopher's brain depends upon the same law. The bodily force, the senses, the observing and reasoning faculties, the moral feelings, can only be improved by habitual exercise.[8]

Applied to moral education, the most important job of the school, this implied training the sentiments to regulate the propensities. Just as soon as they could walk, infants had to be grouped in miniature societies and kept under the eye of a superintendent. Encouragement would then be given "to the practice of generosity, mercy, kindness, honesty, truth, and cleanliness in personal habits" so as to ensure "all occasions of quarrel, cruelty, or fraud, or falsehood" were "minutely and patiently examined into . . . and the moral balance . . . restored."[9]

Intellectual education would also begin during infancy as children learnt to discriminate the objects and events of their environment. Carefully nurturing the organ of wonder, teachers were to encourage the child's exploration of the world—words, such as *reading* and *writing*, being introduced as instruments to further this natural process. To extend and systemize the child's knowledge, Simpson turned to the object lesson, meshing Mayo's activities with the needs of the unfolding faculties. Children would exercise their perceptual organs by observing the basic qualities of objects and bring the faculty of comparison into play by classifying things according to their resemblances and differences. As Combe had argued in the *Lectures,* there was no place for either the Calvinist economy of fear and punishment or the crude utilitarian regimen of places and prizes: phrenological pedagogy demanded that all learning be tied to the natural appetites of the mind and supported by the law of kindness.

Between ages seven and fourteen, Simpson advocated a common elementary school where children could acquire knowledge that would equip them for work and provide "just notions of social life" necessary to render them "enlightened and willing co-operator[s] with yet higher intellects, in plans for the general welfare."[10] Once they understood God's laws of nature, mind, and society, he reasoned, the working classes would surely work hand in hand with the higher ranks for the common weal. This demanded a largely scientific curriculum. Extending earlier object lessons, Mayo's later courses would be used to trace the industrial processes by which raw materials are transformed into socially useful products, an exploration of the physical world that led seamlessly into chemistry, geography, mechanical science, geometry, and natural history. Psychological, social, and moral laws would be investigated through physiology, civic history, political economy, and the rudiments of phrenology. Above all, he demanded, "pupils . . . *must* become natural theologists," able to appreciate "the exquisite order and beauty" of nature's laws, and understand how "the wisdom, power, and goodness of the Creator . . . inhere in every part of the stupendous fabric."[11] As the *Constitution* taught, they would come to understand that following this moral order was the only path to human happiness.

The first step in the implementation of Simpson's scheme was the establishment of a Board of Education. Able to draw upon the latest intelligence from home and abroad, he explained how a central governing body could disseminate knowledge of improved pedagogical methods through a code of instructions and a standardized curriculum. It would also oversee the erection of schools for children in every parish and, following the example of Prussia, set up a ring of Normal schools around the country. Such a large-scale engineering project demanded a careful study of demographic data and the cooperation of architects alert to the principles of instruction. To this end Simpson offered some suggestions about the size and placement of rooms, playgrounds, and equipment. He also stressed the importance of combining infant, elementary, and secondary schools (where appropriate) on a single campus. Boys and girls, he believed, should attend the same classes but be seated separately. Financed initially from government funds, schools would then be maintained by local rates. At this point the Board would turn to management, supervising the training of teachers and monitoring the performance of schools through the reports of local officials and its own cadre of inspectors. In such a well-regulated system, Simpson was confident that teaching, once viewed with disdain, would become a socially valued profession, offering intellectual rewards and the promise of public service to a new generation of talented and eager young men. As in Germany, women would only be allowed into the elementary classroom as assistants.

Of all the obstacles to a national system of education—public indifference, expense, fear of a politically conscious underclass—it was the religious problem that presented the greatest challenge. Paying lip service to the right of conscience, he charged that the Church of England, in particular, had abused its authority over education and transformed schools into instruments for proselytizing. In fact, Simpson pointed out, the church had shown little or no interest in schooling the poor until Joseph Lancaster, a Quaker, started promoting monitorial education. The British and Foreign School Society then came under attack for the threat it posed to religion—even though the Scriptures were taught and the Bible read without comment. Embracing similar methods, the church's NSS set up a parallel system of schooling, placing the Catechism and liturgy at the center of the curriculum and insisting that all children, irrespective of their faith, memorize the dogmas of the Anglican creed. Denigrating dissent, by the end of the 1820s, with its greater recourses, the church had easily outstripped its rival, with around 2,500 schools to the BFSS's 450.

Radicals, he observed, had made their greatest gains in the field of adult education, opening Mechanics Institutes, the Society for the Diffusion of Useful Knowledge, and London University. But even this created uproar! The idea of a university devoted to science and useful knowledge was vehemently opposed until the church established its own sentinel of learning, Kings College, to combat the godlessness in the capital. And now, Simpson warned, the church was awakening once more from its dogmatic slumbers, more angry than ever, as the call for a national system of education gained ground. The repeal of the Test and Corporation Acts in 1828, and the Reform Act in 1832, suggested the possibility of fundamental progress: the public mind was at last opening to the benefits of education. Most promising of all were the developments in Ireland. So long a battleground in which a fiercely Protestant establishment struggled to convert a predominantly Catholic population, sectarian ambitions had been put aside and a system of secular schools established. If the religious question could be solved in such a denominationally divided society, could not the same scheme be acceptable on the mainland? Somehow the impasse that had developed between the various denominations had to be crossed. The issue had come down to the stark conclusion "EDUCATION TO EMBRACE ALL SECTS, OR NO EDUCATION."[12] Surely, Simpson reasoned, the political and economic needs of the nation could not be ransomed to sectarian pride.

The situation in Ireland, however, presented important differences to that in the rest of Britain.[13] During the 1820s, as popular discontent for English rule started to boil, the Catholic Church began to question the motives of the BFSS, which, since its founding in 1812, had used annual government grants of £30,000 to establish more than a thousand monitorial schools around the country. The Kildare Place Society (as it was commonly known) followed Lancaster's strategy of excluding all doctrine and Catechisms, but Catholics resented the Society's predominantly Protestant makeup, the practice of reading Scriptures, and the use of clergy to oversee the running of the schools. Separate Catholic Societies were founded, but the government refused to provide matching grants. Finally, an 1828 select committee concluded that the only way education could be established for all children was to confine common schooling to secular subjects. Catholic and Protestant students could study the basic branches together four days a week, and then receive separate doctrinal instruction on the remaining days. Promoted by Thomas Wyse and carried through Parliament by Lord Stanley, legislation was adopted ruling out religious tests in the hiring of teachers and promising textbooks acceptable to all denominations. But the key feature of the bill was the establishment of an Irish Board of Education. Comprising commissioners from Anglican, Catholic, and Presbyterian churches (thought not proportionally representative of the population), it had the authority to distribute grants to any group that could raise one-third of the money necessary to build and equip a school. Priority was to go to joint denominational schemes, but given the realities of life in Ireland, these were rarely seen. Stanley's act was strongly supported by Catholics and strongly opposed by Anglicans: the dissenters were split. Forced to choose between its traditional allegiance to the Church of England and the possibility of rebellion, the government's religious principles gave way to political expediency. The church may have lost its power, but at least there was no Catholic system of schooling in Ireland.

Could a similar compromise be agreed to in England? Simpson was optimistic. True, the 1833 proposal of Mill and Bentham's disciple, J. A. Roebuck, had been withdrawn in the face of objections from both Whigs and Tories that state-run schooling would undercut religious freedom and de-Christianize society. But there was widespread sympathy for some action. A month later, this sentiment bore fruit. Following Henry Brougham's recommendation, the Whig spokesman Lord Althorp offered a rapprochement. In a late-night debate on the budget, he proposed an annual treasury grant of £20,000 to the two leading school societies. However paltry—the same year £50,000 was allocated for the restoration of the royal stables—here at least was a measure on which all parties could agree. Passing into law by a majority of fifty to twenty-six, the British government was now directly involved in the education of the nation, even if the majority of members did not want to usurp the role of the church. Renewed by the Peel ministry, the grant was continued when the Whigs returned to power in 1835—and shortly thereafter, a second sum of £10,000 was approved for the development of a Normal school.

Although not intended to favor one denomination over the other, the school grant was never divided equitably. Under the auspice of the Treasury, funds were distributed according to a number of conditions, the most significant being that all awards had to be matched by local contributions and that priority be given to the construction of urban over rural schools. But with few applications received from towns, the majority of the aid went to village schools sponsored by the NSS. Catholics had to accept the nondenominational but clearly Protestant schools of the BFSS. Equally troubling was the complete lack of fiscal accountability. Once checks had been distributed, the ministry had no mechanism to ensure that public funds were being used appropriately. Dismayed that their grand scheme had come to so little, Roebuck's supporters quickly recognized that their call for a national system of education had been premature. Fundamental change would only be achieved when Parliament realized the limits of the voluntary system and the consequences to the nation of another generation born into ignorance.

By the time he published the second edition of *The Philosophy of Education* in 1836, Simpson happily reported the work of two select committees: the first, initiated by Roebuck in 1834, to inquire into the state of education in England and Wales, and the effects of the government's £20,000 grant; the second, after the change of government, by Wyse, to continue the investigation. Led first by Lord John Russell, then the Lord Kerry, Simpson reported that the former committee had gone beyond its charge and, as he wrote, was engaged in the more extensive exploration of the whole issue of popular education. He had the "most cheering anticipations" because, as he explained in a footnote, "he had the honour of giving evidence before Mr Wyse's Committee" in an "examination that occupied the entire sittings of seven days."[14] Exploring the "practical details . . . which would not suit a general treatise," Simpson's evidence was considered so important that Lord Kerry, who sat on both committees, included it in the appendix to the English and Welsh Schools Report.[15]

THE RADICAL PLAN

Introducing himself as an advocate at the Scottish bar, Simpson explained how his work as a legal assessor for the city of Edinburgh had brought him into contact with the deplorable conditions of working-class life and helped inform his long-standing conviction that the physical, moral, and intellectual state of the population could only be raised through education. To this end he had become a director of the city's Lancasterian and Model Infant schools and had lately published a work on "The Necessity of Popular Education as a National Object," which was enjoying a "considerable circulation both in England and America."[16] A follower of George Combe, he stood before the committee ready to defend his cause on principle and the weight of experience. And, over the next seven days of intense and detailed questioning, he was not found wanting. For example, on the first day, after laying out his three-tier system of infant schools, common elementary schools, followed by academies and colleges for the higher classes, he was asked about the wisdom of removing young children from the home, the logic of combining the different classes, the danger that intellectual training might sour workers to a life of labor, the advantages of coeducation, the justice of assessing rates for education, and the reason that the voluntary system was unable to meet the nation's educational needs. Letters received at the Edinburgh Infant School, he reported, indicated without exception "that the best feelings of the children are improved, their respect and affection increased, and that comfort which parents enjoy in having the little creatures home after six or eight hours in the school and playground, is such a contrast to the weariness and plague of having them constantly with them, that the infant school is found to be the greatest promoter of happiness of the domestic circle."[17] Why should children not meet to learn as they meet to worship? Common schooling was essential to knitting harmony between the classes and would, moreover, help fit students for occupations according to merit rather than the accident of birth—not that Simpson envisioned wide-scale social advancement. Biological differences in intelligence and character would perpetuate divisions for generations to come. Could academic instruction make the prospect of physical labor distasteful? Surely not. After schooling, children would appreciate the importance of work to the social weal and their own livelihood. Citing the familiar radical line, he insisted that they would "know and feel that the goods of this world cannot be so distributed as to make every one rich; that the vast majority must labour in order to live; and that labour is not only no evil, but, when properly regulated, may be, and really is, a pleasure."[18] As for coeducation, with the exception of classes for sewing and knitting for girls, he was adamant that boys and girls should receive the same elementary schooling. As Combe had suggested in his *Lectures,* after fourteen, females could then be tutored in the domestic arts. One clear advantage of this scheme would be that students of both sexes would have the advantage of a male teacher. In contrast to women, "men had about them a greater moral influence, a power by which to work up a better and more beneficial exertion of the faculties."[19] The whole scheme demanded a massive investment. Hundreds of schools had to be constructed and nearly thirty thousand teachers prepared. The voluntary system simply could not meet such demands. The masters of the Edinburgh Infant and Lancasterian schools both reported that any increase in the existing school fees would result in a massive reduction in attendance. Even the better-placed working-class parents could not afford more than two or three pence a week. This left the schools in the precarious position of relying on the public philanthropy, which in Edinburgh meant the pockets of some 1,500 enlightened citizens amid a population of 150,000. With government money to fund construction and local proportionally assessed rates to meet their running costs, the shared burden would not be onerous, and those that complained—even those without children—would soon recognize the social benefits of their modest investment. However, he did add that "he would double the rate upon the married, both as a check upon early marriages, and as the married have a more direct interest in its application, and the benefits to be derived from it."[20]

And so Simpson's testimony continued. On the second day he answered more detailed questions on his proposed method of taxation; compared his scheme to the school systems of France, Prussia, and America; discussed the training and licensing of teachers; and concluded with a spirited defense of a child's civic right to a state-supported secular education. Many of these topics flowed over to day three, in particular the policies developed by other countries and the issue of compulsory attendance, which he saw as a necessary but temporary evil. Simpson had learnt much from his own visits to France and Germany and was greatly impressed with François Guizot's 1833 report on primary instruction. He had also profited from extensive conversations on American schooling with the mayor of Philadelphia during the latter's sojourn in Edinburgh. But he was adamant that his views flowed mainly from his theory of mind and insisted that if schools were built around these principles Britain's education system would be the envy of all other nations.

The first step toward this end was the formation of a Board of Education and the establishment of local school committees. Simpson spent a good part of the fourth day detailing the respective powers and duties he envisioned for these bodies. But he reserved the majority of his time for the topic most fundamental to the phrenologist's plans: the founding of a central Normal school—and similar institutions across the country—necessary to prepare the thirty thousand or so teachers needed for his system. Enrolling up to two thousand, "seminants" from the age of sixteen would learn the rules of practice and moral training from galleries above a giant schoolroom. The only limitation of scale, he thought, was the size of the building and the range of the instructor's voice. On occasion, students would rotate down to give demonstrations and assist the teacher and later, after much supervision, would be evaluated for their ability to conduct classes by themselves. All of this sounded quite mechanical to the committee, but Simpson insisted that uniformity was the key to a perfect system; all elementary school teachers, public or private, had to earn a certificate of competence. However, for those who wished to pursue the scientific study of education, he envisioned university courses under a Chair of Didactics. Education, he hoped, could then join literature, law, theology, and medicine as one of the learned faculties.

Day four also saw an interesting discussion of school facilities; teaching apparatus, and the need to establish affordable and comprehensive school libraries accessible to children and the community at large. There was no more cost-effective way to "enlighten and humanize the whole neighborhood."[21] Pointing to the great steam presses of the Chambers' publishing company, he explained how a whole library of books could be furnished for just £20. Indeed, under the supervision of the Board, Simpson also suggested the adoption of a series of textbooks Chambers was preparing for the education of children from birth to age fourteen. Based on sound educational principles, these would be superior and cheaper to any similar course yet available, including the texts produced by the Kildare Place Society in Ireland.

The fifth day opened with Simpson explaining his understanding of the relationship between religion and science and his plan, following the Irish system, of combined secular education and separate denominational studies. He would not accept any religious tests for Board members, district committees, or teachers, but saw no problem in employing local clergy, especially in rural areas, to help oversee the progress of schools. Simpson also read into evidence prepared remarks outlining more systematically the pedagogical methods that he recommended in his book and the phrenological principles upon which they were based—all of which he supported by citing the writings of Combe and Brigham and the successful practices implemented in the two Edinburgh schools. There was some debate about whether the faculties Simpson identified were psychologically real, or merely linguistic conventions that generalized the commonplace practice of shaping behavior to conventional norms. Simpson steadfastly stood by his theory and insisted that with a greater knowledge of the human mind, teachers could bring scientific precision to their duties. "It is certainly perfectly true that a judicious teacher will observe evil manifestations and curb them, and foster good ones; but he will do so less intelligently, less precisely, and less in relation to the particular modifications of dispositions in his pupils, than he will do if he has got a precise and clear analysis of the faculties of mind as his working instrument, and knows the various objects in nature which have their pointed relations to those very faculties, so specifically distinguished."[22] So much had been proven in the Edinburgh Infant School, where, in addition to regulating "air, exercise, proper warmth, and cleanliness" according to physical law and training the observing and knowing powers, as nature had intended, the master carefully managed "the abuses of the animal and selfish propensities."[23]

Perhaps the biggest surprise of Simpson's testimony was his insistence that a national system of education should employ monitorial schooling—a position on which he differed from Wyse. This had not been clear in his book, although Spurzheim had endorsed Lancasterian methods in his *Education*. Several questions from the committee reflected incredulity that a perfect education for all classes could be adequately achieved on such a plan. But having seen how effectively Pillans (at the Edinburgh High School), Dorsey (at the Glasgow High School), and Dun (at the Edinburgh Monitorial School) utilized rational methods with classes containing well over 100 pupils, he was confident that with the right training, an average teacher could be expected to instruct 150 students of all ages from six to fourteen. Had not the Germans dispensed with monitorial schooling because of its tendency to degenerate into a set of mechanical operations? If so, Simpson replied, there must have been some error in its mode of application; a properly conducted system, with qualified instructors, was perfectly adapted to intellectual education.

Most importantly, as he explained the following day, when liberated from instructing students en masse the teacher could then pursue the vital task of "incidental education," observing and modifying the manners and dispositions of the children in his charge. But Simpson could not endorse the system of artificial rewards and punishments employed in most monitorial schools. Learning ought not to be grounded in the glorification of the self and the degradation of one's fellows. Nor was it wise to excite acquisitiveness, after all, nine-tenths of society's laws were directed against the abuse of this organ. The key to proper and effective school discipline was to follow the natural economy of pleasures that the Creator had crafted into the human mind. If a student stole another's toy, it was the epitome of folly to correct their criminal act by appealing to love of property, the animal propensity they had just abused. Rather, the teacher should invoke the faculties of justice, benevolence, and veneration by demonstrating to the child the degree of their selfishness, the suffering they had inflicted upon others, and the offence they had caused to God. As one committee member recognized, the effectiveness of this moral code depended on the monitors being instructed in the principles of phrenology. Simpson agreed and emphasized that, in response to another challenge, far from sacrificing their education for the instruction of others, the monitor's own cerebral development would be greatly enhanced by their duties.

On the penultimate day of testimony, Simpson addressed the religious question. Having been raised by a minister of the Presbyterian Church, he was as zealous as any other in his own faith. And yet he found it completely "unphilosophical," indeed dangerous, to insist that religious education should form the basis of the entire curriculum: as Brigham warned, children with particularly excitable religious feelings could be driven to fanaticism, even insanity. He too wanted to make the most perfect provision for education in revealed religion but, drawing upon the parable of the sower, this demanded the careful preparation of the soil so that the seeds of Christianity could flourish. Some theologians believed that the seed itself was sufficient. But Simpson was adamant that resting all truth on the authority of the Bible undercut the scientific foundation for faith. Knowledge of God, moral principles, and the duties of life had to be grounded in both theology and the study of nature: hence the division of schooling into the separate but complementary spheres of secular and sectarian instruction. An "ultra secularist" himself, he would not even allow the Bible into the classroom.

THE BIBLE, THE WHOLE BIBLE,
AND NOTHING BUT THE BIBLE

When, in 1832, James Kay published his shocking exposé *The Condition of the Working Classes in Manchester,* the magnitude of the social problems in Britain's industrial heartland became a matter of national concern.[24] With a population of one hundred forty thousand, the city had forty-five thousand paupers and more than a thousand "haunts of intemperance"; half the children died before the age of five, and those that survived were severely weakened and degraded by the living hell into which they had been born. Immediate action was needed. The government, Kay insisted, had to regulate child labor and provide funds for infant schools where the vice and prejudices of the home could be combated. This argument was clouded two years later when, at the request of Lord Kerry, the city's school returns were presented to Parliament. Convinced that these reports, by under- and overstatement, severely misrepresented the situation, the Manchester Statistical Society conducted its own survey of the city's educational provisions. Their findings were as damning as Kay's. More than one-third of the children between five and fifteen had no education whatsoever, while the schools that did exist were so woefully inadequate as to be nearly useless. Similar reports published the following year on Bury, Salford, and Liverpool revealed the same bleak conditions across Lancashire. In the face of these social ills, many radicals held out a simple cure: the Irish System, as adapted in Liverpool's North and South Corporation Schools.

As James Murphy explains in his classic study, *The Religious Problem in English Education,* in 1827, the Liverpool City Council had financed the opening of two NSS schools to serve its burgeoning underclass.[25] But with a curriculum built around the Catechism and the King James Bible, few in the ever-increasing Catholic population were willing to enroll their children.[26] Leading the Liberals to power in the first elections after the Reform Act, William Rathbone took the office of mayor in January 1836, promising to provide adequate schooling for all of Liverpool's children. By the end of May, the education committee he chaired recommended that the town council sever its links with the church and adopt a system of management and teaching that scrupulously avoided "anything sectarian or exclusive in the regulations or the religious instruction imparted."[27] The goal was not simply to meet local needs, however, for as Rathbone explained the plan, "As soon as our arrangements were carried well into effect and the Schools in order" they would "make them Model Schools for the training of Masters and Mistresses" so as to benefit the country and "prove the practicability of a National system which should include religious education *for all*."[28]

At the same time it submitted its report, the committee also invited Simpson to deliver a series of ten lectures on moral and educational philosophy. Addressing more than two thousand of the working classes, Simpson's presence at this auspicious time created much excitement in the nation's second city—and, in nearby Manchester, where at Richard Cobden's request he repeated the course to similar audiences between May 2 and May 20. After this engagement, a public dinner was then arranged to celebrate Simpson's service and, more importantly, to form an association that would take the cause of education to the nation. With Cobden unable to take the chair (his sister had died the previous night), Wyse and Rathbone hosted the proceedings. Presenting himself as a pupil of others, and as an instrument in the cause of education, Simpson was first to take the stage. He laid out his philosophy of mind, his educational principles, and his scheme for a national system of schooling, much as he had presented it to the Committee on Education in Ireland. Then Wyse rose to praise his coworker in reform and toast the health of Cobden. This meeting, he remarked, "was the first in any part of England, for the promotion of the great and general object of a national system of education."[29] Contrary to the "closet speculators" in the Commons, the people were not inert on this issue; in Manchester, at least, a very different sentiment prevailed. They knew that virtue went hand in hand with education. While civilization created wealth, it also excited the selfish propensities, which led to crime and vice. But as schools and asylums across the country were demonstrating daily, the law of kindness could help redeem even the most wretched. God's laws, he maintained, demanded the full and harmonious development of each child's faculties and the establishment of a meritocratic social order. Public schooling was the key to this happy state, and he urged the workingmen of Manchester to join with Cobden and other leaders in establishing a society dedicated to raising intelligence and promoting a national system of education. The evening concluded with a series of toasts, including one by Rathbone to the "health of George Combe, Esq., President of the Phrenological Society, and author of that admirable work, 'The Constitution of Man,' with success to his efforts to gain the Professorship of Logic for Edinburgh."[30]

A month later Wyse, Simpson, and a number of other supporters met in London to establish their own lobby group, the Central Society of Education. As Wyse had told the meeting in Manchester, during the hearings of 1835, he had been struck by the lack of coordination among the country's many educational societies. Finding them united in sentiment but with "no means of connection with the metropolis" and no "channel of communication with each other," he had proposed a central agency to collect and diffuse information, a source of illumination to aid the government in its efforts to advance the cause of education. Seeking to strengthen their hand, the group decided to petition for inclusion in the British Association for the Advancement of Science (BAAS), when it met in Liverpool the following year. In the meantime, as its prospectus explained, the Society would publish papers on social conditions of the working classes, educational theory, and schooling in other countries. A wide array of influential subscribers was attracted. The management committee alone contained nineteen members of the Commons, including Lansdowne, Russell, Stanley, and Spring-Rice, and such notable intellectuals and popular writers as Augustus de Morgan, John Elliotson, Lady Byron, Harriet Martineau, and Maria Edgeworth. With Wyse as chair and Fellenburg's London agent, B. F. Duppa, as secretary, three volumes of papers were published in 1837, 1838, and 1839, respectively, along with *The Educator*, a book of prize essays containing Simpson's "On the Expediency and the Means of Elevating the Profession of the Educator in Public Estimation"—a defense of the teaching profession and description of how phrenology could be used to determine the character of future masters.[31] The first issue contained an introduction by Duppa on the goals of the Society, an assessment of the progress of education in Britain by Wyse, a synopsis of the various Manchester Statistical Society reports, and several papers on schooling around the world. The following issue continued these themes, with more statistical accounts of education among the working poor and articles on education in Ireland and on value of infant schools. The 1838 journal also included a commentary on the BFSS's Borough Road Normal School, which, while positive about the students' achievements, took issue with Scriptural exercises that the writer believed to be unfair to children of different sects. The BFSS secretary, Henry Dunn, responded in kind, characterizing the Central Society as a state party that would choke voluntary efforts, and Simpson's secularism as a dangerous doctrine that ignored the practical lessons contained in the Bible. Given the ties of many leading Whigs with the BFSS, this was not a good sign for those seeking a national coalition on the question of education.

Back in Liverpool, as the education committee got down to details, Rathbone's experiment started to face serious opposition.[32] Accommodating to the Catholic desire to avoid Anglican prayers and Bible readings, it was agreed that each school day should start with a common hymn drawn from the list approved by the Irish Commission. Teachers would also utilize the Commission's textbooks and its selections from the Scriptures, and denominational instruction would be delivered in the final hour of the day, *after the school closed.* The Liverpool clergy were incensed: excluding the Good Book from the classroom was the first step to popery! Inflamed by the blistering oratory of the Reverend Hugh McNeile, they held a public meeting to demonstrate the church's outrage and announce their intent to combat the council by establishing their own religious schools in the district. The teachers resigned, taking their students to makeshift classrooms, and, most damagingly, a letter was produced from Stanley explaining that although he had authorized non-sectarian education for Ireland, he found the idea of implementing the Irish System in England an anathema. He even enclosed £20 toward the fund.

With only thirty-one students remaining in the Corporation schools, the council acted quickly. New teachers were hired, and Wilderspin was engaged to organize infant education. Mass enrollment quickly followed, and although Catholics were the first to attend, by September 1837, one-third of the 1,500 students in the two schools were Protestant. The council clearly hoped that, once the clergy saw the nature of the common nonsectarian religious teaching and the daily denominational lessons, they would warm to the system. But this was no time for compromise. With municipal elections approaching, Conservatives turned the "school question" into a political issue. Rhetoric escalated. Letters, newspaper articles, and pamphlets were circulated claiming that the Bible had been banned from the schools. On one side, McNeile vehemently attacked the council for embracing Romanist practices; on the other side, defenders of the schools insisted that all students profited from the common Scriptural lessons and that Protestant pupils did indeed read the authorized version of the Good Book every day.

The Liberals prevailed, albeit with a reduced majority. But this, Murphy explains, was only a taste of things to come, as the general election the following summer turned into a bitter and seemingly mindless contest over the exclusion of the Bible—Rathbone even published letters charging respected members of the city's clergy with spreading deliberate falsehoods. Disinformation circulated and passions were excited in order to stir up deep religious animosities. Wilderspin sadly reported that a drunken mob had paraded behind candidates; hooting and howling "the whole Bible and nothing but the Bible."[33] Conservative victory, he charged, had been won by prostituting the Holy Volume. Viscount Sandon, Liverpool's new Tory representative, also acknowledged that the Bible controversy had given him the election. This, he warned, was only the first battle in a far greater war. "The experiment which has been tried here is but a sample of that system which her majesty's government will be anxious to introduce into every town and hamlet in the empire," he maintained and vowed to fight the spread of secularism to his last breath.[34]

It was into this cauldron of animosity that Wyse and Simpson stepped a month later when they traveled to Liverpool for the annual meeting of the British Association. As McNeile tells the story, he attended a preliminary gathering set up to discuss the Central Society's petition. Acting as a lone protestor, he responded to Simpson's speech in favor of inclusion by promising to attend every meeting and "declare my conviction that any system not based upon the Word of God would prove a curse not a blessing to the nation."[35] Seeking common ground, Wyse spoke of the importance of scientific knowledge and the need to develop the intellect as the basis for religious instruction. But McNeile would not be swayed. Wary of embroiling their proposal in a political and religious controversy that would surely alienate the BAAS, Wyse and Simpson withdrew. McNeile, the *Liverpool Courier* boasted, deserved thanks of the whole Protestant community for crushing "a project in the egg which might have grown into a viper."[36]

During the same month Simpson also came under attack from an even more influential opponent, the Conservative member for Kilmarnock and longtime critic of phrenology, James Colquhoun. In an election speech, published in the *Scottish Guardian* on August 7, Colquhoun read what he represented as quotes from Simpson's testimony. Simpson, he claimed, had told the Select Committee

I would have EDUCATION without religion, I would not admit the Bible into the SCHOOLS; and then the people of this country would come to prefer education without religion. The Bible unfits young people for after life; their minds are weakened by it, and they fall into fanaticism and insanity.[37]

When Simpson returned to Edinburgh he immediately wrote to Colquhoun demanding an explanation for this most egregious misrepresentation of his views. Colquhoun elected to stand by his remarks and, in his reply, quoted sections from the Parliamentary report detailing how he had pieced together Simpson's position. He also added in disgust "that while you would exclude rigorously the Bible from your national schools, you recommend to be introduced into them, and placed in the hands of all the children, such a book as Mr Combe's Constitution of Man."[38] "The simple and touching lessons of our Savior you object to, as likely 'to over-work the infant brain,' as likely to produce in some children 'insanity,' 'disgust in all,' p. 270, but 'the analysis of the human powers,' the metaphysics of Mr Combe, you recommend, as of essential value and of universal application to schools."[39] This book, he concluded, "establishes infidelity in its principles, and would lead in its results to a state of national morals such as we see in France."[40]

Deeply wounded, Simpson charged Colquhoun with selecting and joining detached fragments of his testimony, to which the public did not have access and "divest[ing] these even, of their qualifying and explanatory context," simply "to make a good case against [him]."[41] As for the Constitution, "this operated with the Bible, not against it in accelerating beyond calculation the moral and religious improvement of mankind."[42] To suggest that he "would give this book to infants from whom he would take away doctrinal Christianity" or "substitute that work generally for the Bible" was simply absurd.[43] But Colquhoun was not moved by this reply and in two further exchanges again defended his claim that according to Simpson's "plan, the Bible, and the truths of the Bible, are never to be taught within the national Schools."[44] Unwilling to pursue the controversy further, he told Simpson that "our mutual object has been, I think attained. Yours was to expose what you thought my misrepresentation of your opinions; mine was to present to the public a fuller representation of them."[45] Publish, and let the people decide, he challenged. Simpson duly rushed to press, but it is unlikely that his account of the exchange won him many supporters, given the divisive and heated emotions the debate had stirred.

With the growing Conservative opposition to the secularist movement,

Wyse and Simpson embarked on a lecture tour determined to spread their message and soothe religious tensions. Distancing themselves from the contest in Liverpool, their advertisements stressed only the need for a public discussion on education and not the implementation of any preconceived scheme—a Board of Education and a system of national schooling was the main priority. At their first stop in Salford, Wyse voiced his support, as he had a year earlier in Manchester, for separate denominational schools in areas with large populations of Catholics and Protestants. The Irish System could be reserved for cases where children were forced to meet for a common education. With supporting speeches from Simpson and Cobden, resolutions were approved calling for a petition to present the peoples' desire for an efficient and fair system of schooling free of sectarian rancor. While Cobden set about organizing a similar meeting in Manchester, Wyse and Simpson joined Wilderspin in Cheltenham, who, attempting to defend the Liverpool experiment against McNeile, had become embroiled in a bitter pamphlet war with Francis Close, a local clergyman. A similar situation had also developed in Manchester, as the three men discovered when they joined Cobden at the Theatre Royal. Stressing the themes of the Salford meeting, Cobden had managed to rally support from a wide range of religious groups. But he could not win the cooperation of the Reverend Hugh Stowell, Manchester's counterpart to McNeile, who published a preemptive pamphlet warning of the speakers' intent to commit the city to the Irish System. As Stowell later explained in an exchange with Cobden, by the "exclusion of the unmutilated Bible . . . the whole movement is really irreligious."[46] Suitably warned, the Manchester meeting ended with toasts rather than resolutions, and a few weeks later, when supporters of public schooling met to form the Manchester Society for Promoting National Education, it was the system adopted by the BFSS, not the secular curriculum of the Liverpool Schools, that was embraced.

Encouraged by their success, Conservatives tried to ride "the school question" to victory in Liverpool's municipal elections later that same year. But by November the tide of opinion had shifted. Thanks to positive showings in public exams and the growing endorsement of more liberal clergy, it was simply impossible to defend the claim that the Bible had been banned from the Corporation schools. As in Ireland, the council was able to ride out objections and prove that a mixed Protestant and Catholic population could indeed meet for common schooling with separate religious instruction. This message, however, did not play well in the rest of the country, where, by and large, communities did not face the problems posed by large numbers of Catholic immigrants.

Finally, in June 1838, skeptical that any Select Committee on Education would deliver the recommendations he wished for, Wyse presented his own bill to the Commons. Calling for a Board of Education to supervise government grants and a national teacher training college, his motion was narrowly defeated by seventy to seventy-four votes—with several prominent Whigs, including members of the Central Society, opposing the proposal. Russell, for one, professed himself no friend of secularism and claimed that he simply could not support a plan that excluded religious teaching or, as Allen and Dunn feared, established a civil Board empowered to oversee the work of the two societies. This was the end of the line for Simpson and Wyse, for without the support of such powerful friends the movement for secular schooling was doomed.

Two months later, the sweeping Conservative plan came to light. In a measured response to the concerns of the secularists, a group of idealistic reformers led by W. E. Gladstone (and including Viscount Sandon) sought to rekindle the Church's spiritual mission by establishing a comprehensive national system of schooling infused with religious principles. Alert to the church's lethargy and its antiquated system of instruction, the "Young Gentlemen," as they were known, proposed a massive effort to build schools, train teachers, employ new pedagogic methods, and integrate practical subjects in the curriculum. With Wyse's initiative spent, the BFSS and its political allies now faced a far more daunting challenge. It was at this stage that Russell took up the mantle of reform. A past president of the BFSS, he responded to the pressures of Allen and Dunn by promising to prepare a bill styled on the BFSS policy of nondenominational religious instruction. This comprised a system of rate-aided schools in which the Bible would be presented without sectarian interpretation. Jews and Catholics would be exempt from religious lessons, and, in an effort to capture the cooperation of the NSS, Anglican schools would be allowed to teach the Catechism, providing that dissenters would be excused—a position that obviously frustrated the educational mission of the church. Without committing to a Board of Education or making mention of Normal schools, Russell circulated a draft plan that vaguely promised "a new system supported by new funds and administered by a new authority." When this was leaked to the press, Tories put two and two together: the Whigs were lining up behind Wyse and the Central Society to push the Irish System as a blueprint for the rest of Britain. Francis Close of Cheltenham, for example, wrote articles in the *Times* characterizing Russell as an agent of the Central Society and warning against the evils of centralization and secularism. Murphy claims that there was merit to Close's claims. The previous October, after visiting Ireland, Russell had returned through Liverpool and spent several days with William Rathbone. Touring the Corporation schools, he was deeply impressed by both the quality of the religious instruction and the fact, contrary to the situation in Ireland, that the city's education committee was composed of laymen. Murphy continues that, by the time Russell returned to London, he had warmed to the idea of secular instruction and a government bureau to control and superintend the distribution of grants. Hoping to garner support for this modified scheme, he then met with William Howley and Charles Blomfield, Bishop of London, only to find the church steadfastly opposed to any plan that encroached upon the its sovereign right to conduct the nation's education. Pressure was mounting. On one hand, Simpson published a series of letters in the *Courier* citing the successes of the Corporation schools and demanding that the government take immediate action. On the other hand, Close, McNeile, Colquhoun and other friends of the Bible met at the Freemasons Hall to oppose any system that did not permit sectarian teaching. Three days later, Russell addressed the Commons. Citing his talk with Howley and Blomfield and the recent meeting at the Freemason's Hall, he confessed that his ambition to promote a combined system of schooling in England had been tempered by the resolute opposition of the church, whose representatives had convinced him of the "utter hopelessness" of the cause. However, avoiding the need for a vote, he did report that he had ordered the formation of a government committee "by order of council"—composed of five, later four, ministers of the Privy Council—to "consider all matters affecting the Education of the People."[47] Questioned on what this might involve, Russell mentioned the establishment of national Normal and model schools, a system of state superintendence, and grants for training colleges—he did not envision funds for new buildings and avoided the crucial question of religious instruction. That, he promised, was to be debated. Rejecting Murphy's interpretation, Alexander explains that Russell's true intentions surfaced that April when, in its first act, the Committee of Council published its plan for the establishment of national model and Normal schools. This was immediately seen by Conservatives as a Trojan horse by which to establish the BFSS equation for administering grants.[48] Murphy claims that the Normal and model schools would follow the scheme of religious instruction developed in Liverpool, with the sweetener of an Anglican chaplain for separate denominational instruction. However, the actual wording of the minutes, Alexander reveals, indicates general scriptural instruction on the BFSS together with sectarian teaching at a fixed time by the resident Anglican or visiting ministers of other denominations. Alexander summarizes the response: "To a Tory of 1839 the only responsible interpretation . . . was that he was setting up a state model of the 'system' proposed by the BFSS, and that this model would shortly provide the standard of eligibility for state support."[49] Without regard to the niceties of the various schemes, the government was then bombarded on all fronts for planning to impose the Irish System on the nation. In June, Russell finally capitulated and withdrew the Council's plan. Not content with this victory, the church party then tried to dismantle the Board as Stanley introduced the resolution that the Queen revoke the order of council. Passing by five votes, the motion was strongly supported by the Lords. The Queen, however, refused to rebuff the government, and the Council was spared. Yet its power was further muted when the church, determined not to permit inspection of its schools by civil servants, elected to refuse all grant money until the government agreed—as it effectively did in the Concordant of 1841—to use only the supervisors it appointed.

Ironically, the secular plan could not even survive in Liverpool, where after Conservative victories in the general and municipal elections of 1841, the Council, now staffed with Tories, voted to terminate Rathbone's experiment and turn the Corporation schools over to the church. The church's insistence on common prayer and the reading of the authorized Bible proved totally unacceptable to Catholics, who removed their children when the schools opened in 1842. As for the Committee of Council, Russell's and its secretary, James Kay's, stubborn commitment to religious instruction continued to frustrate the secularists a decade later, when Combe, Cobden, and a new generation of Manchester radicals again pushed for a national system of nonsectarian schooling.

Louis Agassiz. *From The American Phrenological Journal and Life Illustrated: A Repository of Science, Literature, and General Intelligence* 17 (1853): 76.

"The Good Schoolmaster Illustrated." The natural language of Horace Mann's new "soft-line" pedagogy. From *The American Phrenological Journal and Life Illustrated: A Repository of Science, Literature, and General Intelligence* 17 (1853): 12.

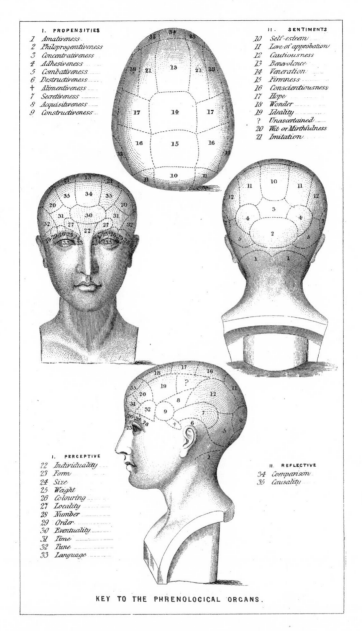

The Phrenological Head adopted by Combe from Spurzheim's list of faculties. From George Combe, *Phrenological Development of Robert Burns, from a Cast of his Skull Moulded at Dumfries, the 31st day of March, 1834* (Edinburgh: W. and A. K. Johnston, 1859).

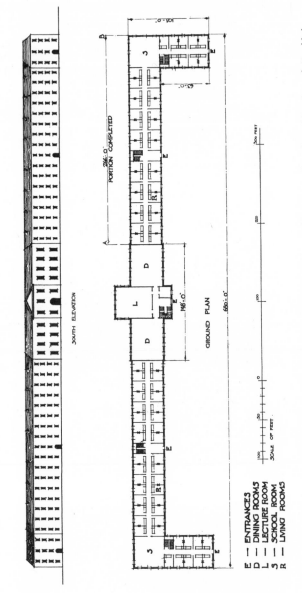

ORBISTON ESTABLISHMENT

COMPILED FROM AN OLD PRINT.

SOUTH ELEVATION

GROUND PLAN

E — ENTRANCES
D — DINING ROOMS
L — LECTURE ROOM
S — SCHOOL ROOM
R — LIVING ROOMS

The blueprint for the main building at Orbiston. From Alexander Cullen, *Adventures in Socialism: New Lanark Establishment and Orbiston Community* (London: A. and C. Black, 1910).

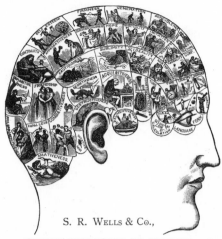

A popular illustration of the natural language of the organs published by Fowler and Wells. From George Combe, *The Constitution of Man: Considered in Relation to External Objects* (New York: S. R. Wells and Co., 1878).

Samuel Gridley Howe. From F. B. Sanborn, *Dr. S. G. Howe: The Philanthropist* (New York: Funk and Wagnalls, 1891).

Johan Gaspar Spurzheim. From *The American Phrenological Journal and Miscellary* 3 (1841).

Amariah Brigham. From *American Phrenological Journal and Miscellary* 10 (1841): 361.

By the 1860s practical phrenologists had integrated the facial angle into the popular view of the moral stages of civilization, even though this index was rejected by Gall and Spurzheim as measuring irrelevant features of the human head. From *The American Phrenological Journal and Life Illustrated: A Repository of Science, Literature, and General Intelligence* 17 (1864): 169.

Mary Swift and Laura Bridgman. Copyright © 1848. Printed by permission of the Perkins School for the Blind.

George Combe. From *The Life of George Combe, Author of "The Constitution of Man"* (London: Macmillan and Co., 1878).

Robert Owen. From Alexander Cullen, *Adventures in Socialism: New Lanark Establishment and Orbiston Community* (London: A. and C. Black, 1910).

Horace Mann. Library of Congress Prints and Photographs Division, Washington, D.C. 20540, USA Library of Congress, Prints and Photographs Division LC–USZC4–7396.

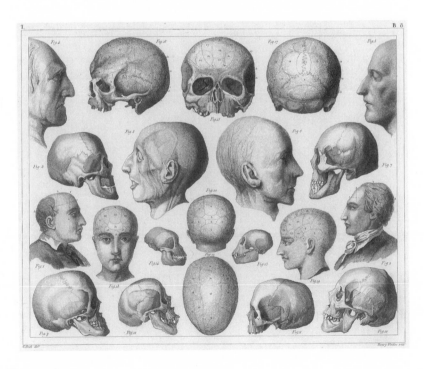

1851 engraving.

Laura Bridgman handwriting sample.

Insanity, Education, and the Introduction of Phrenology to America

You have established universal suffrage, placed supreme authority in the hands of your majorities, and no human means, short of military conquest, can deprive that majority of its way. You have, therefore, only one mode of action left to reach the goal of national happiness: enlighten your people, teach them whatever is necessary for them, in order to guide their faculties right,—train them to self-control,—train them in youth to bend all the inferior feelings under the yoke of morality, religion, and reason. In short, educate them—and educate them well.

George Combe, from *Notes on the United States of North America, During a Phrenological Visit in 1838–9–40*, 1841

When, in 1838, Isaac Ray dedicated his *Treatise on the Medical Jurisprudence of Insanity* "to the Hon. HORACE MANN; To Whose Preserving Exertions, Our Country is Mainly Indebted for One of its Noblest Institutions for Ameliorating the Condition of the Insane," he was recognizing not only Mann's efforts in founding America's first public asylum at Worcester but also the pivotal role he played in legitimating the psychiatric profession and the practice of moral and medical treatment upon which its authority rested.[1] For, no less than the modern high school, the architecture of the first asylums (their internal and external spaces, their division of expertise, labor, and time) was predicated upon assumptions about the causes and control of behavior—practices grounded in the phrenological view of mind that had been developed in the United States by physicians at the Hartford Retreat. As Mann explained in his *Report* (1832) to the Massachusetts Senate, the methods employed at Hartford by Eli Todd and Samuel Woodward demanded that every detail of institutional life had to contribute to a moral environment in which a medical man of high character and scientific knowledge could shepherd patients back to health, reason, and goodness.[2] It was these integrated physical and administrative structures, perfected by Woodward at Worcester and, a decade later, by Brigham at Utica, that became a model for asylums across America.[3] Eventually, Gerald Grob explains, as pressure to accommodate an increasing number of diverse patients and strong hereditarian explanations of insanity started to outweigh faith in the power of moral therapy, these small-scale curative asylums gradually evolved into the custodial warehouses of the late nineteenth century, a transformation that Mann and his fellow phrenologist Samuel Gridley Howe strongly opposed.

David Rothman argues that the asylum was a spontaneous *American* response to the social problems of the New Republic.[4] In a thorough critique of this functionalist claim, Andrew Scull demonstrates that, although the political environment of the New World did color policy toward the insane, the opening of hospitals for the mad owed much to the dissemination of ideas from theorists and practitioners in England and France.[5] Pennsylvania, New York, and Virginia had established custodial hospitals (styled on London's Bedlam) during the nineteenth century, but the first institutions dedicated to the *treatment* of insanity were founded by Quakers hoping to replicate the methods championed by William and Samuel Tuke at the York Retreat and Pinel at the Bicêtré. First in Frankfort, Pennsylvania (The Friends Asylum), and then through the efforts of the New York Quaker Thomas Eddy at Bloomingdale, hospitals were constructed that directly followed the architecture, management, and methods laid out in Samuel Tuke's *Description of the Retreat.*[6] An important development in this movement occurred in 1824, when Todd and Woodward petitioned the Connecticut Legislature to establish a public asylum based on the principles of moral treatment. Todd (whose mother and sister suffered from insanity) collected statistics on the number of mad jailed within the state and described in vivid detail the deplorable conditions of their internment. The English Malady, he warned, was not confined to the new social landscape of industrial Europe; the pressures of life in Republican America were also increasing the incidence of lunacy. Even so, he was confident that the methods developed by French and British psychiatrists had made insanity the most curable of all illnesses, the great success story of modern medicine. A gifted orator, Todd is reported to have brought tears to the eyes of the senators. He also managed to raise sufficient funds from that notoriously frugal body to erect a small institute under his management for both private and public patients. Unlike its namesake in York and the asylums in Frankfort and Bloomingdale, the Hartford Retreat was firmly under the control of physicians, who, asserting their professional competence, maintained that insanity was a physical disorder that must be approached through medical practices. Drawing upon phrenological theory, Todd and Woodward viewed moral therapy as a form of psychosomatic treatment that could complement the doctors' traditional armory of narcotics, purges, blistering, and bloodletting.

Having cut his teeth on temperance legislation as a junior senator to the Massachusetts General Court, Mann became deeply involved with a movement calling for the more humane care of the state's insane. Led by the Reverend Louis Dwight, the Boston Prison Discipline Society (1827) stunned the citizens of Massachusetts with its fearful account of how the mad were housed in the Bay State's jails.[7] Men and women, clothed in rags, were being kept without light, heat, or the use of a toilet. Peering in the small opening through which one inmate had received food during eight years of solitary confinement, Dwight wondered if the creature before him was human. "The hair was gone from one side of the head, and his eyes were like balls of fire."[8] But Dwight's graphic portrayal of wretchedness failed to stir the General Court. It was only in 1829, when Mann added his considerable powers of moral suasion to the cause, that the House agreed to established a committee (under Mann's leadership) to investigate "the practicability and expediency of erecting or procuring, at, the expense of the Commonwealth, an asylum for the safe keeping of lunatics, and persons furiously mad."[9] After conducting a census modeled on Todd's *Report* to determine the number of insane persons within the state, Mann suggested the construction of a public asylum suitable for 120 "furiously mad" patients. Underlying this modest proposal was the assumption that madness was a curable disease. His arguments could have come straight from the pages of Spurzheim's *Insanity*. Citing the York Retreat and the achievements of the Hartford physicians (with whom he had consulted), he confidently asserted that with "the appropriate medical and moral treatment, insanity yields with more readiness than ordinary diseases."[10] The economic and moral lessons were clear: by identifying mental derangement in its early stages, qualified professionals could "soothe and pacify that portion of the mind which had been excited to a frenzy, and so allow those faculties whose action remains undisturbed, to gain the ascendancy," thus saving money and preventing the individual from the terrors of madness.[11] One of the *Report*'s key conclusions concerned the appointment of a superintendent, who, Mann recommended, should "be a Physician, resident at the Hospital, devoting to its interests all his skills and energies."[12]

Todd was the clear choice, but deteriorating health (he died the following year) forced him to decline the position in favor of Woodward. Never was a man more suited to a task. Within five years of his appointment, Woodward had built Worcester into America's preeminent asylum and established himself as the nation's leading expert on the treatment of the mad, an achievement crowned in 1844, with his election as the first president of the Association of Medical Superintendents of American Institutions for the Insane (AMSAII), since 1913, the American Psychiatric Association.[13]

In concert with these institutional reforms, the writings of Woodward's former colleague, Amariah Brigham, helped make the theory of mental derangement a topic of increasing interest for educated New Englanders.[14] Having toured hospitals, prisons, and asylums throughout Europe and having attended the lectures of leading French and English theorists, Brigham was well schooled in the latest psychiatric thought—knowledge he quickly disseminated in America by publishing editions of the two main phrenological texts on insanity, Spurzheim's *Observations on Insanity* and Andrew Combe's *Observations on Mental Derangement*.[15] But Brigham's own thoughts on insanity proved even more influential. Extending the implications of phrenology from the asylum to other social institutions, in *Remarks on the Influence of Mental Cultivation and Mental Excitement upon Health* (1832) and *Observations on the Influence of Religion upon the Health and Physical Welfare of Mankind* (1835), he shocked, frightened, and angered many by explaining how physical conditions, and the excessive emotional and intellectual stimulation of the young mind typical in evangelical meetings and infant school "hothouses," led to sickness and insanity.[16]

Where Todd and Woodward focused on the treatment of insanity, Brigham discussed its prevention. Drawing upon rising fears that the excitement of modern times was causing a dramatic increase in rates of alienation, he opened his *Remarks* with a provocative description of the consequences that result from overtaxing the young brain. Anxiety had gripped the nation. To prepare for success in a world dominated by commerce and industry, parents and teachers were pushing children to acquire intellectual and verbal skills at a dangerously early age. Brigham was particularly disturbed by the infant schools that had sprung up across New England during the late 1820s, boasting accelerated pedagogic strategies without any appreciation of the physiological principles underlying cerebral development. By calling mental organs into operation prematurely, many children were being driven to insanity, others a life depleted of intellectual and physical vigor. Given the woeful ignorance of the science of the mind, he insisted that parents and teachers heed medical theory—and, as the sudden demise of the American infant school demonstrates, it seems that many did.

One had only to look at the "slender, delicate, and pale-faced youths" of the day to see the negative effects of infant education.[17] Not only did the early reading schemes press the brain prematurely, but many schoolbooks contained totally inappropriate material for the immature mind, exciting lower propensities and filling children's heads full of half-truths and facts they simply could not understand.

> Children of both sexes are required, or induced, to commit to memory many verses, texts of scripture, stories, etc. before they are three years of age. They commence attending school, for six hours each day, before the age of four. And often before the age of three; where they are instructed during three years in reading, geography, astronomy, history, arithmetic, geometry, chemistry, botany, natural history, etc., etc. They also commit to memory, while at school, many hymns, portions of scriptures, catechisms, etc. During the same period, they attend every Sunday a Sabbath school, and there recite long lessons: some are required to attend upon divine service at church twice each Sunday, and to give some account of the sermon. In addition to these labors, many children have numerous books, journals, or magazines to read, which are designed for youth.[18]

Add to this the hard-line discipline of many instructors, and, from a medical point of view, the whole economy of schooling appeared tailored to depleting the body and creating lifelong nervous disorders. In contrast, those who were kept from school in early life "and left to follow their own inclinations as respects to study" later manifested "powers of mind which [made] them the admiration of the world."[19] Defending the kind of romantic pedagogy promoted by G. Stanley Hall some fifty years later, Brigham recommended allowing children to follow the inherent appetites of the unfolding phrenological organs expressed in the natural activity of play.

> Let parents not lament, because children do not exhibit uncommon powers of mind in early life, or because compared with some other

children, they are deficient in knowledge derived from books. Let them rather rejoice if their children reach the age of six or seven, with well formed bodies, good health, and no vicious tendencies, though they be at the same time ignorant of every letter of the alphabet . . . for it is a great mistake to suppose that children acquire no knowledge while engaged in voluntary play and amusements. . . . [T]he Book of Nature is the *best book,* and if . . . [a child] is permitted to go forth among the wonders of creation, he will gather instruction by the eye, the ear, and by all his senses.[20]

Brigham thus found himself closer to Rousseau than Locke, whose "Treatise" had "done much injury, by teaching the importance of reasoning with children at a very early age."[21] *Emile,* by contrast, abounded "with many important and practical truths on education."[22]

Although considering it dangerous to reason with children, Brigham did not believe early moral instruction posed any threat to the young mind. Of course, it was possible for the propensities to be overexcited, and fearing the growth of greed, destructiveness, and pride, he warned against the excessive use of rewards and punishments. "The great object . . . in moral education was to call into repeated action those organs that manifest the good qualities, and increase their activity and power."[23] Virtue, as Combe and Simpson taught, was something to be practiced, not preached. If only this rule could be universalized, he was sure that the world would see a revolution in human conduct. Medical knowledge had advanced the length and quality of human life, and intellectual culture had promoted the growth of higher powers, enabling Christian civilizations to rise above the primitive. It was now time to apply science to morals and eradicate the lingering sensuality in human nature. Temperance societies might fight intoxication with the moral force of reason, but the greatest means of effecting social progress was encouraging new interests in children. "Great attention," Brigham urged, must be "given to render the amusements of youth such as will be conducive to mental improvement. They should be seduced, if I may so say, from the haunts of the sensual, by judicious books, pleasing and instructive conversation, well-regulated lyceums, and literary associations; and made to prefer the acquisition of knowledge to the gratification of their appetites."[24] "To give this power to men," it was "not necessary or proper to start with the infant, and task his feeble powers of mind and injure his physical development."[25] All that was required was to keep the child's scientific spirit alive, the natural curiosity that flows from the harmonious action of the faculties. Self-education was thus the means and end of education, "the spirit of inquiry that places reason and conscience on the throne of the human mind."[26]

The same progressive story, charting the rise from sensual and animalistic appetites of the primitive to the rational, healthy, and moral habits of the civilized, also provided the subtext of Brigham's *Observations*. Developing Gall's insight, that the organ of veneration is perhaps the most powerful of all faculties, he traced the historical development of religious belief from the barbaric practices of savages to the balanced harmony of faith and reason in liberal Christianity. But if New Englanders lapped up his exotic tales of human sacrifice, mutilation, circumcision, flagellation rituals, fasting, feasting, and penances, they winced at his insights into the unhealthy effects of contemporary religious practices. Brigham's description of the dangers posed to mind and body by poorly ventilated churches, badly designed seats, bell ringing, night meetings, long sermons, and emotional revivals were simply too radical for his audience.[27] Whatever their view of education, the orthodox could not tolerate the prospect of religious practices being supervened by physiological laws. The firestorm that ensued severely damaged Brigham's reputation, and it was only in 1840, in the wake of Combe's visit to America, that Brigham was viewed as an acceptable candidate for superintendent of the Retreat. Two years later, he was offered the prestigious assignment of heading New York's newly completed Utica Asylum. Here, at last, he found the institutional setting to continue his writing on the nature and causes of insanity. In his six annual reports, and as editor of the *American Journal of Insanity*, he wove phrenological doctrine with moral practice to describe the cure and prevention of all manner of mental afflictions. Although skeptical of cranioscopy, he confidently asserted in his introduction to the first issue of the journal, in 1845, that the physiological principles of phrenology had become the accepted basis of modern psychiatric practice.

> We infer that the brain is not a single organ, but congeries of organs, as maintained by the illustrious Gall and his celebrated successors Spurzheim and Combe. Thus each mental faculty has a special organ, and therefore certain faculties may be disordered by disease of the brain,

while others are not affected; a fact everyday observed in the Lunatic Asylums, but which we know not how to explain if we believe the brain to be a single organ.[28]

THE BELOVED SPURZHEIM

The doctors of Hartford were not the only promoters of phrenology in the United States. By the 1820s, numerous other physicians and men of letters brought word of the new science from their European travels. British and French journals, medical texts, and popular writings describing the theory were readily available, and, starting in 1822, American editions of Combe's and Spurzheim's works were published along with several books by home-grown authors such as Charles Caldwell. In Boston, for example, the distinguished anatomist John Collins Warren, an interested skeptic, lectured on phrenology to the faculty and students at Harvard. He had followed Gall's work since the *Memoire* of 1808, attended Spurzheim's lectures in Paris during 1821, and, over the years, established a large collection of skulls and casts—to which Spurzheim's own cranium would eventually be added. In 1822, after hearing Gall lecture in London, John Wells returned to teach phrenology at Bowdoin College, and John Bell, together with other leading Pennsylvania physicians, organized America's first Phrenological Society in Philadelphia. Shortly afterwards similar groups were established in Louisville, Nashville, Baltimore, and Washington. By 1840, nearly sixty societies had been formed, including, in 1832, the Boston Phrenological Society, which issued the country's first journal, the quarterly *Annals of Phrenology*. And yet without an American Combe or Spurzheim to spark popular attention, phrenology remained the province of medical and literary scholars. Caldwell came closest to igniting a popular movement, his numerous books and articles demonstrating the application of phrenological laws to penal reform, medicine, education, anthropology, and self-culture—his greatest notoriety coming in the 1840s with his staunch defense of phrenology against the *North American Review*, the *Christian Examiner*, and Thomas Sewell, professor of anatomy at Washington's Columbian College. But despite all his energy, in print and at the podium, Caldwell's caustic and confrontational style did not sit well with New Englanders.

For American physicians, who looked toward Paris as the seat of medical learning, Spurzheim was a far more potent figure.[29] A prominent theorist of insanity and one of the world's leading anatomists, he was also viewed as a defender of reason against aristocratic privilege, a professional persona greatly admired by New England intellectuals. One might even say he had a certain kind of nobility—his disinterested benevolence, the "amiable, winning simplicity of his manners, and his unpretending good sense, and good feeling" certainly impressed Yale's Benjamin Silliman.[30] Bringing such a respected teacher to the United States would not only help advance medical science in the New World, it would also promote the standing of American institutions in Europe.

In addition to promoting phrenology, Nathun Capen tells us, Spurzheim braved chronic seasickness and a month-long voyage across the Atlantic in order to meet William Ellery Channing and "study the genius and character of [the] nation."[31] He was particularly interested in "the various tribes of Indians, and . . . the mental and physical conditions of the slaves at the South."[32] Spurzheim did meet Channing, briefly. He also visited the Smith School for Black Children in Boston. But his planned two-year tour ended with his death in Boston after only 71 days. As it turned out, Spurzheim faced sickness from the very start of his ill-fated journey. Leaving L'Harvre on June 20 aboard a sailing ship with no doctor, he helped contain an outbreak of fever among the émigrés, only to land in New York amid an epidemic of cholera. Two days later he journeyed on to New Haven, where Silliman reports, he dazzled the scientific faculty at Yale with the "unexampled skill and the perfectly novel manner" in which he dissected the brain of a child who had recently died of hydrocephalus.[33] Continuing to Hartford, Spurzheim was escorted by Brigham around The American School for the Deaf, the state penitentiary at Weathersfield, several local schools, and, of course, the Hartford Retreat, where, according to Capen, he found Todd's organ of benevolence to be the size of a mountain.[34] Everywhere he went Spurzheim amazed his audience with the accuracy of his phrenological readings. The prison warden, Brigham recounts, confessed that Spurzheim "gave the characters of many of the criminals, especially the noted ones, as correctly as he himself could have done who had long known them."[35]

A similar story unfolded in Boston. Quickly embraced by the city's leading men, he spent his days meeting luminaries and visiting institutions. With lectures scheduled every evening and manuscripts to prepare for publication, he rose to edit his works before breakfast. The social rounds began at nine. Warren, James Jackson, Josiah Qunicy, Nathanial Bowditch, and Daniel

Webster all attended his rooms, and within a few weeks he had formed a deep bond with John Pierpont, Joseph Tuckermann, and Nathaniel Taylor—along with Channing—the city's leading liberal ministers. More important for the development of the science, he also found lifelong disciples in Howe and Capen. Capen, who became Spurzheim's financial secretary, biographer, editor of the *Annals,* and the most active publisher of phrenological works in the years before the Fowlers, sought out Spurzheim for philosophical guidance. Deeply interested in the nature of the mind, he had just finished a tract on metaphysical systems viewed through an analysis of the faculties. Phrenology and Spurzheim dovetailed perfectly with his worldview. Howe also was seeking intellectual direction. A Harvard doctor, who, having gained notoriety as the American Byron for his exploits in the Greek Revolutionary War, had recently embarked on a more pacific crusade as director of the New England School for the Blind (later the Perkins School for the Blind). Inseparable companions, Howe and Capen witnessed Spurzheim's examination of heads at the Massachusetts State Prison and several of the city's schools—including, in addition to Smith, the Female Monitorial School run by William Fowle (future president of the Boston Phrenological Society and coeditor of the *Common School Journal*) and the Hancock School (whose principal, Barnum Field, was one of the thirty-one masters who famously attacked Mann's *Seventh Report*). Fowle was enormously impressed with Spurzheim; Barnum was not, caustically reporting that Spurzheim was highly critical of "the mode in which our primary schools were conducted: he said that the children learned to read and to spell in a mechanical and old-fashioned way; that their intellect received attention to excess, while their feelings were neglected, and that they were too much confined. He thought it too much for the health of the young beings to be confined six hours a day on the benches," the same objections, it turns out, that Mann would raise against Barnum a decade later.[36]

The friends of education also had the opportunity to hear Spurzheim's ideas on schooling when, at the invitation of the American Institute, he presented his first public lecture in the city. Two weeks later, he commenced a series of seminars to the medical faculty at Harvard and a course of eighteen public lectures at the Masonic Temple. Although no record of his university class remains, the advertisements for Spurzheim's lectures suggest he gave the same talks he had offered to English audiences two years earlier. As recorded in the eighteen chapters of *Lectures on Phrenology,* this comprised establishing the brain as the organ of the mind; pointing out the various faculties, their cerebral location, and peculiar manifestations; distinguishing phrenology from other philosophical approaches; tackling the thorny issues of fatalism and atheism; and revealing the practical implications of phrenology for the care of the insane, the treatment of criminals, and the education of children.[37] Attended by the city's "most distinguished physicians, lawyers, divines, and citizens best known for their scientific and literary attainments," the *Boston Medical and Surgical Journal* was so enthused by the event, it predicted that "the efforts of Dr. S. will form among us a new era in education, and open, to the minds of the most intelligent, new and correct views of their moral and intellectual powers, and the best means of cultivating them all, in the most rational and successful manner."[38]

It was during Spurzheim's penultimate lecture that signs of his fever began to distress the audience. Unable to schedule the Masonic Temple for his final talk, he concluded by asking, "In what place shall we meet next time?" A question, Capen comments, "it pleased the Almighty Disposer of events to answer in the council of his own will,—leaving man to dwell upon the infirmities of human nature, and to wonder at the inexplicable decree of Divine Providence!"[39] Rejecting all medication and bleeding, Spurzheim gradually sank into a morbid state and died on October 30. A public autopsy was conducted by Warren and a funeral service held before some three thousand mourners: Tuckermann addressed the congregation, Charles Follen delivered a twenty-eight page eulogy, and Pierpont composed an ode sung by the Handel and Haydn Society.

Immediately after Spurzheim's burial at Mount Auburn, Howe and several other converts met at Capen's office to form the Boston Phrenological Society (BPS). Among the officers, Pierpont was elected president, Howe corresponding secretary, and Capen recording secretary. Fulfilling Spurzheim's expressed wish that "when I die, I hope they will not bury my skull" in order that it may "prove what my dispositions were, and afford the best answer to my Calumniators," Winslow Lewis and "several of his professional brethren" removed the head, brain, and heart from the corpse.[40] Combined with Spurzheim's own collection of skulls and casts, these prize possessions became the centerpiece of the new society's cabinet. According to a catalog published in 1835, this comprised some 416 pieces, including face masks of Napoleon, Bentham, and Saint Simon; total head casts of Cromwell, Brougham, Coleridge, and Godwin; and the skulls of Fredrick the Great and Descartes.[41]

There were crania of native peoples from Africa, Asia, Polynesia, and the Americas, the heads of idiots, criminals, and numerous different animals. It even boasted the head of Joseph Guillotin! The BPS, however, was not for the merely curious. From the outset its highly educated membership decried popularization. At the first meeting, vice president John Barber recognized the potential of phrenology to improve human welfare, but strenuously cautioned that the group's first object should be to prove the truth or falsity of the science.[42] This was clearly recognized as an important challenge by the city's leading men. By 1833, the BPS had around 130 members, including, Capen tells us, twenty-five physicians, ten or twelve lawyers, nine clergymen, and several teachers (including Fowle, Orestes Brownson, George B. Emerson, and Bronson Alcott).[43] Soon recognized around the world as one of phrenology's leading organs, Brigham even wrote to Howe for the group's bylaws, promising in return the skulls of two soon-to-be-executed murderers.

And yet, by 1841, the Society had effectively disbanded. Because this coincides roughly with Thomas Sewell's attack on phrenology and the rise of practical phrenologists such as the Fowlers, some have concluded that the scientific community finally came to see the measurement of heads as a pseudoscience. Not according to Anthony Walsh, whose dissertation study of the Society points to just the opposite conclusion. Having effectively countered antiphrenological critics and answered Barber's challenge, the majority of the BPS's members, Walsh argues, simply tired of studying the brain and the manifestation of the faculties. Combe indicated as much, when in 1839, he addressed the Society on the occasion of its seventh anniversary. Commending the group for their scholarly efforts, he noted that

> many phrenological societies have perished from having prescribed to themselves objects of too limited a nature. They have undertaken chiefly the duty of verifying the observations of Drs. Gall and Spurzheim and other phrenologists, in regard to the organs of the mind and their functions; and have too seldom embraced, in their sphere of action, the application of this knowledge to the physical, moral, and intellectual improvement of themselves and their fellow-men.[44]

No doubt thinking of the debates in Edinburgh, Combe challenged the BPS to dedicate its labors to the field of moral reform. In America, where power rested with the population, the stakes were high. People had to be trained to understand the rhetoric of the sophist and to resist the appeals to their passions. Imploring them "to teach the young generation a sound philosophy of mind," he presented phrenology as "the handmaiden of a pure and practical religion," the only sure means to ensure political liberty. While this call to action did not save the BPS, it did stir Combe's practical disciples, Horace Mann and Samuel Gridley Howe.

SOWING THE SEEDS OF VIRTUE

Without an acknowledged leader to carry the movement forward, American phrenologists looked to George Combe to complete the work Spurzheim had begun. Letters from Caldwell, Howe, and Capen all spoke of his popularity and the great contribution he could make to the future of the New World. Particularly important were the letters of William Ellery Channing. Famous for his stand against Old School Calvinism, Combe no doubt saw him as a kindred spirit. Certainly, Channing was interested in Combe. His brother, the Harvard physician Walter Channing, had edited the first American edition of the *Constitution* in 1828. After reading the work for himself, he initiated a decade-long correspondence in which the two men shared their views on human nature and religion. For example, on June 18, 1830, Combe wrote Channing an extensive prospectus for his *Lectures on Moral Philosophy.* Explaining that "morals and religions" were currently "in the same state as that in which the physical sciences existed prior to the practice of Baconian philosophy," he proceeded to elaborate the physical, organic, and moral laws governing human nature and to deduce the duties of men and women as individuals, members of society, and God's subjects.[45] Channing politely claimed not to have studied phrenology, but found himself "entirely in accord" with its practical conclusions and encouraged Combe to continue his efforts publicizing the laws of physiology.[46] When Combe finally met Channing in 1838, his earlier assumptions were confirmed. Writing to his brother Andrew, he disclosed that "intellectually" Channing was "not a great man; but morally, a very great and good man."[47] "He is a great thinker because the moral sentiments are the fountains of truth, and he follows them. He has *faith,* but he appears to me to want that strong intellectual conviction which the new philosophy gives to us."[48] Evidently, his inability to accept phrenology resulted from his moderate organs of causality and comparison.

Combe's account of his visit to the United States is contained in his three-volume *Notes on the United States of America during a Phrenological Visit in 1838–9–40*. This much criticized and much praised work tells a peculiar story. Originally intended as a private journal, Combe compiled details about the weather, road conditions, hotels, diet, and manners of the nation. But scattered among the pages of this travelogue are penetrating analyses of American history, institutions, and habits that offer a unique, albeit phrenological view of the time. Foremost on his mind were the problems he had faced in Britain. Did American schools, prisons, asylums, and political institutions offer any insights for British reformers? But Combe also wrote his book for his New England audience, presenting in the final volume a kind of progress report on American civilization.

Six years after Spurzheim's harrowing month at sea, passengers could now cross the Atlantic in less than two weeks aboard Brunel's *Great Western*. But if Combe and his wife expected luxury with speed, they were quickly disappointed. Quartered in a minute cabin and relegated to the bottom table of the cramped dining room, they were unable to escape a rather bawdy group of fellow passengers. Not that everyone aboard spent their days and nights at the free bar next to Combe's bedroom; he notes the pleasant vocals of Mr. Wilson and Miss Sharriff; a humorous mock court staged to reprimand one of the revelers; and the company of Nicholas Bache, who was returning to America with plans for the construction of Girad College, a nonsectarian school for Pennsylvania orphans. Combe found Bache to be "liberal and enlightened" and, the following year, when the two met in Philadelphia, recognized his report as "probably the most valuable account of the European Institutions for education which exists."[49]

After meeting with Brigham to set up a series of lectures for late November, Combe left the sweltering heat of New York and traveled up the Hudson to meet his brother William, now a brewer in Albany. From there, he proceeded by carriage to Worcester, and, after touring the State Lunatic Hospital with Woodward ("an enlightened phrenologist"), he took the train to Boston. Even with the "annoyance of constant showers of tobacco saliva squirted on the floor," this was a far more relaxing journey than his three-day trek across the Berkshires.[50] The next day, Sunday, October 7, he attended the Baptist Chapel and on Monday morning, met with Capen to collect a chest of skulls from the harbor, passing an hour with George Bancroft discussing the relationship between phrenological organs and Kantian categories. In the evening he accompanied Howe and Mann to the Perkins Institute to witness the annual demonstration of pupil learning and music, and on his third day, joined Mann and Governor Edward Everett at a common school convention in Taunton. Combe was greatly impressed by Mann's address "on the necessity of education for improving the human mind."[51] A marvelous day was then capped by a sumptuous dinner with the Reverend Bigelow. Returning to Boston the next morning, Combe commenced a course of sixteen 2-hour lectures at the Masonic Temple. Mann, who by this time was Combe's confidant, attended the whole series. Also in the audience were twenty-four blind students who had prepared for the occasion by reading a raised-type edition of "Outline of Phrenology" specially prepared by Howe.

While covering much the same ground as Spurzheim, Combe placed far more emphasis on the moral implications of phrenology, annotating his arguments with detailed advice about personal conduct, penal reform, insanity, and, of course, education. Mann thought these last talks so important he arranged for Combe to give a series of free lectures to common school teachers across the state. Serious but not stodgy, practical but not pedantic, Combe's philosophical message offered a clear and accessible justification for the political and religious convictions central to the Whig ideal of social progress shared by Mann and others of his station. Although only 250 attended his first lecture, by the close of the series he was drawing upward of 500. One correspondent noted that audiences were won over by Combe's "simplicity, earnestness, and directness of expression": he convinced them "in the most unequivocal manner, that he was illustrating what they had *seen* and *felt.*"[52] Mann was particularly struck by Combe's discussion of moral responsibility. He wrote a friend,

> Heads badly organized, dragged down into vice by the force of evil passions, he considered *moral patients;* those which were balanced and hung poised between good and evil, he held liable to triumph or to fall according to circumstances; but on those, nobly endowed, to whom heaven had imparted the clear sightedness of intellect and the vehement urgency of moral power, he imposed the everlasting obligation of succoring and sustaining the first in their weakness and temptation and of so arranging the institutions of society as to withhold the excitements of passion and supply the incentives to virtue for the second class. It was like the voice of God.[53]

Eager to show their appreciation, more than 100 leading citizens gathered at Tremont House for an evening of "sobriety, joy, and merriment."[54] Combe was presented with a silver plate and numerous testimonials to the value of his labors. Clearly delighted by this newfound eminence, he wrote eagerly to his brother. "The educated men here really know and appreciate our philosophy highly, and are most anxious for its diffusion. You are widely known and everybody has read the 'Constitution.' We are prophets here; while Dr. Channing in Boston is very much what I am in Edinburgh."[55] He was equally complementary about the elite circle that embraced him. "My eyes," he continued, "never rested upon such a collection of excellent brains."[56] "The hereditary descent of the moral and intellectual organs has been favored by their habits and institutions, and they are the bigheaded, moral, intellectual, and energetic Pilgrims."[57] But "among all the excellent men who we met with at Boston, none entwined themselves more deeply and closely with our affections than Horace Mann."[58] He even compared Mann's head to that of his beloved brother. George Combe and Horace Mann clearly had much in common. Both were lawyers, rising from the lower-middle ranks to positions of public prominence; both struggled in their youth against the terrors of Calvinism; and both, through their faith in reason, embraced a vision of an ordered universe governed by a benevolent God. In Mann's estimation, no one had expressed these truths so clearly as Combe; for Combe, no one had done so much to realize them in practice as Mann.

Yet Mann's work was only just beginning. For, as Combe soon found out, the much-vaulted New England common schools were very deficient. Attendance was seasonal, facilities primitive (even dangerous), resources minimal, and the teachers unprepared for their duties. On several occasions during his tour, he entered classrooms only to find students of all ages crowded into a single room aimlessly occupied in separate studies. Even in the better schools he bemoaned the almost total emphasis on literature, and where science was taught, it was usually presented in a piecemeal and uncoordinated manner. What disturbed him most, however, were the infant schools, which in America were given over to promoting early literacy. Attempts had been made to introduce the object lesson, but, as one teacher explained, if instruction was not directed to acquiring reading skills, parents regarded it as a waste of time and withdraw their children. Wilderspin's infant school manual was unknown. The result, Combe agreed with Brigham, was an excessive intellectualism that focused on words rather than meaning, thereby neglecting health and the most important goal of early education, moral training. The best course of action, he concluded, was to bring Wilderspin to America so that he could set up a model school to demonstrate the beauty of the system. But Combe's pleas fell on deaf ears. Wherever he went—Philadelphia, Boston, or New York—he received the same response: Americans did not want schools designed for the working-class children of urban Britain. Even reforming the common schools seemed politically impossible; the people were against any increase in taxation, and Democrats opposed the extension of state control over what they regarded as a district matter. With decrepit buildings and teachers who earned less than laborers, education needed an infusion of money and talent. And this, Combe reasoned, demanded a reasonable wage and "proper normal schools in which teachers may be instructed in the philosophy of mind, and in the art of training and teaching."[59]

THE RACIAL ECONOMY OF AMERICA

With Combe's busy schedule of social engagements—visiting the prison at Charlestown and a house of refuge for juvenile offenders, attending a second educational convention, examining Warren's anatomical collection, and traveling to the U.S. Marine Hospital (with Mann and Howe) to dissect the brains of Henry Nye (a sailor from the Sandwich Islands) and Daniel Freeman (a Native American)—he barely had time to examine Spurzheim's skull before traveling to deliver the lectures organized by Brigham in New York. From there, Combe set out on the second leg of his tour, a circuit through Philadelphia, Baltimore, and Washington, D.C., that brought him face-to-face with the grim realities of American race relations. Already apprehensive about visiting the South, Combe was shocked by the social prejudice he witnessed even in the Free States. The situation in Philadelphia was especially disturbing. During his stay in the city of brotherly love, as chance would have it, Combe's apartment was in a building managed by a former slave, whose son, a man by the name of Rob Roy, had a keen interest in phrenology. The father, he reported, "although a complete Negro, has a brain that would do no discredit to a European. It is of full size; the moral and intellectual regions are well developed; and his manner of thinking, speaking, and acting, indicates respectfulness, faithfulness, and reflection."[60] But even such civilized blacks were barred from public events, and Combe, who was determined to get Rob Roy into his lecture, was forced to pass him off as a servant waiting

at the back of the auditorium. "So intense is the aversion even of many humane and educated persons in this city to the coloured race," he despaired,
"they would shrink back from the gate of heaven, if it were opened by a
coloured man."[61] But this animus could not prepare Combe for the flesh
markets of the nation's capital. The thought of "children and young men and
women . . . forced to labour to the limits of their strength, till toil and misery
send them to their grave," he revealed, "haunted my imagination, until the
whole subject became deeply depressing."[62] Contrasting the debates of Congress, "in which the most high-tone appeals were made to justice, and the
noblest sentiments were uttered in favor of universal freedom" with newspaper
advertisements for "the purchase of Negroes from Louisiana and Mississippi,"
Combe "could not avoid the idea that [he] was looking on the representation
of a drama written by a madman."[63] This indeed was not far from the truth,
for the peculiar institution had distorted the mental organs of both slaves and
slaveholders. Compared with the larger heads of northern blacks, he observed
that in some slaves "the brains are so small, that their mental powers must be
feeble indeed."[64] "It is a reasonable inference," he continued, "that the greater
exercise of the mental faculties in freedom has caused the brain to increase
in size"—a conclusion he later verified in his examination of the *Amistad*'s
crew.[65] With the exception of their leader Cinquez, whose "brain indicated
considerable mental power, decision, self-reliance, prompt perception, and
readiness of action," he found the other "genuine Africans presented heads,
on the whole, inferior to the negroes whom I had previously seen in the
United States."[66] As for the supporters of slavery, phrenological observation
satisfied him that their views followed from the diminutive "size of the organs
of Conscientiousness and Benevolence in relation to Acquisitiveness and Self-
Esteem."[67]

Back in Philadelphia, Combe extended his analysis of racial organization to the brains of Native Americans. Having been enlisted by Samuel
Morton to write an appendix on head shape and character for his soon-
to-be-published *Crania Americana,* Combe set out his views on the moral
and intellectual capacities of Anglo Saxons, African Americans, and Native
Americans. Morton had surveyed the world's peoples attempting to establish
a relationship between moral traits and the volume of the skull. The result
was a patchwork of anecdotes and traveler's tales similar to Combe's *System.*
The "Eskimaux" of Greenland, for example, were described as "crafty, sensual, ungrateful, obstinate and unfeeling. . . . [T]hey devour the most dis-

gusting ailments uncooked and uncleaned, and seem to have no ideas beyond providing for the present moment."[68] "Polynesian islanders are characterized by a volatile disposition and fugitive habits. . . . [T]hey act from the impulse of the moment, without reflection and almost without motive" and are thus "kind or cruel, loquacious or taciturn, active or indolent, according to the promptings of caprice or passion."[69] "They have been truly said to possess the foibles of childhood with the vices of men."[70] Worst of all were the Fiji Islanders and New Zealanders, vying for notoriety in "treachery, cruelty, and cannibalism."[71] As for the Hottentots, they were "one of the most singular varieties of the human species, and the nearest approximation to the lower animal."[72] Praising the project, Combe took issue with Morton's methods and his chief conclusions. Measuring the volume of a skull did not reveal the relative size of the moral and intellectual organs within the host brain. This could be seen in Morton's ranking of the African below Indians. Phrenological examination clearly demonstrated that "the brain of the Negro . . . shows proportionately less Destructiveness, Cautiousness, Self-Esteem, and Firmness, and greater Benevolence, Conscientiousness, and Reflection than the brain of the Native American."[73] Indeed, Combe believed, it was exactly these moral and intellectual differences that explained the respective fates of the two races. The American Indian escaped "the degradation of slavery because he is a wild, vindictive, cunning, untamable savage," whereas the African is "deprived of freedom and rendered 'property' . . . because he is by nature a *tame* man, submissive, affectionate, intelligent, and docile."[74] It was Combe's conviction, therefore, against the arguments of men like Henry Clay that "the very qualities which render the Negro in slavery a safe companion to the White, will make him harmless when free."[75] He simply could not understand how Anglo Americans could turn the scales of nature and invest the "Indian character . . . with a kind of nobleness and dignity . . . even boast of their inheriting Indian blood; while the Negro is despised, hated, and by some even abhorred, as scarcely belonging to the human species."[76] Moreover, he found Morton's defense of polygenesis absurd. "When Providence intends to prevent the races from mingling, he renders the product of their union unprolific, as in the case of the mule. The slave-holders have impressed upon the slave population striking evidence that no such prohibition exists between African and European races."[77] Combe also thought that "the whiter the skin, the closer the approach of the individual to European qualities of mind."[78] This was a radical conclusion, even for such a fervent abolitionist as Howe. While serving as a member of the American Freedmen's Inquiry Commission in 1863, he would agree with Combe's estimation of the African character but, seeking to allay fears of social integration and misogyny, side with Morton in presenting the mulatto as an unnatural and sickly creature that would eventually fade from the continent when the races were left to follow their own instincts and the dictates of nature.

REFORMING THE DEVIANT AND TRAINING THE DEFECTIVE

While in Philadelphia, Combe also sought to bring phrenology to bear on one of the most contentious reform issues of the day, the relative merits of the separate and congregate systems employed at Pennsylvania's Eastern Penitentiary (where inmates were secluded for their entire sentence) and New York's Auburn Prison (where inmates were allowed to meet, but always in silence). Combe was most impressed by the administration at Eastern and its broadly humanitarian regime, but objected that despite numerous calls from wardens and inspectors, little or nothing had been done to rehabilitate the prisoners. The solitude of the cell, he noted, may subdue the nervous system, but it could not elevate the higher powers. "When the sentence is expired," Combe predicted,

> the convict will return to society, with all his mental powers, animal, moral, and intellectual, increased in *susceptibility,* but *lowered in strength.* The excitements that will assail him, will have their influence doubled, by operating upon an enfeebled system. If he meet old associates and return to drinking and profanity, the animal propensities will be fearfully excited by the force of these stimulants, while his enfeebled moral and intellectual powers will scarcely be capable of offering any resistance.[79]

The laws of phrenology dictated a more proactive course. "If well constituted minds require extensive moral and religious training and instruction to preserve them in the paths of virtue, ill constituted minds need much more."[80] "Labor," he insisted, "must be bestowed in the cultivation of their moral and intellectual faculties proportionate to their ignorance and wickedness."[81] As in the asylum, prisons had to be placed under the leadership of a professional man of high character who could superintend the culture of the inmates' faculties. Freedom and responsibly could then be "increased in exact proportion to the advancement of the convicts in morality and understanding," until, suitably reinforced to resist temptation, they could be realized into society with the assurance of "continuing in the paths of virtue."[82] Three years after these remarks were published, Mann, Howe, and Charles Sumner entered into a fiery debate on prison discipline with advocates of New York's congregate method, promoting a modified version of the separate system in line with Combe's arguments on moral insanity and the medical treatment of prisoners. Perhaps because of his own six-month incarceration in a Prussian jail, Howe was deeply sensitive to the plight of the prisoner, the torment of his own solitude being matched by his fear of mingling with the wicked creatures who shared his internment. Phrenology justified these concerns and sustained his lifelong campaign—the first at Perkins Institute and then as chair of the Massachusetts State Board of Charities—to prevent the negative effects of unnatural communities.

The third phase of Combe's American tour took him north through New York State. After a rendezvous with Channing at Niagara, he traveled on to Buffalo, Montreal, and Maine, uniting with Mann in Portland for seven days of physical and spiritual recuperation. "Never," Mann wrote, "have I spent a week in a way more congenial to my coronal region."[83] It was hardly as pleasant for Combe, who, covered with mosquito bites, passed much of the time laid up on the couch. Continuing on to Hartford, Combe then delivered a series of lectures organized by Henry Barnard and, along with Brigham and Thomas Gallaudet, retraced Spurzheim's footsteps at the Weathersfield State Prison, the Hartford Retreat, and the American Asylum for the Education and Instruction of the Deaf and Dumb. He was particularly interested in the education of the hearing impaired, not least for the light such instructional practices might shine on the nature of the mind. After her visit to Hartford, Harriet Martineau had affirmed the popular opinion that the deaf were also mentally defective. Gallaudet angrily rejected this assertion and presented several of his students as proof that, when taught how to sign, the deaf could attain extensive practical knowledge and become "amiable and happy in their dispositions."[84] They could, he insisted, learn to name objects and events, make abstractions, generalizations, and comprehend the human emotions. Gallaudet even described how, in just two years, students ignorant of all languages had been taught five thousand words, making them equal, "with regard to the expression of their ideas, with the most intelligent persons among those heathen nations who have nothing but an oral language."[85] To support these claims he pointed to examples of how the deaf were able to communicate complex meanings with people who shared no common language. Laurent Clec, now a teacher at Hartford, had learnt many interesting facts from a Chinese visitor and several Native American children, while, as Combe tells the story, Gallaudet himself

> had conversed with the Africans of the *Amistad,* and learned many particulars of their history and opinions. . . . For example, to discover whether they recognized a God, he assumed the natural language of veneration, looked up as if beseeching and adoring, and pointed to the sky. "Goolly!" said the Africans, "Goolly, Goolly!" then looking grave they imitated thunder, uttering the words "Goolly—Bung! Bung!" There could be no doubt that they gave their name for God.[86]

The methods employed at Hartford clearly demonstrated the falsity of empiricist theory: the loss of one or more senses did not inevitably lead to idiocy. By devising alternative channels of communication between the brain's organs and the external world, there was every reason to expect students could receive a full, if slower, education. This did not mean Combe endorsed signing over oralism. He was highly impressed with Gallaudet's and Clec's achievements, but none suggested that a manual language could elevate all the mental powers—the point that Mann and Howe would make in their determined effort to supplant the natural language of the deaf with oral methods of instruction. In fact, Combe was far more interested in returning to Boston to examine the students at the Perkins Institute who, under Howe's phrenologically grounded instruction, were demonstrating equally remarkable advances. Sitting in the dark, like the blind themselves, Mann, Combe, and Howe marveled as the students "read, ciphered, demonstrated mathematical propositions, traced the courses of rivers, seas, and mountains on their maps," revealing not only "great acquirements in knowledge," but also "well cultivated powers of reasoning."[87] But it was Howe's success with the deaf, blind, and mute Laura Bridgman that most impressed Combe. Her mind, entombed by scarlet fever since infancy, was now, thanks to Howe's ingenuity, at last free to explore the world. In the space of just one year, Combe observed a distinct "increase in the size of her brain," noting in particular that "the organs of the domestic affections [were] . . . in the best feminine proportions."[88]

While in Massachusetts, Combe delivered the previously arranged lectures on education in Boston, Salem, Lowell, Worcester, and Springfield—"sowing the seeds," as he put it, "which Mr. Mann may ripen into a lovely and abundant harvest of morality and intelligence."[89] Combe also attended "Mr. Mann's excellent address on 'corporal punishment.'" Containing "a philosophical exposition of the objects of punishment, and of its effects on children of different natural dispositions," together with "admirable illustrations of his principles, in which wit and logic were gracefully combined . . . interspersed with passages of touching eloquence . . . the lecture was a moral and intellectual treat."[90] As his visit drew to a close, Combe recognized that the time was ripe to pass the mantle of phrenology to his "much valued American friend."[91] Mann's higher education in moral philosophy would be completed during their joint tour of the Mississippi Valley. Mann was ecstatic: "To enjoy for a month the society of that man will familiarize great truths to my mind, if it does not communicate many new ones. The *utile et dulce* could rarely be more happily united."[92] After four weeks of phrenologizing the Western frontier and its inhabitants, Mann's estimation of Combe became almost sycophantic. After seeing the philosopher depart for Liverpool, he recorded in his diary,

> I have never been acquainted with a mind which handled such great subjects with such ease and as it appears to me with such justness. My journeyings with him have been to me a great source of advantage and delight. He has constantly gratified my strongest facilities. The world knows him not. In the next century I have no doubt that he will be looked upon as the greatest man of the present.[93]

Mann could not have been more mistaken. "The greatest man of the present" is almost unknown to historians and hardly ever mentioned in accounts of Mann's work and thought.

One can only imagine Mann's disappointment on reading the first volume of Combe's *Notes on America*. Together with Howe, he scolded his mentor for publishing a catalog of minutiae, "commonplaces and truisms" about climate, food, and lecture attendance, rather than bringing his organs of causality and comparison to bear on the people and institutions of the New

Republic. Fearing the loss of Combe's friendship, Mann was unduly kind in his assessment of the second volume. "You have emerged from the gastric and sensuous regions of the common tourist, and the great light of *Causality* begins to shine."[94] The analysis Mann most wanted did not appear until the third volume, where Combe included his farewell "Address to the American People." Setting out the effect of political systems on the organization of the brain, Combe compared the despotic governments of Austria and Prussia, the aristocratic and church hegemony in Britain, and the institutions of the New World. Only in a democracy, he argued, could human beings achieve the greater happiness that results from the full and free exercise of the mind's organs. And yet, he cautioned, excessive liberty in itself resulted in a different kind of servitude:

> Our affective faculties, both animal and moral, are in themselves blind impulses . . . that . . . stand in need of constant guidance. There must be subordination, restraint, self-denial, the power of self direction, in short there must be *government,* and enlightened government before happiness can be attained. We have seen that your institutions have done everything to set your faculties free: but what have they done to guide them in the right path? So far as I can discover, the answer must be—too little.[95]

America, he warned his hosts, had

> only one mode of action to reach the goal of national happiness: enlighten your people, teach them whatever is necessary for them, in order to guide their faculties aright—*train* them to self-control—*train* them in youth to bend all the inferior feelings under the yoke of morality, religion, and reason. In short educate them—and educate them well.[96]

Such a task demanded public leaders with recognized physical, moral, and intellectual qualities: "men with high temperaments, large brains, and large lungs" who would guide popular opinion and mold the future citizens of a virtuous Republic.[97] This, as the following chapters illustrate, was a call to duty that Howe and Mann could not resist.

II

Phrenological Mann

> I look upon Phrenology as the guide of Philosophy and the handmaiden of
> Christianity. Whoever disseminates Phrenology is a public benefactor.
>
> Horace Mann, *The American Phrenological*
> *Journal and Miscellany,* 1848

The origins of the Common School Revival, the movement to modernize
education in Massachusetts for which Horace Mann is justly famous, can be
traced to 1824, when James G. Carter called public attention to the abysmal
conditions in the majority of the state's schools. Having worked his way
through Harvard by teaching, Carter was well placed to decry the decline in
class discipline and academic standards. In a number of articles published in
the Boston press, he exposed poor facilities, incompetent instructors, inadequate textbooks, and uncoordinated school committees. The common school
had betrayed its historic mission, and radical reform was urgently needed.
The first step in this revival, he reasoned, had to be the establishment of a
seminary to prepare teachers with the knowledge and skills necessary for their
duties—an understanding of the subjects to be taught, the science of mind,
and the means by which to communicate ideas to the developing child.

The situation Carter described had arisen from a number of changes made
to Colonial law. By the act of 1647, towns of 50 or fewer families were required to maintain schools where children could learn to read and write;
towns with 100 or more families had to provide schools with teachers "able to
instruct youth so far as they shall be fitted for the university."[1] Laws of 1789
and 1824 had eroded these requirements. Districts were enlarged, schools permitted to meet for just six months out of the year, and, dropping knowledge
of Latin and Greek, the master had only to be "well qualified to instruct
youth in orthography, reading, writing, arithmetic, English grammar, and
geography, and good behavior."[2] With the traditional ends of schooling subverted, and with no standard by which to judge the competency of teachers,

local school committees fell into the habit of employing whoever was willing to work for the least remuneration. Teaching the "common branches," it was assumed, required no special abilities. Chaos and mediocrity ensued. Absenteeism rose and wealthy parents started sending their children to private academies. But while many in the legislature were concerned by the unraveling of the common school, the majority was even more troubled by the prospect of raising taxes or ceding local control of education to a government agency. As a result, Carter's petition to establish a state-run teacher training college was defeated by a single vote. However, his concerns over teachers and books were taken up the following year by the State Committee on Education, which carried through legislation, first in 1826 and then 1827, requiring each town to elect a school committee charged with employing qualified teachers and selecting suitable textbooks—adding the amendment, tacitly adhered to by the vast majority of districts, that they "shall never direct to be purchased or used, in any of the town schools, any school-books which are calculated to favor the tenets of any particular sect of Christians."[3] In the years after the schism of orthodox and liberal churches, sectarian struggles had been kept out of the classroom, a state of affairs the Committee found fully in accord with the spirit of religious freedom spelled out in the Bill of Rights. But given the nature of knowledge, this nonsectarian stance often resulted in a rather narrow focus on the common branches that many thought neglected the traditional mission of inculcating piety and morals.

To carry his reforms forward, Carter joined with George B. Emerson, Samuel Hall, and a number of other like-minded friends to establish the American Institute of Education. Commencing in 1830, its five-day annual conventions and numerous publications did much to promote awareness of the urgent problems facing schools in the New England states. Several important legislative acts followed. In 1834, having received a sizable reimbursement from the federal government for Massachusetts's services in the War of 1812, and money from the sale of land in Maine, the General Court established a permanent school fund, initially of 1 million dollars. Income from this account was then distributed among those districts that raised taxes to support schooling and filed yearly reports detailing their educational progress. Two years later, the directors of the Institute petitioned the legislature for a superintendent of common schools and, in January 1837, again called for the establishment of a teachers' seminary. Both memorials lay in committee until

Edward Everett was appointed governor. A Whig, Unitarian, and longtime advocate of education, Everett used his inaugural address to propose the establishment of a State Board of Education. The legislature approved, and the measure was passed into law on April 20, 1837. Of the eight men appointed to join Everett and his lieutenant governor, George Hull—Edmund Dwight, Horace Mann, James Carter, Robert Rantoul, Jared Sparks, Edward Newton, Thomas Robbins, and Emerson Davis—the majority were Whigs and Unitarians. As every student of education knows, Mann, who had just signed the bill into law, was convinced to pass up presidency of the senate to become the board's first secretary (his place on the committee being passed to George Putnam, also a Whig and a Unitarian). Despite years crusading for public education, Carter, it seems, was not the man for the job. As Edmund Dwight and other leading strategists recognized, Mann had the intellect, the will-power, and, having just revised the state's legal statutes, a knowledge of the law necessary to stir local districts from their lethargy.

Invested with no formal authority, only the power, to quote from the official charge, "to diffuse as widely as possible throughout every part of the Commonwealth, information of the most approved and successful methods of arranging the studies, and conducting the education of the young," the position of secretary was hardly a promising move for Mann.[4] Quite why he should give up his prestigious office and lucrative legal practice for such an indeterminate role has been the object of much debate. Traditionally, historians have lauded his benevolent spirit; more recently, revisionists have painted him as a zealot, determined to maintain the status quo at a time of rapid social change. But this psychological accounting has uniformly overlooked the influence of Combe's moral philosophy, which captivated Mann's imagination at the very time he was drawn into the cause of education. According to Mann's journal, on May 18, 1837, Edmund Dwight nominated him to the Board and pleaded that he become its first secretary. On May 25, he spent the day reading "that most valuable book, 'Combe on the Constitution of Man.'"[5] And on May 27, he greeted the official announcement of his membership in the eight-man body by recording his sense of gravity for the important work that lay before them. Over the next few days, his thoughts reveal a growing awareness of the relationship between schooling, civic order, the passions, and virtue. When his office building was firebombed on May 30th, he questioned, "Is it possible that such things could be, if moral instruction were not infinitely below what it ought to be?"[6] On June 11, as members of Boston's Irish community rioted, he considered the dangers of the untrained mind to the Republic.

> The educated, the wealthy, the intelligent, may have a powerful and decisive voice in its formation; or they may live in their own selfish enjoyments, and suffer the ignorant, the vicious, the depraved, to form that public opinion. If they do the latter, they must expect that the course of events will be directed by the licentious impulse, and that history will take its character from the predominant motives of action.[7]

By the end of the month, his mind was set. He had chosen the path of usefulness and dedicated himself to "the improvability of the race."[8] "My jurisdiction has changed! I have abandoned jurisprudence and betaken myself of the larger sphere of mind and morals. Having found the present generation composed of materials almost unmallable [*sic*], I am transferring my efforts to the next. Men are cast-iron; but children are wax."[9]

Reflecting on this period in her husband's life, Mary Peabody Mann recalls that "his interest and action in the cause of insane hospitals had deepened his insight into the primary causes and hindrances of human development: and the study of 'Combe's Constitution of Man,' which he met with in 1837, added new fuel to the fire of his enthusiasm."[10] As even a cursory reading of Mann's work reveals, this rekindled enthusiasm went hand in hand with a religious awakening, a recognition, similar to Combe's, that the laws of mind and nature were the key to reconciling a benevolent God with the evils of life. Mann's biographers rightly emphasize the impact of his adolescent rejection of Calvinism (as taught by his "New Light" pastor, Nathaniel Emmons) and his crisis of faith during the 1830s (following the tragic loss of his first wife). In the depths of his grief, Mann struggled mightily to restore a sense of meaning to his world. Phrenology, it seems, played a part in this reconstruction, transforming the cause of education into a religious mission and the role of secretary into that of a martyr—as he frequently described it. Sacrificing his worldly goods, his reputation, even his health, he would use the same laws that cured the deranged minds of the mad to engineer virtuous and rational citizens and so realize, in America, the kind of practical faith that Combe had pictured in the *Constitution*. Phrenology, as Mann neatly described it, would be "the handmaiden of Christianity."

The secretaryship may have had little formal power, but Mann proved an irresistible force. A distinguished orator, a seasoned politician, one of the state's leading lawyers, and, as all who knew him understood, a person who would not compromise any principle, what he lacked in legal authority was more than compensated for by his power of moral suasion. Turning to Simpson's *Philosophy of Education,* Edgeworth's *Practical Education,* and a host of current articles on schooling, he spent much of June familiarizing himself with the new pedagogy and the issues facing the state's common school system. No reading could have been more "delightful," "nothing more congenial with all my tastes, feelings, and principles."[11] And while his friends chided him for abandoning his political career, Mann set his sights on higher pleasures. Rising in confidence, he contemplated the enormity and the importance of his task. "If I can be the means of ascertaining what is the best construction of houses, what are the best books, what is the best arrangement of studies, what are the best modes of instruction; if I can discover by what appliance of means a non-thinking, non-reflecting, non-speaking child can most surely be trained into a noble citizen," then, he reasoned to his sister, "may I not flatter myself that my ministry has not been in vain?"[12]

The legislature had charged the Board with just two duties, preparing an annual abstract of the common school returns and reporting their deliberations on how the condition and efficiency of the state's schools might be improved. The secretary's role, "under the direction of the Board," was to collect these facts and help diffuse, "as widely as possible, throughout every part of the Commonwealth, information of the most approved and successful methods of arranging the studies and conducting the education of the young."[13] The Board promptly assigned its first task to Mann and, after deliberating how he might fulfill the second, came up with the scheme of holding educational conventions in each of the state's fourteen counties. Attended by local teachers, friends of education, leaders within the community, and whichever members of the Board were available, Mann would deliver a lecture and stage debates on important educational topics. The questions he sent to participants, like the queries he fed the school committees, reveal just how carefully these discussions were managed.

Composing his first lecture in July, Mann spent the best part of August arranging his upcoming tour, printing circulars and soliciting the help of local officials and prominent sympathizers. By the end of the month, he was ready for his first official duty. Traveling to Worcester, he addressed the annual meeting of the American Institute, and, a few days later, with the help of Woodward, Calhoun, and Putnam, staged his own opening convention. Buoyed by the positive reception at both forums, he returned to Boston to finalize his plans. Saddling his mare on September 1, he then set out on the three-day trek to Springfield, the first leg of his month-long circuit. With the exception of the meeting at Pitsfield—which had not been promoted by his fellow Board member, Edward Newton—Mann's labors appear to have been extremely successful. His speech was warmly received and the discussions he staged productive. Most importantly, he was able to buttress his cause by establishing county associations throughout the state that could pressure school committees to enact the recommendations of the Board.

THE PHRENOLOGY OF EDUCATION

In the introduction to *Lectures on Education* (1850), a collection of seven annual addresses, Mann claimed that the overarching purpose of his speeches was to explain the "motives and objects of the Legislature in creating the Board."[14] Intended for "popular and promiscuous audiences," he set out, in the most general terms, the basic principles of his educational crusade. More technical issues relating to teaching filled the volumes of the *Common School Journal,* first published in 1839, while his yearly reports provided the opportunity for him to explore "some of the relations which that cause holds to the interests of civilization and human progress."[15] In each of these forums, the influence of Combe and Simpson is simply unmistakable.

After describing the events that led to the establishment of the Board, Mann opened his first lecture by spelling out the basic metaphysical assumptions underlying phrenological theory. "The entire succession of events, which fills time and makes up life," he explained, "is nothing but causes and effects."[16] God had given human beings the power of reason so that they could understand these laws and "foresee the future consequences of present conduct."[17] Nowhere was this more evident than in the development of a child's character. Noting that "all forms of direct and indirect education, affect mental growth," he explained that "the mobs, the riots, the burnings, the lynchings, perpetrated by the *men* of the present day, are perpetrated because of their vicious or defective education, when children."[18] For, "by an irreparable law of Nature," not only were "the iniquities of the fathers . . . visited upon the children, onto the third and fourth generation," but the "ignorance" and "neglect" of parents "whelped and suckled" the "tiger-passions" that generated such "havoc."[19] "Education," he continued, "demanded a scientific acquaintance with mental laws," in particular the paramount rule that "acquirement and pleasure should go hand in hand."[20] God had given the brain an instinctive appetite for learning, so teachers, like gardeners, had to follow the "voice of Nature" by tailoring the physical, intellectual, and moral environment of the school to the implicit wisdom of the learner. Not only did this imply improving the furniture, heating, and ventilation of schoolhouses, but, he continued, "school studies ought to be arranged, as to promote the harmonious development of the faculties."[21] Following this "natural order and progression" prevented "precocious growth" and the dangerous consequences that follow from cultivating organs in the wrong sequence—as the verbal instruction and abstract rule lessons of current teaching practices did.[22] In place of words, learning had to commence with the senses: by manipulating objects that please the eye and spark curiosity, building from concrete to abstract, general truths would be grounded in a knowledge of experience rather than mere sounds.

Throughout the lecture, Mann returned time and time again to the use of punishment as a means for maintaining discipline. Like Combe, he had a deep personal aversion to Calvinistic child-rearing practices and the vicious treatment of children in the traditional classroom. He was equally opposed to emulation. Given that the propensities acted independently of one another, he recognized, as Simpson had argued, that "the intellect may grow wise while the passions grow wicked."[23] Teaching children to prize knowledge for material gain would only make individuals slaves of their instinctive desires: "the noblest part of [man's] nature—his moral and social affections, held captive in the retinue."[24] In a republic where government was based on the principle "that every man, by the power of reason and the sense of duty, shall be fit to be a voter," education had to imbibe "the minds of children with a love of pure and beautiful things" and produce "godlike men who can tame the madness of the times, and, speaking divine words in a divine spirit, can say to the raging of human passion, 'Peace, be still;' and usher in the calm of enlightened reason and conscience."[25]

By the second week of November, his lecture tour complete, Mann got down to the formidable task of composing an abstract from the hundreds of school returns that filled his office. The statistics, of course, fell neatly into the categories he had defined in his earlier circulars. As he read his *First An-*

nual Report before the Board on January 1, 1838, he unfolded the same areas
of concern that had driven the debates of his conventions, only now Mann
gave the whole problem a distinctively moral spin. Plagued with deplorable
facilities, ineffective school committees, community apathy, and incompetent
teachers, the common school had become a seedbed of vice and ignorance.
Skirting the topic of school architecture—which he worked up into a book-
length study the following year—Mann scolded local authorities for the
wanton neglect of their public duties. Children were allowed to skip school
at will; there was no standardization of textbooks and almost no effort to
supervise teachers. He did not mince words. On the matter of schoolbooks,
for example, he accused the district committees of abrogating their legal responsibility to ensure that children were inculcated in basic religious and
moral values. In the whole state he found only three books, used in six
schools, that attempted to teach "the beautiful and sublime truths of ethics
and of natural religion."[26] "One of the greatest and most exigent wants of
our schools at the present time," he continued, was to identify texts written

> to supply children at an early age, with simple and elementary notions
> of right and wrong in feeling and in conduct, so that the appetites and
> passions, as they spring up in the mind, may, by a natural process, be
> conformed to principles, instead of principles being made to conform
> to appetites and passions.[27]

His travels revealed a familiar scene, students of all ages and abilities sitting
in the same room, each working separately from whatever books their parents
had provided. This hodgepodge had to be addressed. Committees had to
insist on common texts, and students had to be graded according to their
abilities. Mann admitted that the blame did not rest solely with the committee members, who, he observed, typically served without remuneration. The
real problem was the widespread public apathy for education. More enlightened parents, alert to the importance of moral and intellectual culture, sent
their children to private academies. But this greatly aggravated the situation.
Removing leading students from the classroom generated an uneconomical
twin system and fostered social divisions that undermined Republican ideals.
Don't think just of your own boys and girls, Mann warned reflecting parents,
"for those children, whose welfare they discard, and whose associations they
deprecate, will constitute more than *five sixths* of the whole body of that

community, of which their children will only be a feeble minority, vulnerable at every point, and utterly incapable of finding a hiding-place for any earthly treasure, where the witness, the juror and the voter cannot reach and annihilate it!"[28] Finally, Mann turned to the competence of masters. "Teaching," he asserted, "is the most difficult of all arts, and the profoundest of all sciences."[29] In its "practical sense, it involves a knowledge of the principal laws of physical, mental, and moral growth, and of the tendency of means, not more to immediate, than to remote results."[30] As he had argued in his lecture, reason and conduct in later life depended on the philosophic wisdom of the teacher. But sadly, supply had answered demand, and the public had gotten the teachers they were willing to pay for. Without knowledge of the machinery with which they worked, armies of incapables were flowing from the schools. Academic learning was obviously important, but, Mann reminded the Board, this was only a small portion of schooling. State law demanded that every child receive a moral education. Values had to be changed, money raised, buildings improved, books and apparatus purchased, and teachers' salaries increased.

The Board agreed, and thanked the secretary for his labors. His circuit, they noted, had awakened a new spirit of enthusiasm in the state, and his *First Annual Report* had skillfully generalized the range of problems facing the common school system. But cognizant of their limited authority, they could do little more than draw the legislature's attention to Mann's recommendations. Funds had to be found for the construction of better schools; members of school committees ought to receive a modest stipend for their service; and institutions should be established for the education of teachers. In addition, the Board solicited shelving and cases to encourage the development of school libraries. They recognized the need to provide suitable works of science, history, and morals, although they shied away from suggesting particular texts in the belief that the marketplace would ensure the free flow of ideas. However, they did propose the publication of a journal, devoid of party spirit and sectarianism, that could diffuse intelligent opinion on educational matters. On the issue of textbooks, they were more dogmatic. Clearly seeking to extend their legal authority, the Board argued for the power to hold back the school fund from any district that did not adopt the books it recommended. As Mann found out from his returns the following year, school committees welcomed the Board's guidance, but bristled at the prospect of having to submit to the directives of a centralized autocratic agency—a localist sentiment that was also starting to build against the Board among the newly elected Democratic legislature.

The General Court responded to the Board's appeal by mandating a number of small changes in the work of the school committees—committee members would be paid for their services, and reports, now due at the end of the academic year, had to be read or distributed to the local community. But Mann had his sights on far more radical reforms, and, in the first quarter of 1838, he persuaded the Board to pursue two initiatives: the publication of library books and the establishment of Normal schools. Gaining control of the means and content of education was not going to be easy, and, by the end of the year, he was deeply embroiled in a religious and political struggle that very nearly resulted in the termination of the Board. Mann's ability to weather these disputes and carry both measures forward is a testament to his legal ingenuity and the persuasiveness with which he wielded phrenological theory and secular logic. Whatever the official charge of the Board, by 1841, Mann had achieved de facto control of education in the state and set up a bureaucracy to carry his reforms into practice.

THE FOUNDATION OF MIND AND MORALS

At their January meeting in 1838, Mann had persuaded the Board to organize the publication of a series of affordable books that would form the basis of a school library. School committees, he promised, would not be compelled to purchase any work they found objectionable. Bids were tendered, and Capen's firm—which would also publish the *Common School Journal*—won the contract. The guiding principle was to provide books, as Mann later put it, "adapted to [children's] moral and intellectual wants, and fitted to nourish their minds with the elements of uprightness and wisdom" without falling foul of sectarian controversy.[31] Removing a potentially volatile debate from the public arena, the Board agreed to follow the example of Ireland and establish a subcommittee comprising all political and religious interests to select appropriate texts. Baptists, Congregationalists, and Unitarians, Democrats and Whigs, need not worry, Mann claimed, for each had representatives armed with a veto, "watchful sentinels, to guard [their] social and spiritual rights against aggression."[32]

The group's chair, Thomas Robbins, shared Mann's enthusiasm for the project. Having pushed the Board to pursue reintroduction of the Bible into the classroom, he was most concerned that the library, while nondoctrinaire, have a decidedly "religious cast." Evidently, the secretary proposed including the *Constitution*. In a letter thanking Mann for "the large bundle of books" that had arrived for his consideration, Robbins reported having "no predilections for Phrenology, apprehending that its tendency might be something Athiestical; but I have been looking over Combe's work & find it better than I expected, & have no objection to it being admitted," beyond the fact that it seemed a little philosophical for the average student. Curiously, Combe's work did not appear in the series, although, along with other phrenological texts, it was required reading for students in America's first Normal school.

As announced at the beginning of Mann's *Third Annual Report* (1839), the Massachusetts School Library comprised two sets of fifty volumes: the first, designed for children between ten and twelve years of age, the second for more advanced scholars and their parents. The goal, according to Capen's introduction, was to present

> every branch of "Science and Literature . . . without sectarian or denominational character in religion, or of partisan character in politics . . . in a popular garb, that they may prove so attractive, as to lure the child onwards, fix his attention, and induce him, subsequently, to seek information from other more recondite works, which, if put into his hands at the onset, would alarm him, and induce a disgust for that which would appear dry and unintelligible, and of course, uninteresting.[33]

Ten volumes were already in print, and leading scholars had been lined up to complete the remaining works. At just forty cents each, Washington Irving, Benjamin Silliman, and Francis Wayland, *The Lives of Eminent Americans*, Paley's *Natural Theology*, texts on chemistry, astronomy, and natural philosophy, and *The Pursuit of Knowledge under Difficulties* could hardly have been refused by any patriotic community, especially if they considered Mann's eloquent and compelling case for the importance of serious reading to the development of the individual and the race.

In Mann's opinion, the "'fictions,' 'light reading,' 'trashy works,' 'empherial,' [*sic*] or 'bubble literature'" that most people read did little or nothing to elevate the mind or refine morals. No doubt they had value as a form of amusement. He conceded that "in feeble health, or after sickness, or severe bodily or mental labor, an amusing, captivating, enlivening book, which levies no tax upon the powers of thought for the pleasure it gives, is a delightful recourse. It is medicinal to the sick and recuperative to the wearied mind."[34] But woe to those who turned to such books for common enjoyment! It was not just the loss of wisdom, but the effect on the brain that worried Mann. For, "in reading merely for amusement the mind is passive, acquiescent, recipient, merely."[35] Mental effort, he asserted, "is just as indispensable, in order to strengthen any faculty of the intellect, as a series of muscular exercises is to strengthen any limb of the body."[36]

Without this exertion, the power of clear, orderly, coherent thought,— the power of seeing whether means have been adapted to ends,— become inactive, and at length withers away like a palsied limb; while, at the same time,—the attention being hurried over a variety of objects, between which nature has established no relations,—a sort of volatility or giddiness is inflicted upon the mind, so that the general result upon the whole faculties, is that of weakness and faintness combined.[37]

"*Light reading makes light minds.*"[38] Even more problematic was the fact that many popular novels were written solely to excite the emotions. Putting the intellect to sleep while the mind surrendered to pleasure, the imagination escaped into a fantasy world that numbed people to the duties of life and sufferings of their fellows. "In all healthy minds," he observed, "judicious action flows from virtuous impulse."[39] Tales of romance, the impossible exploits of heroes, and valorizations of criminals with wit, intelligence, and humor all undermined the necessary relationship between behavior and the moral consequences that underwrote the order of experience. Most destructive of all were the cheap comic books sold by peddlers. Designed to prey on the untutored appetites, the "moral venom" they spouted ate away the "ever-during foundations of conduct and character" necessary for "a free government" and a "Christian people."[40] How could one prepare good parents, good neighbors, and good citizens from children weaned on such an irrational diet? He was also troubled that "so many excellent young persons" should reenact the age-old folly of the court and seek cultivation, grace, and refinement through a knowledge of literature. Fine arts and the ornaments of civilized life were important, but in a world where "utility still outranks elegance," no gentility or gracefulness of mind and manners, however exquisite and fascinating, is any substitute for practical wisdom and benevolence. Without copious recourses of useful knowledge, in our young men and young women; without available, applicable judgment and discretion, adequate to the common occasions and ready for the emergencies of life,—the ability to quote poetic sentiments, and expiate on passages of fine writing, or on a connoisseurship in art, is but mockery.[41]

Finally, to the objection that the average person could get all the information they needed from newspapers or the lecture theatre, Mann responded that however useful and entertaining these mediums were, they tended to present loosely associated facts rather than a coherent philosophy fusing the laws of nature and the duties of life. Such an understanding, he insisted, could only be taught through the steady and systematic engagement with serious texts.

Children needed libraries that would help form mind and character and provide positive knowledge of the world. But one obstacle remained: religion. In a state that had more churches per person than any other comparable population; in which there were more volumes and periodicals devoted to religious issues than any other topic; in which almost every family had a Bible, and those that did not could obtain one free from the government; and in which everyone agreed that religious education was of the first importance, there was also a need for knowledge of the "domestic, social, economical, political, literary and scientific" duties of life under a free government.[42] Cast on a barren soil with a burgeoning population, Massachusetts had to harness the forces of nature—steam, wind, water, and electricity. There was not a single art that could not be made more productive with an understanding of the constitution of events; not a single task, however lowly, that could not be achieved more efficiently with intelligence of God's laws. Take health and nutrition, for example. If every individual knew the structure of the body and the mind, disease and premature death would be greatly averted. How could such knowledge contradict the doctrines of any religious sect?

To know something of nature, children had to develop "their observing and comparing faculties" at the time they were most active, "storing in the mind an abundance of materials, for the judging and reasoning powers to act upon."[43] To know something of morality, they should read biographies of great and good men, who would supply models of virtue to guide conduct when reason lacked the time or power to reflect on events. And, to know something of society, they should study the history of the free institutions that first germinated in New England, among men and women devoted to civil and religious liberty under God's ordinance. But by far, the largest field for improvement, in Mann's estimation, lay with knowledge of the human mind.

> When an ignorant man regards the operations of the mind, he discerns only a tumultuary, conflicting tide of wishes and terrors, of pleasures and pains, of doubts and purposes, rising, contending, without order or law. He takes no cognizance of the different powers and faculties with which he has been endowed, of their relative supremacy, of their different spheres of action, nor of their adaptations to his temporal condition; and hence, when he obeys their impulses, it is without the approval of the conscience, and when he commands them, it is without the discrimination of reason. Every child, towards the close of his minority, has time and capacity enough, could he be furnished with the means, to acquire much of the knowledge, enjoined in that ancient percept, so universally celebrated and sanctioned, "Know thyself."[44]

What more pressing religious duty could there be?

As his critics soon discovered, Mann would pursue his cause to the death. Breaking arguments down to their very atoms, he built his case with a logic none could assail and with a withering rhetoric even the most resolute ego could not withstand. Ever willing to escalate the argument and increase the invective, he simply would not bow to another viewpoint. His was the word and will of God. The first to feel the sting of Mann's razor was Francis Packard, a bitter rival who would still be bent on revenge fifteen years after Mann's death.[45] The best account of this contest is still Raymond Carver's classic *Horace Mann and Religion in the Massachusetts Public Schools*.[46] Around the time Mann wrote to Robbins, Carver explains, Packard, then a representative of the American Sunday School Union, had written to Everett promoting his society's own Select Library. Mann responded to the group's Boston agent on the governor's behalf that the Union's books were altogether too sectarian for Massachusetts. Sensing a personal bias, Packard sent Mann a copy of John Abott's *Child at Home,* requesting his estimation of its value as a school text. Mann, who was appalled by Abott's orthodox portrayal of a vindictive and merciless God, pointed out that its message of fear and blind obedience would certainly be rejected by Universalists, and so legally could not be adopted. Responding to a follow-up letter, where Packard pressed him to justify how any group could find Abbot's goal of inculcating piety objectionable, Mann reiterated his understanding of sectarianism under Massachusetts law, then added his personal opinion, that evil arose from society's failure to cultivate the moral powers, rather than the child's nature, and that the Bible should not be read until the reflective faculties had developed. Packard seized upon this response and, before a meeting of Congregational ministers, painted Mann as an antievangelical determined to impose his own religious convictions on the children of the state. Secularism, he maintained, with some justification, was simply Unitarianism in disguise, and the Normal schools Mann sought to build, nothing less than seminaries for a new priesthood. The orthodox, he warned, should beware lest, once again, the Unitarians stole the rug from under their feet. Robbins responded on Mann's behalf that, as of yet, no decisions had been made about any library book. When Packard then threatened to read Mann's letter, other friends of the secretary objected to the use of the podium for personal attacks, and Packard lost the stage. After all, he was only there to sell books! Acrimonious letters passed back and forth in which Mann challenged the propriety of Packard's actions, Packard questioned the obligations of Mann's office, and the two locked horns on issues of doctrine and public education. As they ground to an impasse, Packard took his attack to the pages of the *New York Observer*. In "Triumph of Infidelity," and then shortly after in two letters addressed to Herman Humphrey, president of Amherst College, he claimed that the Board were engaged in a conspiracy to banish the Bible from the state's schools and to replace religion with the naturalistic ethics of Mann's "new fangled philosophy of Education." There was some sympathy for this view. Newton, for example, had resigned from the Board earlier that month, refusing to be a party in the spread of secularism. Alert to the danger of a sectarian rift, other members of the Board worked behind the scenes to shore up the support of leading orthodox ministers. Davis wrote to the editor of the *Observer* rebutting Packard's claims and requesting that the paper not print any more letters until the secretary's *Second Annual Report* had been published. The Board, he insisted, should be judged by its actions, not by innuendo. Robbins, aided by John Calhoun, persuaded Humphrey of the same point. But Packard would not be contained. Just days before Mann's report was due, he issued his "suppressed" letters in a twenty-five-page pamphlet that warned of the Board's secret agenda and their "invisible all-controlling influence." Now *The Boston Recorder* entered the fray. Opposing the Board's reforms, a December 28th editorial claimed that "sectarianism" was synonymous with spiritual faith and that Mann's efforts to ban the reading of scripture were part of a plot to banish religion from schools. Two weeks later the *Recorder* published an anonymous review of Packard's pamphlet and the first of five letters from a respected orthodox minister named Storrs. Although Storrs took exception to the vehemence of Packard's attack, he nonetheless found a grain of truth in his claims. Mann was not duplicitous, merely mistaken in his belief that the common school could thrive without the Bible. All learning had to revolve around the dangers of moral ruin, the possibility of redemption, the duties of life, and the rewards and punishment in the hereafter. In any case, Storrs maintained, the separation of church and state demanded such decisions be left to the town, not to the government. Concerned not to escalate the debate, Mann wrote to Storrs in order to clear up any misapprehensions that may have arisen between them. He did not embrace the *Recorder's* definition of sectarianism, nor was he on a crusade to exclude religion from the curriculum. Indeed, it was he, in his *First Annual Report,* who had drawn attention to the lack of Christian books and the schools' legal duty to inculcate religion and morality. Storrs, he assumed, had been mislead by Packard's wicked pamphlet. Only towns had the authority to choose texts, including the Bible. Finally, he assured Storrs that where he did have jurisdiction, in the Normal schools, Scripture would be read daily. Mann and his supporters did a good job discrediting Packard (pointing to his underlying financial motives) and calming the concerns of the orthodox, who, as Messerli points out, were largely supportive of the common school reforms. Even so, the same issues would boil up again within the legislature when a group that Mann characterized as "the ultra-orthodox" took exception to what they saw as the dangerous and unwarranted power of the Board and its encroachment on Massachusetts' historic principle of localism.

THE NORMAL SCHOOLS

Two weeks before he brought the issue of the school library before the Board, Mann had been called to address the House of Representatives. With Edmund

Dwight in attendance, he talked for nearly two hours on the urgent need to improve the quality of teaching within the state. Dwight, a longtime supporter of Carter's reforms, sensed sympathy for Mann's cause, but recognized the legislature's continued reluctance to raise taxes for education. He decided to make an offer no Yankee could refuse: he would commit $10,000 of his own money toward the establishment of Normal schools if the state would match his donation and agree to give the Board complete control over their organization. With the recommendation of the Joint Committee on Education headed by Carter, the General Court approved the measure, and, on April 19, Everett signed Dwight's proposal into law. Mann had to move quickly and carefully. As with the school library, he was at pains to demonstrate the Board's nonsectarian spirit—Packard's criticisms were starting to raise eyebrows. After much political wrangling, balancing geographical and religious interests with the willingness of districts to commit resources, three sites where chosen: Lexington, Barre, and Bridgewater. Lexington, which promised to lease an old academy and contribute $1,000 toward the project, would be the first to open—hopefully, Mann projected, on April 19 the following year, the anniversary of America's great battle for freedom. Next, Mann faced the equally delicate task of selecting principals. After the Board's first choice, Thomas Gaulledet declined the post, Mann cast around for other orthodox candidates. Not surprisingly, given the pay and duties of the position, all of Mann's selections rejected the challenge. Finally, as the dedication approached, and his desperation mounted, Mann turned to Cyrus Peirce, a Nantucket schoolteacher who had impressed him on his first circuit of the state. Accepting the call with great reluctance—he seemed to live in awe of Mann—Peirce rushed to prepare his seminary with the meager resources available to him. Aided by his wife, he was to perform every task from lecturing students to cleaning the floors. Eight weeks after the proposed date, America's first Normal school opened inauspiciously amid a torrential rainstorm, and with only three students. Three more trickled in the following week, but by Christmas more than twenty had enrolled in the all-female academy. After Lexington, Mann had less difficulty finding suitable principals. Two months later, Samuel Newman, an orthodox minister and former professor at Bowdoin College opened the school at Barre; the following year, Colonel Nicholas Tillinghast, an instructor from West Point, took charge of Bridgewater.

Mann explained his objectives for the Normal schools most fully in his second lecture, "Special Preparation, a Pre-requisite to Teaching," attended by Combe at the October convention in Taunton. Extending the philosopher's views on the social duties of women, he drew attention to the distinctive character of the female brain, and asked,

> Is there not an obvious, constitutional difference of temperament be-tween the sexes, indicative of a prearranged fitness and adaptation, and making known to us, as by a heavenly imparted sign, that woman, by her livelier sensibility and her quicker sympathies, is the fore chosen guide and guardian of children of a tender age?[47]

Women, Mann answered, had a "high and holy mission" to "breathe pure and exalted sentiments into young and tender hearts."[48] But such work had to be based on a knowledge of the developing mind, "the laws of organization and of increase."[49] In contrast to empiricist philosophers, he did not believe that "a difference in education is the sole cause of all the differences existing among men," but rather, "certain substructures of temperament and disposi-tion, which education finds, at the beginning of its work, and which it can never wholly annul."[50] "The contrasts among men result, not from the pos-session of a different number of original faculties, but from possessing the same faculties, in different proportions, and in different degrees of activity."[51] This could be seen clearly, Mann believed, in the customs of civilized and barbarian races, and indeed the different "intellectual and moral classes" of society.[52] An "appalling truth" had to be faced; "every child born into this world has tendencies and susceptibilities pointing to the furthest extremes of good and evil."[53] Although "that wise and good man" Samuel Woodward was able to "tame the ferocity of the insane . . . and restore them to the guid-ance of reason," indeed, "can do this not only to one, but to hundreds at a time," Mann observed, "we apply these obvious principles, to everything but the education of our children."[54] As a result, the "ignorant and passion-ate teacher" turns "a hundred gentle, confiding spirits into rebels and anar-chists."[55]

> Unfortunately inflamed or . . . unwisely stimulated by an erroneous education . . . a subordinate power . . . grows importunate, exorbitant, aggrandizes itself, encroaches upon its fellow faculties, until, at last, ob-taining the mastery, it subverts the moral order of the soul, and wages

its parricidal war against the sovereignty of conscience within, and the laws of society and of Heaven without.[56]

Witness how the overdevelopment of the appetite for "nourishing beverages" had led men and women "into the seething hell of intemperance"; how acquisitiveness had produced misery; how ideality created slaves to fashion; and how self-esteem produced people consumed by "pride, conceit, intolerance."[57] Teachers had to understand that "all the faculties have their related objects, and they grow by being excited to action through the stimulus or instrumentality of those objects."[58] As Simpson had argued, so Mann insisted, "the blacksmith's right arm, the philosopher's intellect, the philanthropist's benevolence, all grow and strengthen according to this law of exercise."[59]

Eschewing verbal learning and the traditional curriculum, Mann directed teachers to train the mind's various organs while providing useful knowledge. "Nature, science, art" offered "a boundless variety of objects and processes, adapted to quicken and employ each of the faculties."[60] The perceptive powers would be "exercised in the correctness of observation" and the reflective organs in "comparison and judgment."[61] Turning to the moral sentiments, Mann drew his lecture to a close by assuring his audience that "in the education of children, *motives are everything,* MOTIVES ARE EVERYTHING."[62] Neither the fear of punishment nor the promise of reward could serve the purpose of moral education, for "stimulating a child to the performance of actions, externally right, by appealing to motives intrinsically wrong," ultimately sold the child into the bondage of propensities such as destructiveness and self-esteem. Children had to learn the greater happiness that results from acting out of higher motives. Accordingly, Mann concluded, Normal schools, "by study, by discussion, by practical observation" had the task of disseminating "the art and science of teaching" so that those young women charged with nurturing the delicate souls of children would understand how to "touch the right spring, with the right pressure, at the right time."[63] Given this digest of phrenological theory and practice, it is hardly surprising that Combe would write excitedly to his brother that he had never "listened to a more sound, philosophical, comprehensive, practical, eloquent, felicitous composition."[64]

Although no records appear to have survived from Barre and Bridgewater, Peirce's diary and the journal of his prize student, Mary Swift, provide a fascinating picture of the first year at Lexington, revealing how the principles of mind that Mann espoused were realized in the process of teacher education. In contrast to the public school, the Board had complete authority to determine the studies undertaken by future teachers. As Mann outlined the curriculum in the *Common School Journal,* the Normal schools would develop proficiency in all school subjects (orthography, reading, writing, arithmetic, geography, history, etc.) along with knowledge of natural history, astronomy, physiology, and mental philosophy. Students would also learn the "principles of Piety and Morality, common to all sects of Christians" and "THE SCIENCE AND ART OF TEACHING, WITH REFERENCE TO ALL THE ABOVE NAMED STUDIES."[65] Finally, as he had promised Storrs, a portion of the Scriptures was to be read each day.

The school building had two classrooms and dormitories for twenty. Presumably some of the thirty-four women who attended for the second year's class must have lived at home or boarded out. Starting in the second term, the downstairs class was turned into a model school for thirty local children and kept, in rotation, by three of the senior students. Swift was the first superintendent and two other "Normalites" acted as her assistants. The presence of Mrs. Peirce seems to have served as something of a silent monitor within the classroom. Peirce would observe his students twice a day and, from time to time, teach classes himself to demonstrate his methods in front of the entire school, thus ensuring that his students understood how to integrate "theory and practice, percept and example."[66] Starting the week with a formal lecture on the "qualifications, motives, and duties of teachers, the disciplines, management, and instruction of schools, and the *manner* in which the various subjects should be taught," he presented his philosophy of education and something of the *mission* of teaching that he had evolved in his own thirty-three-year career. Originally a disciplinarian, he now proclaimed "love and kindness" and "the entire exclusion of the *premium and emulation system,* and of corporal punishment."[67]

In the autobiographical sketch he wrote for Henry Barnard, Peirce confessed "the book to which, after the Bible, I owe the most is that incomparable work of George Combe, '*On the Constitution of Man.*' It was to me a most suggestive book: and I regard it as the best treatise on education, and the philosophy of man, which I have ever met with."[68] This is apparent from the daily studies at Lexington. The very first entry in Mary Swift's journal, omitted by Yale University Press, is a "long, detailed abstract of the second chapter of [Andrew] Combe's Physiology."[69] The next day her lessons in physiology continued, and after a class in arithmetic, she was introduced to the delights of Francis Wayland's *Moral Philosophy*. Two days later we find her struggling with the principles of light and refraction and hearing a practical lesson on physiology that included remarks on the tightness of women's dresses. "Father Peirce," it seems, was not aware that fashion had swung in the opposite direction! And so it continued, six days a week: stories from the Scriptures were followed by classes in the common branches, recitations of Combe's *Physiology,* and discussions of natural history and political economy. On Christmas Day students started the *Constitution* and Brigham's *Remarks;* in the spring they read Simpson's *Philosophy of Education* and the works of Maria Edgeworth; and, in their second year, Combe's *Moral Philosophy.*

Swift's notes on fourteen Saturday morning lectures also reveal how freely Peirce drew upon phrenological principles. Education had two components, instruction and training: faculties were strengthened by exercise; and teachers had to aim at the harmonious balance of the mind's organs. More importantly, perhaps, he modeled best practice in his own teaching. Explaining his pedagogical methods, Peirce identified four modes of recitation. "1st, by question and answer; 2nd, by conversation; 3rd, by calling on one, two, three, more or less, to give an analysis of the whole subject contained in the lesson; and 4th, by requiring written analyses, in which the *ideas* of the author are stated in the *language* of the pupil."[70] He was

> ever mingling, or attempting to mingle, at these exercises, theory and example; frequently putting the inquiry to them, not only, "How do you understand such and such a statement, or explain such a principle, or illustrate such a position to a class, which you may be teaching?"[71]

Consider, for example, the 100 questions he presented to the students. Answers were to be researched and defended by the principles cited in the texts. These included such phrenological puzzlers as "If we consider disease & death the natural penalties of the violation of God's established laws, do we diminish the salutary effects of belief in his Superintending Providence?"[72] Of course not! "The Providence of God was displayed, by showing his creatures how they might save themselves from misery."[73] "Question 47th Does the brain give form to the scull, or vice versa?"[74] "52nd If the laws of Combe are correct, among what classes should we expect to find the most frequent instances of deformity?"[75] "79th Is the danger of an insufficiently excited brain well understood in the community?"[76] Yale University Press omitted these and many other answers, but did include Peirce's reply to "question 6th If it is true as phrenologists assert, that the higher the forehead the greater the intellect; why do we so frequently find people with high foreheads & little intellect?"[77] Because, he replied, "sometimes the forehead is high but narrow . . . sometimes the organs of perception as color & form are protuberant & give the forehead a sloping appearance—but" as all teachers should know, "a really flat and low forehead is seldom accompanied with much intellect."[78] Reading character and dispositions from the pupil's head was to be part of the teacher's art.

Typical of Peirce's open discussions were topics such as "can the proper objects of schools be secured without appeal to corporal punishments & rewards or premiums?"[79] "Can a method be devised for a system of exercise which shall be consistent with the plan of this institution and not at variance with the rules of physiology as laid down by Mr. Combe?"[80] And, touching on the question of infant depravity and inherited vice, "At what time does the moral power of the child commence?"[81] Combined with student recitations on assigned readings; the lectures and delineations of visiting phrenologists; the sermons of Charles Follen; talks from Horace Mann; and visits from Howe, Mann, and Emerson, there is little wonder Mary Swift adopted the language of the day. After taking his students to the inauguration of Governor Morton, Peirce even found time for a field trip to Spurzheim's grave. Swift fretted over her small organ of number and her rather larger self-esteem. But she need not have worried. Peirce considered her his finest pupil, and she clearly impressed Howe, who later employed her to educate Laura Bridgman, the most famous experiment in phrenological theory. In later life she would apply these teachings to the education of the deaf, and even became a tutor of Helen Keller.

THE BATTLE FOR SURVIVAL

In contrast to Swift's lighthearted journal, Peirce's diary does not make happy reading. He despaired at the attitudes and abilities of his students and begged Mann to release him from a task he lacked the energy and ability to fulfill. Painting Lexington as a dismal failure, he considered himself the cause's worst enemy. It was only his sense of loyalty to Mann at a time when the

Normal schools were under attack that persuaded him to continue his labors. Not that the opponents of the Normal schools ever showed much interest in the activities at Lexington; Peirce only records visits from friends of education. Their criticisms took a broader sweep, as illustrated by arguments in Orestes Brownson's review of Mann's *Second Annual Report* in the October 1839 issue of *Boston Quarterly*.[82]

Brownson, who paid little attention to the content of Mann's Report, charged that the Board was a machine for spreading Whig philosophy and Unitarian dogma. Raising the specter of Prussian autocracy, he argued that Normal schools and mandated textbooks were gradually eroding the democratic basis of American life. Rejecting all centralizing agencies, he zealously defended the right of local districts to direct their own affairs. All systems of education, he argued, must be grounded in religion and politics, because these "embraced all the interests and concernments of human beings."[83] But the Board's advocacy of Christianity "so far, and only so far, as it was in common to all sects . . . if it means anything, means nothing at all. There was no common ground between all the various religious denominations . . . on which the educationalist might plant himself. The difference between a Unitarian and a Calvinist is fundamental."[84] The same was true in politics. Whigs and Democrats advocated irreconcilable views of human nature. Whigism, he argued, was "based upon materialism, and is atheistical in its logical tendencies."[85] Democrats, on the other hand, "accepted an element of the supernatural in every man, placing him in relation with universal and absolute truths."[86] For Brownson, therefore, the state had no business imposing a single set of views on all children; citizens had the right to organize schools that would inculcate the religious and political values they saw fit.

As Combe saw it, this was just another effort to keep the masses ignorant, the "supernatural" being nothing more than the "unenlightened and untrained impulses of the human faculties, ever ready to take in whatever impressions, and to move in whatever directions, men of bold and ardent minds chose to communicate to them."[87] Surely, he reasoned, no Christian sect disputed "the excellence of the precepts and the practical conduct of Jesus Christ!"[88] Here was a set of truths on which religious and political leaders could agree, for did not the state have the right to instruct its members "so as to accomplish them for their secular duties . . . while having no title to interfere with their private judgments concerning the best means of ensuring their safety in a future life?"[89] Three months later, when Marcus Morton rode the tide of popular resentment against the Fifteen Gallon Law, unseating Everett by a single vote, Brownson's Democratic concerns gained an official voice. Peirce and his students heard no direct attack on the Board at Morton's inauguration, but between the lines, his linking of progress in education to the tradition of democratic localism spelled out a clear message. A month later, acting on Morton's recommendation, the legislature asked the Committee on Education to review the standing of the Board. Four days later a majority report, authored by Allan Dodge and Fredrick Emerson was returned, and four days after that, a minority response was crafted, with Mann's assistance, by John Shaw and Thomas Greene.

Combe, who was in Boston for the whole affair, and may well have helped compose the Whig reply, carefully dissected the argument. The Board, the majority claimed, had "a tendency, a strong tendency, to engross itself in the entire regulation of the common schools."[90] Not true, Combe responded, it had no *legal* power over school districts, merely the authority of intelligence. The majority, of course, knew this, as demonstrated by their obverse question: "Why constitute a body with no legal standing?" Clearly the Board did have power, moral and intellectual power. Surely, Combe pointed out, the most cost-effective use of reason in the state. But then would not teachers' organizations be better equipped for this purpose? Not judging by the condition of the state's schools! Repeating Brownson's arguments, the majority then complained that the very process of centralization undermined the democratic basis of republican institutions. Combe observed that the Board was without power to coerce, or even to veto. It appealed only to reason. How could this undermine democracy unless the rational nature of men and women was denied? Pressing the point, he maintained that sovereignty still resided with parents, for they had the power to elect school committees and superintendents who best represented their interests. If the Board's suggestions were wise, they would be adopted; if not, they would be ignored. Finally, the majority's scaremongering about the indoctrination of religious and political values flew in the face of common wisdom. There was "a vast field of Christian, ethical, and political truth which is highly interesting and instructive to the young, and which, nevertheless, is happily without the pale of contest."[91] As for Normal schools, the majority's views were hardly calculated to sway the undecided mind. First and foremost they denied any science of teaching, maintaining that every person must develop his or her own unique methods of instruction. What was the point of creating a new profession when schools were only in session four to five months a year? And, what could these new institutions offer that existing academies and high schools did not provide? Was it not better, the majority argued, to leave education to the marketplace? As for pleas to see the trial through, they found Mann's arguments flawed in principle. The best course of action was simply to buy out the teachers' contracts, repay Dwight, and close the Normal schools immediately.

Adopting a somber and impartial tone, the minority questioned the wisdom of terminating a trial before it had run its course, especially given that the money had already been spent. Reason and prudence demanded a fair test. Unlike the majority report, the minority response drew upon expert witnesses, Howe and George B. Emerson, to review Peirce's achievements. Lexington, Howe declared, "was the best school he had ever seen."[92] No friend of the Prussians, as everyone knew, Howe claimed to have been suspicious about the dangers of indoctrination, but having visited the school several times, and having examined its students, he was struck by the real learning he had witnessed. Other institutions might match these accomplishments, but Howe preferred America's first Normal school

> because its system of instruction is truly philosophical; because it is based upon the principle that the young mind hungers and thirsts for knowledge, as the body does for food; because it makes the students not merely the recipients of knowledge, but calls all their faculties into operation to *attain it themselves;* and finally, because relying upon the higher and nobler parts of the pupil's nature, it rejects all addresses to bodily fears, and all appeals to selfish feelings.[93]

In response to the majority's "teach by doing" credo, Howe assured the legislature that children would no longer have to suffer as schoolmasters experimented upon them. Future teachers would learn about the child's mind before undertaking to manage it. And, significantly, Peirce had achieved something no other institution could match: he was developing his student's moral nature, instilling into the young women under his charge a real sense of mission for their profession. Emerson continued the chorus of praise, adding his own observations about the quality of teaching in the model school, the proof, as he put it, of the whole system.

These substantive arguments, together with the revelation that the majority report had been written after only two hours of deliberation, without even consulting the committee, helped defeat the measure by 285 to 182 votes. A sound but still, in Combe's view, disturbing victory. As he prepared his final report on the state of American civilization, he was struck by the fact that 182 of the leading men in the most enlightened state had voted against reason and morality. It was hard to imagine a more vivid illustration of public ignorance and justification for the importance of education to the future of the Republic. Other attacks would follow—Dodge, for example, sought to eliminate the Board on the pretext of consolidating government bureaucracy and trimming expenses—but, by and large, the following years offered a period of calm in which Mann could consolidate the authority of the Board. By the summer of 1841, when Combe's anonymous *Edinburgh Review* article on education in Massachusetts was read before the American Institute, Mann and Howe could gloat and declare victory over religious fanatics and the opponents of reason.[94]

12

From Savagery to Civilization

Our belief is, that it has been the blessing of this child to have lost those senses and organs, through which, in the case of other children, the follies and vices and errors of the world find an inlet into the soul.

Horace Mann, *Common School Journal*, May 15, 1843

Having consolidated sweeping changes in the Massachusetts school system, by 1843, Horace Mann might well have listened to the council of Edmund Dwight, resigned the secretaryship, and reentered politics. Evidently, he was still intent on pushing further reforms, of bringing to America the pedagogical advances of the widely vaulted Prussian system. Like others of his day, he had read about Prussian schooling in the reports of Nicholas Bache and Victor Cousin. But Mann also had the council of George Combe, who, after his return to Scotland, had spent the following year in Germany.[1] Long an admirer of the Teutonic brain, Combe hoped that his doctrines would help persuade the nation's leaders to break the chains of despotism and establish free institutions throughout Germany. As he noted on his journey down the Rhine, under the sway of Prussia, a massive effort to build new schools and enlighten the people was already in progress. Given "their large intellect, and coronal region," self-government was sure to make Germany the most civilized nation in the world.[2] Early in 1842, Mann had written to Combe asking him to "furnish me during your residence in Germany with a series of letters in relation to the German schools,—their course of studies, modes of instruction, disciplines, order, qualifications of teachers, attainments of scholars, results, &c. Anything, in fact, where you could write without much labor, & which would be most interesting to our people, & most beneficial to our schools, whose condition and wants you so well know."[3] Combe wrote back suggesting that Mann come see for himself.

By the turn of 1843, with Combe back in Edinburgh promising to return to Germany that May, Mann committed to the trip. Along with Howe, he would join the philosopher on a phrenological tour of the Old World. But as their voyage drew near, events took an unexpected course. Howe, recently smitten with the twenty-three-year-old Julia Ward, announced his engagement and proposed their European tour should also serve as a honeymoon. Mann agreed, even though this would delay their departure by a month—as it turned out, seriously undermining the purpose of the trip. No doubt bringing personal matters to the fore, Mann then followed his friend's example and cemented his own affections for Mary Peabody. On May 1, the two couples, accompanied by Julia's sister, boarded the *Britannia*. On their arrival in Liverpool, Mann sent Combe a message informing him of a change in their plans: the night before leaving Boston Howe had hurt his leg quite badly and was in no condition to travel north. They would go to London, see "the final action on the Education Bill now pending in Parliament," and await Combe's reply. But as the party learned on their arrival in the capital, Combe and his wife had plans to leave for Kessingen (a spa town near Dresden) within the week. There was no way the two parties could unite in Britain. Mann would meet the appointments Combe had arranged (with Wyse, Cobden, Whatley, and Brougham); tour the institutions of England and Scotland; and, a couple of weeks later, meet up with Combe in Germany.

Leaving the Howes in London, Mann and his new wife took the train north. They stopped in Derby, York, and Newcastle, and then continued on to Edinburgh by coach. Here, Mann reported in his next letter, they "were charmed with the picturesqueness of the city, & intelligence of such of its inhabitants as we had the pleasure of meeting," most especially Combe's brother, Andrew. Mann was also "much pleased with some features of the Edinburgh schools" and told Combe he derived "far more advantage from an inspection of them than from all I had seen in England."[4] But even the splendor of Loch Lomand could not take his mind off their reunion. Having journeyed the length and breadth of the country in just three weeks, the Manns urgently departed for Hull and the ferry to Hamburg. From there they sped on to Berlin, only to arrive the very day the schools closed for a three-week summer recess. Mann had repeatedly told Combe in his letters that he was not interested in a superficial tour of German schools—the kind of whistle-stop visits he had conducted in Britain—but a detailed examination of the Prussian system. What should he do? Call on principals and inspect empty classrooms? Ought he remain until the schools opened and miss rendezvousing with Combe, or travel on to see him and visit the "schools in the South," which, he had been informed, "are not so good as those here"?[5] The same letter carried the following appeal for help:

> When I get home I think I shall occupy the greater part of my annual report with an account of what I have seen of the German schools. If you could send to me, either at Liverpool or to Boston, any of those large & comprehensive views which arise so naturally on all subjects in your mind, you would do me a personal favor, & add to the value if any, of such a report as I shall make. I desire to make it impulsive in regard to the Education movement in my own country.[6]

In the end they arranged to meet in Leipzig. Trying not to overtax the ailing philosopher, they toured the city—visiting its prisons, hospitals, schools, museums, and art galleries. But after three days Combe recognized that he could not keep up with Mann's frenetic pace and reluctantly took his leave for Italy. As both guessed, they would never meet again.

While in Leipzig, Mann met with Dr. Charles Vogel, the superintendent of the city's schools. He was completely taken with his new host, "a most intelligent man, full of knowledge as well as zeal."[7] "Under Vogel's administration," he later wrote to Combe, "Leipzig has perhaps the most complete & efficient system of education in all Germany. Certainly, we have seen nothing elsewhere quite equal to it."[8] And what Vogel could not show Mann, he could explain. His son-in-law offered a comprehensive account of education in southern Germany while Vogel described the merits of the country's Normal schools. Suitably informed, Mann changed his plans once more. Bypassing southern Germany, the Manns traveled westward to Frankfort. Here, by a curious twist of fate, they ran into the Howes—themselves heading to meet with Combe in Rome. Joyous at their unexpected reunion, the two couples made their way to Baden Baden, where they stayed with Combe's German translator, Gustav von Struve. Von Struve, Mann reported, confirmed Vogel's descriptions, thus providing "a feeling of security & certainty in regard to my opinions and views which was invaluable."[9] Mann's attempt to take the waters proved less successful: if his own account of the incident is to be believed, he barely made it out of Germany alive! Having axed Switzerland and southern Germany from his itinerary, Mann made his way up the Rhine to Holland, where he toured the schools of Utrecht, Amsterdam, Rotterdam, Antwerp, and The Hague. Traveling south through Brussels to

Paris, the Manns then returned to London. Finally, after a short visit to Ireland, they boarded the *Britannia* in Liverpool for an extremely choppy voyage home. If Mann had not seen the schools he had set out to observe, he certainly witnessed sufficient examples of the positive and negative features of the Old World to strengthen the convictions that Combe had fostered. His report would indeed be "impulsive."

THE SEVENTH ANNUAL REPORT

Readers of the *Common School Journal* were the first to read Mann's reflections on his trip to Europe. In the introduction to his sixth volume, he painted a frightening picture of the stark alternatives for human nature that flowed from the character of a country's institutions. He was particularly appalled by the condition of children in the industrial centers of England. "For the love of gain" the English manufacturers had committed crimes "such as have never before been known in any part of Christendom or Heathendom."[10] Years of hard labor, hunger, cold, poor nutrition, and disgusting living conditions had "dwarfed and deformed" the body "in all its proportions."[11] Deprived not "only of all the joys of childhood and the pleasures of knowledge, but the consolations of religion and the hopes of immortality . . . these victims of avarice and oppression live, less like human beings than like a knot of eels in their slime."[12] "The Fejee Islanders" he scolded, "ought to send missionaries to England, to raise, if possible, the English manufacturer to their own level of humanity."[13] In sharp contrast to England, despotic Prussia had utilized public schooling to elevate its people, achieving, in Mann's eyes, a social revolution equivalent "to the new creation of millions of men."[14] The implication was clear; the pedagogical methods employed in the Prussian system had to be adapted to the schools of Republican America. As he declared in the next volume, nothing could be more important to the future of the nation. All those in favor of the scientific approach to education were "helping to elevate mankind into the upper and purer regions of civilization . . . all those obstructing the progress of this cause are impelling the race backward into barbarism and idolatry."[15]

Having read the literature on European education, Mann was already familiar with the general principles underlying Prussian schooling. His goal in journeying to Germany was to put flesh on these bones by providing detailed descriptions of classroom practices that could be incorporated into the training of teachers in the Massachusetts Normal schools. If he only saw a handful of schools, mainly in Prussia and Saxony, by observing the best throughout the whole day, he could at least claim a more comprehensive and useful understanding of the practical aspects of the system. He was careful not to attack the basic principles of American schooling. He did not, for example, advocate the payment of fees or the differential education of rich and poor that he had seen throughout the continent. And, like many of his critics, he was sensitive to the role education plays in the reproduction of the political system. But he was adamant that Prussian methods could be adopted without embracing the county's autocratic policies. German pedagogy, he maintained, may be turned to the good. After all, "the human faculties are substantially the same all over the world, and hence the best means for their development and growth in one place, must be substantially the best for their development and growth elsewhere."[16] Indeed, given the independence of mental faculties, the teaching of reading, arithmetic, and geography had no necessary relationship to any religious or political dogma. In any case, Mann observed, the authority of the Prussian teacher was not directed at the aggrandizement of the rulers but the cultivation of the child. They governed not by fear and fiat, but by love and reason.

It was not that everything he saw in Germany was better than in America: in particular, he found that school facilities were often poor and that little attention was paid to the laws of health and exercise. But he had seen classroom practices which could transform American education in line with the phrenologically based reforms he had initiated in Massachusetts. In Germany, Mann noted, schools divided children according to age and ability so that teachers could instruct classes in lessons tailored to natural interests and the needs of the developing faculties. Knowledge was not abstract and atomized, as it was in New England schools, but integrated with the events of daily life. Starting at age six with the kind of object lessons Simpson had advocated, students discovered the basic features of their world. They examined the materials in their schoolhouse, learning about brick, glass, wood, and metal and their distinctive properties; how different artifacts were fashioned from raw materials; and the various purposes to which they were put. What was more natural than to direct a child's curiosity for flowers and pets, step-by-step, to the language and principles of zoology and botany? Some in his own country had ridiculed teaching "the higher branches" to children, but this surely flowed from the mistaken belief—woven into the structure of American textbooks—that science was a deductive process in which everyday events were subsumed under technical definitions. In Germany, teachers did not use text-books! Their knowledge was stored in their heads and manifested in their reasoning. And science was the tool by which they effortlessly articulated the meaning of events in a manner that was at once intelligible and practical to their students.

In contrast to the dry and senseless atomism of the abecedarians, German teachers taught reading through the "phonetic" plan that Mann had strenu-ously advocated in *The Common School Journal*.[17] They recognized that sounds, not letters, are the elements of language, that children naturally learn to read when words are associated with pictures and that speech is broken down into phonemes, not built up from the abstract symbols of the alphabet, as the American speller did. This same holistic approach had also revolutionized the teaching of writing and drawing, greatly improving standards of penmanship and the ability to sketch. Children learned number by using manipulatives and were introduced to mathematics through real-life problems rather than the de-contextualized formulae New England children were drilled on. The teaching of geography demonstrated the whole method. Instead of memoriz-ing place names, students were taught the origin of physical features through geologic principles, the role of climate and ecology, and the relationship be-tween the world and society. Ultimately, in all subjects, knowledge of nature and human duties led to an understanding of a loving God and the beneficent universe in which men and women live. A nonsectarian spirit pervaded in-struction, even though time was allocated for denominational teaching in the student's faith, Catholic or Protestant.

The crown jewel of the system was the German teacher. A "dignified, intelligent, benevolent-looking company of men" who knew their subjects, cared for their students, and took pride in their mission.[18] In all his time in Germany, Mann did not see one with a book in his hand, not one sitting at his desk, and not one inflicting physical punishment on children. They gov-erned through the power of their moral presence. Capturing attention by appealing to wit and imagination, they choreographed interest and discipline with the natural language of gesture, deftly exciting the sentiments and knowing organs with their movements and expressions. He was particularly impressed by their ability to excite the mental activity of children. In Scot-land, he had witnessed the extraordinary sight of a class in rapt attention for nearly two hours—jumping up and down in their seats, shooting their hands in the air, fingers quivering with excitement—as they vied to answer their teacher's questions. By the side of these students, he observed, "our pupils would seem to be hibernating animals just emerging from their torpid state, and as yet, but half conscious of the possession of life and faculties."[19] German masters also knew how to excite mental activity, but they kept the attention of their class without punishment and without the mechanism of taking places. "Could a visitor spend six weeks in our own schools without ever hearing an angry word spoken, or seeing a blow struck, or witnessing the flow of tears?"[20] "Whence came this beneficent order of men?"[21] From the training they received in the country's Normal schools, followed the reply. Carefully selected through a series of written and oral examinations, future teachers spent two years mastering subject matter followed by a third learning the principles of pedagogy and their application in a model school. Whereas American teachers were regarded with disdain, in Germany they had earned the professional status of doctors and lawyers.

Given this splendid machinery for public instruction, Mann was forced to explain why "the Prussians, as a people do not rise more rapidly in the scale of civilization," but remain "sluggish and unenterprizing in their character?"[22] Four answers came to mind. The famed promiscuity of Prussian women, which might take generations to prune; the fact that children left school at fourteen just as the reasoning faculties were maturing; the want of district libraries with books adapted to engage and develop the youthful brain; and, most significantly, that upon leaving school, students entered a society that treated them as cattle, stupefying their faculties and rendering their knowledge superfluous. What could be expected of a nation just free from vassalage? The organic and social laws did not work overnight. Change would take time, but echoing Combe's assessment of the German mind, Mann confidently predicted that within a few generations the moral advances brought about by this system of schooling would prepare Prussia for the American ideal of republican government. As for the rest of Europe, his prognosis was bleak. He saw "whole classes of men and women, whose organization is changing, whose whole form, features, countenance, expression, are so debased and brutified by want and fear and ignorance and superstition, that the naturalist would almost doubt where among living races of animals to classify them."[23] "No truth can be more certain than this," Mann exclaimed,

that after the poor, the ignorant, the vicious, have fallen below a certain point of degradation, they become the increasing fund of pauperism and vice,—a pauper engendering hive, a vital self-enlarging, reproductive mass of ignorance and crime. And thus, from parent to child, the race many go on, degenerating in body and soul, and casting off, one after another, the lineaments and properties of humanity, until the human fades away and is lost in the brutal, or demonic nature."[24]

Unwilling to advocate negative eugenic engineering—there were "tribes of the human family, whose existence we may not wish to see continued, provided always, that they dwindle and retire in a natural way, and without the exercise of violence or injustice to expel them from the Earth"—he resigned himself to the unpalatable truth that "to re-edify the frame, to rekindle in the eye the quenched beam of intelligence, to restore height and amplitude to the shrunken brow, and to reduce the overgrown propensities of the animal nature within a manageable compass" would require centuries of life under moral laws.[25] Fortunately, the situation in America was quite different. "In many respects," Mann argued, the colonization of the New World "was like a new creation of the race."[26] The pilgrims who survived the rigors of climate and a barren coastline to found a society grounded in common sense and the word of God effectively established a physical, intellectual, and moral bloodline that advanced "humanity at least one thousand years."[27] As stewards of this inheritance Mann called upon his readers to fulfill their duty by adopting "a more earnest, a more universal, a more religious devotion of our exertions and resources, to the culture of the youthful mind and the heart of the nation," in short, the advancement of American society through a common education grounded in scientific laws of the mind.

But perhaps the most startling section of Mann's report was his description of a revolutionary new way to educate the deaf. Where the deaf and dumb of America were "taught to converse by signs made with the fingers . . . incredible as it may seem," in Germany "they are taught to speak with lips and tongue, . . . a power of uttering articulate sounds," that restored the "helpless and hopeless . . . to society."[28] Like "the extraordinary case of Laura Bridgman, which has compelled consent to what would formally have been regarded as a fiction or a miracle," students of Mr. Moritz Hill, the accomplished instructor of the deaf and dumb school at Wissenfels had the ability to read lips "at great distance, by an artificial light, and even with very little light," and talk so clearly that they could pass as normal speakers.[29] Mann himself had "abundant proof . . . that this can be done, and substantially in all cases," reporting that "though an entire stranger, and speaking a foreign language . . . [he had] been able to hold some slight conversation with deaf and dumb pupils who had not completed half their term of study."[30] Fusing the rationale of the German system with Howe's approach to teaching Laura Bridgman, he noted that the hearing impaired have a natural impulse to express themselves through sounds; that when prevented from signing, they soon accept speech and find learning more enjoyable; and that, in addition to extending their range of communication, the use of words helps cultivate such children as moral beings. "All the deaf and dumb who have learned to speak," he insisted, "have a far more human expression of the eye and countenance than those who have only been taught to write."[31] Initially, Howe (in Europe at the time of publication) sought to distance himself from these outrageous claims, but in later years, as president of the Massachusetts Board of State Charities, he too embraced Mann's radical oralism. The logic of phrenology was unavoidable. Sign language, Howe maintained in 1865, "not only prevents the entire and harmonious development of the mind and character but it tends to give morbid growth in certain directions."[32] As such, the goal in educating the deaf was not to create a special class of people—as many feared the deaf community at Hartford was becoming—but to fashion the deaf "into the likeness of common men."[33] It is not surprising that, reacting to this "dangerous incursion" into the education of the deaf, Laurent Clec should compare the efforts of the oralists to the European treatment of Native peoples.[34] As he saw it, by representing their language and customs as infantile and barbaric, Mann and Howe transformed deaf culture into a brutish stage in the ascent of Christian civilization. The very humanity of the deaf was thus the real issue in the escalating debate over sign language.

THE MIND OF LAURA BRIDGMAN

Europe was not the only source Mann drew upon to justify his reforms. Massachusetts also had institutions that demonstrated his view of human nature and the power of the new pedagogy. At Worcester, Samuel Woodward was using moral therapy to cure the insane, and in Boston, at the Perkins Institute, Howe was using phrenology to achieve the impossible, the education of the deaf-blind girl, Laura Bridgman. Here was an educational experiment no teacher could ignore. Introducing Howe's 1842 report, Mann told the readers of the *Common School Journal* that Laura's remarkable education has resolved important philosophical questions and provided a practical lesson for the power of teaching guided by the proper theory of mind. Philosophers had compared the "young mind to clay in the hand of the potter . . . wax ready to receive any impression . . . [and] marble under the chisel of the sculptor," but such views were only "partially correct," for in addition to the force of experience, there was also the force of nature—character being the diagonal resultant.[35] In the case of Bridgman, however, a unique situation presented itself: encased in a sensory tomb and devoid of almost all external stimulation, a mind had been preserved in its natural state. Uncorrupted by society, this child presented scientists with a pristine view of God's workmanship and thus a chance to put pernicious philosophical doctrines to rest. Taking aim at sensationalism and the associated utilitarian principle that morality could be reduced to a calculus of pleasure and pain, Mann charged that the

> world has been infested with a school of philosophers, so called, one of whose dogmas it was, that there is no rule of right; that there is no fixed principles of duty . . . that all our notions respecting equity, and justice, and honor, and compassion, were conventional, arbitrary, capricious; that there was no original faculty in the human soul which preferred truth or falsehood, fidelity to perfidy . . . that each generation may makes its own laws of benevolence or duty . . . and that the great obligations which are acknowledged by all to exist in some form, have no inflexible, immutable, immortal standard, in the moral constitution of the soul. But out of the living reality of this child's nature God has perfected praise. She exhibits sentiments of conscientiousness, of love of truth, of gratitude, of affection, which education never gave her. She bestows upon mankind, evidences of purity, and love, and faith, which she never received from them. It is not repayment, for they were never borrowed. They were not copied from the creature, but given by the Creator.[36]

Clearly, Mann cannot be read as an "apostle of Lockian psychology," as David Hogan suggests. For although it is true that elements of Mann's thought do resonate with Locke's Baconian faith in science, his rejection of original sin, his ideal of rational and morally autonomous citizens, and his commitment to pedagogic practices that promote learning through pleasure rather than punishment, Mann rejected Locke's underlying egalitarianism, his notion of a *tabula rasa,* and, above all, as this passage suggests, his picture of the child as a morally neutral being. "According to Locke's theory," Howe explained, the narrow range of stimuli reaching Laura's mind (i.e., tastes and touch) seemed to imply that "the moral qualities and faculties of this child should be limited in proportion to the limitation of her senses."[37] But this was simply not the case. Her intellectual development and her "remarkably acute . . . moral sense" demonstrated the existence of "innate intellectual *dispositions;* and moreover, innate *moral dispositions.*"[38] The great strides that Laura was making in her studies, along with her immediate and wide comprehension of emotions, was clear and compelling evidence that each "child has dormant within his bosom every mental quality."[39] Further, contrary to the state of original sin predicted by Calvinism, Laura's spontaneous moral sentiments and joyful disposition was unmistakable proof of the inherent goodness of human nature. Her purity revealed that all vice and wickedness resides in corrupt social institutions, and no institution, Howe contended, was more wicked than Calvinism, which distorted the emotions of the immature mind in the name of orthodoxy.

In a remarkable passage, striking at the very heart of the traditional conception of the child, Mann reflected on the inner beauty of Laura's cerebral organization and the exquisite happiness that flowed from the unpolluted exercise of the moral sentiments.

> Our belief is, that it has been the *blessing* of this child to have lost those senses and organs, through which, in the case of other children, the follies and vices and errors of the world find an inlet into the soul. We say *blessing,* for though we acknowledge she lost much in being deprived of the outward world, yet we believe she has had a thousand fold compensation in having all that was innocent pure and lovely, in the inner temple, kept from desecration and sacrilege by that loss. . . . She was saved until, at last, it was her happy fortune to come under the care of one of those master-minds . . . under [whose] parental . . . skill, she has at length been acquainted with much of what is good in life, without being corrupted by its evil . . . she has tasted the exquisite, divine pleasures of affection, benevolence, duty, instead of being seduced away to live and riot in the coarse pleasures of appetite, of sense, and of the lower propensities of our nature.[40]

Howe even believed that if Laura were isolated from all talk of religion until her reasoning organs matured, then, unencumbered by cultural teachings, she would offer a clear and rational justification of liberal theology. But quarantining even someone as profoundly isolated as Laura proved impossible. Visitors and students often spelled out the word *God* on her hand, sparking great curiosity. Adamant that her questions not be answered, Howe instructed Laura's teachers to defer all her queries with the promise that Dr. Howe would explain everything when she was old enough to understand. If he could not stop the impulse of reverence generated by the organ of veneration, perhaps he could keep Laura's mind free from the emotional terrors of Calvinism.

Despite occasional outbursts, it seems that Laura was indeed a happy child who took great pleasure in learning. By using paper labels printed with raised letters, Howe had harnessed her natural inquisitiveness, patiently teaching her to associate the abstract patterns of words with the immediate objects of her surroundings. When "the truth began to flash upon her" that "there was a way by which she could herself make a sign of anything that was in her own mind, and show it to another mind . . . her countenance lighted up with human expression; it was no longer a dog or parrot,—it was an immortal spirit, eagerly seizing upon a new link of union with other spirits!"[41] The sign, which Helen Keller learned at the water pump, but which Victor barely fathomed, was the key to humanity and the development of the higher faculties. Having quickly mastered finger spelling, Laura's education then proceeded with modified object lessons, as Howe gradually and ingeniously improved Laura's language skills and expanded her knowledge of the world. After two years, by the age of ten, she had learned the principal parts of speech, she knew the names of all the common objects in her environment, and she was freely finger spelling with the other blind students at Perkins.

Howe was quick to see the implications of Laura's achievement for the education of the deaf. "The natural tendency of the human mind," he claimed, "is to express thought by some kind of symbol."[42] "Audible signs by the vocal organs are the first to suggest themselves," but when "this avenue is blocked up, the natural tendency or inclination will be gratified in some other way."[43] For this reason he had taken great care to ensure that the manual alphabet had become her natural language. Comparing "the natural signs, or pantomime" of deaf-mutes to "man in his wild state," he maintained that "spoken language, subtle, flexible, minute, precise, is a thousand times more efficient and perfect instrument for thought."[44] Deaf-mutes may "prefer to express themselves by natural signs, *because they are suggested immediately by the thought,*" but his experience with Laura proved they should be prohibited from developing pantomime, in order that finger spelling (and hence, the English language) would become "so perfectly vernacular, that [their] thoughts will spontaneously clothe themselves in it."[45] Clec disagreed, seeing little value in the crude and slow finger spelling employed by Laura, a method, he observed, that took "ten different hand shapes . . . to convey the single brief sign UNDERSTAND."[46] Whatever Laura's successes—successes Howe was unable to achieve with other deaf-blind children in his charge—Clec was convinced that those born deaf and blind "should be educated among deaf people who see" rather than "hearing people who do not."[47]

Laura's education took a new turn when, at age thirteen, Howe set about teaching her the common school curriculum. Alert to the dangers of institutional life and determined to break the popular image of the blind as helpless beggars, he demanded that every child at Perkins develop the skills necessary to support themselves in the world. An obvious occupation was music; some learned basket weaving, others became teachers of the blind. But over and above such vocational training, he believed a common school education was the birthright of all Americans, irrespective of their disability. It helped train the higher powers and provided knowledge necessary for civic duty and wise conduct in life. Laura was clearly a bright child, and Howe held out high hopes that she too could learn a trade (seamstress) and profit from secondary schooling. But he was not naive. With such a severe handicap, even the most commonplace facts were dizzying abstractions for Laura. The higher branches might never be fully grasped, he admitted, but at least the curriculum would ensure the systematic exercise of her rational and moral faculties. He also recognized that her unique condition demanded certain concessions. History, for example, had to be censored to prevent tales of barbarism from wounding her delicate moral organs, while the fears of "several medical gentlemen" that "the continual mental excitement she manifests . . . [could] endanger her mental faculties" were "effectively counteracted by causing her to practice callisthenic exercises, and to take long walks daily in the open air, which on some days extend to six miles."[48]

As in her first lessons, Laura made remarkable progress. But contrary to Howe's published claims, she did not always show an unqualified appetite for learning or a pure moral nature. Mathematics especially seems to have caused her much anxiety. Sometimes she would try to change the subject with a stream of questions, and on other occasions she threw fits, hitting and biting her teachers. Howe had a solution for this rebelliousness. Every good and bad deed was recorded in her teacher's journal. If he found that Laura had acted well, he would be attentive, if she had behaved poorly, he would withdraw his affection and deliver a stern moral lesson. Given her strong attachment to Howe, and her often-voiced fear of isolation, such emotional pressures provided a powerful stimulus to conform. Laura even learned to start the morning with a period of reflection on how she might perfect her nature by controlling her raging passions. But if this silent monitor structured Laura's moral conscience, Howe's religious experiment proved less successful. His yearlong visit to Europe, the demands of a new family, and his increasing involvement in new reform causes eventually loosened his grip over Laura's world. Mary Swift, who had been Laura's primary teacher during Howe's absence, was the first to face up to her incessant questioning about God. Unable, and perhaps unwilling, to divert her passionate appeals, Swift disagreed with the veil of silence drawn around this curious and unfortunate child. Surely, she reasoned in her letters to Howe, Laura's unremitting inquisitiveness was clear proof of her readiness to learn about God. Yet Laura did not even know the name of Jesus! Howe was inflexible. Extolling Swift to abide by his instructions, he responded to Laura's pleas with a brief description of God as a loving father who had created Heaven and Earth for human happiness. Repeating that her mind was still young and weak, unable to understand hard things, he promised to answer all her questions at the appropriate time. Howe never had the opportunity, for on his return to Boston he discovered that a group of evangelicals, possibly at Swift's behest, had been to Perkins Institute. Her mind was now hopelessly confused, full of absurd doctrines she simply could not understand. It was, Howe later confessed, "the greatest disappointment of my life."[49]

Replacing Mary Swift with Sarah Wright, and limiting Laura's contact with school friends and visitors, Howe attempted to regain control over his pupil's education—directing her religious questioning, in particular, toward his own liberal conception of God. Laura continued to make progress, albeit along a slow and punctuated path. She learned much about the world, but, as Ernest Freeberg reveals, displayed the fragmentary nature of her understanding with questions such as " 'Can birds study?' 'Why do flies and horses not go to bed?' 'Are horses cross all day?' " and " 'What did man make red for?'"[50] Guided by her developing conscience as she matured through adolescence to adulthood, her outbursts and "unseemly" behavior became less frequent; although, in Howe's estimation, she remained excitable, childish, and prone to emotional exuberance. Most troubling for the doctor, however, was Laura's growing acceptance of a deeply personal God—she eventually joined the Baptist Church. God became an important companion in her frequently lonely and isolated existence, no doubt promising eternal happiness as a reward for her goodness and the suffering she endured. But for Howe, Laura's developing spirituality was only further proof of her immaturity. His experiment, he finally conceded, had failed; Laura's mind and morals had not progressed much above that of a child. Again, phrenological laws explained her condition. Building upon his 1848 study of the origins and social dangers of idiocy, he invoked the hereditarian arguments advanced by Combe and Spurzheim to assert that the infringement of natural laws was the root cause of all diseases. The first blind students to enter Perkins Institute had been chosen for their intelligence, and many had successfully navigated the common school curriculum. A decade later, he did not have such a rosy story to report: the majority combined blindness with lassitude, a weak intellect, and a host of other disorders that suggested a depleted or deformed constitution—conditions produced by the vice and ignorance of the children's parents. Even Laura, who was not congenitally deaf or blind, seemed to have been born with a feeble organization that made her susceptible to illness. Her parents, he noted, both had small brains, a telltale sign of degeneracy and idiocy. Not that Laura was an unintelligent child. She was certainly a far superior student to the other deaf-blind children—Lucy Reed, Oliver Cresswell, and Julia Brace—that Howe attempted to educate. But her innate weakness was compounded by the loss of sight and sound, which, he now understood, deprived Laura's brain of the stimulating experiences necessary for the full and harmonious development of the faculties. Howe's social philosophy had hardened. Less convinced of the positive effects of moral treatment, by 1850, he increasingly focused on the causes of disability and the kinds of eugenic policies necessary to combat degeneracy.

REACTION AND CONTROVERSY

The community at Hartford and signing schools throughout the country were clearly shaken by Mann's advocacy of oralism; after all, a powerful ally in the cause of reform had turned into an adversary. Keen not to escalate the division, but adamant that such dangerous talk not be allowed to undermine confidence in the schooling of the deaf, Harvey Peet, former teacher at Hartford and now director of the New York School for the Deaf, published a carefully worded rebuttal in the *North American Review.*[51] Adopting a conciliatory tone throughout, Peet aligned himself with Mann's goals but disputed the means by which they might be attained. "The great end of all the teacher's efforts," he claimed, "was to enable the pupils to converse *by writing.*"[52] The written word would help socialize the deaf and make possible their moral, intellectual, and religious instruction. In the vast majority of cases, he continued, this skill could only be learned through the use of signing. Mann's mistake was simply one of ignorance. The great educator was not familiar with the work of the American Asylum and clearly not competent to judge the achievements of deaf students. Did he understand, for example, that almost all of those who learned to read lips and speak were either semimutes or former speakers, and that their remarkable feats were often limited to the community in which they lived? Beyond the confines of the school, without teachers trained to hear their vocalizations and speak slowly, loudly, and distinctly, they would often be, to use Mann's own phrase, as "hopeless and helpless as ever."[53] Like their European counterparts, American teachers of the deaf had also experimented with articulation and lipreading. But after much effort, they had come to understand the long and weary hours necessary to acquire even the most rudimentary vocal abilities were far better spent learning to read and write, skills almost all deaf children master once the natural language of gesture has been embraced.

Why had Mann made such outrageous claims? The year before leaving for Europe, Howe, as chair of the House Committee on Public Charitable Institutions, unsuccessfully petitioned to establish a school for the deaf at Perkins Institute, where, as Mann put it, "the limited language of signs" would be exchanged "for the universal language of words."[54] "Had the members of the legislature seen and heard what I have now often seen and heard," Mann wrote in his *Seventh Report,* this "application would have found a different fate."[55] But Mann's report did not help Howe's cause. Howe had been unable to convince his colleagues that he could improve upon the results achieved at Hartford, or reduce its costs. Now Mann's exaggerated claims only revealed how shallow the knowledge of the deaf was at Perkins Institute.

Without the practical experience to debate teachers of the deaf, Mann remained silent. Yet the trustees at Hartford and New York understood that his claims would continue to excite unrealistic hopes among parents of the deaf until they were explored firsthand—perhaps they might even learn some new techniques that could help save the voices of semimutes? In any case, in the years that followed, both institutions sent representatives to investigate the deaf schools of Europe; Lewis Weld (from Hartford) and George Day (from New York), in 1844, followed by Peet himself, in 1851. By and large, each told the same story. What little the Germans had actually achieved was purchased at the expense of the profoundly deaf and the general education of the semimute. True, some could speak and lip-read, at least within their immediate community, but their intellectual development was sadly lacking. Only the National Institute in Paris, with its system of mixed methods (signing supplemented with extra-curricular articulation for those with residual hearing) could claim real success. Manual communication had to remain at the core of all deaf education in America, but some accommodation to oralism could be made for those few with residual speech and hearing. And so the debate rested until after the Civil War, when Howe returned to the cause of articulation, this time with money, influence, and a powerful eugenic social philosophy on his side.

Laura Bridgman's education had been conducted to discredit empiricist theories of mind and undercut the Calvinist view of human depravity. It was also clearly intended as a demonstration of the new pedagogy and the power of phrenologically informed practices to revolutionize schooling in Massachusetts. Here was an unmistakable beacon for reform. If Howe could educate a deaf-blind child using these methods, what might a teacher do with normal students? But not all of Mann's readers embraced his vision of individual and social perfectibility, or his argument that Howe's successes with Laura, let alone Woodward's ability to cure the insane, had any relevance for the education of schoolchildren. This became evident when an association of thirty-one masters from the Boston Grammar and Writing Schools rose to engage Mann in a wide-ranging and rancorous debate over the recommendations of his *Seventh Annual Report.* Having watched the secretary's sweeping reforms transform schooling across the state, the group evidently decided that it was time to draw a line in the sand. Mann's "hot bed theories" and sentimental view of children could not be allowed to undermine the authority of Boston's most-seasoned teachers, professionals who understood from years of successful experience the best methods of instructing and disciplining students.

Starting with the masters' *Remarks,* and continuing with Mann's *Rejoinder,* a *Reply*, and finally Mann's *Answer*, the two sides debated Prussian pedagogic practices, the best method of teaching reading, and the value of emulation and corporal punishment.[56] In Katz's influential account of this conflict, the masters were simply trying to preserve teacher autonomy in the face of Mann's relentless efforts to gain administrative control over the Boston city schools. Yet this was more than a struggle for power; it was a clash between two radically opposed philosophies of human nature with important religious implications. Certainly Mann sought to solidify his authority by reining in the masters, but his chief motivation was to "rescue children from a system of government, at once injurious to their bodily health, paralyzing to their intellectual nature, and debasing to their moral sentiments."[57] Old school Calvinists, the masters embraced the doctrine of infant depravity and the prime necessity of bending the child's will to the authority of the teacher. "This doctrine," Mann reflected, "underlies the whole," justifying his antagonists' use of "'emulation,' 'sympathy,' 'the pride of intellect,' or 'the pride of virtue,' . . . and whatever force or fear or pain" necessary to secure subjugation from children of "both sexes . . . all ages, and all dispositions."[58] This was a deeply personal issue for Mann, for he confessed that if his own education

> did not succeed in making me that horrible thing—a Calvinist—it succeeded in depriving me of that filial love for God, that tenderness, that sweetness, that intimacy, that desiring nestling love which, I say, it is natural a child should feel toward a Father who combines all excellence. . . . I am as a frightened child whose eye, knowledge, experiences and belief even, are not sufficient to obliterate the image which an early fright burnt in upon his soul.[59]

All behavior was governed by motives, "from the low motive that controls the craven and the brute,—the pain of bodily smart,—up to social, personal, filial, domestic considerations, and from these to the hallowed and immortal influences of morality and religion."[60] The problem was that teachers such as Joseph Hale at the Johnston School continued to defend the daily beating of children as an honorable method for sculpting a "true heart and a sound mind."[61] Phrenologizing Hale, Mann concluded that his vitriolic attack in the pages of the *Reply* demonstrated the same tyranny of "Self-esteem and Combativeness" that drove his indiscriminate use of the whip within the classroom,

"bodily chastisement" of which "barbarians themselves would be ashamed!"[62]
He would not rest until Hale and his cohorts understand the scientific basis
of moral treatment and embraced a more liberal conception of human nature. Citing "the marvelous success with which children bereft in the providence of God of some of the most important of the physical senses, had been
taught, when their minds were unshaken by the agitations of fear" and presenting religious arguments for the inner goodness and perfectibility of the
child, Mann pressed his case for teaching practices grounded in a knowledge
of the brain and the correct stimulation of its organs. Hale rejected Mann's
use of the disabled to justify his vision of the mind—and printed sections of
the *Twenty-fifth Annual Report* of the New York Institution for the Deaf and
Dumb to prove Mann's lack of expertise even in this area of education.[63]
Most importantly, as a Calvinist, he simply could not accept that children's
impulses could serve as a guide to education. Goodness had to be imposed,
not drawn out, and he steadfastly defended his right and duty to use whatever means necessary to this noble end. Mann, who rarely left a challenge
unanswered, did not respond to Hale's taunts beyond defending the success
of the pedagogic reforms he had championed. All around the state, he maintained, enlightened teachers had proven that discipline could be achieved
through the positive economy of kindness and pleasure. Hale and his like,
Mann decided, would be cut down to size in another forum.

Feeding on a growing sensitivity to the treatment of children, Mann's
vivid descriptions of classroom brutality drew sympathy to his cause. In the
public eye, beating was rapidly becoming an unacceptable method of punishment. The question was how to harness this sentiment to undermine the
authority of the masters? Mann came up with a scheme that Katz has characterized as a ruthless and cynical abuse of power. It was certainly effective.
Friends of his cause would get on the city school board and rid Boston of its
hard-line teachers. The plan worked beautifully. During the fall of 1844,
Howe and several other supporters were elected to the twenty-four-man committee—Sumner, standing for his first public office, was defeated. Responding to the controversy, the Whigs pushed a resolution demanding that all acts
of corporal punishment had to be recorded, "detailing as exactly as may be
practicable, the nature of the offences, the age and sex of the pupil, the instrument employed, and the degree of severity used" for the quarterly inspection of the committee.[64] Given the heat generated by the controversy, this was
a level of scrutiny even the most resolute of Mann's opponents could not

endure. School beatings dropped dramatically. But the fireworks really started the following May, when Howe was appointed to conduct the annual examinations of the city's grammar schools. Breaking with traditional oral exams, he insisted on a written test, to be printed privately and distributed without the masters' foreknowledge. Dissecting the results with a statistical scalpel, Howe's *Report* laid out the real ignorance of the city's students. It made grim reading. Some 154 questions on six subjects had been submitted to the city's top 530 students. "To these," Howe explained,

> there should have been 57,873 answers, if each scholar had been able to answer; but there were only 31,159, of which only 17,216 were correct in sense, leaving unanswered 26,714. The 31,159 answers contained 2,801 errors in grammar; 3,733 errors in spelling; and 35,947 errors in punctuation.[65]

However appalling, numbers did not capture the full magnitude of the problem. Many students had guessed on true and false items, whereas other questions demanding a name or short statement revealed only the power of their memory, not an understanding of principles. Thus, although many correctly answered "when was the embargo laid by President Jefferson, and when was the non-intercourse act substituted for it," only a few could explain "what is an embargo?"[66] The students' inability to define terms was particularly disturbing—thirty-nine of the pupils could not even identify one of twenty-eight words selected from their reading book! The cause of such a systemic failure among Boston's brightest students, Howe concluded, was antiquated pedagogic methods and the excessive reliance on textbooks. The masters had to adopt the improved practices developed in Prussia. Moreover, Howe continued, education in Boston lacked control. Classrooms ought to be graded, female assistants employed to instruct the younger children, a single headmaster appointed for each school, and a superintendent hired to oversee the entire system. Finally, Howe turned to the hot issue of corporal punishment, noting as Mann put it in the *Common School Journal,* that "the proficiency made by pupils will always be greater or less, according to the elevated or degrading character of the motives by which they are governed, and incited to study."[67] Not wishing to appear vindictive, the *Report* noted how the rule on recording physical punishments was already bearing fruit and optimistically predicted that with time even the most avid hard-liners would come to see the greater efficacy of appealing to the child's higher motives. Even so, the school board exacted its own brand of justice later that summer when the teachers came before the committee to renew their annual appointments; four were dismissed and several others reallocated to new positions.

Expanding on the *Report* for the readers of the *Common School Journal,* Mann made sport of student errors and deftly contrasted the education provided by masters earning four times the salary of a typical teacher with the results of the "average" Dudley School at nearby Roxbury. Vast sums were spent annually on Boston schools, equal, Mann observed, to the expenditure of the British Parliament for the education of its 17 million people, yet "if the mean of the merits or comparative excellence of the Boston schools is represented by the decimal fraction .0769, the merits of the Dudley School must be represented by the fraction .1544,—that is, the average rank of the Boston Schools is not quite one half that of the Dudley School!" Why? Seconding Howe's *Report,* Mann cited the organization of the schools and the lack of a superintendent. Most important of all, however, was the effect of punishment on the learning culture of the classroom. Thankfully the measures taken by the school board had radically reduced beatings; Hale, Mann noted approvingly, had reduced the frequency of beatings by 84 percent in the second quarter. The result, according to the subcommittee appointed to oversee the Johnson School, was "a very perceptible improvement in good order, in advancement in studies and in the relation between teacher and pupil."[68]

Hale's public chastisement demonstrates the power of Mann's moral force. But he had an even more fearful weapon to unfurl on the masters: Massachusetts state law. The Commonwealth had statutes demanding that the school committee "shall ascertain, by personal examination, the literary qualifications and capacity for government of the schools" of all teachers they employ.[69] The annual examinations and punishment reports would allow the board to keep an eye on current employees, but in the future, Mann demanded, all applicants for these prestigious positions should undergo a public examination to establish their intellectual skills and moral character. Although such "public" examinations were never implemented, within a few years Mann's recommendations to reorganize the schools, designate a head teacher, and appoint a city superintendent were all adopted. The masters had been purged.

13

Guardians of the Republic

In regard to motives, we use in Antioch College no artificial stimulus. We have no system of prizes, or honors, or place-takings. We appeal to no dissocial motive, where the triumph of one competitor involves the defeat of another. We hold it to be unchristian for us to place children or youth in such relations to each other that, if one succeeds, the other must fail; that if one rival wins the prize his co-rival must envy him or repine his own loss, or both. We would not cultivate the intellect at the expense of the affections; what the world calls greatness at the expense of goodness.

Horace Mann, *Demands of the Age on Colleges,* 1857

During the spring of 1848, certain that "the Common School cause in Massachusetts, was so consolidated . . . nothing could overturn it," Mann agreed to resign the secretaryship and accept the Whig Party nomination to complete the recently deceased John Quincy Adams's term in Congress.[1] He would reenter politics and turn his considerable powers of moral suasion to the greatest issue of the day, slavery and its possible extension to the Western territories. "Recent events," he informed the readers of the *Common School Journal* in his "Editor's Farewell," "had proven the great truth, that before a man can be educated, he must be a free man," and he would do his utmost to ensure that "the vast territories which are now roamed over by savage hordes, may rise from barbarian life into civilization . . . instead of sinking . . . into the abyss of slavery."[2] Personal reasons also played a role in his decision. A father of two young children (soon to be three), he fretted that his health might not withstand the rigorous demands of the secretary's duties for yet another year. And, as he explained to Combe, working under the rule of neutrality was becoming more than he could bear.[3] Yet it was precisely this professional anonymity that secured Mann's election. The previous year Howe, supported by Sumner, had run a deeply divisive campaign—polarizing the party into "conscience" and "cotton" Whigs—in his unsuccessful attempt to unseat Robert Winthrop. In the field of politics, Mann realized, pragmatism was more important than principle. Splitting the Whig Party would only serve to strengthen the power of southern Democrats. Accordingly, trading on his reputation as a person of principle, he cemented a fragile coalition and entered the House of Representatives during March 1848 with no mandate except to be his own man.

Resisting pressure from Sumner and Howe to take an immediate stand against slavery, Mann spent the first months of his term taking stock of the House and the character of its members. He also journeyed through Virginia familiarizing himself with its people and the debilitating effect of slavery on both blacks and whites. And, after repeated appeals from Howe, who even traveled to Washington to press his case, Mann agreed to act as council in the high profile trial of Daniel Drayton and Edward Sayers, two white men accused of trying to ferry escaped slaves to freedom. But events soon forced Mann into action. Much to his disgust, the Whig Party selected proslavery Zachary Taylor as its candidate for the upcoming presidential election. On June 30, 1848, with Massachusetts in a state of uproar, Mann rose in the House to deliver his first speech. Without attacking Taylor or aligning himself with the abolitionists, he fused legal, economic, and moral arguments with a stinging denunciation of southern culture into an hour-long tirade against the westward extension of slavery. While his stand deeply offended a number of southern Democrats, back home, along with his defense of Drayton and Sayers, it was strongly endorsed by both Whigs and the new Free Soil Party, who duly reelected him as their joint candidate in the November election. But if Mann's efforts to stand above politics returned him to the House for two more years, he soon found himself in a situation that forced him to choose political sides among his own supporters.

Completing his *Twelfth Annual Report,* Mann somewhat reluctantly passed on the secretaryship of the Board of Education to Barnas Sears and returned to Washington hopeful that with a Whig in the White House the western territories would enter the Union as free states. Mann was now free to pursue his own mind. An antislavery proponent, if not a radical abolitionist, he drew upon his notes in the Drayton and Sayers case to craft a vehement attack on the trade in human flesh conducted within the boundaries of the nation's capital. Delivered on February 23, 1849, he reported how for more than a year he had witnessed the horrors of men and women being treated as animals— caged, beaten, and sold for profit like cattle.[4] This was hardly the religious duty of a civilized country toward primitive peoples. No doubt, he agreed with Charles Brown, a representative from Pennsylvania, some "slaves are in a better condition in this country than they would have been at home."[5] But he sharply rebuked Brown for thinking that this vindicated the actions of the South. Whatever improvement may have been achieved in the African's nature was not "the result of any system of measures designed for their benefit . . . but is the product of selfish motives."[6] Indeed, referring to the selective breeding of slaves for pecuniary ends, he continued, "Where more gain or more gratification can be obtained by the debasement, the irreligion, the pollution of the slave, there the instincts of chastity, the sanctity of the marriage relation, the holiness of maternal love are all profaned to give secularity and zest to the guilty pleasures of sensualist and the debauchee."[7] Moreover, the degrading and menial practices to which most slaves were subject rendered their "higher faculties . . . irredeemably and hopelessly crushed, extinguished, obliterated, so that nothing but the animal, which the master can use for his selfish purposes, remains."[8] Every individual, Mann insisted, has a right "to develop and cultivate the faculties which God has bestowed upon him, and which therefore he holds under a divine charter."[9] This did not mean social and political equality; each person must "occupy the position to which he should be entitled by his intelligence and his virtues."[10] Nor did it mean the integration of the races. Mann did not support state-enforced separate schooling—although, much to the disgust of the abolitionist Wendall Phillips, he refused to speak out against segregation. Like Thomas Jefferson, he was convinced that blacks and whites could only advance in separate communities. His experience in the South confirmed that when joined in society Africans were downtrodden by the more aggressive and intelligent Anglo-Saxons. Likewise whites, by relying on the labor of others, became lethargic and morally indolent. Thus, while encouraging the free colored population of America to train their children with the manners and skills for the rights and duties of citizenship and whatever work, mechanical or professional, their abilities permitted, he proposed the establishment of a new African state in the West Indies or on the Atlantic coast of Africa. Here the need for teachers, doctors, and other leaders would force individuals to develop their brains as well as their muscles. Fundamentally opposed to the idea of forced expulsion from their place of birth, Mann was sure that free blacks would flock to this new country with a missionary zeal to develop their own independent nation —which, ultimately, as a member of the civilized world, would then exert enough moral pressure on the United States to undermine the institution of slavery and provide a refuge for the captive population of the South.

With no action taken on the territories bill, Mann returned to Washington that December to a delicately balanced and highly volatile Congress. Talk of succession was in the air, and pressure was mounting for some kind of compromise. But as Mann explained in his third speech to the House of Representatives on February 15, 1850, he preferred dissolution or even war to the extension of slavery. Daniel Webster saw things differently. Captivating the Senate with a powerful plea for unity, the Massachusetts Whig advocated the toleration of slavery in the present as the price for preserving the future of the Union, a compromise that ultimately led to the Fugitive Slave Bill and the opening of Texas and California to slavery. Mann was outraged, and the rancorous debates that ensued between the two men did much to fracture the Whig Party into irreconcilable camps. Ousted as the Whig candidate for the 1850 election by Webster sympathizers, Mann stood and narrowly won the Congressional seat as a Free Soiler. During his final term in office, Mann did his utmost to undermine the Fugitive Slave Bill, rallying protests in Boston, speaking out in Congress, and printing an extended attack on its legal and moral standing. But few would listen. It was simply impossible to rouse a government dominated by pro-Webster forces.

THE PURITY OF RACE AND GENDER

Burdened with debt and tiring of Washington politics, Mann turned to the lecture circuit. Increasingly convinced that, after all, education would have to precede freedom, he set about improving his financial position and promoting his moral philosophy. In a number of addresses outlining the rewards of a virtuous life, he delivered the same basic message: a Christian republic can only thrive when citizens and political leaders are taught to understand and follow the ways of God. For example, in his *Thoughts for a Young Man,* and in two parallel speeches on the duties of women, he laid out the essential character of the human condition and described the kind of life to which a young person should aspire.[11] Mann was particularly worried that the excitements of the modern world would accelerate the development of the brain and turn the unreflective adolescent toward the fruitless and destructive quest for wealth. Knowledge was power. Utilizing intelligence, the civilized mind had harnessed the vast energies of the Earth to create unlimited riches. Yet such wealth was also a source of misfortune, subjecting the individual to the tyranny of desire and the state to the feudalism of capital. Fortunately, he explained, "Gall, Spurzheim and Combe, have done for Metaphysics . . . what Bacon did for Physics," revealing laws of mind that demonstrated how true happiness is achieved through the full and free exercise of the higher organs.[12] This ethical philosophy pointed to a new era of justice, honor, love, and truth. A young man should thus seek that "golden mean of property which carries its possessor out of the temptations of want, without carrying him into the temptations of wealth . . . [to leave] the money-making treadmill, and betake himself to some walk of public usefulness," in short, to "orient" himself by "the sublime laws upon which the soul of man was formed" so that he might share in "the power and the wisdom and the blessedness, with which God has filled and lighted up this resplendent universe."[13]

As for woman, Mann noted that the physical and mental organization of females was clearly adapted for a specific social role.[14] Lacking men's strength and intellect, they were gifted with a superior moral character. Men dominated society in primitive cultures, but as civilization advanced, women came to play the increasingly vital role of infusing male intelligence with female virtue. This holy task would only be fulfilled when women were educated to exert their goodness outward from the home into occupations such as nursing, teaching, and social philanthropy. The military, law, and especially government were provinces of men; forcing women to deal with the sordid realities of life would corrupt their nature, though Mann did believe that unimpeachable icons of female virtue, such as Dorothea Dix, could play the special role of promoting social policies through the power of their moral presence. Most importantly, as guardians of the human germ, women needed a sound knowledge of physiology in order to raise families "whose hereditary blood has never been corrupted by alcohol, and whose hereditary brain was never narcotized into solidity by the 'vile weed.'"[15] "Under such an obedience to the laws of health and life," Mann thundered, the "pygmy species who now threaten to reduce the robust Anglo-Saxon manhood to the stature of Aztec children, would disappear carrying with them the whole progeny of floss-silk and lack-brain gentilities and puerilities, of whom any respectable man or woman must marry at least two dozen before violating the law against bigamy."[16] In only "three or four successive generations the earth [would] be glorified with a new race; Anakims, not manikins, Apollos, not orang-outangs, sages and seers, and not our Boeotian millions."[17]

Mann's quest to elevate the mind and morals of society took an important turn in 1852. After five frustrating years in Congress, he longed for a field of useful work closer to his family and unsoiled by the political contests that had soured his life in Washington. Two options presented themselves: he could stand for the governorship of Massachusetts or accept the presidency of a new coeducational and antisectarian college proposed by the Christian Connexion, a New England religious group that shared similar views with the Unitarians. Situated in Yellow Springs, Ohio, its backers envisioned that Antioch, like the classical site of Arian theology, would train Christian disciples to become the future leaders of the new frontier. As it turned out, events forced Mann's hand. When the Connexion revised and modified their plans, diminishing the president's authority and reducing his salary, Mann accepted the nomination as the Free Soil candidate for governor. But his strategy, to split the Whigs and form a coalition with Democrats on issues of temperance and antislavery, proved unsuccessful. With only 25 percent of the vote, Mann's fate was decided. He would head west and reenter the field of education.

Chafing under the restriction that he could only hire two of his own faculty (his niece and nephew, Rebecca and Calvin Pennell), Mann was delighted to find "a most remarkable coincidence of opinion and sentiment" when the new staff assembled in his West Newton home. "We were all teetotalers; all anti-tobacco men; all antislavery men; a majority of us believers in phrenology; all anti-emulation men . . . [and] we agreed entirely in regard to religious and chapel exercises."[18] Together this idealistic band composed the college's first catalog around four guiding aims: the equal education of both sexes, the need to ensure health through exercise and diet, the use of progressive teaching methods, and, most importantly, the fostering of students committed to the moral life. A diploma from Antioch was to be a testament of character as well as learning. In addition to a core curriculum of Greek, Latin, mathematics, English, philosophy, physiology, and other natural sciences, students had the option of specializing in history, art, or pedagogy. According to the catalog, the freshmen class would rise at six o'clock for breakfast and chapel, join the faculty in three hours of physical exercise and five hours of classes, and then retire for up to four hours of independent study. Despite this austere regimen, the harebrained system of scholarships developed by the trustees attracted a large number of students. By September 1853, when Mann took charge of the uncompleted buildings and crippled finances of the college, several hundred young men and women

—along with many mature students—presented themselves for physical, intellectual, and moral elevation. The vast majority, however, were so poorly prepared that Mann was forced to open a high school within the college and limit his first university class to only eight students.[19]

Alert to the gravity of his task, Mann prepared a sweeping inaugural address that Jonathan Messerli calls his *Weltanschauung*. Before a crowd of some three thousand assembled from all parts of the state, he drew together the threads of his eugenic philosophy to justify the role of education in the religious and biological progress of humankind. Equating civilization with Christianity, he identified two conditions for advancement in a moral universe governed by the unbending relation of cause and effect, "finding out the laws of God and obeying them."[20] In the six thousand years since the fall of Adam, men and women had broken every rule of health, thus bequeathing offspring through the laws of inheritance with arrested physical and mental development. God had not made humans infirm; rather, as the Bible showed, starting with polygamy in the third generation, harlotry, drunkenness, incest, and indeed "two thousand years of the combined abominations of appetite and ignorance . . . of outrageous excesses and debauchery," humankind had bred "all these vile distempers which now nestle, like vermin, in every organ and fiber of our bodies!"[21] "From such causes," he continued, have

come our present diluted and depleted humanity; effete, diseased and corrupt of blood; abnormal, wasted and short lived; with its manliness so evaporated and its native fires so quenched, that our present world, compared with what it should be, is but a Lazar house of disease, and an Asylum for the Feeble-minded. The imbecile races of Italy and Spain, the half grown millions of India and Mexico, like river mouths, are only the foul drainage of ancestral continents, all gushing with fountains of debilitating and corrupting vices.[22]

Not until

all concoctions for the titillation of the palate, until all stimulants for the excitation of the brain, are made subordinate to the soundness of the stomach and the purity of the blood; until reason and conscience shall rise in majesty above the subject propensities and bind them, like hounds in the leash, and until men shall have reference, in their matrimonial connections, to the physical laws of hereditary descent, they have no right to call themselves civilized or Christian, in their treatment of the body.[23]

Only in their intellectual nature were men and women finally becoming civilized, as the development of science revealed how "the crude substances of nature" could be transformed into "comfort, beauty and blessedness," the rewards of life under God's laws.[24] Even so, Mann warned his freshman class, the cultivation of intelligence had to go hand in hand with moral education in order to ensure that the "inventive and constructive" faculties were not made servants of the lower passions—fearful instruments of destruction that would rape the world under "the love of power and the despotism of pride."[25] The students must surely have been reassured by Mann's pledge that, in regard to their morals, like Jacob, "having wrestled all night with the angel of God, 'I will not let thee go, until thou bless me.'"[26] As many found out, he was not joking. The coeducational environment at Antioch also provided a splendid setting for intelligent matchmaking. In contrast to "the dinner-party, the assembly or the ball-room," the college's "architectural arrangements"—studiously designed to "preserve the relations of delicacy and purity between the sexes"—enabled Mann's students to transcend their passions and "make the most solemn of contracts on the highest of considerations."[27] Extending from the individual to the social, he brought his oration to a close by sketching out a kind of phrenology of spirit, in which the absolute would be achieved by infusing women's "subtler and diviner essence into all the elements that go to make up the Body-politic, or the mystic body of Christ."[28] By man's side, he promised, woman would help to "restore the beauties of Paradise to earth, and to usher in the era of millennial holiness and peace."[29]

As this mission statement illustrates, Mann had not journeyed westward simply to pasture after a long and distinguished career. His greatest work lay before him—cultivating the future guardians of a truly Christian republic, men and women who, like Plato's philosophers, not only understood the social plan on which God had created the human race but had the power and character to bring it into being. This implied a totally new role for higher education: moral training. "The RELATION WHICH COLLEGES BEAR TO THE COMMUNITY," Mann wrote in 1858, "is but little different from that which the brain bears to the rest of the body."[30] "As even the moral tendencies of the child are, to no small extent, inherited from the mother, so every graduate will carry through all his futurity, stamped on his mind and on his soul, impressions, characters, emblems, of the peculiarities, the mental mannerism of the institution whose plastic hand has given shape to his manhood and from whose copious bosom he has drawn his intellectual and moral nutriment."[31]

Surveying college life at the famous sites of classical scholarship and religious teaching, Mann saw only the ornaments of learning and the proselytizing of faith that perpetuated the ignorance and bigotry of doctors, lawyers, politicians, teachers, and other so-called leaders of society. America's colleges were "factories for turning rich, good-for-nothing boys into worse than good-for-nothing men."[32] For when

> a college sends home a great Dragon of intellect into the community, who by force of erudition and talent reaches the high places of judicature or statesmanship, and there perfidiously prostitutes his logic and eloquence to dethrone national justice and enthrone national iniquity; who debauches the public morals by suborning religion to become the nursing mother of national crimes; and who sets the most contagious and fatal of all examples before the young—that union of talent and intemperance or licentiousness—that college inflicts a wound upon the very vitals of the state for which the graduation of a thousand men of commonplace virtues can never atone.[33]

"Have we no interest . . . what manner of men shall preside over these functions of the body-politic?"[34] Was not "their character of more consequence than their learning; their honesty and uprightness of deeper import than their attainment or talent?"[35] Society, he insisted, had a right to demand graduates "trained and indoctrinated in all the cardinal virtues of life," future leaders who could transform "theoretical Christianity into a practical one."[36] The physician's "noble office," for example, was to enter homes, schools, and the workplace in order to dispel ignorance and promote the Christian care of the body. He had a religious duty to

> drive out the Philistine host of bodily diseases and deteriorations— fever, consumption, blindness, deaf-mutism, imbecility, idiocy, lunacy, and all the foul progeny of scrofulous and cancerous blood. All these came into the world through the violations of God's laws; they can be

sent out of the world by obedience to them. They are the terrible punishments that God launches against physiological sins, personal or ancestral. For however it may be in theology, there is no such thing as salvation without works in physiology.[37]

Likewise, Mann believed that "the function of the legal profession is to organize righteousness in the transactions and relations of men."[38] According to this logic, duty to God came before duty to the client, and Mann was adamant that "a lawyer ought never to espouse or prosecute a cause in order that a plaintiff or defendant may prevail, but only in order that justice may be done."[39] Any lawyer, he reasoned, "who knowingly screens the guilty or defends the unjust becomes an accessory after the fact."[40]

Nothing promised to elevate the morals and manners of collegiate halls more than the introduction of woman's "refining, adorning, purifying, and spiritualizing" nature (i.e., when arranged under the guiding principle "association of the sexes *under supervision; non-association, without it*").[41] If educated together, the two genders would exercise "a salutary influence upon the other," promoting both intellectual stimulation and moral restraint.[42] This did not imply the absurd and "promiscuous" doctrine that they should receive the same course of studies—as if to blend the beauty of Hermes and Aphrodite into "*a loathed Hermaphrodite.*"[43] Each had to be trained, as the phrenologist understood, for different spheres of service revealed by their respective physical, emotional, and intellectual organizations. When men and women were educated together, "all the business affairs of the world, all the utilities of science and the beauties of art, will gradually sort themselves into two great classes: into the severer, sterner, harder, robuster occupations for him; into the more peaceful and gentle, the more reserved and unostentatious for her."[44]

To produce a practical rather than a theoretical Christian, disciples who would elevate society rather than simply preach to it, demanded more than a knowledge of religious texts. "Christ never wrote a 'Tract' in his life, but he *went about doing good.*"[45] To do good in their age, Mann's future leaders had to both understand God's laws and have the moral fiber to enact them. Contrary to tradition, this implied that religion and science had to be "reconciled, harmonized, and led to work lovingly together."[46] Much as Combe argued in his *Inquiry into Natural Religion* (1853), so Mann believed "the academy and the church" were simply "different apartments canopied by the same dome—the all-comprehending dome of divine Providence!"[47] When married in this holy nonsectarian union, the offspring of faith and science would "enrich mankind with grander discoveries, pour new light upon the heavenward path of duty, and supply stronger and nobler motives to live in obedience to the will of God."[48] As history demonstrated, religion without science only yielded ignorance and bigotry.

> The effects of continued intermarriages by persons related by consanguinity, the cognate blood unenriched and unstimulated from other fountains, soon breeds weakness, disease, and imbecility. Just so it is with a sect that shuts out truth because it was not embraced in the scheme of its founders. The ideas of such a sect have no alternative for their continued existence but *to breed in and in,* and this, by a psychological law as immutable as the physiological, soon begets a progeny of faith erroneous, absurd, imbecile, and idiotic.[49]

During his final years at Antioch, the quest for biological perfectibility was never far from Mann's mind.

WARRIORS OF VIRTUE

To achieve his educational goals, Mann drew upon the same arguments for content and methods that had informed his common school crusade. True to the prospectus, for instance, he insisted on joint daily exercises for both faculty and students, along with the study of physiology and hygiene. Physical education at Antioch was limited to noncompetitive sports that would not excite self-esteem or promote combativeness. A sound body was necessary for a productive mind, and an informed mind led to a healthy body. In contrast to the sickly graduates of eastern colleges, Mann was adamant that students would leave Antioch with the habits and wisdom essential for a long and vigorous life. The rest of the academic program followed the broad course advertised: the twin branches of the humanities and the sciences converging in the senior year with a series of classes taught by Mann on moral philosophy and natural theology. Rejecting the lectern for the seminar, as one student reported, Mann typically assigned projects to pupils "giving each some question, some theory, some matter-of-fact inquiry, on which each could pursue investigations at leisure, and prepare a paper to be read before the whole class and commented upon by himself."[50] He taught an evening Bible class, where, as his wife explains, "he attempted to make a fair representation of the various interpretations, by different sects, of all the disputed portions of the Scriptures," leaving it to "his hearers to decide that which seemed to them most correct"—and presented students with his own natural theology in a series of rather flowery Sunday lessons, later collected as *Twelve Sermons*.[51]

Financed mostly by credit, Antioch's grandiose campus was only half complete when students arrived for their first semester. There was no heat, classes were scheduled in the dining room, and the Manns, waiting for the construction of the presidential mansion, were forced to take rooms in the dormitories. With many more students than the cut-price scholarship system could support, there was little money for equipment and books. Mann even had to withhold faculty salaries for a time. Eighteen months after its opening, the college was $75,000 in debt and, with soaring interest rates, losing $1,000 a month. Mann begged friends for financial support and spent months on the road fund-raising and lecturing. But affairs went from bad to worse. Fueled by internal rivalries and sectarian bickering, two faculty members opposed to Mann's liberal views attempted to undermine his leadership, igniting a dispute that spilled over into the press, further eroding confidence in the project. On the brink of bankruptcy, Mann sought to restructure Antioch on a sound economic and spiritual basis. Drawing on friends from the East (led by Harvard president Josiah Quincy and Massachusetts governor Salmon P. Chase) he pieced together a financial lifeboat for the college, only to see his plans sink at the final hour, as, with worsening economic conditions and mounting religious distrust, subscribers defaulted on their promises. Forced to foreclose the property, the trustees presented Antioch for auction in June 1859. There was just one bid, the $40,200 raised by Quincy's group. Rising phoenix-like from the ashes, with a charter prohibiting debt and eschewing sectarianism, the future of Mann's experiment was secured just two months prior to his death.

Mann's struggle to ensure the financial and religious independence of Antioch was matched by the incredible battle of wills he conducted with the student body. Life on the western frontier was a good deal more rough-and-ready than that of genteel Boston. To craft intellectual and moral leaders out of the raw material that enrolled in Antioch's first class must have appeared a daunting task, even for someone blessed with Mann's single-mindedness. Determined to curb uncouth frontier habits, Mann had all his male students pledge abstinence from alcohol, tobacco, and profanity. He also banned gambling, frowned upon coffee and dancing, and prohibited students from gathering in local grocery stores. It was said that he could hear a card drop anywhere on campus. Wrestling such vices from 150 men driven by "the impulses of unrestrained appetites, in strong organizations" proved no mean task.[52] Evening after evening he persisted, "exhorting, explaining, arguing, and ridiculing" until only three incorrigibles remained, and these, he reported to Combe, were dismissed at the end of the first year.[53] The rule of virtue, Mann boasted, had been won by moral suasion without recourse to physical coercion or emulation. His chief weapon, at least for the most recalcitrant of his charges, was what Messerli has called a secular confessional, one-on-one "private, intimate, and often confidential conversations" in which Mann attempted "to pass into [a student's] consciousness, and try to make him see mine," to feel, as it were, the pleasures and pains of his own moral organs.[54] He "always shed tears."[55] One can only imagine the effect of this psychological journey on the student. By 1858, he could tell Combe, "We really have the most orderly, sober, diligent, and exemplary institution in the country."[56] Not only was a diploma from Antioch a mark of academic excellence, but, as he announced in convocation of graduates, the degree was conferred "*in further consideration also of the reputable character you have maintained and the exemplary life you have led.*"[57]

Believing that Antioch could be a model for other institutions, Mann attempted to export his vision of a wholesome moral environment to schools and college across the state. In 1856, at the December 27th meeting of the Ohio State Teacher's Association, he presented a resolution calling upon school examiners "never, under any circumstances, to give a certificate of qualification to teach school to any person who habitually uses any kind of intoxicating liquors" and for teachers to "use their utmost influence to suppress the kindred, ungentlemanly, and foul mouthed vices of uttering profane language and using tobacco."[58] Two days later at a convention for delegates of Ohio state colleges, Mann presented a parallel set of resolutions, recommending that all colleges in the state of Ohio "dismiss or expel students who, without permission of their respective teachers, use any kind of intoxicating beverages."[59] Mann also called upon faculty to root out the so-called code of honor, the system of bullying and intimidation that protected misconduct, bred distrust, and undermined the feelings of respect and obedience that students should afford to their teachers. Like the honor among thieves, this law ruled by a terrible despotism, inflecting severe punishments on those virtuous individuals brave enough to confront wrongdoers. Students had to understand that the acts they sought to hide out of loyalty to a friend were actually contributing to their friend's ruin, incubating seeds of vice that would blossom as a corrupt character in later life. Far from hiding evil, students had a duty to monitor and report misconduct, a practice that, Mann predicted, if ever instituted, would itself "save nine-tenths of the occasions for informing."[60]

Many of these arguments found their way into Mann's first baccalaureate address the following July, as he explained his view of the relationship between the college and society to his first graduates. Phrenological laws justified happy, healthy, and physically strong students developing their intellectual faculties and cultivating their moral nature. These principles also underwrote a growing social mission, as Plato-like, promising young men and women transcended "the coarse allurements of sense for the serene and refining joys of sentiment."[61] Having viewed the everlasting, immutable, and beneficent laws of Creation, Mann felt confident that Antioch's graduates would hear the call to duty and experience the sweet rewards that flowed from leading humanity to a more Christian life. Not everyone could follow this path, but Mann, like other college faculty, was on guard lest individuals dominated by their appetites attempted to curry their education into a position of prominence. Judges, lawyers, doctors, and teachers had to be ambassadors of God's will, not self-serving individualists. "In the august presence of these dignitaries," and "in the presence also of Almighty God," Mann implored his young warriors of virtue, "to make now a vow of self-consecration to a life of work and duty and beneficence" and "to wind up your resolution to such a pitch of intensity that its spring will not uncoil until the fruitions and securities of eternity are substituted for the motives and efforts of time."[62]

Starting in the summer of 1856, the pressures of the presidency began to exact a toll on Mann's health. Prone to insomnia and plagued by hemorrhoids, he suffered a minor stroke that for a short time impaired his speech. Anticipating death, especially after hearing of Combe's passing in 1858, Mann drew upon what was left of his energy to secure Antioch's future and promote his vision of its non-sectarian mission. By the occasion of his third baccalaureate address in July 1859, his powers were all but spent. As much a moral accounting of his own life as a call for service, he talked of his burning passion for reform trapped within his feeble frame. If only he could fight one more battle for God! The only way to carry the fight forward was to transfer his enthusiasm, his experience, and his knowledge into younger, more athletic bodies. Spelling out the paths of misery and happiness in this world, he presented the human predicament and the guiding star of God's natural order. Continuing the military imagery, he maintained that "nothing today prevents this earth from being a paradise but error and sin. These errors, these sins, you must assail . . . the disability of poverty; the pains of disease; the enervations and folly of fashionable life; the brutishness of appetite and the demonisms of passion."[63] Barely audible, he concluded his last oration with the oft quoted plea, "I beseech you to treasure up into your hearts these my parting words: *Be ashamed to die until you have won some victory for humanity.*"[64] Mann himself was not ashamed, when, two months later he succumbed to a continuing fever. On his final day, having been told he had no more than three hours to live, he summoned students to his bedside to implore them one more time to consecrate their lives to the obedience of God's laws. Supremely confident in the care of his own soul, he left instructions for Henry Barnard to publish his phrenological chart as the best testament to his own life and character.[65]

14
The High Tide of Secularism

In every step of [secular] instruction we should direct the emotional faculties of wonder, reverence, benevolence, conscientiousness, and the love of the beautiful, to God as the Author of all, and train these faculties practically with the faith, that, in conforming to His laws, we are paying him the highest homage that can be offered by a rational being to his Creator; and at the same time expanding, elevating, and improving our own minds.

George Combe, "On Secular Education,"
Westminster Review, July 1852

Combe and he wife returned to Britain physically and mentally exhausted by their two-year tour of the United States. Retiring to a cottage just outside Edinburgh, they spent the next six months trying to obey the laws of nature, George leisurely composing his *Notes on America* and revising his *Lectures on Moral Philosophy* and Cecy enjoying the countryside and visits from friends. Phrenology had prospered in his absence. The laws of mind, he told the National Association of Phrenologists that September, were at last starting to bear fruit in fields as diverse as medicine, jurisprudence, criminology, anthropology, and education, although he cautioned that to be considered scientists they would have to move beyond mere observation to the precise measurement of the head and challenged the group to develop instruments that could quantify the size of the brain's various organs. He was particularly cheered to report the progress of phrenology in America and across the continent—even Italy was starting to embrace his doctrines. The one dark spot was the almost complete ignorance of God's laws in Germany, the country of phrenology's origin.

Determined to fulfill his pledge to introduce phrenology to the land of Gall, Combe recommended lessons in German and started planning for a yearlong visit to the Rhineland. In the meantime, a most important and pressing duty had to be completed—the popularization of Mann's work in

Britain. Still relatively unknown in the United Kingdom, Combe was hopeful that Massachusetts' common school revival could provide a blueprint for the advancement of education in a nation still bitterly divided by religious differences. The free institutions of the United States, he reasoned, with their unique combination of sectarian impartiality and limited legal authority, were far more congenial to the Anglo-Saxon mind than the autocratic and centralized machinery of despotic Prussia.

Published anonymously in the *Edinburgh Review* in June 1841, Combe's "Education in America—State of Massachusetts" presented a compelling digest of Mann's first four *Reports,* his *School Returns,* the opening issues of the *Common School Journal,* and the 1840 contest to dissolve the Board.[1] Starting with a clear description of the main legal statutes governing the powers and responsibilities of school districts, taxation, and religious neutrality in education—including the edict that "the school committee shall never direct to be purchased or used, in any of the town schools, any schoolbooks which are calculated to favor the tenets of any particular sect of Christians"—he explained how, without centralized guidance, Massachusetts' famed localism had failed to meet the state's historic educational mission.[2] Responding to this situation, the government had created a Board of Education and appropriated funds for school construction. Without any legal power to compel reform, the Board's secretary, Horace Mann, had spread practical knowledge across the state and without party or cant awakened the public to the advantages of education. As a result, Massachusetts was now engaged in a massive revitalization of its schools; teacher-training colleges were being built and library books disseminated to elevate the population. Combe also drew attention to Mann's advocacy of female teachers and to the effectiveness with which he had used the school returns—not only did these abstracts contain a "vast amount of valuable information," but by "informing each district what all the others are doing," it operated "powerfully on the spirit of emulation."[3] "Even the most callous," he reported, are roused into sensibility and shame, when they see their own imperfections exhibited to the public gaze."[4] It was true that political opponents had attempted to crush this movement, but not, Combe noted, for any infringement of religious feeling. In all the thousands of pages of reports, many written by local clergymen of different denominations, there had not been a single call for sectarian teaching. Surely, he concluded, these facts, the potent combination of perfect impartiality and the absence of compulsion, demonstrated "strong evidence of the possibility of operating on the public mind by means of an organized system, and authorized functionaries, wielding moral powers alone"—a lesson, he added pointedly, that appears highly "instructive to ourselves."[5]

Not only were the free institutions of the United States better adapted to the English temperament, but, as Combe had discovered on his American tour, by stimulating the faculties, they were also the most effective means of raising the public mind. This became obvious later that summer as Combe made his way from Hamburg to Mannheim. For, despite the overall superiority of the German brain, it was evident from the poor intellectual and moral state of the country that Germany's autocratic regime was still stifling the development of the higher powers. The new schoolhouses he saw on his travels demonstrated the government's desire to enlighten the people, but without the freedom to think and act for themselves, he was convinced that the population would remain mired in their old habits. If only he could persuade a few leading men to consider his teachings, Combe was sure "from their large intellect" that "the Germans would make better use of free institutions than either the Americans or the English have done."[6]

In the four years since his previous visit, "steamboats and railroads" were starting to break "the despot's chains."[7] Never was there a more propitious time to disseminate the truths of phrenology. Yet the weight of this mission lay heavily upon him. For the best part of a year he worked with tutors and von Struve, practicing his language skills and adapting lectures to the tastes and manners of a German academic audience. By May, with the enthusiastic support of von Struve, he had gained sufficient confidence to present himself to the faculty at Heidelberg. Aided by Mittermair and Chelius, professors of law and surgery, he battled anxiety and an unremitting headache to present a course of twenty-two lectures. Whether or not he made any important converts is unclear. But his efforts were appreciated. Even Friedrich Tiedemann, whose "Brain of the Negro Compared with that of the European and the Orang-outang" had been roundly criticized by Andrew Combe, thanked him for his labors.[8]

Combe had pushed his "powers to their utmost."[9] Writing to his brother, he described how "nervous excitement" caused "so much pain . . . [he]could not even hear the *Scotsman* read without great suffering."[10] "I had deep breathings, and my nerves tingled to the ends of my fingers, which once lost sensation."[11] With neither spirit nor energy to continue, he forwarded his casts and skulls to Dresden, hoping he would recover sufficiently to lecture there the following year, and headed home to recuperate during the winter. After several months of better health Combe again entertained the possibility of resuming his mission in Germany, but reluctantly submitted to medical advice that even reading a prepared paper would seriously jeopardize his delicate organization. Rather than lecture the Germans, he would take the waters and winter in Italy. "Taking the waters" seems to have been an excellent excuse for an expensive European vacation. Still, as explained earlier, he did manage to meet with Mann in Leipzig before traveling on to join the Howes in Rome. Pursuing his new interest in the fine arts, he then spent the best part of a year examining how well the great masters had captured their subjects as measured by the principles of phrenology.[12]

Two anonymous publications occupied Combe's attention after his return to Edinburgh in the summer of 1844. First, *The Vestiges of the Natural History of Creation,* which arrived at his door without a note. Written by his friend Robert Chambers (who zealously hid his identity to protect the family publishing business), many thought this sweeping account of the evolution of life could be attributed to Combe. After all, it did culminate with an endorsement of phrenology. Except for Chamber's assertion that organic life arose from chemical processes, Combe was in complete agreement with the book and, one senses, a little jealous of its celebrity. Even so, the *Vestiges* became something of a talisman for Combe, indicating through its reception that the public was now ready to hear more advanced doctrines. The second work, a pamphlet titled "Who Should Educate the Prince of Wales?" was published later in the year. Combe and his brother were objects of special interest at the palace, especially among the German members of the British court. In 1836, on the advice of the queen's physician, James Clark, Andrew Combe had been appointed doctor to Leopold I, King of Belgium. Ill health forced him to resign after only a few months, but during his short stay in Brussels he treated then Prince Albert of Saxe-Coburg and made a strong impression on his council, Baron Stockmair. Two years later, George Combe was introduced to the baron at Clark's house. Not only did his head reveal "large *morale* with a fair intellect," but, after engaging him in conversation "on ideas in general," he reported to Andrew that Stockmair was "more perfectly of our way of thinking in morals, religion, and politics than any man, who was not a thorough phrenologist, whom I have ever seen."[13] Over the next few years, the baron became fully committed to Combe's doctrines and, together with Clark, helped promote phrenology among the royals—Albert was so enamored with Combe's teaching, and his love of all things German, he even presented copies of *Moral Philosophy* and *Lectures on Popular Education* to leading politicians. Stockmair was thus keen to know Combe's views on the article—largely pleas not to appoint a clergyman as the young prince's tutor and to follow what Combe saw as a rather utopian curriculum suited to a child savant. Combe, of course, warned against overtaxing the child's mind and recommended an instructor schooled in phrenology who could teach Edward scientific knowledge of the world in accordance with the needs of his developing faculties. Special care had to be taken not to strengthen the organs of self-esteem and love of approbation already enlarged by the prince's unique upbringing. But beyond this typical digest of phrenological wisdom, Combe's long, detailed letter also explored a weightier set of questions about the relationship between government and religion, issues he would develop more thoroughly over the next few years in the important trio of papers "Remarks on National Education," "On the Relation between Religion and Science," and "What Should a Secular Education Embrace?" as he pushed the logic of his secular faith to its apogee.[14]

Basically, Combe was concerned that the future authority of the sovereign not be grounded in the irrational doctrines of revealed religion. In the past, royalty had turned to the church, believing that faith in the supernatural was the only instrument by which to maintain social order. But the Bible was too vague a book to ensure stability in the modern world; government had to be grounded upon the universal truths of morality crafted into the human constitution. From his conversation with the most enlightened minds of Germany, America, and Italy, Combe assured the baron that "Christianity is merely a republication of the religion of nature, and that its pure and comprehensive morality is the solid foundation on which all the supernatural portions of its structures rest."[15] That is, the Scriptures provided a guide to conduct only insofar as they captured the essence of natural laws. As future king, Edward would have to be schooled in the doctrines of the Anglican Church, but this did not mean his mind could not be opened to the moral foundation of social life. No longer a divine figurehead, Combe pictured the ideal sovereign as a living representative of the moral and intellectual powers that would lead the country toward prosperity and civilization.

During the summer of 1846, Combe was invited to explain his ideas at Buckingham Palace. Victoria, more skeptical than her husband, was growing concerned that Prince Alfred, now two years old, was not making satisfactory progress. Combe's delineation of the royal head seemed to ease her fears, but contrary to his hopes, Victoria stuck with convention and appointed Bishop Wilberforce to oversee Edward's education. Several years later, in 1850, after a second visit and much prodding from Stockmair, Clark, and Prince Albert, a German phrenologist named Ernst Becker was retained to supervise the young prince's recreational activities. Combe was ecstatic at the opportunity to prove the benefits of phrenology and entertained high hopes that the wisdom of the first family would soon be embraced by the rest of the country. He brought Becker to his house in Edinburgh during the winter of 1850–51 for three months' instruction in physiology and, from then until 1854, maintained a detailed biweekly correspondence on Edward's progress. At this time, an even more important colleague, William Ellis, was hired to tutor the royal children in social science and political economy. As it turned out the "palace project" had little, if any, direct impact on the course of education in Britain, but Combe was always grateful of his patron's support and maintained that the "Queen and the Prince Consort [had] risen far above the prejudices of the age in the education of their family."[16]

LIFE IN GOD'S SECULUM

The phenomenal sale of the *Vestiges* was not the only indication that more rational attitudes were developing toward the relationship between science and religion. Industrial expansion, the growth of the railroads, and numerous other technological advances all demonstrated the advantages of harnessing the laws of nature. Combe even saw cracks appearing in the orthodox façade of the church and signs of reasonableness among the aristocracy. Never had he "known England and Scotland, morally and physically, in a more promising condition."[17] But by far the most exciting event of 1846 was the repeal of the Corn Laws. Seventy years after Adam Smith, "Richard Cobden had taught the public and the peers the power of reason."[18] The principle of free trade stood as a sublime proof of God's providential economy: could Cobden not be persuaded to elevate other truths of reason? In particular, could he not be persuaded to become the English Horace Mann and carry the cause of public education to the nation?

Like Mann, Cobden was also a committed disciple of Combe's teachings—the *Constitution,* he declared, "read like a transcript of his own familiar thoughts."[19] Since 1837, when he invited Combe to lecture in Manchester, the two men had been frequent correspondents and strong friends. Cobden was particularly impressed when Combe identified his large organ of veneration— "that," the free trader confessed eleven years later, "was a triumph for phrenology."[20] For despite "possessing a strong logical faculty, which keeps me in the path of rationalism," he admitted to "a strong religious feeling" and "a sympathy for men who act under that impulse."[21] Indeed, it was this sympathy that had tempted him to believe that he might engineer some compromise to the problem of education. But the fundamental divisions he had encountered during Simpson's campaign a decade earlier were still in place. The best policy, he cautioned Combe in 1847, was to first push the extension of the franchise and then promote public schooling. Dogmatic minds, already starting to thaw, would finally come to their senses when they realized that the working classes were destined to become their masters.

But Combe was in no mood to wait for the passing of geologic time, especially given the rift between the denominations generated by the Tory's abortive effort to pass the Factory Bill of 1843, which would have placed working children in schools under the administration of the church. Taking stock of the government's plans, nonconformists found themselves caught between two equally unpalatable axioms: education without religion (which was unconscionable) or public schooling with religion (which was bound to favor Anglicanism). The only way forward was voluntaryism. As promoted by Edward Baines, editor of *Leeds Mercury,* and Edward Miall, Herbert Spencer's mentor at the *Nonconformist,* dissent took the increasingly militant stance that any government involvement in schooling would be immoral. Public charity and the principle of laissez-faire, they believed, were sufficient to meet the country's educational needs.

Kay's ambition to create state-run normal schools, institute teaching certificates, and tie government grants to inspection and the standardization of the curriculum were thus seen by dissenters and secularists alike as a blatant effort to favor the hegemony of the church. Could the government not find a domain of religious, moral, and intellectual knowledge that all sects could recognize as essential to life in the modern world? Facing the retrenchment of old animosities, Combe decided the time was ripe for a new look at the central concepts at the root of the impasse. Each side, he argued in his *Remarks on National Education,* whether favoring secular, sectarian, or combined instruction, was committed to certain views of "the nature of man, of the origin and objects of society, of the powers and duties of government, and of the connection between practical morality, secular prosperity, and religious belief."[22] Yet no party had provided a systematic analysis of these fundamental relationships, and without such conceptual clarification, hope of an agreement on public education was impossible.

Building on the basic premises of the *Constitution,* Combe demonstrated that social life imposed certain expectations on the behavior of citizens, including the obligation that every individual develop physically, morally, and intellectually in such a way that their health, conduct, and civic understanding contributed to the well-being of all. They had a duty, for example, not to pass vice on to their progeny. But Combe also made the stronger claim that governments ought to train the religious sentiments. Of course, spiritual commitment was a matter of individual conscience, but it was justifiable, he believed, to insist that men and women learn to revere the divine directives woven into the fabric of nature. As he had told Stockmair, given "that no law is laid down to man in the Bible for his guidance in temporal affairs, which is not inscribed as clearly in the book of nature," who could object to "the conclusion that the state has a right to teach the practical doctrines of natural religion recognized in Scripture, to all?"[23]

Combe identified two opponents of his views: voluntaryists and arch-conservatives—such as Robert Ingles (humorously known in Parliament as "the member for heaven"), who criticized any and all talk of secular schooling as rank infidelity. In response to free market nonconformists such as Edward Baines and Edward Miall, he argued that for all its good intentions, the voluntary scheme had proven itself incapable of coordinating a system of schooling that attended to the educational needs of all children. Only the state could examine the workings of the whole system, discover social laws, and disseminate information essential to the public good. As for Ingles, in castigating the study of nature "as a gigantic scheme of godless education," did he believe "that God was author of a great system of infidelity?"[24] Ingles own constituency, Oxford, seemed to bear this prejudice out, for at England's most eminent seat of learning, apart from the Thirty-Nine Articles of the Church of England, the study of science was virtually unknown. This divide between faith and reason was a cause of grave concern. "The notion that morality and religion rest EXCLUSIVELY on the Bible as their basis, [had] produced something like a divorce, not only between religion and science, but between religion and literature, religion and legislation, religion and history," a separation, he insisted, that "left religion in a kind of ideal desert, from which she issues only to disturb the march of mundane affairs."[25] The same error was also evident in the work of many scientists, who, leaving theological concerns to the church, failed to consider the presence of God in the works of nature, rendering knowledge of the world devoid of religious significance.

> Until science shall discover her own character and vocation—that she is the messenger of God, speaking directly to (the religious) sentiments in strains calculated to thrill and rouse them to the most energetic action—she will never wield her proper influence over society for the promotion of their moral, religious, and physical welfare. Never, until she do so, will she take that place in social esteem and veneration which, as the fountain of divine wisdom, she is entitled to possess.[26]

Science, then, had to be understood as a form of religion. Fortunately, Combe predicted, with orthodoxy in decline, the time would soon come when men and women would stand up to the church "and shake the theological fabric in this country to the ground."[27] Reconciling "the morality of nature with that of scripture," they would then infuse daily life with science and religion "to the infinite advantage of both and of the people."[28]

There was no better proof of Combe's doctrines than the history of education in Ireland. For more than a century, the English church had excluded all but doctrinal teachings in the vain attempt to eradicate Catholicism. But starving the Irish mind of practical knowledge had resulted in the most fearful state of physical, moral, and intellectual depravity. Only since the legislation of 1828 was this situation being reversed. For the past eighteen years the same winning formula employed in Massachusetts—combined secular studies and separate religious instruction, reading of the Holy Scriptures without note or comment, and an interfaith board to select textbooks—had met the approval of all sects. With a four-fold increase in pupils and clear evidence that the practical curriculum was developing intelligent and moral scholars adapted for success in life, there was every reason to hope that secular schooling would transform the country. Why could this system not be adopted with similar results in the rest of Britain?

In 1848, Combe intensified his attack in "The Relation between Religion and Science," a stinging critique of sectarian education that called for a new reformation in religion to "recognize man and the natural world as constituted by Divine Benevolence and Wisdom, and adapted to each other for man's instruction and benefit."[29] The first duty of this new faith would be "to communicate to the young a knowledge of that constitution and its adaptations, as the basis of their religious faith and practice . . . and train them to realize in their own minds and bodies, and in the society to which they belong, THE NATURAL CONDITIONS on which health, prosperity, purity, piety, and peace depend."[30] Until this was accomplished, Combe was convinced that the world would remain as the *Shorter Catechism* presented it, a theater of pain, misery, and suffering. Witness the despair of Ireland, the spread of disease in English cities, and the shocking mortality rates among the laboring classes. It was time for those enlightened clergymen who privately recognized a more rational and beneficent order in nature to stand against orthodox fanatics and openly advocate secular instruction. Christianity, Combe continued, resided in the large body of truths common to all sects, not the fine and irresolvable disputes that separated them—most dogmas, even the devout had to acknowledge, must be largely riddled with error. "To vote money, therefore, as is done by the Minutes of Council of August and December, 1846, to every sect, to enable it to educate its own members in its only religious doctrines, is actually to endow discord. It is deserting the shrine of reason and of moral and religious principle, and bowing at that of prejudice and bigotry."[31]

Combe's third, and in many ways most compelling article, presented a strictly theological justification for secular education. Recalling the experiences of his youth—the physical and mental tyranny of Luke Fraser's classroom and the dismal predictions of Calvinism—he revealed the great mystery that had driven his life's work. How could the truth of God's government, imprinted on his mind at an early age, be reconciled with events in the world? The *Catechism,* while insisting on God's authority, did not explain the manner of His administration. Gradually, as Combe's mind opened to the principles of physics, chemistry, political economy, and physiology, he started to apprehend the lawful structure of nature. But it was only through phrenology that he came to realize how human beings were adapted to the world through the structure of the brain's organs. Struggling with the problem of fatalism, he finally accommodated the physical and the moral. God had provided men and women with the rational abilities and free will to understand and improve their nature. His own key insight had been that veneration and other religious sentiments must be trained to regard the laws of nature as God's commandments—a reverence to the principles of physiology and political economy that provided middle-class social values the ultimate sanction, the divine will of God. What, then, should secular education embrace? "Instruction," he replied, "in the qualities, modes of action, relations, and purposes of things and beings by means of which the government of the world is maintained; and also TRAINING of the whole faculties, animal, moral, and intellectual, to ACTION in conformity with the order of Providence."[32] Getting down to specifics, this entailed the same basic curriculum that Simpson had presented some fifteen years earlier, suitably infused with lessons on the religious significance of nature.

SECULAR SCHOOLING

Combe's three pamphlets created a good deal of excitement among supporters of secular schooling. But none was more enthusiastic than William Ellis. A member of John Stuart Mill's Utilitarian Society, as a young man Ellis had begun a promising career as an economic theorist, publishing articles in the *Westminster Review* and lecturing to adult classes at the London Mechanic's Institute. One set of talks, presented in 1835, so impressed Brougham, he hired a speaker to have them read to workingmen's audiences around the country. However, an early marriage, modest financial recourses, and the demands of managing the failing Indemnity Mutual Marine Assurance Company curtailed Ellis's scholarly work. The academic world's loss was the business world's gain. After twenty years at the helm, Ellis turned Indemnity Mutual into a highly successful company and made his own fortune in the process. By 1846 he had the time and the financial resources to return to his most passionate concern, promoting the moral lessons of economics as a guide to human happiness and social well-being. Convinced that the basic principles of his social science could be understood by children, he presented a series of lessons, later published as *Outlines of Social Economy,* to the students of the BFSS school in Camberwell.[33] His efforts confirmed his fondest expectations, and the following year, on the advice of Francis Place, he joined with the Chartist leader, William Lovett, to open London's first secular school at the National Hall in Holburn. Funded by Ellis, the school commenced in 1848 with close to 200 students. Shortly thereafter, Ellis and John Runz opened the first of seven "Birkbeck" schools (named for George Birkbeck, who helped found the London Mechanic's Institute) in Chancery Lane. Ellis

312 / Chapter 14

had hoped to lecture in the BFSS Normal school, but when his request was refused, he instituted his own night classes and instructed dozens of teachers in the philosophy of secularism and his own distinctive method of instruction, a form of interrogative questioning that led students to construct economic principles for themselves.

Quite when Ellis became a convert to the doctrines of the *Constitution* is unclear, although it is evident that by 1848, when he wrote to Combe with a copy of *Questions and Answers,* he embraced both the phrenological view of mind and the principles of natural theology.[34] Instruction, he maintained, had to follow the laws governing the brain by utilizing practices "that strengthen, develop, and rightly direct all its faculties"; religion had to be taught as a social duty, not a set of beliefs; and the curriculum had to acquaint children with positive facts necessary for them to understand their position and duties in life.[35] He also scorned the classics and insisted that teaching eschew all punishment and emulation. Combe was equally sympathetic to Ellis's project. He praised his social economics in the *Westminster Review* and eagerly promoted the National Hall and Birkbeck schools.[36] Combe was also taken by Lovett, whose *Chartism* reads like a digest of his own educational thought. Lovett was not exaggerating when he told Combe that "whatever little good I have been able to achieve I am widely indebted to yourself."[37] He defined education as "*all those means* which are used to develope [*sic*] the various faculties of mind and body, and so train them, that the child shall become a healthy, intelligent, moral, and useful member of society."[38] He argued that because "the *proper* use and exercise" enlarged and strengthened "every part of the mind and body," each faculty had be trained through "a course of discipline" that would "habituate it to form certain operations *with ease and effect*," so rendering individuals happy, useful members of the community, able to "follow the physical laws of their nature, the social institutions of man, and the moral laws of God."[39] And so on, even to the smallest matters of curriculum and pedagogy. Indeed, in a recent article, David Stack argues that Lovett's entire radical philosophy flowed from an environmentally progressive reading of Combe's phrenology that suggested the possibility of significant human improvement through self-help and moral discipline.[40]

Although there is merit in Stewart and McCann's judgment that Ellis "was probably the most influential educator during the mid-nineteenth century," especially given the quarter of a million pounds he is estimated to have

poured into secular schooling, the appeal of practical subjects such as social economics and physiology also owed an important intellectual debt to
Combe's teachings.[41] It was, after all, Combe's view of human nature and the
social good that underwrote Ellis's lessons and provided the epistemic basis
for the dozen or so secular schools that opened during the 1850s. Keen to play
a leading role in this movement, Combe persuaded Ellis to help finance a
school north of the border. In December 1848, with the aid of James Simpson
and the star pupil of Ellis's seminary, William Mattieu Williams, Combe issued a prospectus to the working men and women of Edinburgh announcing
the opening of the Williams Secular School in one of the poorest sections of
the city. With the help of a Miss Carmichael, Williams operated the school
successfully for six years with an average enrollment of 150 boys and girls.
It was undoubtedly the best practical illustration of how phrenological principles could be applied to education. The curriculum flowed directly from the
writings of Combe and Simpson. Children acquired the instrumental skills
of reading, writing, and arithmetic and positive knowledge about the human
constitution and its relations to the social and material worlds. Building on
knowledge of physical properties acquired through object lessons, a host of
explorative activities were employed to teach the basic principles of mechanics, chemistry, and natural history. Geography continued this training of the
perceptive and reflective faculties by extending the study of topographical
features to sciences such as geology and meteorology. Investigating the body
in anatomy and physiology, pupils learned about health, diet, exercise, and
the responsibilities of child care, and, because good citizenship demanded an
understanding of political economy, Williams employed Ellis's lessons on the
realities of supply and demand, wage and labor relations, pauperism, and the
practical doctrines of self-help. Finally, in phrenology, students were introduced to the laws of mental life. Combe taught this last class himself. Mixing
his armchair anthropology with practical ethics, he attempted to instill in his
pupils an appreciation for the exercise of their higher powers and the rewards
of rational self-management. Throughout the entire system, all knowledge
was justified as an illustration of God's beneficent order and the greater happiness that results from acting in accordance with natural laws.

Perhaps the most famous criticism of the Birkbeck schools is found in
Dickens's *Hard Times* (1854).[42] Satirizing the object lesson and the teaching of
political economy through Mr. Gradgrind's call to "form the minds of rea-

soning animals" by instructing "boys and girls in nothing but Facts," Dickens presented the graduates of Ellis's secular schools as a servile automata, devoid of reason and spirit.[43] Although this may be a fair criticism of earlier utilitarian schemes, it hardly does justice to Ellis's ambition to develop informed workers who complied with industrial life out of principled self-interest.[44] Nor does it apply to the kind of lessons taught in Edinburgh. As Williams told parents at the first board meeting, the school's central goal "was to replace the blind memorization of words and dogma . . . with the acquisition of ideas."[45] The verbal rote and rule following techniques of the early Lancasterian system were rejected in favor of a "Socratic method," in which students were encouraged to ask questions and offer their own observations.[46] Some sense of this procedure can be gained from Combe's last publication, *On Teaching Physiology and Its Applications in Common Schools,* in which he utilizes the "mode of teaching [learned] from my friend Mr. William Ellis."[47] Concerned to show how the Creator had adapted the world to human needs and instituted social laws that promote common welfare, he engaged a group of working-class children in an extended dialogue that, in passages such as the following, taught the functions of the body, the provisions of nature, and the importance of performing one's appointed task in life.

Q. Have any of you a knife? Here various pocket knives in various stages of wear were presented. One much worn in the joint and one not perceptibly worn, were selected.

Q. Do you see any difference in the joints of these two knives? They were handed to each pupil and examined. "Yes Sir; one is worn round, and the other is quite straight in the joint."—Q. Right: but *what* caused that one to become round? "Much opening and shutting; this wore away the iron of the joint by rubbing against the spring."—Q. Does the axle of a cart-wheel wear away? "Yes Sir."—Q. Why? "Also by rubbing."—Q. Do they put grease on it? "Yes."—Q. For what purpose? "To make the wheel move easy and rub less."

Q. Now does anything resembling this go on in your body? A. Pause; no answer.—Q. Strip off your jackets. This was instantly done, accompanied by a shout of laughter.—Feel with your left hand the shoulder joint of your right arm, and swing the right arm, extended at full length, round and round.—Q. What do you feel? "The top of the arm moving at a joint."—A diagram of the human skeleton was here unrolled, and the structure of the ball-and-socket joint of the shoulder explained to them.—Q. Now suppose that this were a real skeleton of bone, and I should swing the arm round and round for a day, what would ensue? "The motion would wear the bones in the joint."—Here the secretion, in the socket of the joint, of oil to lesson the friction of the cartilages covering the bones, was explained.—Q. Will this altogether prevent the waste? "No; the cart axle has oil, yet it wears."[48]

God had created the body so that, with the correct diet and exercise, it would function productively for a good number of years. Combe had little problem bringing his students to understand a similar lesson: people born with different abilities were appointed to distinct tasks in life.

Q. When a farmer is ploughing all day, is he doing a necessary duty? "Yes he is." Q. Is he respected or despised for working in this manner? "To be respected; he is doing what is right."—Q. If he had in mind all the steps that we have followed, would he feel that in ploughing he was doing a religious duty? "Yes."—Q. Why so? "Because he would understand that God had appointed him to do it, that he and others might have bread to enable them to live." Right.[49]

Interestingly, in his explanation of this method, Williams noted that because boys were endowed with larger causality, they more readily understood philosophical points. The trick in teaching a coeducational class, therefore, was to move the group forward by calling on girls to recite facts and boys to explain principles—an intellectual union complemented by the powerful moral influence females had on the behavior of boys.

As Williams's five annual reports show, his primary concern was not so much learning as moral training. And on this subject he became an enthusiastic herald of Combe's psychological management. Instead of adapting the child to the system, the system had to be adapted to the child. With little experience in the classroom, he confessed to having accepted the position of master only on condition that he may resort to corporal punishment until the moral tone of the school made it superfluous. But knowledge of phrenology and experience had revealed that the "direct and exclusive appeals to the nerves of sensation and the Sentiment of Fear, are not only unnecessary, but decidedly mischievous."[50] "All that is required," he explained, is to exercise the faculties manifested in deficiency, or to repress those manifested in excess. Such training is necessarily painful, but this pain is instituted by the Creator as an element of the human constitution, and is a sufficiently intense, and a far more effective, appeal to selfishness and fear, than any of the artificial devices for inspiring terror, which are commonly resorted to.[51]

When children sought the attention of their peers, they were placed in a corner. Pupils who chattered were sentenced to silence, and those who were tardy or fidgeted in class forfeited their recess. The ones that could not keep quiet were separated, and those that quarreled were forced to hold hands "until angry feeling gave way to cheerful friendliness."[52] "Children who came dirty to school [were] publicly washed."[53] Most importantly, the moral lesson was always explained and, in the case of egregious behavior, made an object of class study through a jury of the offender's peers. Under this system of moral restraint, Williams boasted, the child learns to weigh options, consider consequences, and "feel that he lives under Divine laws, and that natural punishments await his transgressions, which he cannot escape, although no human avenger be present."[54] God Himself would become their silent monitor.

James Simpson died in 1853. The following year Williams accepted a lectureship in Birmingham, and despite its service to the community, the school was forced to close. Combe, increasingly constrained by his own fragile health, struggled in vain to appoint a new principal. In part, the problem was financial. By refusing to include doctrinal religious instruction in the curriculum, the Williams School, like other secular schools around the nation, was ineligible for government grants and had to rely on fees and philanthropic donations—which were hardly sufficient given the poverty of the people and the prejudices against secularism and phrenology. Passing the baton to the recently formed Manchester Secular School, Combe could only hope that other more energetic spirits would carry his reforms forward.

THE NATIONAL PUBLIC SCHOOL ASSOCIATION

At the same time Combe was working to establish the Williams School in Edinburgh, a new movement for a national system of secular education was forming in Manchester.[55] The brainchild of Samuel Lucas and several members of the now defunct Anti-Corn League, a plan was published in 1847 calling for free, state-supported secular schooling in Lancashire.[56] Guided by Combe and his 1841 article on the Massachusetts system, Lucas proposed infant, elementary, industrial, and evening schools superintended by local school committees, committees of Lancashire's six administrative Hundreds, and a county school board. As in Massachusetts, local committees would be responsible for hiring teachers and reporting statistics in annual returns. "Nothing [was to] be taught in any of the schools which favors the particular tenets of any religious sect."[57] This meant excluding all books that did not meet the approval of an interdenominational panel empowered to veto objectionable material. Finally, the board, which would have no legal authority to interfere in the management of schools other than settling disputes, would supervise a Normal school and employ a secretary to disseminate the latest intelligence.

Carefully massing materials (Combe provided Mann's *Reports,* issues of the *Common School Journal,* and letters from America), the group attempted to garner support for their plan among local clergy concerned by mounting educational problems within the county. But while sharing their enthusiasm for free schools, Hugh Stowell announced in a public meeting during March 1849 that the church could not sanction "any system of general education of which the Christian religion is not the basis."[58] Even a conscience clause seemed impossible. Schools, he cautioned, could be secular or sectarian, but not both—and if the former were approved, what would become of the existing voluntary institutions? Despite this setback and the failure of W. J. Fox's bill in Parliament, the Lancashire Public School Association (LPSA) believed they had enough support to move the scheme forward, even to the whole country. On September 3, 1850, a conference was called at the Free Trade Hall to establish a national movement for secular schools. It was evident, however, that some compromise had to be made on the religious question, and Lucas, now coordinating operations from London, suggested the Irish System of reading sections from the Scriptures that met the approval of all denominations. Others supported including optional periods in the curriculum devoted to sectarian teaching. But even with these provisos, Cobden, reluctantly drawn into the leadership of the group, was convinced that a campaign for "secular" schooling would still be read as endorsing a godless education, given that the majority understood secular to mean nonreligious. W. E. Forster, the future author of the 1870 English Elementary Education

Act, proposed nonsectarian, but Cobden won the day and the National Public Schools Association (NPSA) was born.

While the NPSA was attempting to build momentum, north of the border, a group composed of Free Church, Presbyterian, and liberal public leaders formed the National Education Association (NEA) in order to promote tax-supported religious schooling in Scotland. Attempting to extend the traditional network of parish schools, they suggested dividing the country into local districts and establishing a rate to hire teachers and build schools. Because there was less concern over doctrine—all Scottish denominations taught the Shorter Catechism—than which sect might gain government power, their manifesto called for heads of households to meet and determine the subjects to be taught in each township. Keen to move forward, many liberals, including James Simpson, supported the measure. By sending a bill to Westminster, he later explained, Simpson expected at least the addition of a conscience clause and was hopeful that national agitation would rouse the government to solve the religious problem once and for all by mandating a national system of secular instruction. Combe was less optimistic and published a pamphlet explaining why he dissented from the plan. Convinced that the various sects would combine to impose their religious views on the minority, he tried to rally interest around the NPSA plan. The following year, as the NEA struggled to accommodate the interests of the various Scottish denominations, Combe and Simpson attempted to capitalize on the popular interest in educational reform. In a series of lectures to workingmen's groups around Scotland, they explained the benefits of secular education and the inherent fallibility of theological dogmatism. Combe was particularly severe on the Shorter Catechism, which, he suggested, would become the sole content for what the manifesto called "sound religious instruction." On April 18, together with NPSA secretary Robert Smiles, they attended a meeting called to inaugurate the newly formed Glasgow Public Schools Association and encourage support for the secular education movement at its most crucial hour. After explaining all the issues and informing the four thousand crowded into the auditorium of the success of the Birkbeck and Williams secular schools, Combe announced that, coordinating with petitions from Manchester, the Liberal member of Parliament, Lord Melgund, was about to present a bill for Scotland. He had every reason to expect that the rising voice of an informed public would at last push the government to act for the greater benefit of the nation. Two months later Combe was in Westminster to witness his fondest hopes dashed by a Tory majority of thirteen votes. Shocked by the ineptness of the debate, he was left with the impression that "the House consists of common-place men with common-place information; excepting a few superior spirits whose influence is extinguished by the inert mass with which they are associated."[59] Even Lord John Russell, whom he called on a few days later at Pembroke House, seemed to have little understanding of the basic issues. More had to be done to enlighten the public and the nation's leaders. To this end, Combe continued his lectures in Scotland and prepared for what would be his last public address, the grand meeting of the NPSA in Manchester that December. Called to organize a "monster" petition on behalf of the city's working men and women, the event restored Combe's confidence that the realization of his plan would soon be at hand.

Cobden was not so sanguine, for by this time a new cloud had appeared on the horizon. As the NPSA struggled to bring their plan before Parliament, Stowell and a coalition of clergy and dissenters formed the Manchester and Salford Committee in Education (MSCE) to further their own vision of a tax-supported religious education in the area. Announced in January 1851, their proposal insisted on religious choice, with the administration of schools under the aegis of the main denominational bodies. "The local plan," as it became known, had powerful supporters across the religious spectrum, including Kay, who, as he pointed out in a letter the previous year, shared the same political goals as the Lancashire movement, but found himself "fundamentally opposed to a system of daily schools separate from the superintendence of the great religious bodies of his country, and in which the religious influence shall not pervade the whole discipline and instruction."[60] Others in the MSCE rejected the alleged superiority of the Massachusetts system and reacted testily to American descriptions of the British workingman's depravity—including Horace Mann's claim that the New England bloodline was one thousand years ahead of the Old World's.[61] The NPSA sought a rapprochement, but the MSCE, seeing little advantage in compromise, proceeded to present their own bill to Westminster, which was roundly rejected by both Liberals and Tories.

Encouraging Lord Melgund to counter their opponents and take his bill before Parliament yet again, Combe was still hopeful that further debate would raise understanding of the issue in Parliament. Even more important was the establishment of a national movement similar to the Anti-Corn League. Privately and publicly he pleaded with Cobden to emulate Horace

Mann. "Having been one of the grand instruments for insuring a constant supply of food for the bodies of the people," Combe wrote in the *Westminster Review,* Cobden had still more important work before him, "to bring his great moral and intellectual power to bear on the supply of useful knowledge and moral training for their minds. Success in this," Combe predicated, "will form the crowning merit of his life."[62] But Cobden had little stomach for another seven-year crusade. As he had told the NPSA a few months earlier, although watching their agitation "with the utmost interest," he did not think he could serve any further role "unless it be to act in a mediatorial capacity."[63] The problem of education, he concluded, was now more intractable than when Simpson visited Manchester in 1837.

To resolve the matter of education in Lancashire, a select committee was appointed under the leadership of Lord John Russell. Dissolved, then reappointed amid the political debacles of the early 1850s, the committee eventually published the testimony it had gathered without comment. One important outcome of this process was the founding of the Manchester Secular School.[64] Set up by the NPSA in 1854 to demonstrate the practicality of their scheme, it followed the example of the Williams School with a curriculum comprising instrumental skills, the object lesson, physiology, Ellis's social economics, and, while not mentioning phrenology, the kind of moral philosophy and natural theology developed by Combe.[65] The principal, Benjamin Templar, also rejected corporal punishment for moral suasion and the rule of kindness. But, as in Scotland, Manchester's experiment in secular schooling soon ran afoul of the Committee of Council's stricture that government money would only be granted when the doctrines of revealed religion were taught. Unable to meet its expenses, the school finally capitulated and, in 1861, commenced teaching the Scriptures.

Events were not going well for the secularists. In 1853, when Russell introduced his own "Borough" bill aimed at empowering municipalities over five thousand to levy an educational rate, he spoke of the need to raise the level of scientific and technical training in the nation. But he firmly rejected any move that would undermine the central role of religious instruction. The NPSA plan, he told the House of Commons, was unacceptable because it took religion out of the schools, whereas Combe's "new scheme" to replace Christianity with natural theology was even more pernicious. Combe was incredulous. When he first argued in favor of secular education he was charged with infidelity; after responding that "nature is a Divine institution and in these schools we shall teach God's natural laws established to regulate human well-being" he was pictured as offering something, to use Lord John's words, "far more dangerous!"

Other education bills were submitted in the remainder of the decade—notably by Parkington for England and Moncrief for Scotland—that attempted in various ways to frame some form of religious compromise acceptable to all denominations, but with the excitement generated by the Crimean War and problems such as the Maynooth Controversy, there was little a weak government could do to fashion unanimity. Both the NPSA and the MSCE ran out of steam, although in efforts to carry legislation they came close to reconciliation. In the end it was Parliament that proved the sticking point, justly earning Frank Smith's condemnation of Westminster during this period as "the great cemetery for the internment of defunct Education Bills."[66]

By 1860, the monolithic grant system was collapsing under the weight of its own gross inefficiency—each school had to deal directly with Westminster, and there were no checks on the effective use of public money. In response to these and other problems, the Newcastle Commission (and later the Argyle Commission in Scotland) recommended a continuation of the denominational system—the nation, it found, was opposed to secularism—with payments keyed to the performance of students. As enacted in the Revised Code of 1862, grants were then distributed as a single sum to school managers according to a formula that weighed attendance, teacher certification, and student performance in reading, writing, and arithmetic. The state was not about to examine sectarian instruction. Two important consequences followed. The need to secure funds increased the time denominational schools devoted to secular instruction, while, despite rising enrollments, government grants diminished. Finally, recognizing the limits of public charity, the voluntaryist party capitulated. In a spectacular about-face, Baines and Miall admitted the need for public secular schooling. Government supported religious education, they feared, would inevitably come under the control of the church. Citing the 1867 extension of the franchise to over a million more working men, they now believed it imperative to educate the nation for democratic citizenship. Combining with secularists and the rising union and workingmen's groups, a new coalition was formed around the Birmingham-based National Education League. Opposed by the church's National Education Union, the country was finally divided by issues—such as the conscience clause—on which compromise was possible. And, after much acrimonious debate, Forster's 1870 bill at last found a formula acceptable to both sides in the essentials of the system that Combe had brought back from America. England and Wales were divided into school districts with elected officials, a local rate was levied, and instruction was constrained by the mandate not to teach the doctrines of a particular denomination—sectarian lessons were scheduled for fixed periods in the day to permit instruction from leaders of different religious sects. Far from happy with this compromise, the League continued to challenge the use of public funds for denominational teaching and fought bitter battles to block the election of sectarian candidates. But the common school had been established, and from this and similar legislation in Scotland in 1872, the modern school system gradually emerged, as over the following years laws were passed to ensure free schooling, compulsory attendance, and more standardized bureaucratic control. It is worth noting, however, that British schools, unlike their American counterparts, were never designed to be truly common. An essentially working-class institution, they were to live side by side with more elite private schools in a rigidly divided class society.[67]

THE ENDS OF LIFE

The major intellectual and personal achievement of Combe's final years was the completion of *On the Relation between Science and Religion* (1857).[68] Extending the arguments of his "Remarks on National Education," he composed and privately published an explorative essay, *An Inquiry into Natural Religion,* to sound out his theological views among his most trusted friends. The resulting comments were then used to strengthen his thesis, which finally arrived at the publishers, largely rewritten, the year before his death. Curiously, the *Inquiry* became the source of some discord between Combe and Mann. Lost in the move to Yellow Springs, Mann eventually wrote to Combe confessing that he had only read the first half of the book, but was gravely concerned over what he took to be his friend's denial of human immortality. Somewhat annoyed by Mann's superficial reading, Combe responded that he did not "deny immortality to man."[69] It was merely that he was unable to "penetrate into [God's] design in calling me into existence so completely as to discover that it certainly embraces a future life," but he could "see nothing that necessarily contradicts it."[70] His faith, however, was so perfect that he felt no anxiety about the matter.

Combe's views were shaped by several important distinctions. By "religion," he meant "a sentiment, an emotion, or a state of feeling . . . distinct from intellectual conception."[71] "Theology," on the other hand, was the conceptual views men and women "form concerning the objects which excite the religious emotion; and it springs from the intellectual faculties stimulated by that emotion."[72] Different people had different theories because they were born with different faculties. In practice, the two were intimately related. "As the shuttle adds the woof to the warp to make the cloth, the intellect adds theology, or particular notions about God, to the emotion; and the two combine to what we commonly call religion."[73] Threaded in infancy, the composition of this web bound thought and emotion so tightly that it often led to incredible degrees of fanaticism. Progress in faith thus rested on grounding religious feeling in a sound knowledge of the human condition. On this score, Combe sought to demonstrate that men and women were naturally intelligent, religious, and moral beings who could learn much about the world and the responsibilities of life. But beyond the existence of a Creator, the faculties indicated nothing of God's "form, his substance, his size, his place of residence, or his mode of being."[74] They did, however, reveal something of His intentions through the pull of duty and the greater pleasures of the "higher life." Spiritual contemplation often produced ecstatic feelings, but this did not imply that faith required some otherworldly object. Combe saw no reason why human beings should not ground their religious feelings in a reverence for God's works. "Nature . . . [was] sufficient to produce all the hopes, joys, consolations and feelings of resignation and endurance."[75] Indeed, reflecting on the history of barbarism and savagery, of error and superstition, Combe defended natural theology as the key to Christian progress. In contrast to the fierce and muddled stories of the orthodox, the practical faith he had taught at the Williams School helped cultivate the intellect and perfect the moral sentiments, producing a "more pure and beneficent religion . . . [which] more effectively . . . operated on the minds of its votaries as a stimulus to social improvement."[76] This did not mean rejecting the Bible. A new creed, "Combeism," could be formed out of scriptural doctrines that went beyond reason without contradicting it. One thing was certain— Christianity as it was now taught would soon perish. If only the clergy would embrace his views, "every church would become a focus of Divine light, radiating blessings on humanity, and every school a vestibule to the church."[77]

As Mann's Twelve Sermons reveals, he was teaching natural theology to the students at Antioch, albeit with a great deal more ideality than causality.[78] Interpreting Biblical lessons as prescriptions for earthly conduct, he defined the Kingdom of Heaven as the joy experienced by those who lived their life in accord with God's laws, and miracles as the deeds of great servants to humanity—the works of Dix, Howe, and Woodward, for example. As for immortality, he simply extended Combe's argument for God's existence to induce, from the faculties themselves, a promise of the hereafter. It was inconceivable that, after a lifetime battle with evil dispositions inherited from the crimes of his ancestors, he would stand before God, "his soul purified and rejunvenated," and not receive "the victor's palm" and "'well done good and faithful servant.'"[79]

Whether or not Mann ever finished reading the *Inquiry,* he seems to have been sufficiently soothed by Combe's letter to seek a rapprochement and assure his ailing friend of his fundamental commitment, even in the face of his own mortality, to the doctrines that had given meaning and purpose to his life. Apologizing that the duties of a college president left him little time for correspondence, he assured Combe that he should not fear that he would "have forgotten one who have done my mind more good than any other living man—a hundred times more? I not only think of you, remembering you, but in a very important and extensive sense, *I am you.* You are reproduced in my views of life . . . and in that understanding of the wisdom and ways of Providence which vindicates God to man."[80] And so it was that both men met their maker, united in hope for the future of their cause, totally unaware of how, in just a few short years, the science and faith for which they devoted their lives would be consigned to the graveyard of history.

Combe's whole thought was based on a single assumption, an assumption he found so obvious to be beyond serious doubt. The world, as he phrased it, was an institution administered by God for human well-being. The year after his death, the unimaginable happened: this metaphysical axiom fell before the theory of evolution. The world was not adapted to human faculties; rather, the mind had adapted to nature in order to ensure survival. Stripped of design and purpose, the laws of nature no longer held the religious and moral imperatives that Combe had preached. In one stroke, without an economy of providence, phrenology and secularism lost their intellectual foundation. A new basis for middle-class values, positive knowledge, and scientific training had to be forged from the reality of an adaptive mind. Perhaps the most successful intellectual synthesis to meet this challenge was

Herbert Spencer's synthetic philosophy. Arising from his own early commitment to phrenology, Spencer's evolutionary naturalism and social evolutionism rescripted much of Combe's moral philosophy around a new set of scientific assumptions that promised ethical and rational progress through the logic of evolution. Spencer, of course, did not share Combe's view of a paternal state, but his *Education: Intellectual, Moral, and Physical* (1861) revealed very similar ideas about the aims, methods, and content of schooling. He recapitulated Andrew Combe's writings on physiology, adapted the use of the object lesson to his own associationist psychology, and, in his famous "What Knowledge Is Most Worth?" offered a naturalistic justification for the kind of scientific curriculum presented in "What Should a Secular Education Embrace?"[81] With little difference in their practical recommendations, it is not surprising, given the anachronistic character of phrenology and secularism, that Combe's name was forgotten from the educational debates of the second half of the nineteenth century. But however strange his arguments may have appeared to his successors, they were plausible, indeed compelling to the moderate reformers of his day and merit his recognition as one of the most important and influential educational theorists of the nineteenth century.

15
The Education of Littlehead

The existence of so many idiots in every generation must be the consequence of some violation of the *natural laws;*—that where there was so much suffering there must have been sin.

Samuel Gridley Howe, *Report Made to the Legislature*
of Massachusetts, Upon Idiocy, on Idiocy, 1848

One of the most prominent and influential Americans of his day, Samuel Gridley Howe has received remarkably little scholarly attention. Since Harold Schwartz's biography was published in 1956, there has been no comprehensive account of his life and only a handful of studies detailing specific aspects of his work—such as his efforts to educate the blind, his experiment with Laura Bridgman, and his campaign to establish oralism among the deaf.[1] Significantly, only one of these works, Ernest Freeburg's *The Education of Laura Bridgman* (2001), has come to terms with the theory behind Howe's reforms. For example, Harlan Lane's influential history of the deaf ignores phrenology and presents Howe as a self-serving power monger, a man "committed to the struggle" but "well-nigh indifferent to the cause."[2] This neglect is not surprising, for Howe left no treatise explaining the philosophy behind his mission. The guiding commitments of his long and eventful life remain buried in a scattered sea of official reports, letters, and journal articles. Like the philosophy of mind he espoused, his thought and work remains largely unknown.

After gaining notoriety as the "American Byron" for his exploits in the Greek Revolutionary War, Howe became famous around the world as director of the Perkins Institute, the teacher of Laura Bridgman, and later the founder of the New England School for Feebleminded and Idiotic Youth. In addition to these duties, throughout the 1840s, 1850s, and 1860s, Howe was drawn into the cauldron of party politics and the abolitionist movement. Along with Charles Sumner, he became a leader of the Conscience Whigs, a tight group of moral reformers bent on undermining the interests of Cotton and effecting radical change in the state's policies toward its dependent classes—his relentless efforts to establish scientific practices of schooling, care of the insane, and the treatment of prisoners were matched only by his deep-seated opposition to the spread of slavery. Outraged by the annexation of Texas and the prospect of an unjust war with Mexico, Howe mounted an unsuccessful bid for the Whig nomination in the 1846 Congressional race. Then, in 1848, as the party splintered over the selection of the proslavery Zackary Taylor for its presidential candidate, he became a fervent Free Soiler, editing the *Commonwealth* and campaigning for Sumner's election to the Senate. Howe also played a leading role in establishing a Vigilance Committee to protect runaway slaves from southern bounty hunters, and, in 1854, with the passing of the Kansas-Nebraska Act (which repealed the Missouri Compromise and left the spread of slavery up to the territories), he raised funds for the Massachusetts Emigrant Aid Company, supplying guns and money for northerners willing to stem the expansion of slavery by settling in the West. He even ventured to Kansas, braving the Border Ruffians and Marauders, to distribute $10,000 among these settlers. Finally, convinced that matters would have to be decided by force rather than reason, he became one of the Secret Six who supported John Brown's ill-fated raid on Harper's Ferry. This was a low point in Howe's life. Publicly humiliated before a congressional committee, in the eyes of many, he had abandoned the field of morality for a treasonous act of violence. He narrowly escaped prison. Howe's reputation was restored somewhat during the Civil War when his long-time friend John Andrews, then governor of Massachusetts, asked him to inspect sanitary conditions in the state's army encampments, a service he and Dorothea Dix later provided for the War Department. As important as this work was, Howe was more concerned with the fate of the South's soon-to-be-freed slave population. In a series of reports to the secretary of state, Howe, Robert Dale Owen, and James McKaye compiled anthropological evidence to argue that Africans were capable of supporting themselves and living decent moral lives. Calling for immediate civil rights, they proposed the establishment of an Emancipation Bureau (later the Freedmen's Bureau) that would coordinate schooling and provide the work-related training necessary for self-sufficiency.

After the Civil War, Andrew appointed Howe to the Massachusetts State Board of Charities. Under his ten-year leadership, this agency invoked the hereditarian and environmental laws of phrenology to enact sweeping reforms in the state's welfare policies and institutional practices, including the establishment of a deaf school dedicated to oralism. Determined to revenge Mann, Howe mounted a vicious attack on the signing community at Hartford that, as Schwartz observes, "reached heights of bitterness even for him."[3] During these last years, Howe had one other notable foray in the field of reform. Nominated by President Grant to the Santo Domingo Commission, he sought to extend American hegemony through the West Indies. From the strategic foothold of Samana Bay, he believed that the United States could promote commerce, eradicate slavery, and bring Christian civilization to the region. Mired in the tangled and dubious finances of unscrupulous property speculators, a corrupt dictatorship, and a revolutionary people's movement, the scheme fell stillborn. Physically weak, Howe returned to Boston to detail his work at Perkins Institute in his final "Forty-third Report." Mann had died in 1859, and Sumner, with whom he had split over the Caribbean fiasco, passed away in 1874. Weak, angry, and disillusioned, Howe lingered on two more years before finally succumbing in 1876 to a long and painful illness.

The "Hero of Greece," the "Chevalier," the "Cadamus of the Blind," Howe was a man of powerful character and seemingly limitless energy. Fierce and vitriolic, he pursued his goals with the conviction of a religious crusader. He would not give an inch—all who stood in his way were heretics to be cast into the flames of damnation by his scathing and unremitting oratory. As with Mann, the source of this certainty was an unwavering belief that the practical Christianity underwritten by the phrenological laws of exercise and descent had to be extended into every area of social policy. This goal is transparent in his reports on prison discipline and ex-slave communities; it guides his reflections on the education of the deaf and the blind and directs the approach to welfare reform he promoted through the Massachusetts State Board of Charities. Nowhere, however, is Howe's mission to institute physiological principles of virtue more clearly articulated than in his efforts to educate the feebleminded and protect society from the scourge of idiocy and its associated social problems.

TRAINING FEEBLE MINDS

The deaf, once thought to be dumb, irredeemable brutes, had been taught to communicate through a language of gestures; Jean-Marc Itard had socialized the Savage of Aveyron, and, in America, Howe had educated the deaf, blind, and mute Laura Bridgman. In 1848 Howe embarked on an equally fantastic experiment. Following the methods developed by Itard's student, Edward Séguin, he set out to prove that even the mentally retarded could be trained.

Although certainly motivated by humanitarian concerns, Howe's interest in the mentally retarded has to be seen in context with his broader ambition to ground social and institutional policies in the laws of phrenology. As Horace Mann used Laura's education to justify the adoption of new pedagogic practices, so Howe, in chronicling the progress of his idiotic students, constantly directed attention to larger political concerns. The problem of idiocy, he told the Massachusetts state legislature, "was not limited to the hundred or thousand unfortunate creatures in this generation who are stunted or blighted by it," for even if the means could be found to alleviate their suffering and "cut off [this] outward cancer," its "vicious sources" would remain in the system.[4] "Idiocy," he maintained, was "a diseased excrescence of society . . . an outward sign of an inward malady."[5] A true disciple of Spurzheim, he was as concerned to justify the basic principles of his eugenic social philosophy as he was to perfect methods for training the feebleminded.

Howe first became interested in the feebleminded during 1839 when a blind idiot was admitted to the Perkins Institute. Despite his limited success with the boy, Howe was convinced that such children were "not beyond the saving reach of the divine laws which promise improvement as the sure return of every kind of cultivation."[6] Perhaps he visited the Bicêtre on his European tour or heard of Séguin's achievements from Mann, who toured the Frenchman's school in the rue Pigalle during 1843. In any case, when he returned to America the following year, Howe was fully apprised of Séguin's work and eager to start a similar experiment in Massachusetts. Together with Samuel Woodward he published a series of letters in the *Boston Advertiser* citing Séguin's spectacular achievements as evidence that idiots could indeed be educated.[7] But it was only in 1845, when the *American Journal of Insanity* published a remarkable letter from John Connolly (superintendent of the Hanniwell Asylum and Britain's leading specialist on the institutional care of the insane) detailing the successes at the Bicêtre, that the movement to establish an idiot asylum within the state really got under way. Particularly startling was Connolly's description of a fifteen-year-old boy named Charles Emile, who had entered the hospital "wholly animal" just one year earlier. "Idiotic in his inclinations, sentiments, perceptions, faculties of perception and understanding, and also of his senses," Charles Emile was "unfit to harmonize with the world without."[8] He had "a voracious, indiscriminate, gluttonous appetite" and "a blind and terrible instinct of destruction."[9] He "overturned everything in his way, but without courage or intent; possessed no tact, intelligence, power of discrimination, or sense of propriety; and was awkward to excess."[10] "His moral sentiments are described as null, except the love of approbation, and a noisy instinctive gaiety, independent of the external world."[11] Devouring everything, however disgusting; brutally sensual; passionate,—breaking, tearing, and burning whatever he could lay his hand upon; and if prevented from doing so, pinching, biting, scratching, and tearing himself, until he was covered with blood."[12] "This same poor idiot boy," Connolly continued,

> is now docile in his manners, decent in his habits, and capable . . . of directing his vague senses and wandering attention, so as to have developed his memory, to have acquired a limited instruction concerning various objects, and to have become affectionately conscious of the presence of his instructors and friends. . . . Nature has placed limits to the exercise of his powers which no art can remove. But he is redeemed from the constant dominion of the lowest animal propensities; several of his intellectual faculties are cultivated, some have even been called into life, and his better feelings have acquired some objects and some exercise.[13]

"A wild, ungovernable animal, calculated to excite fear, aversion, or disgust, has been transformed into the likeness and manners of a man."[14] Armed with this evocative tale and a letter from Charles Sumner's brother describing Séguin's methods, Howe persuaded the influential senator Judge Horatio Byington to bring the issue before the General Court. Its recommendation prompted Governor Briggs to appoint a commission (comprising Howe, Byington, and Gilman Kimball) to "inquire into the condition of the idiots of the Commonwealth, to ascertain their number, and whether anything can be done on their behalf."[15]

Howe's resulting *Report upon Idiocy* (1848), Charles Rosenberg observes, became "by far the most widely quoted" empirical study of the biological origins of mental retardation during the nineteenth century.[16] It certainly made sensational reading. After two years struggling with the legal and medical definitions and collecting statistics from towns across the state, Howe compiled a shocking chronicle of physical and moral decay. Extrapolating from the 420 "true idiots" he had examined in seventy-seven towns, he estimated that Massachusetts had up to 1,500 idiots within its boarders. Since a report filed in 1840 had arrived at the smaller population of 600, Howe's study raised the commonly voiced fear that, like insanity, idiocy was on the rise, a product of the pressures of modern life and the influx of Irish immigrants.[17] Repulsed by the physical condition and "the mental and moral darkness" of these pitiful creatures, Howe highlighted the real magnitude of the problem: the burden to the Commonwealth of future generations "sunk in brutishness." In Howe's Christian physiology, idiocy—indeed, all diseases— were the product of the "ignorance, vice, and depravity" that led individuals to transgress God's laws. Only when armed with the techniques of moral treatment and the laws of hereditary, he warned, could the retarded be redeemed from their animal existence and the state equipped to combat the future spread of degeneracy.

Like the accounts of his protégée Dorothea Dix, Howe's description of filthy, half-witted children, clothed in rags soaked with sweat and excrement, driven by insatiable appetites to gorge on animal scraps and, through neglect, to "descend into moral depravity and mental degeneration" (incessant masturbation) was clearly designed to shock the gentlemen of the General Court into action.[18] Their duty was clear. Given that educators in Europe had demonstrated that "idiots may be trained to habits of industry, cleanliness, and self respect; that the highest of them may be measurably restored to self-control, and that the very lowest of them may be raised up from the sloth of animal pollution in which they wallow . . . the humanity and justice" of the legislature demanded they follow suit and "take immediate measures for the formation of a school or schools for the instruction and training of idiots."[19] Economically, such schooling would turn a dependent class into one capable of earning their own livelihood; morally, it would remove from society the "spectacle of beings reduced to a state of brutishness"; and, religiously, it would fulfill the imperative of all Christians to redeem the forsaken souls of lost children. It would also create a laboratory in which to study the laws governing the disease.

EDUCATING THE WILL: EDWARD SÉGUIN'S
PHYSIOLOGICAL PEDAGOGY

It was a "singular and interesting fact," Howe observed, "that the first regular attempt, upon record to educate an idiot was made with a view to prove the truth of the sensualist school of philosophy, which was so much in favor in France during the revolution."[20] According to this theory, "by causing certain sensations, certain ideas would be generated, and from these a given kind of character produced."[21] But Itard's valiant efforts only proved the opinion of many—notably Howe's own intellectual forefathers, Gall and Spurzheim— that Victor was not a savage, but a congenitally retarded idiot, incapable of learning because of the abnormally small size of his brain. Even so, Itard's humanitarian efforts were not lost, for, thanks to his student Edward Séguin, the many pedagogic strategies he had devised for Victor had been perfected for the education of idiots in the asylum schools of the Bicêtré and Salpêtrière.

Even so, Howe was careful to explain that it was not Séguin but the celebrated French physiologist Felix Voisin who had done the most to forward the cause of the idiot.[22] A founding member of the Paris Phrenological Society, Voisin had written extensively on the problem of idiocy and, after opening two private schools, had been appointed physician to the incurables at the Bicêtré in 1839. Three years later he was joined by Séguin, then a twenty-six-year-old student of Esquirol. Having impressed a government commission by successfully educating several feebleminded children at the Salpêtrière, Séguin was given a year to demonstrate his methods with the 100 or so children under Voisin's charge. But although Voisin was impressed with Séguin's pedagogical innovations, the two men were poles apart on questions of theory. This became an issue when a committee comprising Pariset, Flourens, and Serres, all antiphrenologists, reviewed Séguin's memoir on the education of idiots for the Academy of Sciences and roundly praised him for all the successes at the Bicêtré. In 1843 events came to a head: Séguin's celebrity, his radical politics, and his questioning of medical authority proved too much for Voisin and the hospital administration. With rumors circling about maltreatment and cruelty, he was dismissed from the school and forced to establish his own institution on the rue Pigalle.[23] Howe, of course, sided with the phrenologists. "It is due," he admitted, "to Edward Séguin, to say that, to him more than any other person, seems to be owing the great and rapid improvement which has been made in the *art* of teaching and training idiots."[24] Yet he warned against the wholesale adoption of Séguin's work. He was, Howe reported, "unconsciously biased in his judgment" and "rather disposed to disparage everything said or done by others beside himself."[25] Most importantly, Séguin held that intellectual incapacity was not the criterion of idiocy, but rather *"an infirmity of the nervous system, which has the effect of removing the organs and faculties of the child from under the control of the WILL, and giving him up to the domain of his instinct, and cutting him off from the moral world."*[26] The will, as Howe read Séguin, was thus a separate, immaterial faculty acting independently of the cerebral organization, unable to function because of the morbid state of the body. For a phrenologist, this was pure heresy. Howe simply could not allow Séguin's achievements to undercut the assumption that insanity and idiocy resulted from a diseased or deformed brain.

Esquirol had adopted Laromiguière's revision of *Idéologie,* in which attention was elevated from a property of sensation to an active power of the soul. It was this "will" that made learning possible. It also explained mental retardation. "Idiots," Esquirol observed, were unable to concentrate—they "cannot focus their senses; they hear but they do not listen; they see but do not observe."[27] "Deprived of memory they cannot retain impressions that come to them from external objects; they compare nothing; they form no judgments, [and] as a result they desire nothing."[28] Finally, having "no need of signs that serve to express things and desires," idiots "could not learn to speak."[29] Their condition, Esquirol concluded, was simply incurable.[30]

Rejecting this negative prognosis, Séguin approached Itard in the hope that he could learn the pedagogic skills to prove Esquirol wrong. His timing was perfect. In the last year of his life, the ailing Itard had been asked to work with a retarded mute from the Paris Children's Hospital. Lacking the strength necessary for the task, he agreed to direct the boy's training if Séguin would take the role of teacher. Séguin clearly revered his new mentor. Despite frequent periods of intense pain, Itard shared his pedagogical insights and engaged Séguin in debates on the nature of mind. It was from these lessons, Séguin recalled, "I learned the secret of his influence over the idiots" and "his weakness in philosophy."[31] As George Sumner put it, where Itard held with Condillac "that all simple ideas are the result of sensation alone," Séguin, following Esquirol, insisted "on the existence of an internal, intelligent, reflective power, which seizing the notions furnished by the senses, reasons upon them and produces ideas."[32]

Since the experiment with Victor, Séguin later complained, those who studied idiocy had been more concerned with proving or disproving "Gall's system . . . [than] the benefit of the poor idiot, whom they declared incurable."[33] Under Itard's guidance he proved the theorists wrong. After only fourteen months, Esquirol was forced to testify that Séguin had "taught his pupil to make use of his sense, to remember, to compare, to speak, to write, to count, etc.," adding "that from the character of his mind and the extent of his knowledge, M. Edouard Séguin was capable of giving this system of education all desirable extension."[34] And this Séguin did, first with a group of ten children at the Salpêtrière, and then with the students under Voisin's care at the Bicêtre.

Itard had always maintained that Victor was a savage, not an idiot. But according to Séguin, he had secretly come to accept Pinel's diagnosis shortly after presenting his *First Report*—as the amended scheme for Victor's training demonstrated. "When the first philosophical programme of Itard had partly succeeded against what was savage in his pupil," Séguin reported, he "conceived after Pereire and Rousseau, the physiological terms of his second one, which adapted themselves exactly to the functional incapacitates of the idiocy of his pupil, so admirably described by Pinel; so that *nolens volens,* the great teacher began to treat the idiot in the savage."[35] Itard's revised scheme of developing the senses, the intellectual faculties, and then the affective functions thus became the manual for Séguin's physiological curriculum. Physical degeneracy was not the result of a defective organization but the rule of animal instincts. Combined with a history of poor nutrition, lack of exercise, and emotional rejection, it was hardly surprising that idiots would assume the appearance of brutes. Their muscles had to be activated, their senses trained, and their will asserted. The longer a child had been allowed to sink into this state of atrophy the harder it would be to resurrect his or her soul, but, in many cases, remarkable progress was possible, and Séguin held out hopes of training idiots to become self-supporting and contributing members of society.

Starting with physical education, Séguin adapted a variety of gymnastics exercises to tone up his students, excite interest, and overcome the "negative will" that kept them in a slumberous state. Games were particularly useful.

Arousing social sympathy and the pleasure of success, they provided an ideal opportunity to teach moral conduct and cooperative behavior. Just as Itard worked on Victor's sensitivity, so Séguin introduced objects with a variety of tactile properties (such as roughness, temperature, and weight) to engage, even force, the child's interest and stimulate attention. To become more than mere receptors, idiots had to turn their perceptions into concepts and demonstrate a functional understanding of how things are related in the world. Music was also an important tool. By teaching rhythm, it helped children discriminate sounds and prepared them for the more difficult task of learning language. Once again, inactivity explained mutism. Students had to be led, step by step, from the basic atoms of speech to words and sentences. Moving from simple to complex, as Pestalozzi had done, they were drilled first in the production of consonants, then consonants combined with vowels, words, and finally sentences. The teaching of higher skills progressed in a similar fashion. Once the rudiments of drawing lines and angles had been mastered, letters were introduced and their combination associated with signs. The more able pupils were then taught reading, arithmetic, and other school subjects. In line with the doctrine of moral treatment, the authority of the teacher was all important—overcoming resistance often demanded submission to another's will. This was particularly evident in the third and most demanding of Séguin's curricula goals: instilling behavior that would permit his students to act in accord with social mores.

PHRENOLOGIZING THE IDIOT

Having rejected the metaphysical underpinnings of Séguin's approach, Howe set about assimilating his pedagogy to the phrenological view of mind. Most importantly, given his views about the origins of disease and social deviance, Howe wanted to demonstrate that idiocy was caused by a physical condition of the brain that could be passed on to subsequent generations through the laws of hereditary transmission. The will, he maintained, was not separate from the body but, as Spurzheim taught, simply "that desire, which *prevails* for a time, over all other desires" in the cerebral economy of propensities, sentiments, and intellectual faculties.[36] Inextricably tied to their material organization, men and women were part of the animal kingdom, and the idiot, limited by impaired organs, simply a mutation of nature. In Howe's assessment, idiots looked and behaved like monkeys because they thought and acted with monkeylike brains. Only when their damaged faculties were care-fully and correctly trained could they rise from brutality and attain the dis-tinctive expression of humanness.

To substantiate this claim, Howe drew heavily from Connolly's report and Sumner's letter. Connolly was a man of science better able even than Séguin to appreciate the achievements of the idiot school. He was also a phrenolo-gist. Sumner, much to Howe's chagrin, was not. Accordingly, Howe was care-ful to quote only those sections of the letter that pertained to Séguin's edu-cational innovations, not his theoretical views of mind. Sumner, it seems, had become rather too enamored with Séguin. Opening with a discussion of competing theories of idiocy, he quickly slid into an attack on Gall, who, he claimed, had "condemned to perpetual imbecility all those whose volume of brain failed to fill his insatiable calipers."[37] "Gall," Sumner continued, declared

> that one whose head presents certain dimensions *must necessarily be an idiot.* "Never has an exception to this rule been found; never will an exception be found." Unfortunately for Gall's theory, but fortunately for those suspected of imbecility, many exceptions *have* "*been found;*" fortunately, also, for the poor idiots, the error of those who denied them all intelligence, and who pronounced them incurable, has been proved, the interdict against them revoked, and the fact triumphantly estab-lished that, however deranged their condition, however devoid of hu-man faculties they seem to be, they carry within them the Holy spark which intelligent sympathy may inflame.[38]

Combining patience, talent, and scientific wisdom, the teachers at the Bicêtre had proven once and for all

> that idiots may be educated,—that the reflective power exists within them, and may be awakened by the proper system of instruction; that they may be raised from the filth in which they grovel to the attitude of men; that they may be taught different arts, that will enable them to gain an honest livelihood and that, although they may never, perhaps, be developed to such a point as to render them authors of those gener-ous ideas and great deeds which leave a stamp upon an age, yet, still,

they may attain a respectable mediocrity, and surpass in mental power the common peasant of many European states.[39]

Howe could no more embrace this exaggerated faith in progress than he could accept the idea of an immaterial reflective power. Acknowledging Séguin's achievements, he thus set out to defend Gall's rule—a pivotal plank in his overarching claim that degeneracy resulted from transgressing physiological laws. The small brain hypothesis was thus what philosophers of science call a critical experiment, a fact of nature upon which competing theories would stand or fall. The lengths Howe went to in order to save this thesis indicate the magnitude of what was at stake in this argument. If the material basis of idiocy was undercut, the causal relationship between illness and morality would collapse, and Howe's eugenic social philosophy would tumble. He would have no scientific basis for the medically based reforms he wished to carry to the General Court. Howe's project thus embraced two goals; first to prove that the shape and size of the head was an index of mental ability and second, given this constraint, to show that idiots could indeed profit, albeit in a limited way, from Séguin's educational methods.

Howe approached his task with a spirit of scientific disinterestedness. "The close personal examination of so many idiots presented too rare and important an opportunity for ascertaining their craniological as well as other bodily peculiarities, to be lost."[40] The Senate would have to forgive his use of phrenological terms, but behavior had to be categorized systematically. He would not, he promised, pursue the question of whether such traits were related to the development of particular regions of the brain. Rather, he would simply measure heads, report affective, intellectual, and physical development, and tabulate the results against the morals of the parents to reveal the hereditary link between vice and physical degeneracy.

Quoting from Spurzheim's book on *Insanity*, Howe argued that "qualities of mind correspond to the deranged state of the body."[41] Identifying "various degrees of stupidity," he then set out a typology by which to categorize the mentally retarded according to the degradation of their faculties. Idiots, he asserted, were "MERE ORGANISMS, MASSES OF FLESH AND BONE IN HUMAN SHAPE . . . WITHOUT ANY MANIFESTATION OF INTELLECTUAL OR AFFECTIVE FACULTIES," fools that had a "BRAIN AND NERVOUS SYSTEM . . . SO FAR DEVELOPED AS

TO GIVE PARTIAL COMAND OF THE VOLUNTARY MUSCLES,"
and imbeciles that had "NORMAL POWERS OF ANIMAL ACTION . . .
AND REASON ENOUGH FOR THEIR SIMPLE INDIVIDUAL GUID-
ANCE, BUT NOT ENOUGH FOR THEIR SOCIAL RELATIONS"[42]
His own insatiable calipers—or rather those of the practical phrenologist
Enos Stevens—would then show, in the lowest grade at least, that "an obvious relation is seen between the size and development of the cranium, and of
its different parts, and of the amount of intellectual power, and the different
kinds of mental manifestation."[43] Such comparisons demanded a system for
quantifying mental and moral traits according to their deviation from a normal, healthy state. To this end, he reported the abilities of idiots on an as-
cending scale from 0 to "the tolerably harmonious action of the various mental faculties . . . in ordinary persons" represented by the number 10. If an
idiot is examined and found to have "no sense of property, no idea of right,
no benevolence, no affection or regard for anybody, he is marked 0. If he
has some faint idea of property, he is marked 1, if he has affections, 2; if
he manifests rudiments of veneration, respect for others, 4, or 5, &c."[44] Pre-
dating mathematical measures of variation, the resulting record of cepha-
lograph readings and family traits that Howe and Stevens compiled for some
574 idiotic persons throughout the state illustrated clear correlations between
the development of the phrenological organs, skull, health, and parental history. In the majority of cases, idiocy was easily traced to parental scrofula,
near-relative marriages, alcoholism, lack of cleanliness, and masturbation.
Take for example subject number 370, a nine-year-old male idiot with a very
small head, "the least and lowest of a constantly degenerating breed."[45]

> The grandparents were intemperate and depraved. The children born
> unto them were puny and weak-minded, and they sank still lower into
> the slough of vice and depravity. The mother of this boy was herself a
> simpleton; and this was her second illegitimate child. Though of feeble
> health, she gave herself up to excessive licentiousness, her passions be-
> coming almost maniacal.[46]

The result, a pathetic child who "has no muscular contractility; he cannot
stand, nor sit upright, nor even turn over. . . . He has not even the power to
masticate his food."[47] And so it was, in case after case, as Howe put flesh on
his numbers with detailed accounts of parentage, biological functions, mus-

cular vigor, the subject's senses, instincts (to reproduction, destructiveness, secretiveness, and self-esteem), knowing faculties (color, time, tune, imitation, and language), reasoning powers (causality and comparison), and moral sentiments (such as veneration and benevolence). Little was left to the imagination.

Turning to the issue of head size, Howe cautioned that

> some writers have hastily concluded, that because a few idiots, whose heads were smaller than the measure which had been laid down as the minimum of brain by which intelligence could be manifested, have nevertheless been partially educated; and because many others, with heads of normal size and shape, are hopelessly idiotic; therefore the doctrine of the dependence of mental manifestation upon the structural condition of the brain is overthrown.[48]

"Size," he contended, "is only one of the structural conditions of the brain upon which mental manifestations depend;—*quality* of fiber, health, exercise, &c., are others."[49] Referring to Gall, he then maintained that an "anatomist and philosopher, who wrote fifty years ago, saying that a man with a head below a certain measurement must necessarily remain an idiot in spite of any means of education then known, would still be right in his general conclusions, notwithstanding means are now discovered to educe considerable intelligence out of such a supposed idiot."[50] His own "close and extensive observations of idiots" strongly confirmed "not only the doctrine of the volume of the brain being one important element in the means of manifesting mental power, but all the main doctrines of that school of philosophy which teaches that God gives us the body not merely as the handmaid of the soul, but weds and welds the two together in bonds of dependence that death alone can sever."[51]

This remarkable fusion of science and value, of republican ideology and liberal Christian progressivism became, as Russell Hollander notes, "the most influential statement on idiocy available in the United States for the next quarter of a century."[52] It certainly persuaded the Massachusetts legislature, who quickly, if cautiously, approved a three-year annual stipend of $2,500 to fund an experimental school under Howe's supervision in a wing of the Perkins Institute. A local teacher, James Richards (his future son-in-law), was quickly dispatched to Paris to learn Séguin's methods, and in October of the same year, twelve children were enrolled into Howe's study (two private students joining the ten funded by the state). In the years that followed, the educational successes of Howe and Richards were overshadowed only by the remarkable achievements of Laura Bridgman. Reflecting on their first twelve months, Howe claimed marked results with the "the great majority" of students. "In some cases," he noted, "the change in appearance, condition, and habits of the children has been so great as to amount to a new creation. From sickly, gluttonous, stupid, slothful creatures, they have become healthy, self-controlling, active, and comparatively bright."[53] "Some have been rescued from the category of idiocy, by which they had fallen by reason of disease, neglect, or unfavorable circumstances, rather than been born to it. Others have been so far improved as to become inoffensive even to the most fastidious persons, and to be capable of earning their livelihood under the care of kind and judicious persons."[54] A year later he reported even more fantastic advances. His students

> had improved in heath, strength and activity of body. They are clean and decent in their habits. They dress themselves, and for the most part sit at the table and feed themselves. They are gentle, docile and obedient. They can be governed without a blow or unkind word. They begin to use speech, and take great delight in repeating the words of simple sentences they have mastered. They have learned their letters, and some of them, who were speechless as brutes, can read easy sentences and short stories! They are gentle and affectionate with each other; and the school and the household are orderly, quiet, and well regulated in all respects.[55]

Although the teaching methods employed at Perkins differed little from those developed by Séguin, they followed a very different philosophy, as became evident in 1850 when Séguin came to work for Howe—his appointment only lasted two months! Where Séguin worked against a morbid body to engage the will, Howe and Richards sought to invigorate the system and train the faculties. Given the low state in which many students entered the school, physical exercise took precedence in the curriculum. A nutritious diet, walking, gymnastics, and various sports were all used to promote health and fitness. For those capable of thought, intellectual training was pursued through the object lesson. "Balls made of different materials, of wood, woolen, leather, India-rubber, etc." were used to stimulate the senses and awaken the perceptive faculties.[56] Progress was slow, often painful. It might take days for names and qualities to be learned, but with great patience pupils could be taught "positive and directly useful knowledge."[57] Sense-based learning was an essential first step; after all, these were the memories that the weak reflective faculties would have to work with. Howe described, for example, how hard it was to train the organ of number. Hour after hour, students were "made to pour two successive pint measures into a quart measure, and their feeble intellect taxed to comprehend that . . . one and one makes two."[58] When teaching reading, Howe departed from Séguin's procedure and adopted Mann's whole language approach, as he had with Laura. The mind, he argued, could understand hat as a sign more readily than it could assemble *h a t*. The most important and difficult task facing the school was to strengthen the moral sentiments, diminutive organs dominated by the overriding power of the animal passions. Idiots would never appreciate moral principles, but, nurtured within a loving environment, the most able, he predicted, could learn to act virtuously and feel the glow of humanity within them.

A FINER CLAY

Seeking a celebrity case to promote his cause, Howe drew particular attention to George Rowell, a child with an extremely small head—though possessing "much vitality and energy."[59] Entering the program at age seven, he exhibited "the gait of a monkey."[60] "Speech, that peculiarly human attribute, and the surest test in such cases of the degree of intellect, was wanting. . . . [H]e was to all intents and purposes as dumb as a brute."[61] "He had no sense of decency or duty, and no regard for the rights or feelings of others."[62] "In only two and a half years George had become a new being, a human being neat, orderly, able to eat at the table with other children, make his bed, and do various household chores."[63] Most importantly, he was beginning to speak and read with understanding. He could even arrange letters into the sentence "*Our Father who art in heaven, hallowed be thy name.*"[64]

In the biography of her father, *Letters and Journals of Samuel Gridley Howe,* Laura Richards remembers George Rowell well. "'Littlehead,' his playmates called him . . . a tall youth, busy, happy, and useful; his life a round of simple duties and pleasures thoroughly performed, thoroughly enjoyed."[65] "Littlehead" was just the success story Howe needed to excite public sympathy and open the purses of politicians. Suitably impressed, the 1851 Joint Committee on Public Charitable Institutions recommended a permanent annual stipend of $5,000 to support what would become the Massachusetts School for Idiotic and Feeble-minded Youth. Four years later, the legislature granted $25,000 for a new building, and Howe's school left Perkins Institute for a new location in South Boston (much to the relief of Laura Bridgman, who despised being associated with the retarded).

But this new star pupil clearly presented something of a dilemma for Howe, who, only two years earlier, had tried to equate brain size with intelligence. With a skull measuring less than fifteen inches in circumference, George must have appeared a perfect test case for Gall's hypothesis. Howe even admitted that his head "falls short of the size supposed to be necessary for manifestation of any intellect by physiologists who have written upon the subject."[66] He clearly had some explaining to do.

Revisiting the issue in his 1850 *Report,* Howe recognized the need for a few "physiological remarks upon the effects of the size of the brain upon idiocy."[67] The (now) thirteen students in his study had larger than average craniums for their age—normal, if a hydrocephalic boy was excluded. But there were two children, George and Edmund, with skulls so small that it appeared they simply "did not have enough brains for the manifestation of common sense."[68] (Edmund had a seventeen-inch head.) This was an unusual condition: out of the 388 heads measured in 1848, there were only 98 such "true type" idiots. Naturally, Howe wanted to know why. And naturally he found an answer in phrenology. There were, it seems, two different branches of the disease. The majority of cases resulted from inherited congenital imperfections that distorted or deformed the brain's organization. While "uncouth in their appearance, and strange in their ways," these children were nonetheless "like men, and not animals, in their looks."[69] The second, less frequent cause of the disease, from which George and Edmund suffered, was tied to head size. In such cases the brain was not diminished evenly, yielding "a man in miniature," but rather, as phrenological readings showed, predominantly in the intellectual and moral regions, rendering the child subject to the appetites and propensities common to animals—as the natural language demonstrated. Such an idiot, Howe asserted, "generally loses the peculiarly human appearance, and sinks into the likeness of the higher animals in his looks and actions."[70] Talking of Edmund, Howe writes, "one of our pupils . . . has, moreover, the long arms of the ape; he moves about with his head and shoulders stooping, and his arms hanging forward, as though he was going to drop on all fours. One of his pleasures is to climb upon a desk or high place, and leap through the air, with outstretched limbs, upon some one's neck, and to cling around him, not as a common child does, with his arms around alone, but twining his legs about him as though he were one of the Quadrumana."[71] This condition, Howe observed, had important philosophical implications; "the true idiot" provided "a clue to the process of development of the race of mankind."[72] Christian societies had evolved from barbarism to civilization as the higher faculties were gradually strengthened. But looking back, beyond "those tribes which still linger behind in savagedom," he glimpsed "animal man," a creature with "the dwarfed brain of the idiot," an "*up-looking* and twinkling eye," "flattened forehead," and "projecting jaws" driven by instincts "which have entirely died out in the race long ago."[73] George and Edmund, for example, while having "good command of most of the voluntary muscles . . . were utterly wanting" in the "peculiarly human attribute, speech," although he noted that the "part of natural language which we call the language of signs, which expresses certain emotions, and which men have in common with the higher animals, was possessed by these boys in about as much perfection as it is by trained monkeys and dogs."[74] Even so, there was a difference in kind "between man, even in his lowest or animal state, and the brute."[75] For although "they could not make the simplest sentence . . . they had the germs of the *capacity* and of the *disposition* to speak,—not as the parrot speaks—not to imitate sounds merely— but to attach *names* or vocal sounds to things, and to use these sounds as *signs of things.*"[76] Watching "the efforts which poor little Edmund makes to repeat over the words that he has learned" convinced Howe that even this brutish form contained an immortal soul "struggling to proclaim his title to a share of human nature."[77]

Struggle as he might, Edmund was no match for George, who, despite his far smaller brain, had made greater progress with language. Littlehead, it seems, ruled the roost at Perkins. "Active, very resolute, and passionate," he "masters all the boys who are anywhere near his own age, and sometimes strives for mastery over the bigger ones."[78] Howe's explanation? Blood. The quality as well as the quantity of brain had to be taken into consideration. As evidenced by his temperament and features, George had "a finer organization" than his lymphatic chum. His brain, although smaller, "could do more *thinking* than a bulky and coarse one."[79] "Best expressed by the single word *blood,* or high blood," he was "an idiot made of finer clay, and in a finer mould."[80]

Howe had saved Gall's hypothesis about head size, demonstrated that even the most desperate idiots could be educated, and, by revealing the physiological laws governing the hereditary transmission of moral traits, proven the importance of his study to scientifically informed social policy. It is simply impossible to untwine fact from value in this synthesis: science, by revealing God's will in the order of nature, *was* morality, a clear imperative to discipline behavior in accordance with the principles of physiology. "The moral to be drawn from the prevalent existence of idiocy in society," Howe announced,

> is, that a very large class of persons ignore conditions upon which alone health and reason are given to men, and consequently they sin in various ways; they disregard the conditions which should be observed in intermarriage; they overlook the hereditary transmission of certain morbid tendencies, or they pervert the natural appetites of the body into lusts of diverse kinds,—the natural emotions of the mind into fearful passions,—and thus bring down the awful consequences of their own ignorance and sin upon the heads of their unoffending children.[81]

But these "terrible evils" were "not necessarily perpetual."[82] As Combe had argued in the *Constitution,* so Howe believed that suffering was "the chastisements sent by a loving Father to bring back his children to obedience to his beneficent laws."[83] No longer ignorant of the laws of inheritance and exercise governing the mind, a happier, more Christian republic could be engineered: politicians could enact physiologically sound legislation, doctors could work to redeem the afflicted, and educators could teach God's "simple, clear, and beautiful order."[84] "If strictly observed for two or three generations," Howe was certain that this moral code would "totally remove from any family, however strongly predisposed to insanity or idiocy, all possibility of its recurrence."[85] Not that he would have supported the negative policies of later eugenicists; moral force and knowledge of God's providential order were the only legitimate instruments of social progress. This unbending belief in the power of moral suasion can best be seen in Howe's efforts to deinstitutionalize state charities and engage the public directly in acts of reform. Fundamentally opposed to warehousing dependents, he constantly warned that the construction of artificial and unnatural societies would strengthen the lower propensities at the expense of the moral sentiments. No doubt those as severely handicapped as Laura Bridgman and George would require close care, but as the following chapters reveal, the idée-fixe of Howe's remaining years was to locate the blind, the deaf, the feebleminded, as well as paupers, criminals, veterans, and even ex-slaves in natural, family-oriented communities that would foster the healthy and harmonious development of their faculties.

16

Race, Science, and the Republic

Now by utterly rooting out slavery, and by that means alone, shall we remove these disturbing forces and allow fair play to natural laws, by the operation of which, it seems to me, the colored population will disappear from the Northern and Middle States, if not from the continent, before the more vigorous and productive white race. It will be the duty of the statesmen to favor by wise measures, the operation of these laws and the purification and elevation of the national blood.

Report of the Secretary of War: Communicating, in Compliance with a
Resolution of the Senate of the 26th of May, a Copy of the Preliminary Report,
and also of the Final Report of the American Freedmen's Inquiry Commission
(Washington, D.C.: Senate, 38th Congress, 1st session, no. 53, 1864)

When the 39th Congress assembled in 1865 to plan the reconstruction of the nation, they faced the historic problem of determining the social and political rights of a people freed from slavery. With a commanding majority in both the House and the Senate, Republicans set the agenda. The radical wing of the party, led by Sumner and Thaddeus Stevens, demanded full citizenship for blacks and supported constitutional reforms and government programs to ensure that states complied with this mandate. In a politically color-blind world, they argued, work and the ethic of self-help would ensure the social, moral, and economic advancement of African Americans. That March, just a month before Lincoln was assassinated, Congress passed an act establishing a Bureau of Refugees, Freedmen, and Abandoned Lands within the War Department to oversee the welfare of ex-slaves for the duration of the conflict, and one year thereafter. The following year, with Johnson as president and reports of "black codes" and widespread discrimination across the South, moderates within the Republican Party presented bills to ensure basic civil rights (not covered in the Thirteenth Amendment) and extend the life and power of what was now known as the Freedmen's Bureau. When Johnson vetoed these modest proposals, the radical agenda was thrust to the forefront. According to Eric Foner, Johnson was bent on driving the radicals from the Republican Party by standing firm on what he believed to be the popular sentiment on the race problem, keeping Africans in their place.[1] He even used the specter of amalgamation as a tool to discredit his opponents. As it turned out, this was a massive miscalculation. Overriding Johnson's veto, Congress rallied around Sumner and passed a series of remarkable legislative acts—including the Civil Rights Bill, the Freedmen's Bill, and the Fourteenth and Fifteenth Amendments—to ensure the political liberties and progress of African Americans. The moral agenda of the old Conscience Whigs had won out over political expediency and the force of public prejudice.

Samuel Gridley Howe played a significant role in the early part of this political contest. In 1862, while serving on the United States Sanitary Commission, Howe and several members of his old Vigilance Committee joined to form the Boston Emancipation League, a pressure group dedicated to petitioning the government for immediate legal action on behalf of the thousands of refugees who were being held in Union camps. Issuing letters to various military commanders, the League questioned the ex-slave's work ethic, morals, religious sentiments, interest in schooling and ability to learn, and, importantly, their desire to emigrate northward. "Could the freemen take their place in society, as a laboring class, with a fair prospect of self-support and progress . . . or would they need preparatory training and guardianship?"[2] The responses made compelling reading. The freedmen, most commanders replied, were orderly citizens and willing workers. Religious, loyal, and peaceable, they harbored little resentment toward whites and showed absolutely no interest in moving north—except to flee slavery. Certainly, the ex-slaves would need some training and temporary guardianship, but, if granted equal rights and protected by the law, there was every reason to believe that they could become productive participants in a vibrant southern agricultural economy. After Lincoln's January 1st proclamation, the League then pressed Congress to form an "Emancipation Bureau" to guard ex-slaves from persecution and exploitation. The government already had a Bureau of Indian Affairs. Was not a similar agency warranted to oversee the millions soon to be released from slavery?[3] With the help of well-placed political allies, Howe's agitation paid off. The following March, with cohorts Sumner and Massachusetts governor Andrews, the Secretary of War, Edwin M. Stanton, appointed Howe—together with the New York abolitionist James McKaye and Robert Dale Owen of Indiana—to the three-man American Freedmen's Inquiry Commission. The group was charged with investigating the condition of the ex-slaves and reporting "what measures will best contribute to their protection and improvement, so that they may defend and support themselves," but as Stanton's private correspondence reveals, the secretary of war was also keen to learn what role the freedmen could play in defeating the South.[4]

The first and most pressing order of business facing the Commission was to determine what should be done with the thousands of refugees who filled the union camps. Fanning out across the South, Howe, Owen, and McKaye toured encampments in Virginia, the Carolinas, and Florida. Each returned with the same enthusiastic story. Published in June, their "Preliminary Report" was emphatic: "With rare exceptions, the Africans were loyal men, who put faith in government for guidance and protection. They were willing workers, docile and easily managed, not given to quarreling, of temperate habits, cheerful and uncomplaining."[5] They also valued education and had a strong religious sentiment. What vices the commissioners found—minor cases of theft, dishonesty, and licentiousness—resulted from the evils of their previous situation rather than any inherent traits of the African character. Although the freedmen were still dependent and "child-like," they did not envision a permanent system of guardianship. African Americans did not need charity, and certainly should not be made wards of the state. All that was necessary was the opportunity to become self-sufficient. To this end, they recommended the establishment of a Bureau of Emancipation or Freedmen (under military control until Congress enacted legislation for a civil agency) to help ex-slaves acquire abandoned lands, to provide basic schooling and agricultural training, and to ensure legal protection in the event of disputes. Responding to Stanton's hopes, the *Report* also strongly endorsed the participation of freedmen in the war effort. True emancipation, they reasoned, demanded that the oppressed participate in the struggle for their freedom. The Union, of course, would also benefit from an additional two hundred thousand troops.

The following May, the commissioners published their "Final Report."[6] Subtitled "Blueprint for Reconstruction," it focused primarily upon the responsibilities of the legislative branch in the years after war. In forceful and authoritative language, Howe, Owen, and McKaye surveyed the origins and nature of slavery, examined the legal justification for emancipation, and predicted the future of the African race in the United States. Reconstruction, they maintained, had to proceed on the twin assumptions that the South was conquered territory and that slavery had been consigned to history. This meant that no state should be allowed to reenter the Union until it established a constitution that recognized the legal rights of freedmen, including, most importantly, the right to vote. The franchise was not only necessary to the future well-being of African Americans, it was crucial to the future of the nation—after all, here were four million loyal voters who would ensure the continuance of the Union. When it came to the distribution of lands, however, the commissioners vacillated. Privately, Owen and McKaye supported the division of plantations among blacks and poor whites.[7] Howe's position on this issue is unclear. Certainly, he wanted to ensure the economic independence of the freedmen, but perhaps, like northern conservatives, he balked at the prospect of confiscating private property. What might be the long-term consequences of such a precedent? In any case, probably fearing the loss of political support, the commissioners avoided the issue of seizure and recommended only the allocation of abandoned lands.

Taken together, the two reports provided just what Howe's political friends ordered: a scientific, legal, and ideological defense of the radical policies that Sumner was pushing through his Senate Committee on Slavery and Freedmen, the legislative counterpart of the War Department's Commission. Indeed, as John G. Sproat observes, a comparison of the commission's recommendations with the details of the Wade-Davis Bill and the constitutional amendments subsequently passed by Congress clearly indicates how "the Senate Committee, the later Joint Committee on Reconstruction, and individual Radical politicians were strongly influenced by the findings and recommendations" of the inquiry.[8] Sproat even points out that, had the commission's ideas "with regard to the land been adopted on anything more than a token scale, the story of the economic reconstruction (and hence, the political and social reorganization) of the South unquestionably would have been altered."[9]

But what Sproat, and others, have not commented on is the pervasive scientific racism underlying the two reports. This is particularly evident in the commissioner's efforts to assuage the prejudices of northern whites about the social consequences of emancipation and answer the vital question of "whether, in the course of human events, with or without the aid of precautionary measures, it be likely that the two races hitherto the dominant and the subordinate shall be able, when both shall be free, persistently to endure side by side, and to live together in one common country harmoniously and with mutual advantage?"[10] The Commission's conclusion? Granting ex-slaves full civic rights would not, as antiabolitionists had predicted, lead to amalgamation or a mass migration northward. New England women and New England jobs were safe, they explained, thanks to the principles of physiology. To demonstrate the workings of these natural laws, Howe had traveled to the free African communities in what at the time was known as Canada West. Collecting statistics from a number of towns in Ontario, he presented data demonstrating the physical, moral, and intellectual progress of ex-slaves and their descendents. The effects of slavery had weakened the black population and swelled its numbers with the effete and sickly mulattos. Yet he was positive: drawing upon the laws of descent established by the American School of Anthropology, suitably adapted to phrenological theory, he reported the inherent aversion of the races and predicted the emergence of a purer African population. Harboring no vindictiveness, blacks would prove themselves trustworthy Christian citizens, fully capable, once set upon their own feet, of adopting civilized habits. Indeed, drawing upon Howe's research, Owen even predicted that the interaction of the races would be mutually beneficial. Dominated by affections, with strong social instincts—"a knowing rather than a thinking race," "its perceptual faculties stronger . . . than its reasoning powers"—the African would temper the cool and rational Anglo-Saxon while "finding respectable positions and comfortable homes."[11]

Although it is difficult to assess the influence of Howe's arguments, his effort to soothe social concerns by invoking the moral order of nature provides an instructive example of the dangers of scientism. It also, rather nicely, illustrates the depth of racism even among the strongest friends of the freedmen. And, as in his postwar campaign to refashion public welfare in Massachusetts to accord with the laws of inheritance, Howe's drive to solve the race problem helps reveal something of the origins of eugenic social thought in the United States.

THE BLACK, THE WHITE, AND THE MULATTO

After delivering their "Preliminary Report," the commissioners again split up, each traveling to different regions of the country to study the problem of race firsthand. Howe elected to investigate the thirty thousand exiles and their descendants who had escaped to Canada.[12] There he found towns comprising "a fair sample of our coloured people," being in "about the same proportion of pure Africans, half-breeds, quarter-breeds, octoroons, and others in whom the dark shade grows fainter and fainter, until it lingers in the fingernails alone."[13] Given the parallels to conditions future freedmen would face, he pointedly asked how this natural experiment in the "capacity for self-support and self-guidance" had fared.[14] It was a success! The communities he visited demonstrated that even in adverse climatic conditions the refugees "earn a living; they build churches, and send their children to schools; they improve in manners and morals—not because they are 'picked men,' but simply because they are *free men.*"[15] In short, blacks displayed all the instincts of family, home, work, and Christian piety necessary for civilized, independent life. But then, what of social amalgamation and its sinful fruit, the mulatto? What lessons could be learned from the Canadian experience about the future relations of whites and blacks in America after the abolition of slavery?

On his return to Boston in early August, Howe struggled to square his experiences north of the border with the social mores of the day. Naturally he approached the problem through the phrenological principles regulating the biological and environmental determinants of human nature. As he argued in his work on idiocy, he was convinced that physiological laws would guide the progressive advancement of all men and women. But while Howe could draw upon extensive statistical records to demonstrate the causal links between sin and degeneracy, he was not sure how such relationships played out in questions of race. Careful consideration of the "natural laws of increase and modification" was central to any policies pertaining to the future emancipation of two million blacks and a similar number of mulattos. In a series of letters to the Harvard naturalist Louis Agassiz—America's leading biologist and staunch defender of polygenesis—he pondered whether blacks could "be a persistent race in this country? Will they be absorbed, diluted, and finally effaced by the white race, numbering twenty-four millions, and continually increased by immigration, besides natural causes?"[16] Would not "the practical amalgamation fostered by slavery become more general after its abolition? If so, will not the proportion of mulattos become greater and that of pure blacks less?"[17] "Such momentous questions demanded the proper consideration of political, physiological, and ethnographical principles."[18]

Agassiz's reply demonstrates how early nineteenth-century views about the character of Africans and other racial groups were embedded in a nest of highly charged religious and political debates over the origin of species and their modification by the environment—the outcome of which, in the years prior to Darwin, was a number of theories about human degeneration, varieties, and hybrids. Howe did not approach his subject completely naive of these arguments. He pointedly asked Agissiz, "Is it not true that in the Northern States at least the mulatto is unfertile, leaving but few children, and those mainly lymphatic and scrofulous?" And again, making his own convictions clear, "If there be irresistible natural tendencies to the growth of a persistent black race in the Gulf and river States, we must not make bad worse by futile attempts to resist it. If on the other hand, the natural tendencies are to the diffusion and final disappearance of the black (and colored) race, then our policy should be modified accordingly."[19]

The first and most influential response to Jefferson's negative appraisal of the African character in *Notes on Virginia* was provided by Samuel Stanhope Smith, Professor of Moral Philosophy and later president of Princeton. Stressing biblical orthodoxy and the Linnaean concept of species, his *Essay on the Causes of the Variety of Complexion and Figure in the Human Species* (1787), expanded and republished in 1810, attempted to prove the essential unity of mankind. Contrary to Jefferson's suggestion that blacks and whites might be distinct species, Smith held that the physical and moral differences between the races were the product of environmental forces. Human beings, he maintained, were the most adaptable of all animals. Starting with the book of Genesis, he explained that all races had descended from a single creation, somewhere in Asia. As men and women dispersed around the world, various geographical, climatic, nutritional, and social conditions worked upon the mind and body—changing appearance and, in many cases, greatly debasing character. This did not mean that blacks lacked the potential for genius. Slavery, like the barbarous civilizations of Africa, had brutified the intellect. But as a freed people, under the positive influence of European culture, they would surely improve in stature and develop the same intellectual powers as Anglo-Saxons.

Others were not as convinced about human plasticity. The classification of races produced by Continental theorists such as Curiver and Blumenbach were easily read as evidence of a hierarchical biological order. Perhaps, as the Manchester physician Charles White suggested, God had adapted different races to distinct locations sometime after the Creation? Certainly, anatomical examination—especially of the skull—suggested innately fixed characteristics. Such arguments, based on measurement and medical expertise, were eagerly embraced by the growing number of American physicians and scholars opposed to abolition. Charles Caldwall, for example, vehemently assailed Smith's credibility, chiding his attempt to curtail scientific inquiry with religious dogma. Why should a student of human nature be constrained by the Mosaic account of Genesis? Were not other options open to a Christian scientist? Samuel George Morton provided one such solution. The founding theorist of the American School of Anthropology, Morton's study of Native American crania seemed to demonstrate that the indigenous peoples of the New World were all part of a single distinct race, not modified Mongols, as Smith taught. Conducting a similar investigation of skulls imported from Egypt, *Crania Aegyptiaca, or, Observations on Egyptian Ethnography, Derived from Anatomy, History, and the Monuments,* he used hieroglyphics copied from temple walls to argue that the heads and behavior of Africans had remained constant since ancient times.[20] If the environment had not produced changes in four thousand years, he reasoned, how could the black population possibly have been formed since the fall of Adam (some six thousand years earlier)? Was it not more likely that what the Bible actually presented was merely an exemplary account of creation, the birth of Caucasians, who, after all, were destined to be the most important of God's creatures? The chief and obvious objection to this white-only interpretation of Genesis, given the Linnaean concept of species as an interbreeding population, was the existence of interracial offspring. For Smith, mulattos were living proof that races were varieties of the same type. Disputing this conclusion, Morton maintained that different species could indeed be crossed to create hybrids or breeds with varying degrees of fertility.

This was no terminological squabble, but a heated political debate over the moral identity of a people with profound implications for the American Republic. Published in the *American Journal of Science,* Morton's "Hybridity in Animals Considered in Reference to the Question of the Unity of the Human Species" laid out the facts at hand. Although interspecies mating was uncommon in the wild, numerous examples of hybrids could be found among domestic animals as different as cows and sheep. Invoking the writings of Josiah Nott, whose "Two Lectures on the Natural History of the Caucasian and Negro Races" pointed to the fecundity of many vegetable and animal hybrids, he described how crossbreeding could produce sterile descendents, offspring capable of union among themselves, and, on some occasions, a population that could only mate with the parent stock.[21] The conclusion was clear. It was the artificial proximity engineered by human beings that led to such abhorrent unions—overcoming through the distorted environment the natural instincts of each species. A strong innate antipathy demonstrated, he believed, by the mutual repugnance of blacks and whites. Such feelings were clearly an index of the natural order, for, as the physical degeneracy of the mulatto revealed, far from encouraging new forms, God had placed "a constant tendency in nature to restore and preserve a primitive type . . . by expunging accidental variations."[22] Obviously, a new criterion of species was needed. "After much observation and reflection," Morton presented his own definition "which seemed to cover the whole ground better than those which . . . preceded it: SPECIES—a primordial organic form."[23] Agassiz was delighted. Here was a major scientific breakthrough to rival the work of European scholars. A conceptual advance, moreover, that confirmed his own personal convictions about the moral and physical differences between the races.

RACE HATRED

It was only after he immigrated to America, in 1846, that Agassiz met an African, an encounter completely different to that of Combe's. Writing to his mother about the servants in his Philadelphia hotel, he freely expressed a visceral reaction that would underwrite all his subsequent thoughts on race. Recounting "the black faces with their thick lips and grimacing teeth, the wool on their head, their bent knees, their elongated hands, their large curved nails, and especially the livid color of the palm of their hands," he found it impossible to "repress the feeling that they are not of the same blood as us."[24] "The feeling that they inspired in me is contrary to all our ideas about the confraternity of human types and the unique origin of our species."[25] "What unhappiness for the white race—to have tied their existence so closely with that of negroes in certain countries. God preserve us from such a contact!"[26] Within five years, Agassiz had added his considerable authority to the cause of the American school. In lectures and articles, he warned the country about the dangers posed by a race with the "brain of a seven year old."[27] He was not a defender of slavery, nor did he think (as, after Darwin, many race scientists would argue) that blacks were subhuman; every species of mankind shared the same moral and intellectual powers, albeit in different degrees. He even accepted that as spiritual beings they could look forward to eternal redemption. Earthly affairs, however, were a different matter. Zoological investigations demonstrated that, although now populating the whole world, the various races were uniquely adapted to particular climatic regions; whites to the temperate regions of Europe and blacks to the more torrid zones of Africa. As such, freed slaves could not hope to compete with the stronger white population of the northern states. Such considerations had led Nott to conclude that the only rational solution to the problem of race was the continuation of slavery. This, as he saw it, was the South's moral duty, for whatever the evils of the institution, it kept a childlike people happy and content under the moral influence of a religious culture.

No doubt Agassiz would have preferred some scheme for returning Africans to their natural home at the time of Cain, but this seemed impractical given the numbers, and the apparent failure of the Liberian experiment. As he told Howe, the problem was to find a way of combining two different species of humans within a single social organization that ensured the legal rights of all. Never was there a more pressing need for scientific knowledge.

Two problems loomed large for the legislator: how to deal with pure blacks, and the policies most appropriate for mulattos. After describing the two competing theories of human diversity, Agassiz confirmed the received view that blacks were well suited to life in the South, a climate in which, he believed, the two or more million slaves of pure stock could propagate "*ad infinitum.*" And because the imitative and submissive African would readily accommodate to the Anglo-Saxon, he did not envision blacks falling before whites as the more combative and destructive Native American had. In short, it appeared that blacks and whites were destined to be cotenants on the American continent. As for mulattos, given that crossbreeding "produced sterility or at least a reduced fecundity"—the punishment for transgressing the natural repugnance between races—Agassiz believed physiology and morality demanded that everything should be done to reduce their number. Amalgamation was simply out of the question. Free from the unhealthy intimacy brought about by slavery, he thought the races would naturally avoid one another. Social policies, he continued, had to ensure the progress of each pure race according to its various needs. This was a complex issue. No doubt sensitive to his own Gallic pedigree, Agassiz indicated that physiological laws

revealed the mixing of different nationalities within a single race had positive effects; the problems of "breeding-out" were not at all like the problems
of "breeding-in." Consider carefully, he told Howe, the consequences of indiscriminate liaisons among the peoples of Central American and the implications "for republican institutions" if instead of the "manly population descended from cognate nations the United States should be inhabited by the
effeminate progeny of mixed races, half Indian, half negro, sprinkled with
white blood. Can you devise a scheme," he warned, "to rescue the Spaniards
of Mexico from their degradation? Beware then of any policy that may bring
our own race to their level."[28]

Emancipation should bring legal rights to blacks, but not, Agassiz protested, social union or political equality. "They should be entitled to their
freedom, to the regulation of their own destiny, to the enjoyment of their life,
of their earnings, of their family circle," but not the franchise, especially in
the South, where blacks outnumbered whites. Political rights had to be
earned by demonstrating civilized behavior. And, on this matter, history was
not on the side of the African. It was a significant fact that "while Egypt and
Carthage grew into powerful empires and attained a high degree of civilization; while Babylon, Syria, and Greece were developed to the highest culture
of antiquity, the negro race groped in barbarism and *never originated a regular
organization among themselves.*"[29] Morton's research proved that "the natural
propensities and mental abilities" of ancient Africans were "pretty much as
we find them at the present day—indolent, playful, sensual, imitative, subservient, good-natured, versatile, unsteady in their purpose, devoted, and affectionate."[30] How could such a people ever be equal members in a civilized
community? "As to the half-breeds, especially in the Northern States," he
restated his opinion that "their very existence is likely to be transient, and
that all legislation with reference to them should be regulated with the view,
and so ordained as to accelerate their disappearance."[31] There would be a
permanent race of Africans in the Americas, but he was confident that it
could exist independently of white New England. Through the prudent observance of physiological laws, an ecologically and morally sound distribution of races could be constructed. Preventing the unnatural amalgamations
fostered by slavery, the number of half-breeds would diminish, northern
blacks would migrate to their own communities in the South, and southern
whites, naturally unsuited to the hot and swampy lowlands of Dixie, would
gradually move north or west.

WHITE MAKES RIGHT

After thanking Agassiz for his advice, Howe went straight to the core of his friend's letter, the relationship between science and morality. He could not accept Agassiz's rejection of political equality for blacks. True to the Republican ideology pushed by Sumner, he maintained that given the opportunity to work, Africans (if not mulattoes) would develop the moral traits necessary for full citizenship. But, as his many cutting and painful remarks reveal, he too disliked the African and longed for a racially pure homeland. What, then, should be the guide of policy, the head or the heart? On this matter, Howe asserted the primacy of moral intuition. Not only would he "advocate entire freedom, equal rights, privileges, and open competition for social distinction, but what seems to me the shocking and downward policy of social amalgamation."[32] Even so, he reassured Agassiz, sentiment would not contradict reason—their different means would lead to the same end. "The heavens are not going to fall, and we are not going to be called upon to favor any policy discordant with natural instincts and cultivated tastes."[33] "God does not punish wrong and violence done to one part of our nature, by requiring us to do wrong and violence to another part."[34] Republican values were synonymous with the natural order. Left to themselves, the laws of Providence would work their beneficent magic. "Slavery," he argued

> has acted as a disturbing force in the development of our national character and produced monstrous deformities of a bodily as well as a moral nature, for it has impaired the purity and lowered the quality of the national blood. It imported Africans and to prevent their extinction by competition with a more vigorous race, it set a premium on colored blood. It has fostered and multiplied a vigorous black race, and engendered a feeble mulatto breed. Many of each of these classes have drifted northward, right into the teeth of thermal laws, to find homes where they would never live by natural election.[35]

As he prepared to write the most important report of his life, Howe had quite a balancing act to perform. On one hand, he would use the law of exercise to justify the progress of an industrious and moral race. On the other hand, he would invoke natural instincts and the laws of descent to dispel fears of social amalgamation. He would show that without social constraints pure Africans could thrive in Christian society, that they would not be attracted to whites, and that they would flee the cold for the more temperate South. On the other hand, agreeing with Agassiz that "mulattoism is hybridism," he explained the eventual eradication of the "half-breed," the living symbol of human sin and degeneracy. Again he refused to infringe upon natural rights and civil liberties. Some had recommended biological amalgamation, he observed, in the hope of diluting black blood, but "a pint of ink diffused in a lake is still there, and the water is still less pure."[36] "Others," with whom he concurred, believed "that mulattoism is not and cannot be persistent beyond four generations. In other words, that like some other abnormal and diseased conditions it is self-limiting, and . . . the body social will be purged of it."[37]

To help justify these momentous arguments, Howe toured several more army camps and, with the help of Edward Jarvis, sent out a series of questionnaires to doctors and other public officials gathering vital statistics on whites, Africans, and mulattoes—although his plan to study the achievements of freed Africans in the West Indies had to be canceled when the War Department refused to fund another expedition. Confident, however, that all his hypotheses were confirmed by the data he did collect, Howe put his thoughts to paper and presented his conclusions to Stanton at the end of December. When Stanton—who was sympathetic to the radicals but not overly fond of the commissioners—refused to publish it, Howe issued copies at his own expense and made sure it was included in the appendix of the Commission's *Final Report,* which was delivered three months later, in May 1864.

Howe's description of the free black communities of Canada West presented compelling empirical proof that Africans were not a threat to white society. They clearly demonstrated the ability to build a Christian culture and to be economically independent, and, when carefully interpreted, the statistics on births, deaths, and marriages revealed the unnaturalness of social amalgamation and the inherent weakness of the mulatto. Thanks to some slick reasoning, nature vouched completely for Howe's ideological convictions on race and society. He found free blacks who had succeeded in business, demonstrated competence in agriculture, and, contrary to received stereotypes (the mulatto apart), were hard and industrious workers. They had a deep if sentimental religious spirit and were rapidly acquiring civilized morals and manners. Crime was of a petty rather than violent nature, women were afforded great respect, and everywhere he observed a profound love of children. Most surprisingly, he found little anger or resentment toward whites for the immense suffering they had caused—he even recorded cases of escaped slaves wracked with remorse for betraying the trust of their former masters. These were indeed a forgiving and loyal people. Howe was also struck by their "childlike" capacity for amusement—a disposition that "grows out of their very organization."[38] Perhaps this cheerfulness was "among those marvelous arrangements by which Providence prepared races for the parts they are to bear in the drama of existence?"[39] The same logic he applied to the minds of the deaf, the blind, and the feebleminded also explained the African character. Unable to accept polygenism—which, as Combe argued, violated the basic assumptions of phrenology—Howe found a physiological basis for black and white differences in the stages of evolutionary development. "The Caucasian race, during the uterine and infantile growth, *passes through* 'certain stages of form,' which are so much more persistent in the African race as to be characteristic of it."[40] That is, "the white man seems to pass out of that phase of young life abounding in mirth and jollity, when he passes beyond boyhood, while the negro remains longer in it, if indeed he ever gets out at all."[41] This same process also governed the development of the intellectual faculties and explained the widely accepted imitative character of blacks. Many Canadian teachers reported no race-related differences in their students' performances; there were even cases of exceptional black scholars. But allowing for "liberal sympathies," Howe concluded that "observation and *a priori inferences*...pointed to the mental inferiority of half-breeds, if not of the negroes."[42] Like "some teachers of colored schools in the Northern States," most Canadians agreed that their "scholars advance as fast as whites in all the elementary studies, but fail when they come to studies which tax higher mental powers or the reasoning and combining faculties."[43] This, Howe pointed out, was because "the perceptive faculties are more nearly allied to the instincts, which men share equally with other animals; while the reasoning and reflecting faculties are superior to them, and are midway between that animal nature common to man and the brutes which holds us down to earth with them, and those higher qualities, or particularly human attributes, which lift us toward the heaven."[44] On this account, "mulattos seem to be, among the races, what eunuchs are among individual men"—"they have less animalization than blacks, and less spiritualization than whites."[45] And Africans, with "sharp eyes and ears . . . are quick of perception . . . very imitative; and they rapidly become intelligent. But they are rather a knowing than thinking people. They occupy useful stations in life; but such as require quick perceptions, rather than strong sense."[46] Given these qualities of mind and character, Howe concluded that blacks should not be allowed to form colonies or gather in urban enclaves. The influence of white civilization was essential to their material, moral, and intellectual progress. Moreover, as the different experiences of Canada's various cities demonstrated, racial tensions were minimized by the diffusion of refugees. Equally racist as their southern neighbors, Canadians had learned to accept blacks when they were integrated into society, but rejected them when they formed a rival community.

Turning to the second political objective of his report, Howe had to confess that despite these achievements Canadian blacks were not thriving as they should. "Births never equaled the deaths," and "without constant immigration the colored population" would surely "diminish and soon disappear."[47] Even the mulatto was proving more resilient than he had anticipated. But thanks to a remarkably flashy piece of ad hoc reasoning, Howe was able to save his thesis. Echoing Agassiz, he observed that if left to nature the mulatto would have faded and the black population would have been restored, "for there is in the social system, as in the individual body, a recuperative principle that tends to bring men back to the normal condition of their race."[48] Physiological laws, of course, had not been followed.

> The offspring of the cross between the small number of pure Africans formally slaves in the Northern States and the whites would have dwindled, and by this time nearly disappeared, by reason of the effect of climate, of further crossing between half-breeds, and their comparative infecundity, but for continual accessions from the South. There in a more favorable climate, fruitfulness greater than follows intercourse between mulattos was and is kept up, by constant crossing with the white race. From this central source in the South, then, comes the flood of adulterated blood, which spreads, whitening a little as it flows, but which reaches the North, and helps to retain there the taint which was fast vanishing.[49]

The situation was also compounded by interracial unions in Canada, but again Howe had a neat answer. Because of the difficulties of escaping slavery, the first emigrants were predominantly male. As always happens when one sex predominates, "natural tastes and dispositions, unduly thwarted . . . [were] perverted into morbid and monstrous passions," driving men outside their group—mostly into the arms of foreign domestics.[50] Even so, he was able to reassure his readers that as more black women entered the community, "negroes true to human instincts, began to be drawn together by more natural affinities than existed between them and another race. They grouped themselves in families, sanctified by marriage."[51] In sum, free from the disruptive effects of slavery, natural laws would eradicate the mulatto and leave a hardworking, sober, and congenial race of blacks. Drawn south by love of home and the warmer climate, these responsible moral citizens posed no threat of amalgamation and indeed would "co-operate powerfully with the whites from the North in re-organizing the industry of the South."[52]

Contrary to Agassiz's hopes for a racially divided nation, Howe did not think it "desirable to have [blacks] live in communities by themselves."[53] Drawing upon the Canadian experience, he noted that when combined "with whites in not greater proportion than one thousand to fifteen or twenty thousand, antagonism of race will hardly be developed, but negroes will imitate the best of white civilization, and will improve rapidly."[54] Ex-slaves did not need a massive welfare program or paternal institutions. Not prone to pauperism or laziness, blacks could rise through self-help. "The white man has tried taking care of the negro, by slavery, by apprenticeship, by colonization, and has failed disastrously in all; now let the negro try to take care of himself"—as long, that is, as he stayed in the South.[55]

Written by Owen, the Commission's "Final Report" incorporated all of Howe's major conclusions. The freedmen were essential to the war effort and to the future of the nation; after all here were four million "loyal citizens to assist in reconstructing in a permanently peaceful and orderly basis the insurrectionary states."[56] Could the ex-slave thrive in a free and open competition with the more robust and intelligent Anglo-Saxon? Yes. Evidence from Canada and the northern states proved that despite extreme hardship, they were honest and productive citizens committed to the habits and institutions of Christian civilization. Would they swarm north? No, not unless emancipation was revoked. Indeed, given the African's great love of home, their aversion to the cold, and the greater prejudice of the northern states, Owen predicted a black streak southward and, within a few years, "half the free Negro population now residing among us crossing Mason and Dixon's line to join the emancipated freedmen of the south."[57] Social harmony demanded that blacks not settle in colored enclaves. But this, of course, raised the specter of amalgamation—some even considered it a proper solution to the race problem. Not for Owen. As Howe's research clearly showed, the mulatto was an unnatural and physically degenerate being that, given emancipation, would soon be effaced from the land—a conclusion he further justified, albeit with some very tenuous reasoning, by examining the relative rates of births, marriages, and deaths among whites, blacks, and mix-breeds.[58] "A physical evil injurious to both" races, amalgamation was "rightly discouraged by public opinion, and avoided by all who consider it a duty as parents, to transmit to their offspring the best conditions for sound health and physical well-being."[59] Legislating personal relationships was beyond the orbit of the government, but Owen happily cited Howe's studies to prove that with the abolition of slavery, the free play of natural laws would make such liaisons an anathema to both races. "Without the injurious mingling of blood," Owen was confident that the social influence of the two races on each other, as "soon as their reciprocal relations shall be based on justice, will, beyond question, be mutually beneficial."[60] He was, of course, talking about the South. The North, he promised, could look forward to a future free from the problem of race, confident that the laws of nature would not impose any relationships on southern whites that infringed upon good morals. Sumner's political prayer had been answered. Physiological laws provided a scientific justification for the Republican approach to reconstruction and the social prejudices necessary to sustain it.

Ministering to the Body Politic

Phrenology teaches, that all the institutions and regulations of society . . . should be formed with a view to the development of all the propensities, faculties and sentiments of man in their due proportion, and in their natural order; or, in other words, should cultivate and develop his physical, moral, and intellectual nature. The society which effects this to the greatest possible number of its members is in accordance with the principles of phrenology, and is good: that which calls into action any of these natures, and stimulates it to such a degree as to repress or prevent the due development of either of the others, is unphrenological, and bad.

Samuel Gridley Howe, *A Discourse on the Social Relations of Man,* 1837

As the Massachusetts legislature took stock of the changing economic and social climate in the years after the Civil War, it became apparent that many of the reforms achieved during the antebellum period were ill-adapted to current needs. Like vestigial organs, the institutions founded to care for the insane, the poor, the criminal, and the dependent were outmoded relics of a previous time. A complex, costly, and confused network of aid had evolved in which the state was administering welfare through a dozen or so large asylums, almshouses, and hospitals, while more than 200 towns and cities provided small-scale relief in community houses, local jails, and private homes.[1] These two systems had to be brought in line. It was also evident that more specialized facilities were needed for the Commonwealth's dependent classes. In particular, the almshouses, constructed in response to the flood of Irish refugees during the first half of the 1850s, had become mass receptacles, crowding in one building the physically and mentally incapable, criminals, paupers, and orphans.[2] Work had to be found for the able-bodied and appropriate care given to those who required it. And, perhaps most importantly, with the rising generation of urban youth, the state had to take preventative measures to stem what many saw as a frightening spread of vice and degeneracy.

In 1863, Governor Andrew formed the State Board of Charities to address this plethora of concerns. Officially charged "to investigate and supervise the whole public charitable and correctional institutions of the Commonwealth, and to recommend such changes and additional provisions as they may deem necessary for their economical and efficient administration," the committee of six set about collecting information and correcting obvious abuses. However, with Howe's appointment the following year and his immediate election as chair, the group quickly adopted a far more radical agenda. In addition to questions of efficiency and order, the Board now proposed to investigate the origins of abnormality and deviance. If every arm of state charity collected statistics on the physical and mental causes of degeneracy, Howe wrote in the Board's *Second Annual Report,* the "attention of the legislature and the people" could be drawn to "those natural laws and social conditions upon which so surely depend, in every community . . . the numerical proportion to the whole population of the defective or infirm class . . . the dependent or pauper class, and . . . the vicious and criminal classes."[3] Special attention had to be paid to family ties in order "to illustrate the laws of descent."[4] When the consequences of breaking such physiological principles were more widely known, he confidently predicted a decrease in the number of malefactors and dependents. Asylums, reformatories, prisons, and workhouses would still be needed, at least in the short term, but they would have to undergo fundamental changes in accord with the principles governing the development of human character. Most importantly, Howe was adamant that public institutions not create unnatural communities: housing inmates in confined spaces, he believed, led to unhealthy associations that further strengthened already dominant propensities. Congregation had to be replaced by separation and diffusion. Convinced that the greatest instrument for the proper management of the mind was the family, he proposed a sweeping de-institutionalization of public charity: the blind, the deaf, and the insane would live in ordinary homes while receiving specialized daytime training. He was particularly distressed by plans to build institutions for the disabled soldiers of the Civil War. Congregating hundreds of men within single-sex dormitories would deprive them of their most important social needs and create a totally unnecessary institutional bureaucracy. Better by far to have "five hundred maimed veterans stumbling about the towns and villages of Massachusetts, living partly on their pensions and partly by their work, than shut up in the costliest and best structure that art could plan and money could buy."[5] Howe's policies demanded a far greater degree of public involvement—indeed, the kind of practical intimacy with the dependant that characterized his own life's work at Perkins. But in Howe's mind there was no such thing as vicarious virtue. The work of charity had to be

> done by the people themselves, directly, and in the spirit of Him who taught that the poor ye shall always have with you,—that is near you,—in your hearts and affections,—within your sight and knowledge; and not thrust far away from you, and always shut up alone by themselves in almshouses or reformatories, that they be kept at the cheapest rate by such a cold abstraction as a State government.[6]

UNNATURAL COMMUNITIES

"Massachusetts," Howe explained in the *Second Annual Report,* "contains (in round numbers) about five hundred blind, four hundred deaf mutes, three thousand insane, twelve hundred idiots, and ten thousand paupers, who, with a few exceptions, are supported by the public or their friends. Add to this those who have become dependent through illness, those who have developed bad habits," "the hideous army of drunkards," "the fallen women who minister to the evil passions and lust," and the other "parasites of the body social," and it became apparent that the state had at least forty-five thousand "helpless, dependent, idle consumers, and destructives."[7] The situation was not as bad as Howe had witnessed in Europe, but still, immediate action had to be taken. Sympathy needed guidance. Schools had to teach physiology, legislators had to be trained in the laws of society and political economy, and the population had to be informed about the causes of human degeneracy. Once citizens realized the importance of a stable family, regular work, good nutrition, comfortable housing, and the other essentials of life to the development of mind and character, Howe was sure that the community would support a whole infrastructure of educational institutions—schools, libraries, churches, lecture halls, and public festivals—dedicated to promoting the health and intelligence of the population. Moral suasion had worked well in the case of the mad—it was "the *people of Massachusetts* who took the insane out of the garrets, the cellars, the cages . . . when through the pleadings of Horace Mann and other philanthropists, they came to understand their real condition and wants"—why should it not also work for the pauper and criminal?[8]

Everyone, Howe assumed, knew the importance of breeding and training animals. They knew, for example, that "it is hard to teach the pup of an untrained pointer to point, while it is easy to teach the pup of a trained dog. And further, if several generations are trained, the last pups will point almost instinctively, and without special training."[9] The same knowledge had to be applied to human beings. The chief cause of social degeneracy was "inherited organic imperfection,—vitiated constitution,—or *poor stock.*"[10] As Spurzheim taught, the helpless, the worthless, and the wicked could be partitioned into two broad categories: the dependent and pauper class (which lacked vital force), and the criminal class (which inherited "vicious habits of thought and action").[11] Although "poor nutrition . . . and the abuse of functions" on the part of parents depleted the vital force of their children, the greatest factor in the creation of the first group was the abuse of alcohol. Spirits, wine, and beer (even coffee and tobacco) modified the human constitution, exciting the passions and diminishing the higher faculties until "habitual weakening" of the "will, reason, and conscience" resulted in "a morbid condition, with morbid appetites and tendencies" that was "surely transmitted to the offspring."[12] Howe further subdivided this class into the feeble, sick, insane, and drunkards (who were able to work under guidance) and those with severe physical and mental defects (who were utterly incapable of personal industry). The number in the first division compared to the size of the general population provided an index of society's intelligence, and the ratio of the second group to society yielded a measure of its biological purity.

Turning to the criminal class, Howe warned of a far more dangerous problem than lack of vigor—children born with powerful propensities and torpid moral sentiments. "Bodily monsters," he observed, do not "perpetuate their monstrosities," but "spiritual monsters multiply, like the devil that took to himself seven other devils."[13] The law of extinction would not deplete this stock, and he feared that the "hot-bed growth of the cities" would yield "a baleful crop, unless we strive to prevent the seed from sprouting. Once up we cannot cut them down; but only strive to direct their growth aright. This is the good work of reformation; but prevention is a better one."[14] Weeding out this bad seed would be difficult work, especially among those who bore the greatest responsibility for its germination. Unwilling to sanction sterilization, he rested his hopes on the power of moral suasion. There was, he believed, at least one sentiment that could be reached even in the most vicious characters, the love of offspring. "Many a man who will not forgo his . . . desires . . . through respect for human or divine laws—through love of father, brother, wife, or friend—through fear of prison here, or eternal hell hereafter . . . would sooner lay hands on his own life, than knowingly hurt his little child, even if it be yet unborn."[15] The perfection of the race, therefore, depended upon educating the lowest element of society about the consequences of their depravity.

Why were the laws of descent constantly violated? Did men and women think themselves immune to the inevitable and inflexible order of Providence? Perhaps those with a large individuality might, but in most cases, the problem was simply ignorance. While Europeans could see the effects of inheritance in the ghettos of the Continents' large industrial cities, New Englanders had to look carefully at the pauper class or examine the causes of "idiocy, and its cognate infirmities."[16] The situation was also muddied by the multiplicity of effects that attended sin. Oftentimes skipping generations, producing different symptoms depending upon sex, temperament, and vital energy, it was hard to see a direct correlation between vice and its physiological consequences. "*Likeness in variety*" was the fundamental law of nature.[17] But ultimately, with appropriate statistical records, Howe was confident that all these factors could be quantified and controlled. Take for example the fearful infant mortality rates, touching 50 percent in some years. If farmers could rear 96 percent of their livestock to maturity, could not society preserve its children? Death at such an early age resulted primarily from an inherited lack of vital energy. Fortunately, as he had claimed in his report on the ex-slaves of the Canadian West, there were "innate recuperative powers" that would return the social system to its natural condition, "providing individuals did not stray too far from the Creator's ordained path."[18] "In a few generations, with temperate life and wisely assorted marriage, the morbid conditions disappear."[19] This would demand careful management of a class driven mostly by animal appetites. But Howe was optimistic, for, contrary to popular opinion, he found that "persons in this condition are docile and easily governed."[20]

Having laid out the nature and causes of human deviancy, Howe turned to the kind of physiologically informed practices that should constitute the state's approach to charity. In all domains, he presented the same basic poli-

cies: the biological classification of types, the separation and diffusion of inmates, and the direct participation of the public in the reform of the degenerate. The key instruments in his plan were the twin moral agencies of work
and family life. The first developed attitudes of self-reliance and industry, the
second, through ties of blood and place, honed the sentiments essential to
social order.

Howe's criticism of the state's reformatories provides an example of this
logic. As prisons evolved from punitive to correctional institutions, he noted
that special hope had been placed on the possibility of reforming the juvenile
offender. Although removing children from the influence of vicious and
hardened criminals was a positive step, congregating them in large institutions produced its own problems. Howe was especially concerned by the
School Ship, which squeezed dozens of teenage boys in such cramped spaces
that they could barely move their elbows. Devoid of domestic morals and
womanly influence for weeks on end, the pure mind could only shudder at
the wicked thoughts these youths must have entertained. Things were hardly
better on land. Despite their best intentions, there was little the understaffed
faculty of Massachusetts' reformatories could do with hundreds of young
offenders—if it was not for the cooperation of the "better boys," Howe was
sure they would be quite overwhelmed. Of course, there were success stories,
accounts of wayward boys and girls being transformed into good and productive citizens. But such celebrity cases, Howe insisted, were probably explained by a child's natural tendency to virtue, not the school's discipline. To
devise effective policies, reformers had to look to the laws of physiology, and
these suggested, repeating the phrenologists' hierarchy of brains, three basic
types of juvenile offenders. First, the good child, the "Little Nells and David
Copperfields" who because of "their strong moral tendencies . . . gravitate
naturally toward virtue."[21] Second, those who are "so unhappily organized,
who have such innate activity of the animal propensities and passions, and
with such feeble moral sense, they tend naturally to vice."[22] In between these
two extremes was a far larger third class that, while inheriting "unfavorable
moral tendencies," was not prone by nature either to vice or to virtue. This
was the group that would profit most from the positive effects of a nurturing
community and suffer most from the negative culture of institutional life.
Howe was silent on the fate of innately bad boys and girls. Believing them to
be irredeemable, he offered the rather chilling assessment that any improvement in their behavior should not be taken as evidence of a reformed character, merely the strengthening of love of approbation or the organ of imita-

tion. In the case of the majority, however, reformation was possible through the realignment of the propensities. This was best achieved when children formed loving attachments with moral guardians. The offender

> must have companionship; and if he cannot draw others into his own way of thinking and feeling, he will, perforce, fall into theirs. . . . As new faculties, feelings, and emotions are brought into play, those formally too active subside, and he begins to get into sympathy with the public feeling of the household. . . . The cravings of the old propensities grow less and less, as pleasure is found in the exercise of the new ones; he gradually acquires a certain harmony of mental action, the average result of which is a new character.[23]

Even more pressing than the overhaul of the reformatory system was the need to address the hundreds of orphaned children living as wards of the state in Massachusetts' three great almshouses: Tewkesbury, Monson, and Bridgewater. Although well fed, well dressed, clean, and schooled in the common branches and religious precepts, these children inherited dangerous tendencies that had to be counteracted by education. Where other boys and girls learned the values of work and friendship within the family and community, inmates of the almshouses imbibed the "pauper atmosphere," strengthening their animal nature as they congregated with society's worst elements. Howe bristled at the suggestion of the Tewkesbury superintendent that, rather than indenturing children, they should be retained in the institution and taught a trade. This would "intensify their abnormal tendencies" and "cut them off from the healthful and purifying influences of family life, country life, and of general society; of early friendships and of local attachments."[24] Who would send their own sons and daughters to such establishments?[25] As yet, America did not have a pauper or criminal class, but if the inherited tendencies of these children continued to become habitual, as typically happened in institutional life, Howe was convinced that it soon would. The most informed approach, he suggested, was to relocate the insane and idiotic inmates to a central facility, exclude all vicious and criminal types, place the better children in care, and put the deserving poor under the positive moral regimen of the workhouse. The money saved by closing reformatories and almshouses could then be used to fund superintendents and pay families willing to foster wayward boys and girls.

As Howe boasted in the opening pages of the Board's *Fifth Annual Report*

(1869), the committee's recommendations led to radical changes in the state's welfare system.[26] A vast amount of statistics had been gathered on the nature of social degeneracy and, in place of a hodgepodge of uncoordinated and expensive charities, an organized system was emerging around the scientific classification and effective treatment of criminals, paupers, the insane, and other classes of dependents. Legislation lowering the number of poor entitled to state (as opposed to local) relief had led to the closure of a hospital and two almshouses. Bridgewater was transformed into a workhouse, and Tewksbury became a home for the chronically insane. All able-bodied paupers were now forced to work, and upwards of 400 children had been relocated to a boarding school at the Monson facility, free from the harmful influence of vicious and depraved adults. The Board had also been instrumental in constituting a new system of supervision to oversee the apprenticeship of reformatory and almshouse children. But more could be done. Pressing his phrenologically based policies, Howe was more adamant than ever that the dangers of congregation must not be ignored. In argument after argument he sought to justify the extension of the family system to almost every arm of public welfare. Like Horace Mann, he now believed that "woman's power" was the most effective weapon of reform. They had the larger social duty of infusing "the immense moral force" of female nature throughout the welfare system. Here was a field where woman could "undoubtedly excel man, because it includes nurture and admonition of children, the treatment and reformation of youth, the oversight and direction of perverse women, the care of the sick, the constant consolation of the old and the dying."[27] The *Fifth Annual Report* also announced one other reform measure dear to Howe's heart, the establishment of a new school for the education of deafmutes. The children of Massachusetts would no longer be forced to learn the "lower" system of sign language used at Hartford; the Clarke School in Northampton was now open to teach them human speech.

WORD AND MIND

After lying dormant for more than ten years, the articulation-signing debate reignited in the early 1860s when a wealthy lawyer, Gardiner Hubbard, sought Howe's help with the education of his daughter Mabel—the future wife of Alexander Graham Bell—who had lost her hearing at age four after a bout of scarlet fever. As Harlan Lane tells the story, concerned to preserve her speech, Hubbard had taken Mabel to the American Asylum, only to be informed that she could not enroll before age ten. Mabel, Hubbard learned, would soon lose her voice, but could eventually look forward to acquiring "the beautiful language of signs." Determined to avoid this fate, he turned to Howe, who told him exactly what he wanted to hear. Mabel could be taught to read lips and her speech could be saved. The key, as with Laura, was to prevent the girl from signing. All that Hubbard had to do was to hire a private tutor to help Mabel's mother provide round-the-clock oral instruction. No special skills were required, only womanly patience and perseverance.

Howe, it seems, had given similar advice a few years earlier to a couple from Providence, Rhode Island. Their daughter, Jeannie Lippitt, had become quite adept at lipreading, but had made little progress in vocalization. Resolving to give Howe's scheme a fair trial, Hubbard and his wife enlisted the services of a teacher, Mary True. Without any background in deaf education, they followed Howe's recommendations to the letter. Gradually their intensive efforts bore fruit, as Mabel became proficient at reading lips and improved her ability to articulate words. After two years, Hubbard could report that his daughter "spoke imperfectly but intelligently, and understood those around her."[28]

By now a zealous convert to oralism, Hubbard, joined with Howe, the State Board of Charities secretary, F. B. Sanborn, and Harvard president Thomas Hill to press the Massachusetts legislature to establish a state school for the deaf. A bill was drafted and the issue directed to the Committee on Education. Here it came under the scrutiny of Lewis Dudley, the member for Northampton, whose own congenitally deaf daughter, Teresa, was a student at Hartford. After five years of private tutoring, Teresa had entered the institute accomplished in sign language and with a good command of written English. Highly appreciative of her achievements, Dudley was an enthusiastic supporter of the manual method. Howe, Hubbard, Sanborn, and a number of other supporters—including Laura Bridgman's former teacher Mary Swift Lamson—all spoke in favor of oralism, but Dudley's testimony and the arguments of Hartford's principal, Collins Stone, won the day. There was simply no good reason to reject the practices developed at Hartford, the committee's report concluded, for "a theory of visionary enthusiasts that had been repeatedly tried and abandoned as impractical."[29] Incensed by this judgment, Hubbard and Howe determined that a practical experiment was needed to show just how visionary their claims actually were.

By a curious twist of fate, it was Dudley who helped bring about this practical trial and who, as a newfound advocate for oralism, ultimately convinced the General Court to establish a school for the deaf in Massachusetts, an institution dedicated to speech that radically changed the course of deaf instruction in America. Interested to learn more about Laura Bridgman's education, Dudley set up an appointment with Lamson. As he was leaving his office for the meeting, a Mrs. Cushing showed up seeking advice on how to educate her own deaf daughter, Fanny. Dudley invited her along. Much to his annoyance, Cushing was completely persuaded by Lamson's advocacy of lipreading and vocalization and agreed, despite his warnings, to submit Fanny to a course of oral training. After some discussion, Harriet Rodgers, sister of another of Bridgman's teachers, Eliza Rogers, was persuaded to undertake the project at her home in Billerica. At first Rogers taught Fanny finger spelling, but after a trip with Cushing to see Jeannie Lippitt in Providence, she dedicated herself to speech. Within a few months she too was a convert and, with the help and financial support of Hubbard, announced her intention to open a private school for the deaf. By the summer of 1866, Rogers and four students were ready to start Howe's experiment.

After years of pressing for reforms, Howe knew exactly how to win support for his cause. In concert with Hubbard, he lined up political friends to push the measure in the legislature; he used the Board's *Second Annual Report* to explain the implications of the two methodologies, for the development of both the individual and the state, and, as with Bridgman and the idiotic children that he had trained, he planned public exhibitions to demonstrate the sensational achievements of his pedagogic methods. The only thing missing was a wealthy philanthropist willing to help finance the project. This part of the puzzle fell into place that fall when Hubbard, together with Rogers's brother-in-law, Lieutenant Governor Thomas Talbot, went to present the argument for oral education to Howe's longtime friend and fellow member of the Secret Six, Governor Bullock. Fully apprised by Howe and Sanborn, Bullock supported their initiative and promised to raise the issue at the beginning of the year when he addressed the legislature. He also disclosed that John Clarke, a Northampton banker who had himself suffered from a loss of hearing, was willing to donate $50,000 toward the establishment of a Massachusetts school for the deaf.

True to his word, Bullock voiced his concerns for the intellectual and moral development of the deaf and appointed a special joint committee to investigate Hubbard's proposal. "I know not to what supervision we may more safely intrust the delicate and intricate," he told the legislature, "than to the matured experience which has overcome the difficulty of blindness superadded to privation of speech and hearing."[30] Given the stakes, this was sure to be a highly controversial debate. But with the publication of the *Second Annual Report,* the contest also became ugly. Collins Stone issued a rebuttal on behalf of the friends of Hartford, and Howe followed with remarks defending his conclusions. By the time the committee convened—comprising Dudley and Talbot, along with Howe's close friend Francis Bird, representing the governor's council—the apparently practical question of providing the best schooling for the deaf had boiled into a bitter contest of basic philosophies. Never was the debate between environment and biology so polarized. Caught between promoting a language of signs and a deaf community capable of transmitting its own culture and the physiologically grounded arguments of Howe's eugenic theory, politicians were left to decide what it is that makes us human.

Like all his other social reforms, Howe's arguments for the education of the deaf flowed directly from his commitment to the basic phrenological principles of inheritance and exercise. Both blindness and deafness resulted from the infringement of natural laws. But where blindness typically had a functional cause, producing an inherited lack of vital energy, deafness was more likely a congenital defect—the product of an inappropriate marriage— that also rendered the child prone to vicious tendencies. This distinction had implications, especially for the education of the deaf. The powerful propensities they inherited could only be controlled "by intimate intercourse with people of sound and normal condition—that is, by general society," where they would "be *strengthened by associating closely and persistently with others having the like infirmity.*"[31] Language was the key. "In its largest sense," Howe observed, "this is the most important instrument of thought, feeling, and emotion; and especially of social intercourse."[32] Fortunately, the blind, although weak, had strong social instincts that impelled them to develop their linguistic facility and participate in the general population. Not so with the deaf, who, without speech, could not communicate and form healthy relationships. Of course, the "rudimentary and lower parts of language, or pantomime, [were] open to mutes," but this mode of communication only served to harden the animal propensities, brutifying the deaf and perpetuating their isolation in an impoverished culture.[33] The development of mind and character depended on the complexity of the language. Those who talked in English and thought in English, unlike speakers of less civilized tongues, exercised their higher faculties more thoroughly. Sign, with its obvious physical commonality to the communication of animals, did not excite the higher powers and thus prevented the deaf from becoming rational beings. This is why Howe was so disturbed when he heard of the formation of a deaf church in Boston.

> If our mutes, educated at Hartford, had been taught articulation, and taught as well as children are taught in the German schools, they might attend public worship in our churches; they would all partake the common spirit of religious devotion (which public worship does so much to strengthen;) most of them would seize the sense and meaning of the service and sermon; and the intelligent ones would catch enough of the very words of the preacher to understand his discourses.[34]

"This statement," he added, "is not made hastily or thoughtlessly."[35] The further prospect of an autonomous community of deaf families, breeding an increasing number of deaf children, was simply beyond the pale.

Stone was quick to reply. In his annual report of 1866 he took issue with nearly all of Howe's claims, especially the assertion that only 40 percent of the school's students were born deaf. In fact, 95 percent of Hartford's pupils were congenitally deaf, and for them, Stone insisted, articulation was a pipedream.[36] The long, tedious and ultimately futile lessons in speech only stole valuable time from their general education, leaving the child isolated and ignorant of the world. Howe's fears about congregation were misplaced. The asylum provided a positive moral culture that disciplined children in the manners of Christian life. As for the financial concerns that Howe had raised, the one-on-one tutoring required for oral instruction would be far more expensive—especially because, contrary to Howe's claims, such specialized work could not be left to the untrained but conscientious woman. Finally, Stone defended the integrity of signing and stood behind deaf societies and deaf churches. Why should honest and hardworking citizens not meet to worship in their own language? Nobody denied these rights to French or Italian Americans.

Unmoved, Howe responded with a scathing pamphlet defending all the claims made in the *Second Annual Report*. The stage was set for a fiery debate before the joint special committee. Were the fruits of articulation really worth the effort? Could speech and lipreading be taught without special training? Should the deaf be separated or congregated? Ought the government to intervene to stop the emergence of a deaf race? The two sides passionately presented all the arguments they had exchanged in print. But what seems to have swayed the members, especially Lewis Dudley, were the sensational presentations of deaf students schooled in lipreading and speech. As discussed by Harlan Lane, Howe and Hubbard set up several carefully choreographed performances, first at Lamson's house, where more than seventy people witnessed the verbal skills of Rogers's pupils, and later at Josiah Qunicy's home, where an even larger crowd saw Jeannie Lippitt hold a spoken conversation with Lamson's cousin Roscoe Green, another of Rogers's pupils, who had lost his hearing at age eight. Other children spelled words, took dictation, and solved arithmetic problems. According to Lane, these acts were achieved mostly with smoke and mirrors. The selectively invited and uncritical audience were not informed that the majority of students were semimutes, nor were they allowed to question the pupils for themselves. The situation was different, however, when Mabel Hubbard appeared before the committee. Although Lane does not record the event, her father claims that she was freely questioned in arithmetic, history, and geography, answered "satisfactorily," and was found to be "equal in intelligence to most hearing children of her age."[37] Hubbard reports that when asked, "Can you tell me who laid the first Atlantic cable, she quickly and smilingly answered 'Cyrus Field.'"[38] Dudley was impressed, but still not convinced. His pivotal defection was cemented when, at his wife's insistence, Teresa was allowed to visit Rogers's home for a few days of instruction. When she returned able to voice several words, albeit indistinctly, Dudley's heart melted. Given her ability to read, write, and sign, perhaps he thought that a course of oral instruction could not hurt his daughter—lipreading especially would be a valuable skill. Perhaps also he now saw articulation as a viable alternative for the semimute, but he still did not think it was an option for the congenitally deaf. Persuaded by Howe and Hubbard's arguments, especially the claim that language learning had to be keyed to the maturing structures of the child's brain, Dudley suggested a compromise. Massachusetts should open local schools for the deaf, close to the family home, in order to prepare students for admittance at the American School for the Deaf when they reached age ten. How could Stone and the trustees at Hartford object?

The committee's report, brought before the legislature in June 1867, by and large favored education through sign—the congenitally deaf and those who lost their hearing during infancy could not profit from oralism. It did not endorse Howe's argument that Massachusetts had an obligation to school her own students, nor did it accept his fears about the evils of congregation. But it did advocate making the most of Clarke's bequest by establishing an experimental primary school for the instruction of children too young to attend Hartford. Finally, as if to lay the issue to rest, the responsibility for overseeing the education of the deaf was transferred from the Board of State Charities to the Board of Education. With no stipulation as to the mode of instruction, Dudley, Hubbard, Talbot, and the other members of the appointed incorporation committee moved fast. Rogers was persuaded to take charge of the enterprise, Clarke was convinced of the superiority of oralism, and, with buildings rented from Dudley, the Clarke School was opened in Northampton that fall, with Hubbard as its first president.

It was decided that admittance would be restricted to "two classes of state pupils," those "who were partially deaf" and "those who had lost their hearing when over four years of age."[39] Further, responding to Howe's strictures, the Clarke Institute was to be organized as a family in which teachers worked, played, and shared their homes with the students. Yet despite these mandates, several of the twenty pupils who enrolled in the first class, including Teresa Dudley, were beyond primary age, and eleven "were either congenitally deaf, or had lost their hearing at two years or under, and before they had acquired any language."[40] The number continued to rise. In 1893, Catherine Yale wrote in her "Principal's Report" that 70 percent of those attending were born deaf, the conviction having "grown very strong that every deaf child should have the opportunity to learn to speak and read from lips."[41] Even so, remarkable achievements were soon reported: by the end of the first year Dudley, now a complete convert to oralism, was recommending articulation for the congenitally deaf, and, reporting on his visit to the school, Philip Gillett of the Illinois State Asylum told a meeting of his fellow principals that despite his prejudice against oralism, he had seen "semi-mutes readily comprehended the remarks of teachers or others from the motions of the organs of speech . . . and [use] their own voice and organs of speech intelligibly and intelligently."[42] Mutes were also "quite expert at lip-reading, and conversed with comparative ease and fluency in articulate speech, which was understood by the strangers present without difficulty."[43]

THE HEGEMONY OF ORALISM

Howe had reason to gloat. In the *Fifth Annual Report* of the State Board of Charities he rejoiced that the authority of the American Asylum had finally been broken. Historically wedded to outmoded practices and held back by lethargy and egoism, Hartford had attempted to maintain its funding and its position of dominance by suffocating all rival ideas. With the chains removed, however, Rogers's school demonstrated exciting new possibilities for the deaf and great economies for the state. "Two or three years of training in articulation . . . [during] the tender years of childhood," he predicted, "will enable some mutes to attend common schools, especially in towns where a class of them can be formed."[44] Most importantly, Rogers was teaching human speech. At Hartford and similar institutions there was always "*visible* uproar . . . a struggle for expression, a vehemence of manner, an eagerness of gesticulation, and an anxiety of countenance not pleasant to behold."[45] There the deaf "seem like human beings under the spell of silence, trying with emphatic gestures, flashing eyes, and beseeching looks, to express their thoughts through the lowest form of human language, which is but little above the highest form of the language of animals, and not without something of their expression."[46] At Clarke, where all signs were forbidden, a more pleasant and controlled scene greeted the visitor. True, the children made strange sounds, but at least these were "*human utterance[s]*" as they reached up to the highest form of language.[47] All this could be explained through the laws of the mind. Clarke "has proven . . . by practice," he affirmed, "the correctness of inferences drawn from *a priori* considerations, that mental powers and faculties must be developed at certain stages of physical development, or they will never be developed."[48] Signing, as Howe argued previously, failed to excite the higher moral and intellectual organs, leaving the deaf in the brutified condition that he had described. This principle also explained the relative merits of the two modes of instruction and the real reason that the American Asylum would not enroll students under the age of ten. Children, he continued, are born with a natural instinct to talk, not to express themselves in the gestures of monkeys. The fact that the ear cannot capture sounds did not mean that oral communication was impossible, for, at the height of their development in early childhood, the lower perceptive faculties had the power—lost in later years—to distinguish the visible distinctions between words as they appear on the lips and face of the speaker. But rather than make use of these abilities, teachers of sign forced younger students to suppress their spontaneous interest in articulation. It was far easier for them to wait a few years until other powers took precedence. By then, of course, several of the mind's organs would have atrophied and the child would be unable to learn. Oralism, not signing, was thus the most natural method for educating the deaf. Indeed, so great was the child's hunger for speech, Howe was convinced that most dedicated mothers could teach those born deaf to speak, or at least preserve the voice after scarlet fever. Such children would then attend special classes in the common schools, thus avoiding institutionalization and all the evils of congregation. No doubt this would require some accommodation; teachers might have to take special lessons in Normal schools. But at the very minimum, he demanded, "all whose parents desire it, should have opportunity for a fair trial of their [child's] capacity to acquire human speech," noting that "no such opportunity *can* be presented in an institution where sign language is used as the medium of instruction and of common conversation."[49] By 1887 his wish had come true; a parents' right to choose between oral and sign schools had been enacted into Massachusetts state law.

HOWE'S LEGACY

Howe's *Fifth Annual Report,* together with the well-publicized accounts of the successes at Clarke, soon generated a new enthusiasm for lipreading and articulation that the principals of the nation's deaf institutes could not ignore. Mindful that an alternative system of schooling could undermine the future of signing and the vibrant deaf community, the principals agreed to classes in oralism for semimutes as, in fact, Weld had done twenty years earlier in response to Horace Mann's criticisms. These experiments had failed, but Edward Gallaudet, recently back from his own fact-finding tour of European schools, rallied for a more strenuous and determined trial. Having witnessed a variety of efforts to teach speech, he was convinced that signing was an absolute necessity for the deaf. Like Howe, he bemoaned their separation by language from the broader community and was even opposed to deaf marriages. But prohibiting manual communication was pointless. It did not lead to superior verbal skills, and the huge amounts of time it occupied totally undermined the possibility of teaching students about the world in which they lived. Concerned to promote a fuller participation in society, Gallaudet thus advocated a "combined system" of instruction, based on American Sign Language (ASL), that united lessons in articulation and lipreading with finger spelling and an increased emphasis on reading and writing English. Deaf educators were ready to move with the times. Following Gallaudet's council, by the end of the decade there were a dozen oral instructors teaching in deaf institutions across the country.

But this effort to contain oralism to a complementary role proved futile. Even as Collins Stone was reintroducing articulation classes at Hartford, a new day school, named for Horace Mann, was opened to teach speech in Boston. Growing rapidly under the energetic leadership of Sarah Fuller, by 1875, it enrolled sixty-three students to Northampton's sixty. Most importantly, Fuller brought Alexander Graham Bell to the United States to experiment with the exciting new technique of visible speech. A strict oralist, it was Bell more that any other figure who turned Howe's theoretical program into a practical reality. With his invention of the telephone in 1876, he had the time, means, and public authority to gain control of deaf education. Bell shared virtually all Howe's views on language, physiology, and pedagogy. He believed sign was too concrete and idiomatic a medium to serve as an effective instrument for abstract thought. He was concerned that signing separated the deaf from normal society.

Drawing upon similar eugenic principles, updated to conform to evolutionary theory, he echoed Howe's belief that, through their association in residential schools and their use of an alien language, the deaf were forming unhealthy isolated communities that promoted intermarriage and thus the birth of defective children, even, he feared, the emergence of a degenerate variety of the human race. After reviewing statistics indicating that more than 30 percent of the students at Hartford and similar institutions had deaf relatives, he called for immediate legislation to ban deaf marriages. He also campaigned vigorously to replace residential asylums with day schools that would allow the deaf to stay in the family home and mix with normal children. Repeating Howe's claim, he promised that "special teaching" was to "be a matter only of the first few years of life"; after that, deaf children could be mainstreamed[50]—reforms that Bell used his money and influence to steer into public policy over the next two decades. Equally important, Bell combined with Catherine Yale to start an oral teacher-training program in Northampton. And, in 1891, fulfilling a long-standing ambition, he organized and richly endowed a rival organization to the Convention, the American

Association to promote the Teaching of Speech to the Deaf (AAPTSD). In concert with the instructors and publications flowing from Clarke, the AAPTSD's meetings and *Review* (later named the *Volta Review*) effectively gave control of deaf education to oralists. By 1900, Bell had ensured that the majority of America's teachers of the deaf were oralists, three-fourths of instructors were hearing, and half of all students were banned from using sign in school. In 1920, only one in five teachers were deaf, and 80 percent of students were prohibited from signing—a dominance that continued until the 1960s and 1970s when the merits of ASL, kept alive by generations of the deaf, would be seriously explored.

By the time of his death in 1876, Howe could take solace that the cause of oralism was in good hands. He could also witness the impact of his social philosophy on public welfare policy. By the 1870s, optimism about the power of moral treatment to harmonize the brain's disordered faculties had largely evaporated. Increasingly convinced of the hereditarian determinates of behavior, reformers stressed the prevention of degeneracy by implementing legislation to regulate public morals. In America, the annual reports of the Massachusetts State Board of Charities set this agenda, and, as in so many other areas of institutional policy, other states were quick to follow suit. The same year Howe brought his eugenic philosophy before the General Court, he and Sanborn also established a national organization to promote their vision of statistically grounded and physiologically based reforms—what eventually became the American Social Sciences Association (ASSA).[51] In annual meetings, public officials and political leaders gathered to hear lectures on record keeping, the determinates of abnormality, and the need for a professional core of experts to coordinate scientifically grounded social policies. Ten years before he wrote *The Jukes* (1877), Richard Dugdale attended the ASSA and heard Howe explain his method of classifying biological types, collecting statistics, and inferring the laws of propagation governing degeneracy—and no doubt reflections on the threat of the deviant and the advantages of preventative reform.[52] Such arguments—readily available in Howe's many official reports—became something of a blueprint for public officials, as, by 1874, eight other states followed Massachusetts' lead and established their own boards of State Charities. Supported by Bell's influential arguments on the hereditability of deafness, and several sensational studies of social degeneracy, Howe's teachings easily meshed with the hardening mindset of late nineteenth-century social scientists. Without a theory of genetics or the sophisticated statistical methods devised by Francis Galton and his followers, Howe could only rely upon the crude point-by-point comparisons revealed in his tabulations. His typologies, like the physiological laws that he identified, were all based on superficial inductions and common prejudices—"lack of vigor" and "morbid tendencies" were hardly the stuff of science. However, they were sufficient to make a potent political case for physiologically in-formed welfare policies and helped create a field of prescientific professional knowledge and practices upon which the eugenic movement could build.

Notes

FRONTAL MATTER

1. Horace Mann, *A Few Thoughts for a Young Man* (Boston: Tickner, Reed, and Fields, 1850), 38.

2. Ibid., 38–39.

3. John Dewey, *Later Works, 1925–1953*, 17 vols. (Carbondale: Southern Illinois University Press, 1981–1991). Horace Mann, *Lectures on Education* (New York: Arno Press, 1960), 118.

4. George Combe, *The Constitution of Man: Considered in Relation to External Objects* (Boston: Allen and Ticknor, 1834).

5. On Combe's educational thought, see William Jolly, ed., *Education, Its Principles and Practices as Developed by George Combe* (London: MacMillan and Co., 1879); and Stephen Tomlinson, "Phrenology, Education, and the Politics of Human Nature: The Thought and Influence of George Combe," *History of Education* 25 (1996): 235–254.

6. Horace Mann, quoted in Jonathan Messerli, *Horace Mann: A Biography* (New York: Knopf, 1971), 351.

7. James Simpson, *The Philosophy of Education: With Its Practical Application to a System and Plan of Popular Education as a National Object* (Edinburgh: A. and C. Black, 1836). Originally published as James Simpson, *Necessity of Popular Education as a National Object; with Hints on the Treatment of Criminals, and Observations on Homicidal Insanity* (Edinburgh: A. and C. Black, 1834).

8. George Combe, *Lectures on Popular Education, Delivered to the Edinburgh Philosophical Association for Procuring Instruction in Useful and Entertaining Science, in April and November, 1833* (Edinburgh: J. Anderson, 1837).

9. Combe's record of this tour is contained in George Combe, *Notes on the United States of North America, During a Phrenological Visit in 1838–39–40*, 3 vols. (Edinburgh: Maclachlan and Stewart, 1841).

10. Harold Silver, *Education as History* (London: Methuen, 1983), 22.

11. Lawrence Cremin, *The Republic and the School: Horace Mann on the Education of Free Men* (New York: Teachers College Press, 1957), 14.

12. Michael B. Katz, *The Irony of Early School Reform: Educational Innovation in Mid-Nineteenth Century Massachusetts* (Cambridge, Mass.: Harvard University

Press, 1968); David Hogan, "Modes of Disciplines: Affective Individualism and Pedagogical Reform in New England, 1820–1850," *American Journal of Education* 99, no. 1 (1990): 1–56.

13. The best introductions to phrenology in Britain are Roger Cooter, *The Cultural Meaning of Popular Science: Phrenology and the Organization of Consent in Nineteenth Century Britain* (Cambridge: Cambridge University Press, 1984); and David De Guistino, *The Conquest of Mind: Phrenology and Victorian Social Thought* (London: Croom Hill, 1975); and in the United States, John D. Davis, *Phrenology, Fad, and Science* (New Haven, Conn.: Yale University Press, 1955).

14. Mary Mann, *Life and Works of Horace Mann,* 5 vols. (Boston: Lee and Sheppard, 1891), 59.

15. George Combe, *The Life and Correspondence of Andrew Combe, M.D.* (Philadelphia: A. Hart, 1850), 368.

16. Quoted in Angus McLaren, "A Prehistory of the Social Sciences: Phrenology in France," *Comparative Studies in Society and History* 23, no. 3 (1981): 3–21.

CHAPTER 1

1. Frank E. Manuel, *Freedom from History: And Other Untimely Essays* (New York: New York University Press, 1971), 221.

2. On Cabanis and the *Idéologues,* see Martin S. Staum, *Cabanis: Enlightenment and Medical Philosophy in the French Revolution* (Princeton: Princeton University Press, 1980), *Minerva's Message: Stabilizing the French Revolution* (Montreal: McGill-Queen's University Press, 1996), and " 'Analysis of Sensations and Ideas' in the French National Institute (1795–1803)," *Canadian Journal of History* 26 (1991): 393–413.

3. Pierre Jean Georges Cabanis, *On the Relations between the Physical and Moral Aspects of Man* (Baltimore: Johns Hopkins University Press, 1981).

4. *The Philosophical Writings of Etienne Bonnot, Abbé de Condillac,* 2 vols. Trans. Franklin Philip and Harlan Lane (Hillsdale, N.J.: Lawrence Erlbaum Associates, 1987). On Condillac and sensationalism see Isabel Knight, *The Geometric Spirit: The Abbé de Condillac and the French Enlightenment* (New Haven, Conn.: Yale University Press, 1968); and John C. O'Neal, *The Authority of Experience: Sensationist Theory in the French Enlightenment* (University Park, Pa.: Pennsylvania State University Press, 1996).

5. *Philosophical Writings of Condillac,* 2: 453–454.

6. Ibid., 454.

7. Ibid., 480.

8. Condillac, quoted in Harlan Lane, *The Wild Boy of Aveyron* (Cambridge, Mass.: Harvard University Press, 1976), 82.

9. *Philosophical Writings of Condillac,* 2: 556.

10. Massieu, quoted in Harlan Lane, *When the Mind Hears* (New York: Vintage, 1984), 38.

11. Sicard, quoted in Lane, *When the Mind Hears,* 34.

12. Cabanis, quoted in Elizabeth A. Williams, *The Physical and the Moral: Anthropology, Physiology, and Philosophical Medicine in France, 1750–1850* (Cambridge: Cambridge University Press, 1994), 85.

13. Cabanis, quoted in ibid.

14. Cabanis, quoted in Robert J. Richards, *Darwin and the Emergence of Evolutionary Theories of Mind and Behavior* (Chicago: University of Chicago Press, 1987), 28.

15. Cabanis, quoted in ibid., 28–29.

16. Ibid.

17. On Pinel, see Jan Goldstein, *Console and Classify: The French Psychiatric Profession in the Nineteenth Century* (London: Cambridge University Press, 1987); Williams, *Physical and the Moral;* and Dora B. Weiner, *The Citizen-Patient in Revolutionary and Imperial Paris* (Baltimore: Johns Hopkins University Press, 1993).

18. Philippe Pinel, *Treatise on Insanity* (Washington, D.C.: University Publications of America, 1977).

19. *Philosophical Writings of Condillac,* 2: 475.

20. Goldstein, *Console and Classify.*

21. Pinel, quoted in ibid., 100.

22. Pinel, quoted in ibid.

23. Tracy, quoted in ibid., 99.

24. On Victor, see Lane, *Wild Boy of Aveyron;* Roger Shattuck, *The Forbidden Experiment: The Story of the Wild Boy of Aveyron* (New York: Farrar Straus Giroux, 1980); Michael Newton, *Savage Girls and Wild Boys: A History of Feral Children* (London: St. Martin's Press, 2003); and Julia Douthwaite, *The Wild Girl, Natural Man, and the Monster: Dangerous Experiments in the Age of Enlightenment* (Chicago: University of Chicago Press, 2002).

25. Jean Itard, "The Wild Boy of Aveyron," in Lucien Malson, *Wolf Children and the Problem of Human Nature* (New York: Monthly Review Press, 1972), 138–39.

26. Lane, *Wild Boy of Aveyron.*

27. Quoted in ibid., 47.

28. Condillac, quoted in ibid., 25.

29. Itard, "Wild Boy of Aveyron," 99.

30. Ibid., 101.

31. Ibid., 103.

32. Ibid., 105.

33. Ibid., 106.

34. Ibid., 109.

35. Ibid.

36. Ibid., 117.

37. Ibid., 126.

38. Ibid., 122.

39. Ibid., 137.

40. Ibid., 141.

41. Ibid., 167.
42. Ibid., 169.
43. Ibid., 178.
44. Ibid., 174.
45. Ibid., 141.
46. Francois Joseph Gall, *On the Functions of the Brain and of Each of Its Parts,* 6 vols., trans. Winslow Lewis Jr. (Boston: Marsh, Capen and Lyon, 1835), 1: 165.
47. Ibid.
48. Ibid.
49. Ibid., 162.
50. Ibid., 166–67.

CHAPTER 2

1. John Dewey, *The Living Thoughts of Thomas Jefferson* (New York: Fawcett Publications, 1957).
2. Ibid., 23.
3. "Notes on the State of Virginia" in *Thomas Jefferson, Writings,* ed. Merrill D. Peterson (New York: Library of America, 1984).
4. On Jefferson, see Joseph Ellis, *The American Sphinx: The Character of Thomas Jefferson* (New York: Alfred A. Knopf, 1996).
5. See, for example, William Adams, *The Paris Years of Thomas Jefferson* (New Haven, Conn.: Yale University Press, 1997).
6. Jefferson, quoted in Gilbert Chinard, *Jefferson et les Ideologues* (Baltimore: Johns Hopkins Press, 1925), 203.
7. Winthrop Jordan, *Black over White: American Attitudes toward the Negro, 1550–1812* (Chapel Hill: University of North Carolina Press, 1968).
8. "Notes on the State of Virginia," 263.
9. Ibid., 264.
10. Ibid., 266.
11. Ibid.
12. Ibid.
13. Ibid., 269.
14. Ibid.
15. Ibid., 267.
16. Ibid.
17. Ibid., 270.
18. Ibid., 264.
19. Jefferson, quoted in Saul Padover, *Jefferson: A Great American's Life and Ideas* (New York: Harcourt, Brace and World, 1952), 70.
20. *The Adams-Jefferson Letters: The Complete Correspondence between Thomas Jefferson and Abigail and John Adams,* 2 vols., ed. Lester J. Cappon (Chapel Hill: University of North Carolina Press, 1959), 2: 390.

21. Peterson, *Thomas Jefferson*, 901.

22. Ibid., 901–2.

23. "Notes on the State of Virginia," 273.

24. Ibid.

25. *Adams-Jefferson Letters*, 388.

26. Ibid.

27. "Notes on the State of Virginia," 272.

28. Ibid.

29. Ibid., 277.

30. Peterson, *Thomas Jefferson*, 43.

31. Antoine Louis Claude Destutt de Tracy, *A Commentary and Review of Montesquieu's Spirit of Laws* (New York: Burt Franklin, 1969).

32. Ibid., iv, o.

33. Ibid.

34. Ibid.

35. Ibid.

36. Ibid.

37. Charles François Dupuis, *The Origin of all Religious Worship* (New York: Garland, 1984).

38. My argument in this section is drawn primarily from R. R. Palmer, *The Improvement of Humanity* (Princeton: Princeton University Press, 1985); Robert J. Vignery, *The French Revolution and the Schools: Educational Policies of the Mountain, 1792–1794* (Madison: State Historical Society of Wisconsin, 1965); Andy Green, *Education and State Formation* (London; Palgrave-Macmillan, 1991); James Bowen, *A History of Western Education*, vol. 3 (London: Palgrave-Macmillan, 1986); Brian Head, *Ideology and Social Science: Destutt de Tracy and French Liberalism* (Boston, Hingham, Mass.: Dordrecht, M. Nijhoff, 1985); Brian W. Head, *Politics and Philosophy in the Thought of Destutt de Tracy* (New York: Garland, 1987); Emmet Kennedy, *A Philosophe in the Age of Revolution: Destutt de Tracy and the Origins of "Ideology"* (Philadelphia: American Philosophical Society, 1978); Isser Woloch, *The New Regime: Transformations of the French Civic Order, 1789–1820s* (New York: W. W. Norton and Company, 1994); Martin S. Staum, "Human, not Secular Sciences: Ideology in the Central Schools," *Historical Reflections* 12, no. 1 (1985): 49–76; Jay W. Stein, "A Scholarly Temple from National to Napoleonic," *History of Education Quarterly* 1, no. 4 (1961): 7–15; and L. Pearce Williams, "Science, Education, and the French Revolution," *Isis* 44, no. 4 (1953): 311–30.

39. See Palmer, *Improvement of Humanity*, 124–29.

40. Stein, "Scholarly Temple."

41. Antoine Louis Claude Destutt de Tracy, *Observations sur le Système Actuel d'Instruction Publique* (Paris: Ve Panckoucke, 1801).

42. Antoine Louis Claude Destutt de Tracy, *Éléments d'Idéologie: I, Idéologie* (Paris: Courcier, 1804); *Éléments d'Idéologie: II, Grammaire* (Paris: Courcier, 1803); *Éléments d'Idéologie: III, Logique* (Paris: Courcier, 1805).

43. *The Writings of Thomas Jefferson*, 20 vols., ed. Albert Ellery Bough (Washington, D.C.: Thomas Jefferson Memorial Association, 1907), 13, 178–79.

44. Ibid., 177.

45. Antoine Louis Claude Destutt de Tracy, *A Treatise on Political Economy* (Detroit: Detroit Center for Health Education, 1973).

46. Jefferson in Chinard, *Jefferson et les Ideologues*

47. Chinard, *Jefferson et les Ideologues*, 105–6.

48. Ibid., 203.

49. *Adams-Jefferson Letters*, 491.

50. Ibid.

51. Elie Halévy, *The Growth of Philosophic Radicalism* (Boston: Beacon Press, 1966), 435.

52. *Adams-Jefferson Letters*, 568.

53. Peterson, *Thomas Jefferson*, 1122.

54. Ibid., 1214.

55. Ibid.

56. *Adams-Jefferson Letters*, 494.

57. Ibid., 491.

58. Ibid.

59. Ibid., 242.

60. Ibid., 499.

61. Ibid, 501.

62. Ibid.

63. Ibid, 535.

64. Ibid., 538–39.

65. On the political significance of the three-fifths rule, see Garry Wills, *Negro President: Jefferson and the Slave Power* (New York: Houghton Mifflin, 2003).

66. On Jefferson's efforts to establish the University of Virginia, see Cameron Addis, *Jefferson's Vision for Education, 1760–1845* (New York: Peter Lang, 2003); Harold Hellenbrand, *The Unfinished Revolution: Education and Politics in the Thought of Thomas Jefferson* (Newark: University of Delaware Press, 1990); Roy Honeywell, *The Educational Work of Thomas Jefferson* (Cambridge, Mass.: Harvard University Press, 1931); Dumas Malone, *Sage of Monticello* (Boston: Little Brown, 1981); and Lorraine Smith Pangle and Thomas L. Pangle, *The Learning of Liberty* (Lawrence: University Press of Kansas, 1993).

67. Peterson, *Thomas Jefferson* 1348.

68. Ibid., 1346–52.

69. Peterson, *Thomas Jefferson* 706.

70. Ibid., 467.

71. Ibid., 1465.

72. Chinard, *Jefferson et les Ideologues*, 203.

73. Jefferson, quoted in Robert Colin McLean George, *Tucker: Moral Philosopher and Man of Letters* (Chapel Hill: University of North Carolina Press, 1961), 158.

74. Pangle and Pangle, *Learning of Liberty*, 157–84.

75. Jefferson, quoted in Herbert B. Adams, *Thomas Jefferson and the University of Virginia* (Washington, D.C.: Government Printing Office, 1888), 139.

76. Ibid.

77. *Adams-Jefferson Letters,* 605.

CHAPTER 3

1. Etienne Georget quoted in Gall, *On the Functions,* 5: 298.

2. Ibid., 299.

3. On the *Memoire* and the commission's response to it, see "Report on a Memoir of Drs. Gall and Spurzheim, Relative to the Anatomy of the Brain," *Edinburgh Medical and Surgical Journal* 5 (1809): 36–66.

4. Gall, *On the Functions,* 5: 320.

5. The best introduction to Gall in English is John Van Wyhe, "The Authority of Human Nature: The Schädellehre of Franz Joseph Gall," *British Journal for the History of Science* 35, no. 1 (2002): 17-42. See also Wyhe's extensive *The History of Phrenology* on the World Wide Web: http://pages.britishlibrary.net/phrenology.

6. Michel Foucault, *The Order of Things* (New York: Random House, 1994).

7. Charles Bonnet quoted Gall, *On the Functions,* 5: 305.

8. Gall, *On the Functions* 5: 317.

9. Ibid., 312–13.

10. Ibid., 313.

11. Ibid.

12. Herder quoted in Edwin Clarke and L. S. Jacyna, *Nineteenth Century Origins of Neuroscientific Concepts* (Berkeley: University of California Press, 1987), 231.

13. Erna Lesky, "Structure and Function in Gall," *Bulletin of the History of Medicine* 44, no. 4 (1970): 304.

14. Charles Bell quoted in Clarke and Jacyna, *Nineteenth Century Origins,* 216.

15. On Gall's life and works, see "Biography of Gall" in Gall, *On the Functions,* 1.

16. Ibid., 10.

17. Ibid., 16.

18. Ibid.

19. Ibid.

20. Ibid.

21. Ibid.

22. Ibid.

23. Ibid., 7.

24. Ibid., 9.

25. Ibid.

26. Johan Gasper Spurzheim, *Phrenology, or the Doctrine of Mind; and of the Relations between Its Manifestations and the Body,* 2 vols. (Boston: Marsh, Capen and Lyon, 1834), 1: 20.

27. Robert M. Young, *Mind, Brain and Adaptation in the Nineteenth Century:*

Cerebral Localization and Its Biological Context from Gall to Ferrier (Oxford: Oxford University Press, 1990), 24.

28. Gall, quoted in Owesi Temkin, "Gall and the Phrenological Movement," *Bulletin of the History of Medicine* 21, no. 3 (1947): 279.

29. Richard Chevaeux, "Gall and Spurzheim—Phrenology," *Foreign Quarterly Review* 2 (February 1828): 11.

30. The term "cranioscopy" was coined in England to represent Gall's doctrine of the skull, *Schädellehre.*

31. Charles Villers, *Lettre à George Cuvier, de L'Institute National de France, sur une Nouvelle Theorie du Cerveau, par le Docteur Gall* (Metz, France: Colligon, 1802).

32. Walter, quoted in Hollander, *In Search of the Soul,* 2: 326.

33. Ibid., 327.

34. Chevaeux, "Gall and Spurzheim."

35. "Report on a Memoir," 37.

36. Ibid., 38.

37. Ibid., 40.

38. Ibid.

39. Clarke and Jacyna, *Nineteenth-Century Origins,* 34–37.

40. Quoted in Hollander, *In Search of the Soul,* 2: 330.

41. F. J. V. Broussais, *Lectures on Phrenology Delivered in 1836 in the University of Paris* (London: G. Churchill, 1836), 546.

42. Franz Joseph Gall and Johan Gasper Spurzheim, *Anatomie et Physiologie du System Nerveaux en general, et du Cereau en particular,* 4 vols. (Paris: Schoell, 1810–19).

43. Gall, quoted in Temkin, "Gall and the Phrenological Movement," 309.

44. Gall, *On the Functions,* 1: 219.

45. Ibid., 212.

46. Hollander, *In Search of the Soul,* 1: 340.

47. Gall, *On the Functions,* 1: 72.

48. Ibid., 92–93.

49. Ibid., 2: 107.

50. Ibid., 140.

51. Ibid.

52. Ibid., 154–55.

53. Ibid., 155.

54. Ibid., 158.

55. Ibid., 159.

56. Ibid., 1: 163.

57. Ibid., 208–9.

58. Ibid., 211.

59. Ibid., 218.

60. Quoted in Temkin, "Gall and the Phrenological Movement," 285.

61. Gall, quoted in ibid., 286.

62. Gall, *On the Functions,* 1: 218.

63. Ibid., 254.
64. Ibid.
65. Ibid., 258.
66. Ibid., 255.
67. Ibid.
68. Ibid., 147–49.
69. Gall, *On the Functions,* 2: 198.
70. Ibid., 201–2.
71. Ibid., 219.
72. Ibid.
73. Ibid., 224.
74. Ibid., 202.
75. Ibid., 3: 264.
76. Ibid., 265.
77. Ibid.
78. Ibid., 266.
79. Ibid., 278.
80. Ibid., 297.
  81. Johan Gasper Spurzheim, *Lectures on Phrenology* (London: Edward Portwine, 1837), 193.

CHAPTER 4

  1. The Marquis Mosquati, quoted in Hollander, *In Search of the Soul,* 1: 342.
  2. *The Surgical and Physiological Works of John Abernathy,* 2 vols. (London: Longman, Rees, Orme, Brown, and Green, 1830), 2: 44.
  3. Spurzheim revised this work in several editions, resulting in Johan Gasper Spurzheim, *Phrenology, or the Doctrine of Mind; and of the Relations between Its Manifestations and the Body* (London: Treuttel, 1825); *Observations on the Deranged Manifestation of the Mind* (Boston: Marsh, Capen, and Lyon, 1835); *A View of the Elementary Principles of Education, Founded on the Study of the Nature of Man* (Boston: Marsh, Capen, and Lyon, 1832); and *The Anatomy of the Brain with a General View of the Nervous System* (London: S. Highley, 1826). Spurzheim also published a number of smaller, more popular works, such as *The Philosophical Catechism of the Natural Laws of Man* (Boston: Marsh, Capen, and Lyon, 1832) and *Outlines of Phrenology* (Boston: Marsh, Capen, and Lyon, 1832), along with notes and technical articles on exchanges with his critics. A complete list of Spurzheim's writings is found in Roger Cooter, *Phrenology in the British Isles: an Annotated Historical Bibliography and Index.* (London: Scarecrow Press, 1989).
  4. John Gordon, quoted in Nahun Capen, "A Biography of the Author," in *Phrenology, in Connexion with the Study of Physinogomy,* Johann Gaspar Spurzheim (Boston: Marsh, Capen, and Lyon, 1836), 48–50.
  5. Abernathy, *Surgical and Physiological Works,* 2: 44.

6. Ibid., 19.

7. Ibid., 20.

8. Ibid.

9. Ibid., 21.

10. Ibid., 22.

11. Ibid.

12. See Martin S. Staum, "Physiognomy and Phrenology at the Paris Athénée," *Journal of the History of Ideas* 56 (1995): 443–62.

13. Forester, quoted in Roger Cooter, "Phrenology and British Alienists," in *Madhouses, Mad-doctors and Madmen: The Social History of Psychiatry in the Victorian Era,* ed. Andrew Scull (Philadelphia: University of Pennsylvania Press, 1981), 64.

14. Comte, quoted in Temkin, "Gall and the Phrenological Movement," 297.

15. Cooter, "Phrenology and British Alienists," 62.

16. Ibid.

17. George Combe, quoted in "Biography of Spurzheim," *The American Phrenological Journal and Miscellany* 3, no. 1 (1841): 8.

18. Spurzheim, *Phrenology,* 2: 112.

19. Ibid., 119.

20. Ibid., 149.

21. Ibid.

22. Ibid., 150.

23. Gall, quoted in Hollander, *In Search of the Soul,* 1: 341.

24. Spurzheim, *Observations,* 53.

25. Amariah Brigham, "Appendix" in Spurzheim, *Observations,* 233.

26. Spurzheim, *Observations,* 134.

27. Ibid., 135.

28. Ibid.

29. Spurzheim, *Education,* 1.

30. Ibid., 39–41.

31. Ibid., 45.

32. Ibid., 46–47.

33. Ibid., 46.

34. Ibid., 118.

35. Ibid., 132.

36. Ibid., 95.

37. Ibid., 158.

38. Ibid., 96.

39. Ibid., 102.

40. Ibid., 104.

41. Ibid., 240–41.

42. Ibid., 138.

43. Ibid., 185.

44. Ibid., 187.

45. Ibid., 184.
46. Ibid.
47. Ibid., 186.
48. Ibid., 208.
49. Ibid.
50. Ibid.
51. Ibid., 211.
52. Ibid.
53. Ibid., 212.
54. Ibid., 214.
55. Ibid., 216.
56. Ibid.
57. Ibid., 224.
58. Ibid.
59. Ibid.
60. Ibid., 227.
61. Ibid., 230.
62. Ibid., 232. For Spurzheim's influence on Spencer, see Stephen Tomlinson, "From Rousseau to Evolutionism: Herbert Spencer on the Science of Education" *History of Education* 25, no. 3 (1997): 235–54.
63. Spurzheim, *Education,* 232.

CHAPTER 5

1. G. N. Cantor, "The Edinburgh Phrenological Debate, 1803–1828," *Annals of Science* 32 (1975): 195–218; Steven Shapin, "Phrenological Knowledge and the Social Structure of Early Nineteenth Century Edinburgh," *Annals of Science* 32 (1975): 219–43; "Homo Phrenologicus: Anthropological Perspectives on an Historical Problem," in *Natural Order: Historical Studies of Scientific Culture,* ed. Barry Barnes and Stephen Shapin (Beverly Hills, Calif.: Sage, 1979); and "The Politics of Observation: Cerebral Anatomy and Social Interests in the Edinburgh Phrenological Disputes," in *On the Margins of Science: The Social Construction of Rejected Knowledge,* ed. Roy Wallis (Keele, U.K.: University of Keele Press, 1979).
2. Charles Gibbon, *The Life of George Combe: Author of "The Constitution of Man,"* 2 vols. (London: Macmillan and Co. 1878), see 1: 121–22.
3. Quoted in De Guistino, *Conquest of Mind,* 27.
4. Shapin, "Politics of Observation," 168.
5. Silver, *Education as History,* 22.
6. For the twenty-eight years of Combe's autobiography, see Gibbon, *Life of George Combe,* 1: 1–68.
7. Ibid., 53.
8. Ibid., 50.
9. Ibid.

10. Ibid.

11. Ibid., 51–52.

12. Ibid., 40.

13. Ibid., 39.

14. Ibid., 50.

15. Ibid.

16. Ibid., 40.

17. Ibid., 18.

18. Ibid., 49.

19. Ibid.

20. Ibid.

21. Ibid., 59.

22. Ibid., 58–59.

23. Ibid., 59.

24. Ibid.

25. Ibid., 60.

26. Ibid., 65.

27. Ibid.

28. Ibid., 73.

29. Ibid., 85.

30. Ibid., 92.

31. Combe, *Essays on Phrenology, or an Inquiry into the Principles and Utility of the System of Drs. Gall and Spurzheim, and the Objections Made Against It* (Edinburgh: Bell and Bradfute, 1819), lv.

32. Combe, quoted in Gibbon, *Life of George Combe,* 1: 95.

33. Ibid.

34. Combe, *Essays on Phrenology,* 361.

35. Ibid., 368.

36. Ibid.

37. Ibid., 373.

38. Ibid.

39. Ibid.

40. Ibid., 378.

41. Ibid., 385.

42. Ibid., 381.

43. Andrew Combe, *Observations on Mental Derangement* (Delmar, N.Y.: Scholars' Facsimiles and Reprints, 1972), 8–10.

44. Ibid.

45. See Combe, *Life and Correspondence.*

46. Gibbon, *Life of Combe,* 1: 144–76.

47. George Combe, *A System of Phrenology* (Edinburgh: J. Anderson, 1825), 561.

48. Ibid., 563.

49. Ibid.

50. Ibid., 568.

51. Ibid., 564.

52. Ibid., 582.

53. Ibid., 204.

54. Harriet Martineau, *Biographical Sketches* (New York: Hurst, 1876), 133.

55. Ibid.

56. Cooter, *Cultural Meaning*, 102.

CHAPTER 6

1. Robert Owen, *The Life of Robert Owen,* 2 vols. (London: Effingham Wilson, 1857), 1: 4.

2. Ibid., 16.

3. Owen, *Life of Robert Owen,* 1: 1–243.

4. Ibid., 13.

5. Ibid., 30.

6. Ibid.

7. Ibid.

8. Robert Owen, "A New View of Society," in ibid., 289.

9. Gregory Claeys, *Citizens and Saints* (Cambridge: Cambridge University Press, 1989), 33.

10. Godwin, quoted in Brian Simon, *The Radical Tradition in Education in Britain* (London: Lawrence and Wishart, 1972), 32.

11. Ibid.

12. William Godwin, *An Enquiry Concerning Political Justice, and Its Influence on General Virtue and Happiness,* 2 vols. (London: G. G. and J. Robinson, 1793), 1: 644.

13. Owen quoted in Claeys, *Citizens and Saints,* 78.

14. See S. E. Maltby, *Manchester and the Movement for National Elementary Education, 1800–1870* (Manchester, U.K.: Manchester University Press, 1918), 124–27.

15. W. A. C. Stewart and Philip McCann, *The Educational Innovators: 1750–1880* (London: MacMillan, 1967), 65.

16. Owen, "New View of Society," 277.

17. Owen, *Life of Robert Owen,* 1: 136.

18. Ibid.

19. Ibid.

20. Ibid., 138–39.

21. Ibid., 139.

22. Ibid., 141.

23. Ibid., 142.

24. Phillip McCann and Francis A. Young, *Samuel Wilderspin and Infant School Movement* (London: Croom Helm, 1982).

25. See Stewart and McCann, *Educational Innovators,* 241–67.

26. David Hamilton, "Robert Owen and Education: A Reassessment," in *Scottish Culture and Scottish Education, 1800–1980,* ed. W. Humes and H. Paterson (Edinburgh: John Donald, 1983).

27. Robert Owen, *Selected Works of Robert Owen,* 4 vols., ed. Gregory Claeys (London: W. Pickering, 1993), *1: xxi.*

28. David Hogan, "The Market Revolution and Disciplinary Power: Joseph Lancaster and the Psychology of the Early Classroom System," *History of Education Quarterly,* 29, no. 3 (1989): 381–417.

29. James Mill, *Schools for All, in Preference to Schools for Churchmen Only* (London: Thoemmes Press, 1995).

30. James Mill, *The Article Education,* reprinted from the *Supplement to the Encyclopedia Britannica* (London: J. Innes, 1824), 20.

31. Ibid., 39.

32. James Mill, quoted in Brian Simon, *Studies in the History of Education, 1780–1870* (London: Lawrence and Wishart, 1960), 76.

33. Ibid., 32.

34. Owen, *Selected Works,* 1: 9.

35. Robert Owen, *A New View of Society and Other Writings* (London: Penguin, 1991), 75.

36. Ibid., 76.

37. Robert Owen, "Address to the Inhabitants of New Lanark," in *Utopianism and Education: Robert Owen and the Owenites,* ed. John F. C. Harrison (New York: Teachers College Press, 1968), 94.

38. Ibid.

39. Ibid., 84–85.

40. Ibid., 85.

41. Owen, "New View of Society," 1: 317.

42. Ibid., 96.

43. Robert Dale Owen, "An Outline of the System of Education at New Lanark," in Harrison, *Utopianism and Education.*

44. Owen, "Address," 87.

45. Ibid.

46. Ibid., 144.

47. Owen, "Address," 87.

48. Ibid., 88

49. Ibid.

50. Ibid.

51. McCann and Young, *Samuel Wilderspin,* 41–42.

52. Ibid., 133.

53. Ibid., 132.

54. Ibid., 133.

55. Ibid., 134.

56. Ibid., 133–36.

57. Robert Owen, quoted in Margaret Cole, *Robert Owen of New Lanark* (New York: Oxford University Press, 1953), 68.

58. Robert Dale Owen, *Threading My Way: An Autobiography* (New York: G. W. Carleton and Co., 1874).

59. Owen, *Life of Robert Owen,* 152.

60. Owen, quoted in McCann and Young, *Samuel Wilderspin,* 40.

61. Ibid., 49–66.

62. Owen, *Life of Robert Owen,* 153.

63. Ibid.

CHAPTER 7

1. Robert Dale Owen, *Threading My Way,* 101.

2. Owen, *Life of Robert Owen,* 1: 155.

3. Ibid.

4. G. D. H. Cole, *Robert Owen* (Boston: Little, Brown, and Company, 1925), 149.

5. Ibid.

6. Ibid.

7. Ibid., 2a: 115.

8. Robert Owen, *Two Memorials on Behalf of the Working Classes* (Lanark, England: 1818, London, Longman, Hurst, Orme and Brown).

9. Robert Owen, *Report to the County of Lanark, of a Plan for Relieving Public Distress, and Removing Discontent* (Glasgow: University Press, 1821).

10. Hamilton, quoted in J. F. C. Harrison, *Quest for the New Moral World: Robert Owen and the Owenites in Britain and America* (New York: Charles Scibner, 1969), 31.

11. Quoted in Gibbon, *Life of George Combe,* 1: 26.

12. George Combe, *The Life and Dying Testimony of Abram Combe in Favour of Robert Owen's New Views of Man and Society* (London: J. Watson, 1844), 8.

13. Ibid., 9.

14. *The Register for the First Society of Adherents to Divine Revelation at Orbiston,* 2 vols. (Orbiston, Lanarkshire, England: Orbiston Press, 1827), 1: 187.

15. Alexander Cullen, *Adventures in Socialism: New Lanark Establishment and Orbiston Community* (New York: AMS Press, 1971), 201.

16. Abram Combe, *Seven Lessons, Addressed to the Members of the First Society of Adherents to Divine Revelation* (London: Watson, Hetherington and Cleave, 1845), 6.

17. Ibid., 12.

18. Ibid.

19. Abram Combe, *Observations on the New and Old Views, and Their Effects on the Conduct of Individuals: As Manifested in the Proceedings of the Edinburgh Christian Instructor and Mr. Owen* (Edinburgh: James Auchie, 1823), 61.

20. Ibid.

21. Ian Donnachie, "Orbiston: A Scottish Owenite Community 1825–1828," in *Co-operation and the Owenite Socialist Communities in Britain, 1825–45,* ed. Ronald George Garnett (Manchester, U.K.: Manchester University Press, 1972), 162.

22. "Advertisement" in *The Register for the First Society of Adherents to Divine Revelation at Orbiston* (Orbiston, Lanarkshire, England: Orbiston Press, 1827).

23. Abram Combe, *The Sphere for Joint Stock Companies; or the Way to Increase the Value of Land, Capital, and Labour: With an Account of the Establishment at Orbiston in Lanarkshire* (Edinburgh: Bell and Bradfute, 1825).

24. "Rules and Regulations of a Community," *Proceedings of the General Meeting of the British and Foreign Philanthropic Society* (London: A. Taylor, 1822), 53.

25. Combe, *Sphere for Joint Stock Companies,* 31–34.

26. Ibid., 31.

27. *Register,* 2: 30.

28. Combe, *Sphere for Joint Stock Companies,* 34.

29. Quoted in Stewart and McCann, *Educational Innovators,* 162.

30. Frank Podmore, *Robert Owen: A Biography* (New York: D. Appleton and Company, 1924), 353.

31. Combe, *Sphere for Joint Stock Companies,* 47.

32. *Register,* 2: 9–10.

33. Combe, *Sphere for Joint Stock Companies,* 28–29. Just before writing this pamphlet, Abram had helped his brother compose George Combe, "Phrenological Analysis of Mr. Owen's New Views" *Phrenological Journal* 1 (1823/24): 218–237.

34. Combe, *Sphere for Joint Stock Companies,* 53.

35. *Register,* 1: 180.

36. Combe, *Sphere for Joint Stock Companies,* 68.

37. *Proceedings of the General Meeting,* 53.

38. Ibid., 54.

39. *Register,* 1: 121.

40. *Ibid.,* 19.

41. *Ibid.,* 125.

42. Ibid.

43. *Ibid.,* 183.

44. *Ibid.,* 200.

45. *Ibid.,* 181.

46. *Ibid.,* 156.

47. *Register,* 2: 2.

48. Ibid., 5.

49. Ibid.

50. Ibid.

51. *Ibid.,* 18.

52. Ibid., 15.

53. Ibid.

54. Ibid.

55. Quoted in Podmore, *Robert Owen,* 371.

56. *Register,* 2: 69.

57. Quoted in Donnachie, "Orbiston," 156.

58. *Register,* 2: 71.

59. Ibid.

60. Cullen, *Adventures in Socialism,* 324.

61. Robert Owen, *A Development of the Principles and Plans on Which to Establish Self-Sustaining Home Colonies* (London: Home and Colonization Society, 1841).

62. Ibid., Appendix 1: 7.

63. Ibid., 9.

64. Cullen, *Adventures in Socialism,* 206.

65. Ibid.

66. Ibid.

67. Ibid., 92.

68. Owen, *Development of the Principles,* Appendix 1, 10.

69. Ibid.

CHAPTER 8

1. Gibbon, *Life of George Combe,* 1: 131.

2. Ibid., 132.

3. Ibid.

4. Ibid.

5. Ibid.

6. Combe, "Phrenological Analysis," 218–37.

7. Ibid., 236.

8. Ibid.

9. Ibid., 225.

10. Ibid., 225–26.

11. Ibid., 228–29.

12. Ibid., 229.

13. Ibid., 228.

14. Combe, quoted in Gibbon, *Life of George Combe,* 1: 164–65.

15. Ibid.

16. Ibid., 165.

17. Gibbon, *Life of George Combe,* 1: 182.

18. Ibid.

19. Ibid., 182–83.

20. Johan Gaspar Spurzheim, *A Philosophical Catechism of the Natural Laws of Man* (London: Charles Knight, 1826).

21. George Combe, *On Human Responsibility as Affected by Phrenology* (Edinburgh: privately printed, 1826).

22. Quoted in ibid., 186.

23. William Scott, *The Harmony of Phrenology with Scripture: Shewn in a Refutation of the Philosophical Errors Contained in Mr. Combe's "Constitution of Man,"* 2d edition (Edinburgh: Fraser, 1837), 24.

24. Gibbon, *Life of George Combe,* 1: 186.

25. George Combe, "On Human Capability of Improvement," *Phrenological Journal* 29 (1831): 197–212

26. Gibbon, *Life of George Combe,* 1: 239.

27. Ibid.

28. Ibid., 8.

29. Ibid., 4.

30. Ibid., 9.

31. Combe, *Lectures on Popular Education* 26.

32. Combe, *Constitution of Man,* 97.

33. Ibid., 77.

34. Ibid.

35. Ibid.

36. Ibid., 79.

37. Ibid., 103. See also Victor Hilts, "Obeying the Laws of Hereditary Descent: Phrenological Views on Inheritance and Eugenics," *Journal of the History of the Behavioral Sciences* 18 (1982): 62–67, 69.

38. Combe, *Constitution of Man,* 110.

39. Ibid., 112.

40. Ibid., 110.

41. Ibid., 119.

42. Ibid., 135.

43. Ibid.

44. Ibid., 147.

45. Ibid., 159.

46. Ibid., 164.

47. Ibid., 170.

48. Ibid., 172.

49. Ibid., 203.

50. Ibid., 205.

51. Ibid.

52. Ibid.

53. Ibid., 206.

54. See Gibbon, *Life of George Combe,* 1: 213.

55. Ibid.

56. Quoted in McCann and Young, *Samuel Wilderspin,* 112.

57. Gibbon, *Life of George Combe,* 1: 213.

58. Quoted in McCann and Young, *Samuel Wilderspin,* 114.

59. Wilderspin quoted in ibid.

60. Simpson, *Philosophy of Education,* 235.

61. Ibid.

62. Ibid.

63. Ibid., 247.

64. Ibid.

65. Ibid., 236.

66. Ibid., 241.

67. Ibid., 244.

68. Ibid., 244–45.

69. James Simpson, "Phrenological Analysis of Infant Education on Mr. Wilderspin's System," *Phrenological Journal* 6 (1830): 418.

70. Ibid., 419.

71. Ibid., 428.

72. Ibid., 424.

73. Ibid., 426.

74. Ibid.

75. Ibid., 428.

76. Ibid.

77. Ibid.

78. James Simpson, "Lessons on Objects as Given in a Pestalozzian School at Cheam, Surrey," *Phrenological Journal* 7 (1831): 266.

79. Ibid.

80. Jolly, *Education,* 294.

81. Ibid., 268.

82. George Combe, "On Education," *Phrenological Journal* 8 (1833): 451. Combe placed Brougham's challenge on the title page of his *Lectures on Popular Education.*

83. Combe, *Lectures on Popular Education,* 24.

84. Ibid.

85. Ibid., 47–48.

86. Ibid., 91.

87. Ibid., 99.

88. Ibid., 100.

89. Ibid.

90. Thomas F. Gieryn, *Cultural Boundaries of Science: Credibility on the Line* (Chicago: University of Chicago Press, 1999), 147.

91. Ibid, 5.

92. Gibbon, *Life of George Combe,* 2: 27.

CHAPTER 9

1. James Murphy, *Church, State, and Schools in Britain, 1800–1970* (London: Routledge and Keegan Paul, 1971).

2. J. L. Alexander, "Lord John Russell and the Origins of the Committee of Council on Education," *Historical Journal* 20 (1977): 395–415.

3. Simpson, *Philosophy of Education,* 19–21.

4. Ibid., 13–14.

5. Ibid., 28–29.

6. Ibid., 109–10.

7. Ibid., 110.

8. Ibid., 91.

9. Ibid., 98.

10. Ibid., 113–14.

11. Ibid., 124.

12. Ibid., 197.

13. Donald H. Akenson, *The Irish Education Experiment: The National System of Education in the Nineteenth Century* (London: Routledge and Keegan Paul, 1970).

14. Ibid., 204.

15. Ibid.

16. James Simpson, "Evidence of James Simpson, Esq.," in *Report from the Select Committee (of the House of Commons) on Education in England and Wales Together with the Minutes of Evidence, Appendix, and Index* (London: House of Commons, 1835).

17. Ibid., 122.

18. Ibid., 127.

19. Ibid., 129.

20. Ibid., 131.

21. Ibid., 153.

22. Ibid.

23. Ibid.

24. The arguments in this section are informed by Alexander "Lord John Russell"; Richard Johnson, "Educating the Educators: 'Experts' and the State, 1833–9," in *Social Control in Nineteenth Century Britain,* ed. A. P. Donajgrodzki (London: Croom Helm, 1977); Denis G. Paz, *The Politics of Working-Class Education in Britain 1830–1850* (Manchester, U.K.: Manchester University Press, 1980); Murphy, *Church, State, and Schools;* and Simon, *Studies in the History of Education.*

25. Murphy, *Church, State, and Schools.*

26. Murphy, *Church, State, and Schools.*

27. Ibid., 35.

28. Rathbone, quoted in ibid., 86.

29. *National Education: Report of Speeches Delivered at a Dinner Given to James Simpson, ESQ. By the Friends of Education in Manchester* (Manchester, U.K.: Prentice and Cathrall, 1836).

30. Rathbone, quoted in *National Education,* 25.

31. James Simpson, "On the Expediency and the Means of Elevating the Profession of the Educator in Public Estimation," in *The Educator: Prize Essays* (London: Taylor and Walton, 1839).

32. Murphy, *Church, State, and Schools.*

33. Wilderspin, quoted in ibid., 96.

34. Sandon, quoted in ibid., 105.

35. Ibid., 106.

36. McNeile, quoted in Richard Parkin, *The Central Society of Education, 1836–1840* (Leeds, U.K.: University of Leeds Museum of the History of Education, 1975), 3.

37. James Simpson, *National Education, or the Spirit of Secularism Morally Tested* (Edinburgh: Adam and Charles Black, 1837), 8.

38. Ibid., 13.

39. Ibid.

40. Ibid.

41. Ibid., 14.

42. Ibid.

43. Ibid., 16.

44. Ibid., 24.

45. Ibid., 25.

46. Stowell, quoted in Maltby, *Manchester,* 53.

47. Russell, quoted in Alexander, "Lord John Russell," 408.

48. Ibid., 410.

49. Ibid., 411.

CHAPTER 10

1. Isaac Ray, *Treatise on the Medical Jurisprudence of Insanity* (Boston: Little Brown, 1838).

2. Horace Mann, Benzaleel Taft, and W. B. Calhoun, *Report of Commissioners Appointed under a Resolve of the Legislature of Massachusetts to Superintend the Erection of a Lunatic Hospital at Worcester and to Report a System of Discipline and Government for the Same* (Boston: Dutton and Wentworth, 1832).

3. Gerald N. Grob, *The Mad among Us: A History of the Care of America's Mentally Ill* (Cambridge, Mass.: Harvard University Press, 1994).

4. David J. Rothman, *Discovery of the Asylum: Social Order and Disorder in the New Republic* (Boston: Little Brown, 1971).

5. Andrew Scull, *Social Order/Moral Disorder: Anglo-American Psychiatry in Historical Perspective* (Berkeley: University of California Press, 1989).

6. Samuel Tuke, *Description of the Retreat: an Institution near York, for Insane Persons of the Society of Friends* (London: Dawsons of Pall Mall, 1813).

7. *Reports of the Prison Discipline Society of Boston: 1st–29th; June 1826–May 1854* (Montclair, N.J.: Patterson Smith, 1972).

8. Gerald Grob, *The State and the Mentally Ill: A History of Worchester State Hospital in Massachusetts, 1830–1920* (Chapel Hill: University of North Carolina Press, 1966), 22.

9. Quoted in Grob, *State and the Mentally Ill,* 25.

10. Mann, Taft, and Calhoun, *Report of Commissioners,* 19–20.

11. Ibid., 21.

12. Ibid., 29.

13. Gerald Grob, "Samuel B. Woodward and the Practice of Psychiatry in Early Nineteenth Century America," *Bulletin of the History of Medicine* 36 (1962): 430.

14. On Brigham, see Eric T. Carlson, "Amariah Brigham: I. Life and Works," *American Journal of Psychiatry* 112 (1957): 831–36; and Eric T. Carlson, "Amariah Brigham: II. Psychiatric Thought and Practice," *American Journal of Psychiatry* 112 (1957): 911–16.

15. Spurzheim, *Observations;* Combe, *Observations.*

16. Amariah Brigham, *Remarks on the Influence of Mental Cultivation and Mental Excitement upon Health* (Hartford, Conn.: F. J. Huntington, 1832); *Observations on the Influence of Religion upon the Health and Physical Welfare of Mankind* (Boston: Marsh, Capen and Lyon, 1835).

17. Brigham, *Remarks,* 36–57.

18. Ibid., 58.

19. Ibid., 61.

20. Ibid., 56.

21. *Emile,* he added, "has had a great and beneficial influence in Europe, but appears to be little known in this country." Ibid., 72.

22. Ibid.

23. Ibid., 89.

24. Ibid., 98–99.

25. Ibid., 99.

26. Ibid.

27. Brigham, *Observations on the Influence of Religion.*

28. Amariah Brigham, *American Journal of Insanity* 1 (1844–45): 105.

29. On Spurzheim's visit to the United States, see Anthony Walsh, "Johan Christoph Spurzheim and the Rise and Fall of Scientific Phrenology in Boston, 1832–1842" (Ph.D. diss., University of New Hampshire, 1974); and Nahum Capen, *Reminiscences of Dr. Spurzheim and George Combe* (New York: Fowler and Wells, 1881).

30. Benjamin Silliman, quoted in Capen, "Biography of Author," 105.

31. Capen, *Reminiscences,* 8.

32. Ibid.

33. Silliman, quoted in Capen, *Biography of Spurzheim,* 105.

34. For an account of Todd's work at the Hartford Retreat, see Lawrence Goodheart, *Mad Yankees: The Hartford Retreat for the Insane and Nineteenth Century Psychiatry* (Amherst: University of Massachusetts Press, 2003).

35. Brigham, quoted in Capen, *Reminiscences,* 10.

36. Barnum, quoted in Capen, "Biography of Author," 123.

37. Spurzheim, *Lectures on Phrenology.*

38. Quoted in Anthony A. Walsh, "Phrenology and the Boston Medical Community" *Bulletin of the History of Medicine* 50 (1976): 267.

39. Capen, "Biography of Author," 126–27.

40. Quoted in Gibbon, *Life of George Combe,* 1: 277.

41. *A Catalogue of Phrenological Specimens* (Boston: Ford, 1835).

42. Walsh, "Spurzheim and the Rise and Fall of Scientific Phrenology," 330.

43. Capen, "Biography of Author," 120.

44. Combe, quoted in Capen, *Reminiscences,* 213.

45. Combe, quoted in Gibbon, *Life of George Combe,* 1: 220.

46. Channing, quoted in ibid., 1: 222.

47. Combe, quoted in ibid., 2: 63.

48. Combe, quoted in ibid., 2: 40.

49. Combe, *Notes,* 1: 323.

50. Combe, *Notes,* 2: 223.

51. Combe, *Notes,* 2: 51.

52. *American Phrenological Journal* 1, no. 4 (1839), 122.

53. Mann, quoted in Messerli, *Horace Mann,* 352.

54. *American Phrenological Journal* 1, no. 4 (1839): 125.

55. Combe, quoted in Gibbon, *Life of George Combe,* 2: 32.

56. Combe, quoted in ibid., 34.

57. Combe, quoted in ibid.

58. Combe, quoted in Ibid.

59. Combe, *Notes,* 3: 105.

60. Ibid., 48.

61. Ibid., 63.

62. Ibid., 85.

63. Ibid., 86.

64. Ibid., 112.

65. Ibid.

66. Ibid., 139.

67. Ibid., 75.

68. Samuel Morton, *Crania Americana; or, a Comparative View of the Skulls of Various Aboriginal Nations of North and South America* (Philadelphia: J. Dobson, 1839), 54.

69. Ibid., 61–62.

70. Ibid., 62.

71. Ibid., 61.

72. Ibid., 90.

73. Combe, *Notes,* 2: 77.

74. Ibid., 78.

75. Ibid.

76. Ibid., 79–80.

77. Ibid., 79.

78. Ibid.

79. Ibid., 223–24.

80. Ibid., 220.
81. Ibid.
82. Ibid., 227.
83. Mann, quoted in Gibbon, *Life of George Combe*, 2: 72.
84. Gallaudet, quoted in Combe, *Notes*, 2: 93.
85. Gallaudet, quoted in ibid., 94.
86. Ibid., 151.
87. Combe, *Notes*, 3: 204.
88. Ibid., 204.
89. Combe, quoted in Gibbon, *Life of George Combe*, 2: 44.
90. Combe, *Notes*, 2: 169.
91. Ibid., 284.
92. Mann, *Life and Works*, 1: 125.
93. Mann, quoted in Messerli, *Horace Mann*, 362.
94. Mann, *Life and Works*, 1: 145.
95. Ibid., 333–34.
96. Ibid., 336.
97. Ibid, 351.

CHAPTER 11

1. Quoted in [George Combe], "The Massachusetts Common School System," *North American Review* 52 (January 1841): 149.
2. Ibid., 150.
3. Quoted in Combe, *Notes*, 1: 359.
4. Ibid.
5. Mann, *Life and Works*, 1: 75.
6. Ibid.
7. Ibid.
8. Ibid., 81.
9. Ibid., 83.
10. Ibid., 59.
11. Ibid., 85.
12. Ibid., 87.
13. Horace Mann, *First Annual Report of the Board of Education, Together with the First Annual Report of the Secretary of the Board* (Boston: Dutton and Wentworth, 1838).
14. Mann, *Lectures*, vii.
15. Ibid., ix–x.
16. Ibid., 14.
17. Ibid., 15.
18. Ibid., 13.
19. Ibid., 13, 17–18.

20. Ibid., 20.

21. Ibid., 37.

22. Ibid., 38.

23. Ibid., 47.

24. Ibid.

25. Ibid., 55–56.

26. Mann, *First Annual Report,* 65.

27. Ibid.

28. Ibid., 55.

29. Ibid., 58.

30. Ibid.

31. Horace Mann, *Third Annual Report of the Board of Education, Together with the Third Annual Report of the Secretary of the Board* (Boston: Dutton and Wentworth, 1840), 47.

32. Quoted in Combe, *Notes,* 1: 72.

33. Mann, *Third Annual Report,* 24–25.

34. Ibid., 60–61.

35. Ibid., 61.

36. Ibid.

37. Ibid., 62.

38. Ibid, 64.

39. Ibid., 69.

40. Ibid., 74.

41. Ibid., 71.

42. Ibid., 82.

43. Ibid.

44. Ibid., 92.

45. Fredrick Packard, "The Life of Horace Mann by his Wife," *The Princeton Review* 38, no. 1 (1866): 74–94.

46. Raymond Carver, *Horace Mann and Religion in the Massachusetts Public Schools* (New Haven, Conn.: Yale University Press, 1929). See also Messerli, *Horace Mann.*

47. Mann, *Lectures,* 73.

48. Ibid., 74.

49. Ibid.

50. Ibid., 80.

51. Ibid., 81.

52. Ibid., 82.

53. Ibid., 83.

54. Ibid., 85.

55. Ibid.

56. Ibid., 88.

57. Ibid., 88–93.

58. Ibid., 94.

59. Ibid., 94–95.

60. Ibid., 95.

61. Ibid., 96–99.

62. Ibid., 103.

63. Ibid., 111.

64. Combe, *Notes,* 1: 51.

65. Horace Mann, *Common School Journal,* I, no. 2, January 15, 1839, 38.

66. Arthur O. Norton, ed., *The First State Normal School in America; the Journals of Cyrus Peirce and Mary Swift* (Cambridge, Mass.: Harvard University Press, 1926), liv.

67. Ibid., li.

68. Peirce, quoted in Samuel J. May, "Cyrus Peirce," in Henry Barnard, *Memoirs of Teachers, Educators, Promoters, and Benefactors of Education* (New York: F. C. Brownell, 1861), 433.

69. "The Journal of Mary Swift," in Norton, *First State Normal School,* 82.

70. Peirce, quoted in Norton, *First State Normal School,* l.

71. Ibid.

72. Ibid., 140.

73. Ibid., 142.

74. Ibid., 159.

75. Ibid.

76. Ibid.

77. Ibid., 144.

78. Ibid., 145.

79. Ibid., 94.

80. Ibid., 116.

81. Ibid., 157.

82. Orestes Brownson, "Review of Mann's *Second Annual Report,*" *Boston Quarterly* 2 (1839): 393–418.

83. Brownson, quoted in Combe, *Notes,* 3: 135.

84. Ibid.

85. Ibid.

86. Ibid., 138.

87. Combe, *Notes,* 3: 140.

88. Ibid.

89. Ibid., 141.

90. Quoted in Combe, *Notes,* 3: 310.

91. Ibid., 315.

92. Howe, quoted in Norton, *First State Normal School,* 272.

93. Ibid.

94. [Combe], "Education in America—State of Massachusetts," *Edinburgh Review* 73 (July 1841): 486–502.

CHAPTER 12

1. Gibbon, *Life of George Combe,* 2: 137.

2. Ibid.

3. Mann to Combe, February 28, 1842, Mann Papers MSS: Massachusetts Historical Society.

4. Mann to Combe, June 19, 1843, Mann MSS.

5. Mann to Combe, July 11, 1843, Mann MSS.

6. Mann to Combe, September 25, 1843, Mann MSS.

7. Ibid.

8. Ibid.

9. Ibid.

10. Mann, *Life and Works,* 5: 84.

11. Ibid.

12. Ibid., 85.

13. Ibid.

14. Ibid., 92.

15. Ibid., 262.

16. Horace Mann, *Seventh Annual Report of the Board of Education together with the Seventh Annual Report of the Secretary of the Board* (Boston: Dutton and Wentworth, 1844), 22.

17. See "Words, Words, Words," in Mann, *Life and Works,* 5: 177–83.

18. Ibid., 127.

19. Ibid., 62.

20. Ibid., 138.

21. Ibid., 128.

22. Ibid., 155.

23. Ibid., 187.

24. Ibid., 188–89.

25. Ibid., 187–88.

26. Ibid., 191.

27. Ibid., 192.

28. Ibid., 25.

29. Ibid., 31–32.

30. Ibid., 25–26.

31. Ibid., 32–33.

32. Samuel Gridley Howe, *Second Annual Report of the Board of State Charities* (Boston: Wright and Potter, 1866), lii.

33. Ibid., lv.

34. See Lane, *When the Mind Hears.*

35. Horace Mann, "Laura Bridgman," *Common School Journal* 4, no. 10 (May 16, 1842): 146.

36. Ibid., 148.

37. Samuel Gridley Howe, "Laura Bridgman," *Common School Journal* 3, no. 4 (February 15, 1841): 50.

38. Ibid., 49.

39. Ibid.

40. Horace Mann, "Laura Bridgman," *Common School Journal* 5, no. 10 (May 15, 1843): 146–47.

41. Howe, quoted in Ernest Freeberg, "More Important Than a Rabble of Common Kings: Dr. Howe's Education of Laura Bridgman," *History of Education Quarterly* 34, no. 3 (1994): 309.

42. Samuel Gridley Howe, "Laura Bridgman," *Common School Journal* 4, no. 10 (May 16, 1842): 150.

43. Ibid.

44. Ibid., 151.

45. Ibid.

46. Lane, *When the Mind Hears*, 292.

47. Ibid.

48. Howe, quoted in Freeberg, "More Important," 312.

49. Ernest Freeberg, *The Education of Laura Bridgman: The First Deaf and Blind Person to Learn Language* (Boston: Harvard University Press, 2001), 162.

50. Freeberg, "More Important," 312.

51. Harvey Peet, "Seventh Annual Report of the Secretary of the Massachusetts Board of Education," *North American Review* 59 (1844): 329–52.

52. Ibid., 332.

53. Ibid., 337.

54. Mann, *Seventh Annual Report*, 34.

55. Ibid.

56. *Remarks on the Seventh Annual Report of the Hon. Horace Mann, Secretary of Massachusetts Board of Education* (Boston: Little and Brown, 1844); *Rejoinder to the Reply of Hon. Horace Mann, Secretary of Massachusetts Board of Education, to the "Remarks" of the Association of Boston Masters upon his Seventh Annual Report* (Boston: Little and Brown, 1845); Horace Mann, *Reply to the "Remarks" of Thirty-one Boston Schoolmasters on the Seventh Annual Report of the Secretary of the Massachusetts Board of Education* (Boston: Fowle and Capen, 1844); *Answer to the "Rejoinder" of Twenty-nine Boston Schoolmasters: Part of the "Thirty-one" Who Published "Remarks" on the Seventh Annual Report of the Secretary of the Massachusetts Board of Education* (Boston: Fowle and Capen, 1845).

57. Mann, *Answer*, 82.

58. Ibid., 100.

59. Mann, *Life and Works*, 1: 5.

60. Mann, *Answer*, 88.

61. Quoted in Mann, *Answer*, 104.

62. Ibid., 117.

63. *Rejoinder*, 62–64.

64. Quoted in Horace Mann, "Boston Grammar and Writing Schools," *Common School Journal* 7, no. 19 (October 1, 1845): 266.

65. "Reports of the Annual Visiting Committees of the Public Schools of the City of Boston 1845," in Otis W. Caldwell and Stuart A. Courtis, *Then and Now in Education, 1845–1923: A Message of Encouragement from the Past to the Present* (New York: World Book Company, 1924), 171.

66. "Reports of the Annual Visiting Committees," 174.

67. Mann, "Boston Grammar and Writing Schools," 237.

68. Ibid., 268.

69. Ibid., 269.

CHAPTER 13

1. Mann, quoted in Messerli, *Horace Mann*, 455.

2. Mann, quoted in Mann, *Life and Works*, 5: 303.

3. See letters to Combe, April 12, 1849, and November 15, 1850, in Mann Mss.

4. Horace Mann, *Slavery: Letters and Speeches* (Boston: B. B. Mussey and Co., 1851).

5. Ibid., 128.

6. Ibid., 135.

7. Ibid.

8. Ibid., 143.

9. Ibid.

10. Ibid.

11. Horace Mann, *Thoughts for a Young Man* (Boston: Lee and Shepard, 1887).

12. Ibid., 49.

13. Ibid., 80–84.

14. Horace Mann, *Lectures on Various Subjects* (New York: Fowler and Wells, 1859).

15. Ibid., 110.

16. Ibid.

17. Ibid., 112.

18. Mann, quoted in Joy Elmer Morgan, *Horace Mann at Antioch* (Washington, D.C.: National Education Association, 1938), 67–68.

19. Messerli, *Horace Mann*, 553.

20. Horace Mann, "Dedicatory and Inaugural Address," in Morgan, *Horace Mann at Antioch*, 254.

21. Ibid., 207.

22. Ibid.

23. Ibid., 208.

24. Ibid., 241.

25. Ibid., 236.

26. Ibid., 251.

27. Ibid.

28. Ibid., 254.

29. Ibid., 266.

30. Horace Mann, "Relation of Colleges to the Community," in Morgan, *Horace Mann at Antioch,* 539.

31. Ibid., 544.

32. Ibid.

33. Ibid., 559.

34. Ibid., 552.

35. Ibid.

36. Ibid., 555.

37. Ibid., 553.

38. Ibid., 554.

39. Ibid., 556.

40. Ibid.

41. Ibid., 559.

42. Horace Mann, "Report on the 'Code of Honor,' Falsely so Called," in Morgan, *Horace Mann at Antioch,* 529.

43. Mann, "Relation of Colleges," 564.

44. Ibid., 563.

45. Horace Mann, "Demands of the Age on Colleges," in *Horace Mann at Antioch,* 297.

46. Ibid.

47. Ibid., 303; George Combe, *An Inquiry into Natural Religion, Its Foundation, Nature and Applications* (Edinburgh: Neil and Co, 1853).

48. Ibid., 317.

49. Ibid., 313.

50. Quoted in Morgan, *Horace Mann at Antioch,* 94.

51. Mann, *Life and Works,* 1: 435; Horace Mann, *Twelve Sermons: Delivered at Antioch College* (Boston: Ticknor and Fields, 1861).

52. Mann, quoted in Messerli, *Horace Mann,* 568.

53. Ibid., 568.

54. Ibid., 569.

55. Ibid.

56. Ibid.

57. Ibid., 579.

58. Horace Mann, "Report on Intemperance, Profanity, and Tobacco in Schools and Colleges," in Morgan, *Horace Mann at Antioch,* 538.

59. Mann, "Report on the 'Code of Honor,'" 531.

60. Ibid., 527.

61. Mann, "Report on Intemperance, Profanity, and Tobacco," 338.

62. Horace Mann, "Baccalaureate Address of 1857," in Morgan, *Horace Mann at Antioch,* 360.

63. Horace Mann, "Baccalaureate Address of 1859," in Morgan, *Horace Mann at Antioch,* 388.

64. Ibid., 389.

65. Henry Barnard, *Memoirs of Teachers, Educators, Promoters, and Benefactors of Education* (New York: F. C. Brownell, 1861), 397–99.

CHAPTER 14

1. [Combe], "Education in America."

2. Ibid., 261.

3. Ibid., 266.

4. Ibid.

5. Ibid., 264.

6. Gibbon, *Life of George Combe,* 2: 137.

7. Ibid.

8. Andrew Combe, "Remarks on the Fallacy of Professor Tiedemann's Comparison of the Negro Brain and Intellect with Those of the European," *Phrenological Journal* 11 (1838): 13–22.

9. Gibbon, *Life of George Combe,* 2: 148.

10. Ibid.

11. Ibid.

12. George Combe, *Phrenology Applied to Painting and Sculpture* (London: Simpkin, Marshall and Co., 1855).

13. Gibbon, *Life of George Combe,* 2: 22.

14. George Combe, "Remarks on National Education"; "The Relation between Religion and Science;" and "What a Secular Education Should Embrace" in Robert Cox, ed., *Moral and Intellectual Science: Applied to the Elevation of Society* (New York: Fowlers and Wells, 1848).

15. Gibbon, *Life of George Combe,* 2: 194.

16. Ibid., 299.

17. Ibid., 213.

18. Ibid.

19. Ibid., 15.

20. Ibid., 218.

21. Ibid.

22. George Combe, "Remarks on National Education," 15.

23. Ibid., 14–17.

24. Ibid., 27.

25. Ibid.

26. Ibid., 29.

27. Ibid., 32.

28. Ibid., 32–33.

29. George Combe, "The Relation between Religion and Science," 126.

30. Ibid.

31. Ibid., 155.

32. Combe, "What Should a Secular Education Embrace?" 371.

33. William Ellis, *Outlines of Social Economy* (London: Smith, Elder, and Co., 1846).

34. William Ellis, *Questions and Answers Suggested by a Consideration of Some of the Arrangements and Relations of Social Life: Being a Sequel to the "Outlines of Social Economy" By the Same Author* (London: Smith, Elder, and Co., 1848).

35. Quoted in Stewart and McCann, *Educational Innovators,* 333.

36. George Combe, "Secular Education," *Westminster Review* 113 (July 1852): 1–18.

37. Lovett, quoted in Brian Harrison "Kindness and Reason: William Lovett and Education," *History Today* 37 (March 1987): 18.

38. William Lovett and John Collins, "Chartism: A New Organization of the People," in *The Radical Tradition in Education in Britain,* ed. Brian Simon (London: Lawrence and Wishart, 1972): 225–86.

39. Ibid.

40. David Stack, "William Lovett and the National Association for the Political and Social Improvement of the People," *The Historical Journal* 42, no. 4 (1999): 1027–50.

41. Stewart and McCann, *Educational Innovators,* 339.

42. Charles Dickens, *Hard Times* (New York: Modern Library, 2001).

43. Ibid., 1.

44. For a comprehensive discussion of the first and second generation utilitarian educational program and Dickens's criticisms, see Paul A. Olson, *The Kingdom of Science: Literary Utopianism and British Education, 1612–1870* (Lincoln: University of Nebraska Press, 2002).

45. Williams, quoted in Jolly, *Education,* 213.

46. Ibid., 237.

47. George Combe, *On Teaching Physiology and Its Applications in Common Schools* (Edinburgh; MacLachlan and Stewart, 1957), 1.

48. Ibid., 8.

49. Ibid., 11.

50. Williams, quoted in Jolly, *Education,* 683.

51. Ibid.

52. Ibid.

53. Ibid., 684.

54. Ibid.

55. Donald K. Jones, *The Making of the Education System* (London: Routledge and Kegan Paul, 1977); and "Lancashire, the American Common School, and the Religious Problem in British Education in the Nineteenth Century," *British Journal of Educational Studies* 15, no. 3 (1967): 292–306.

56. *A Plan for the Establishment of a General System of Secular Education in the County of Lancaster* (London: Simpkin and Marshall, 1847).

57. Ibid., 7.

58. Maltby, *Manchester,* 71.

59. Gibbon, *Life of George Combe,* 2: 292.

60. Maltby, *Manchester,* 82.

61. See *The Scheme of Secular Education proposed by the National Public Schools' Association Compared with the Manchester and Salford Borough's Educational Bill* (London: Longman, Brown, Green, and Longmans, 1851).

62. Combe, "Secular Education," 17.

63. Cobden, quoted in Wendy Hinde, *Richard Cobden: A Victorian Outsider* (New Haven, Conn.: Yale University Press, 1987), 222.

64. Donald K. Jones, "Socialization and Social Science, Manchester Model Secular School, 1854–1861," in *Popular Education and Socialization in the Nineteenth Century,* ed. Phillip McCann (London: Methuen, 1977).

65. Donald K. Jones, "Working Class Education in Nineteenth Century Manchester: The Manchester Free School," *The Vocational Aspect* 29 (Spring 1967): 22–33.

66. Frank Smith, *The Life of Sir James Kay-Shuttleworth* (London: J. Murray, 1923), 257.

67. See P. N. Farrar, "American Influence on the Movement for a National System of Elementary Education in England and Wales, 1830–1870," *British Journal of Educational Studies* 14 (November 1965).

68. George Combe, *On the Relation between Science and Religion* (Edinburgh: Maclachlan and Stewart, 1857).

69. Gibbon, *Life of George Combe,* 2: 342.

70. Ibid.

71. Combe, *Inquiry into Natural Religion,* 35.

72. Ibid.

73. Ibid., 45.

74. Ibid., 54.

75. Ibid., 63.

76. Combe, *On the Relation,* 216.

77. Ibid., 257.

78. Mann, *Twelve Sermons.*

79. Ibid., 268–69.

80. Mann, quoted in Messerli, *Horace Mann,* 581.

81. Herbert Spencer, *Education: Intellectual, Moral, and Physical* (New York: D. Appleton, 1860).

CHAPTER 15

1. Harold Schwartz, *Samuel Gridley Howe: Social Reformer, 1801–1876* (Cambridge, Mass.: Harvard University Press, 1956).

2. Lane, *When the Mind Hears,* 286.

3. Schwartz, *Samuel Gridley Howe,* 278.

4. Samuel Gridley Howe, *Report Made to the Legislature of Massachusetts upon Idiocy* (Boston: Coolidge and Wiley, 1848), 3.

5. Ibid.

6. Howe, quoted in Schwartz, *Samuel Gridley Howe*, 137.

7. See James Trent, *Inventing the Feeble Mind* (Berkeley: University of California Press, 1994).

8. John Connolly, quoted in "Schools in Lunatic Asylums," *American Journal of Insanity* 2 (1845–46): 336.

9. Ibid.

10. Ibid.

11. Ibid.

12. Ibid.

13. Ibid., 337.

14. Ibid.

15. Howe, *Report Made to the Legislature*, 3.

16. Charles Rosenberg, "The Bitter Fruit: Heredity, Disease, and Social Thought in Nineteenth-century America," *Perspectives in American History* 8 (1974): 189–235.

17. See Edward Jarvis, "On the Supposed Increase of Insanity," *American Journal of Insanity* 7 (April 1852): 333–64.

18. Howe, *Report Made to the Legislature*, 32.

19. Ibid., 53.

20. Ibid., 36.

21. Ibid.

22. Pliney Earle, "European Institutions for Idiots," *American Journal of Insanity* 7 (April 1852): 332.

23. See Trent, *Inventing the Feeble Mind*, 284–85.

24. Howe, *Report Made to the Legislature*, 37.

25. Ibid., 18.

26. Ibid., 19.

27. Esquirol, quoted in Lane, *Wild Boy of Aveyron*, 262.

28. Ibid.

29. Ibid.

30. Ibid.

31. Séguin, quoted in ibid., 258.

32. George Sumner, "Letter to S. G. Howe," in *Twenty-eighth Annual Report of the Trustees of the Massachusetts School the Idiotic and Feebleminded Youth* (Boston: Wright and Potter, 1876): 68.

33. Séguin, quoted in Lane, *Wild Boy of Aveyron*, 261.

34. Esquirol, quoted in ibid., 264–65.

35. Edouard Séguin, *Idiocy: And Its Treatment by the Physiological Method* (Albany, N.Y.: Brandow, 1907), 21.

36. Howe, *Report Made to the Legislature*, 19.

37. Sumner, "Letter to S. G. Howe," 61.

38. Ibid., 61–62.

39. Ibid., 63.

40. Howe, *Report Made to the Legislature,* 65.

41. Ibid., 49.

42. Ibid., 61.

43. Ibid., 66.

44. Ibid., 94.

45. Ibid., 62.

46. Ibid., 62–63.

47. Ibid., 62.

48. Ibid., 66.

49. Ibid.

50. Ibid.

51. Ibid.

52. Russell Hollander, "Mental Retardation and American Society: The Era of Hope," *Social Service Review* 22 (September 1986): 400.

53. Samuel Gridley Howe, "Progress of the Massachusetts School for Idiotic and Feeble-Minded Youth," in *On the Causes of Idiocy* (Edinburgh: Maclachlan and Steward, 1858), 71.

54. Ibid.

55. Howe, quoted in Laura E. Richards (ed.), *Letters and Journals of Samuel Gridley Howe,* 2 vols. (New York: AMS Press, 1973), 214–15.

56. Howe, quoted in Emerson, "Dr. Howe's Reports upon Idiocy," *Christian Examiner and Religious Miscellany* 50 no. 1 (January, 1851): 129.

57. Ibid.

58. Ibid.

59. Richards, *Letters and Journals,* 2: 215.

60. Ibid.

61. Ibid.

62. Ibid.

63. Ibid.

64. Emerson, "Dr. Howe's Reports upon Idiocy," 121.

65. Richards, *Letters and Journals of Samuel Gridley Howe,* 2: 216.

66. Samuel Gridley Howe, "Influence of the Brain upon Idiocy," *On the Causes of Idiocy* (Edinburgh: Maclachlan and Steward, 1858), 63.

67. Ibid., 59.

68. Ibid.

69. Ibid., 60.

70. Ibid.

71. Ibid., 62.

72. Ibid., 61.

73. Ibid.

74. Ibid., 64.

75. Ibid.
76. Ibid.
77. Ibid.
78. Ibid., 63.
79. Ibid., 64.
80. Ibid., 62.
81. Howe, *On the Causes of Idiocy*, 2–3.
82. Ibid., 1.
83. Ibid.
84. Ibid., 3.
85. Ibid.

CHAPTER 16

1. Eric Foner, *Reconstruction: America's Unfinished Revolution, 1863–1877* (New York: Harper and Row, 1988).
2. *Facts Concerning the Freedmen: Their Capacity and their Destiny* (Boston: Press of Commercial Printing House, 1863).
3. *Memorial of the Emancipation League of Boston, Massachusetts, Praying the Immediate Establishment of a Bureau of Emancipation* (Washington, D.C.: Senate, 37th Congress, 3d session; no. 10, 1863).
4. John G. Sproat, "Blueprint for Reconstruction," *Journal of Southern History* 23, no. 1 (1957): 34.
5. "Preliminary Report," in *Report of the Secretary of War: Communicating, in Compliance with a Resolution of the Senate of the 26th of May, a Copy of the Preliminary Report, and also of the Final Report of the American Freedmen's Inquiry Commission* (Washington, D.C.: Senate, 38th Congress, 1st session, no. 53, 1864).
6. "Final Report," in *Report of the Secretary of War.*
7. See Sproat, "Blueprint for Reconstruction," 40.
8. Ibid., 44.
9. Ibid., 43.
10. "Final Report," 25.
11. Robert Dale Owen, *The Wrong of Slavery: The Right of Emancipation and the Future of the African Race in the United States* (Philadelphia: J. B. Lippincott and Co., 1864), 221.
12. Samuel Gridley Howe, *The Refugees from Slavery in Canada West* (Boston: Wright and Potter, 1864), 15.
13. Ibid., 1.
14. Ibid.
15. Ibid., 4.
16. Howe, quoted in *Louis Agassiz, his Life and Correspondence*, 2 vols., ed. Elizabeth Cabot Cary Agassiz (Boston: Houghton, Mifflin, 1886), 2: 592.
17. Agassiz, quoted in ibid.

18. Howe, quoted in ibid.

19. Howe, quoted in ibid., 593.

20. Samuel Morton, *Crania Aegyptiaca, or, Observations on Egyptian Ethnography, Derived from Anatomy, History, and the Monuments* (Philadelphia: J. Pennington, 1844).

21. Josiah Clark Nott, *Two Lectures on the Natural History of the Caucasian and Negro Races* (Mobile, Ala.: Dade and Thompson, 1844).

22. Ibid.

23. Morton, quoted in William Ragan Stanton, *The Leopard's Spots: Scientific Attitudes toward Race in America, 1815–59* (Chicago: University of Chicago Press, 1960), 141.

24. Agassiz, quoted in Stephen Jay Gould, *The Mismeasure of Man* (New York: Norton, 1981), 77.

25. Ibid.

26. Ibid.

27. Agassiz, quoted in *Louis Agassiz*, 2: 606.

28. Agassiz, quoted in ibid.

29. Agassiz, quoted in ibid.

30. Agassiz, quoted in ibid., 605–6.

31. Agassiz, quoted in ibid., 608.

32. Howe, quoted in ibid., 614.

33. Howe, quoted in ibid.

34. Howe, quoted in ibid.

35. Howe, quoted in ibid., 615.

36. Howe, quoted in ibid.

37. Howe, quoted in ibid.

38. "Final Report," 99.

39. Ibid.

40. Ibid.

41. Ibid.

42. Ibid., 82.

43. Ibid.

44. Ibid.

45. Ibid.

46. Ibid., 81–82.

47. Ibid., 17.

48. Ibid., 18–19.

49. Ibid., 19–20.

50. Ibid., 29.

51. Ibid., 30.

52. Ibid., 33.

53. Ibid., 104.

54. Ibid.

55. Ibid., 82.

56. Ibid., 99.

57. Ibid., 102.

58. Ibid., 106.

59. Ibid.

60. Ibid.

CHAPTER 17

1. Schwartz, *Samuel Gridley Howe.*

2. See Edward W. Pride, *Tewksbury—a Short History* (Cambridge, Mass.: Riverside Press, 1888).

3. Samuel Gridley Howe, *Second Annual Report of the Board of State Charities* (Boston: Wright and Potter, 1866), xvi.

4. Ibid., xvii.

5. Ibid., xiii.

6. Ibid., xl.

7. Ibid., xx.

8. Ibid., xxxviii.

9. Ibid., xxxvii.

10. Ibid., xxii.

11. Ibid., xxiii.

12. Ibid., xxv.

13. Ibid., xxxv.

14. Ibid.

15. Ibid., xxvi.

16. Ibid., xxxii.

17. Ibid.

18. Ibid., xxxi.

19. Ibid.

20. Ibid.

21. Ibid., xix.

22. Ibid.

23. Ibid.

24. Ibid., lxxxvii.

25. Ibid.

26. *Fifth Annual Report of the Board of State Charities of Massachusetts* (Boston: Wright and Potter, 1869).

27. Ibid., xi.

28. Gardner Hubbard, "Historical Address," in Edward Allen Fay, *Histories of American Schools for the Deaf, 1817–1893,* 3 vols. (Washington, D.C.: Volta Bureau, 1983), 2: 18.

29. Quoted in Lane, *When the Mind Hears,* 316.

30. Bullock, quoted in Hubbard, "Historical Address," 2: 19.

31. Howe, *Second Annual Report,* lii.

32. Ibid., liii.

33. Ibid.

34. Ibid., lvi.

35. Ibid.

36. See Lane, *When the Mind Hears,* 318–26.

37. Hubbard, quoted in Sarah Fuller, "Mann School," in Fay, *Histories of American Schools for the Deaf,* 2: 20.

38. Ibid.

39. Caroline A. Yale, "The Clarke Institution," in Fay, *Histories of American Schools for the Deaf,* 2: 22.

40. Ibid.

41. Ibid.

42. Philip Gillett, quoted in *Fifth Annual Report of the Board of State Charities of Massachusetts, 32.*

43. Gillett, quoted in ibid.

44. Ibid., lxxxvi.

45. Ibid.

46. Ibid.

47. Ibid., lxxxviii.

48. Ibid., lxxxix.

49. Ibid., xcv.

50. Bell, quoted in Lane, *When the Mind Hears,* 364.

51. Thomas L. Haskell, *The Emergence of Professional Social Science: The American Social Science Association and the Nineteenth-Century Crisis of Authority* (Urbana: University of Illinois Press, 1977).

52. Richard Dugdale, *The Jukes: A Study in Crime, Pauperism, Disease, and Heredity* (New York: G. P. Putnam's Sons, 1910).

Index